AMERICAN RURAL LIFE

A TEXTBOOK IN SOCIOLOGY

By

DAVID EDGAR LINDSTROM

PROFESSOR OF RURAL SOCIOLOGY
UNIVERSITY OF ILLINOIS

WITH AN INTRODUCTION BY
DR. O. E. BAKER

THE RONALD PRESS COMPANY · NEW YORK

To the Rural People
of America

PREFACE

This book has been written for students and professional workers in rural sociology. It should enable rural young men and women to become acquainted with the basic sociology of rural life, in a national rather than a local setting. It should enable these young men and women, and the rural sociologists who work with the social environments which produced them (or didn't produce them!) to become fully aware of the social problems which our increasingly complex civilization has imposed on rural life. These problems are just as important as are the sociological problems of our cities, and correct solutions to them are just as necessary. One, a group understanding of the need for soil conservation, is of such surpassing urgency that the future of our civilization depends, in considerable measure, on just how well we decide to solve it.

The reader of this book will soon discover that I have tried to balance academic objectivity with guidance and help to the student and professional worker. I have, in each chapter, selected problems for discussion which are typical, have set them in their natural social settings, and have then offered suggestions for their solution. Opportunities for further discussion, reading, and study are abundantly provided throughout the book.

I am indebted to Dr. O. E. Baker of the University of Maryland for the stimulating Introduction he has been good enough to prepare, and for his advice. I wish to acknowledge the help of many of my friends and associates who read various chapters in manuscript and gave helpful criticisms: Howard W. Beers, University of Kentucky; Edmund deS. Brunner, Teachers College, Columbia University; Ralph Cummins, Illinois Presbyter; Nat T. Frame, BAE, United States Department of Agriculture; Howard A. Dawson, Rural Department, National Education Association; C. Horace Hamilton, North Carolina Teachers College; John H. Kolb, University of Wisconsin; Charles E. Lively, University of Missouri; A. R. Mangus, Ohio State University; L. J. Norton, University of Illinois; Robert A. Polson, Cornell University; E. H. Regnier, University of Illinois; and Ray E. Wakeley, Iowa State College. My wife read and contributed suggestions to the entire manuscript. I am grateful to Mrs.

v

Stanley Pierce and Mrs. James Ayars for their invaluable help in editing, and to John W. Albig, Chairman of the Department of Sociology, University of Illinois, for his encouragement in submitting the manuscript for publication.

DAVID EDGAR LINDSTROM

Urbana, Illinois
  March, 1948

CONTENTS

ILLUSTRATIONS

TABLES

INTRODUCTION

The land is the foundation of the family and the family is the foundation of the democratic state. Unless the wide difference in reproduction rates diminishes between rural and urban people in the United States—and it has not diminished for many decades—probably two thirds, possibly three fourths, of the citizens of the nation a century hence will be descendants of the rural population of today. During the three years preceding the 1940 census, the last years for which there are adequate data, ten adults in the urban population were rearing about seven children, whereas ten adults in the rural farm population were rearing about fourteen children, and in the rural nonfarm population, eleven to twelve children. Unless there is a profound change in the ideals and the values of the urban people—change which probably would have to be supported by changes in the economic system—most city families of today will be extinct within two or three generations. Their biological heritage, and part of their cultural heritage, will pass away with them.

This will be a great loss to the nation, for urban people have enjoyed greater educational and cultural advantages than most rural people, and should be better able to pass these on, in turn, to their children. Moreover, in general, the more ambitious and better educated rural youth migrate to the cities, especially from the poorer agricultural areas. If there be a correlation of education and ambition with inherited ability (and there probably is, in part), this migration from rural to urban areas will not only gradually deplete the quality of the rural stock, but will also deplete the quality of the national stock, because these rural migrants to the cities soon acquire city ways, including a very low birth rate.

I believe the hope of the nation lies, first, in the retaining of their culture by the rural people, particularly of the family as an institution for continuing the race and transmitting wealth and culture. Secondly, I believe the nation's hope lies in retarding and, if possible, reversing the direction of rural-urban migration. The least we can hope and work for is disappearance of the characteristic differential in education and ambition of the rural migrants, when compared with the nonmigrants.

The trend of science and technique is strongly toward increasing production per worker in agriculture. A century ago about 70 per cent of this nation's "gainfully employed" (to use the census phrase) were engaged in agriculture; today about 14 per cent—only one fifth as many—are so engaged. Despite this tremendous shift, there are twice as many workers in agriculture today as are needed to provide the nation with food and fibers. The 1940 census revealed that nearly half the farmers in 1939 produced less than $600 worth of products per farm, and that these less-productive farms produced only about 6 per cent of the commercial agricultural products. It appears, therefore, that less than 10 per cent of the nation's gainfully employed are not only providing food and fibers for the people of the nation, but are also providing some surplus for foreign lands, notably of cotton and wheat.

There is no hope that we can solve the dilemma of the persistent rural-urban difference in birth rates by increasing materially the number of commercial farmers. We should not forget that the largely self-sufficing or part-time half of our farm families are providing far more than their proportionate share of the children. Perhaps the time may come when children will be considered as valuable as crops and livestock. If that ever happens, then the poor people of the Appalachian Mountains, of the Cotton Belt, of the Upper Lakes Country, and elsewhere, plus the myriad of part-time farmers who tend to cluster nearer the cities, will be held in appropriate esteem, and their numbers may increase. Meanwhile, what solution is there to the problems arising from the declining birth rate in the cities? It is now far below the reproduction level and is likely to fall still lower as the number of marriages diminishes, following the wartime expansion.

The solution, probably only partial, lies in the retention of rural homes by rural youth, and by older people now employed in the cities. It also includes the movement of many city people of rural origin to the suburbs. That such movement is of considerable magnitude is indicated by the 1940 census returns, which revealed a 14 per cent increase in the rural nonfarm population, compared with a 7 per cent increase in the urban population, and a stationary farm population. The 1950 census will almost certainly show a larger rural nonfarm than rural farm population. In reproduction rates these rural nonfarm people resemble the farm people more than the urban people.

The state agricultural extension services, and the departments of agricultural economics in the agricultural colleges and elsewhere, who will probably be the principal users of this textbook, should expand their services to include these rural nonfarm people. Probably half the membership of the Grange (Patrons of Husbandry) are rural nonfarm residents, as is a large proportion of the members of the Farm Bureau Federation. The hope of the nation will increasingly reside in these rural nonfarm (mostly village and surburban) people, provided they retain their rural values as to things worth while. In particular, let us hope they retain their respect for the family as an institution for the reproduction of the race and the transmission of wealth and culture from generation to generation.

I hope those agricultural extension workers, especially youthful home demonstration agents, who have lived in the urban environment which exists in most of our agricultural colleges, or who have so imbibed the subtle propaganda of our popular magazines, particularly the advertisements, that they no longer respect or perhaps even know the native values of rural life, will at least read enough of this book by Professor Lindstrom to pause and ponder before they lead the rural youth in their custody along the path that tends to extinction of the family and the race.

I hope the teachers in the agricultural colleges will read enough of this book to realize that religion is more important than prices in determining success in farming. By religion I mean the ideals, convictions, and attitudes of a people, and the institutions that grow out of religious beliefs.

I hope the professors of sociology in the agricultural colleges and elsewhere will continue to keep in mind the words of William James: "I am done with great things and big things, great institutions and big success, and I am for those tiny, invisible, molecular, moral forces that work from individual to individual, creeping through the crannies of the world like so many soft rootlets, or like capillary oozing of water, yet which, if you give them time, will rend the hardest monuments of man's pride."

O. E. BAKER

AMERICAN RURAL LIFE

Chapter 1

THE IMPORTANCE OF RURAL LIFE AND CULTURE

Despite the increasing urbanization of our civilization, the world's rural people still outnumber those who live in its cities. All over the world, from the corn-hog farm of our Middle West to the rice paddies of China's Kwangtung province, from the sheep station in Australia to the *estancia* on the pampas of Argentina, the world's farmers are producing essential food and fiber materials in huge quantities. Yet their contribution to our civilization does not end there, for they also contribute sons and daughters to our cities. All through history, rural life has been a source of many human and cultural values which have gone into the development of urban civilization. There is, of course, a reciprocal relationship, for many of the things which are now improving the quality of rural life had their origins in urban areas. The study of rural life and culture—and their constant improvement—is the work of rural sociology. The rural sociologist believes that the quality of life in rural areas should be of as much concern to the whole of society as is the wise use of our natural resources. Society as a whole can advance only if its rural people also "live the good life." In this text we shall devote almost our entire attention to the rural sociology of our own country.

A concern for the welfare of rural people and a realization of their great importance to the rest of society are reflected in the writings of social scientists and philosophers all through history. They have realized, as we also do today, that the farmer is the very foundation of a stable social order, that cities must depend on rural populations for their growth and survival, and that small farms cultivated by free farmers are essential to an effective society.

Rural and Urban Interdependence

Rural and urban people have always been interdependent, for our cities and towns grew out of small rural community life. And, although rural people are more directly dependent upon the soil for their livelihood, it is also true that our urban peoples' welfare rests, to an astonishing degree, upon the dependability and efficiency of

3

their rural neighbors in their management of the soil and their production of foods and fibers. As our society has become more and more complex, an increasing amount of rural and urban interdependence has developed. The city and the country depend upon one another for goods and services, and for the welfare of their institutions. Modifications of culture can, and often do, come out of this interdependence and interassociation.

Rural communities create and perpetuate cultural values which are essential to the whole of society. The youth from these communities, as they move into town and city areas, carry with them the special kind of training and the attitude of mind they have gained in the rural community. Rural areas, in turn, are affected by the quality of services, both economic and social, which is provided for them by towns and cities; they may be affected in a far more vital way by the ideas and ideals which are acquired from urban areas.

The problems that arise out of these changing relationships between rural and urban life, and how they may be solved to the mutual benefit of rural and urban people, constitute a large part of the task of rural social scientists. Later chapters will discuss specific educational, health, welfare, recreational, and similar problems facing rural people and the effects their solution will have upon rural and urban people. We must recognize at the outset, however, that there *are* significant differences. An understanding of these differences will help us to meet and solve the peculiar problems facing rural people.

Values Necessary to Good Life in Rural Areas

Earning a Living and Learning to Live.—In a democratic society the values of any kind of group life need to be tested in the light of the fundamental values held most dear: the worth of the individual and his right to "life, liberty, and the pursuit of happiness." Most of our time is spent in earning a living. It is considered a distinct social value if an individual is able to earn his own living; the better he does this, the higher is the repute in which he is held by his neighbors. At one time it was thought to be a disgrace if one asked for charity, and in rural areas this is still largely true. Students of rural life realize, however, that earning a living is not all that is necessary. They know that learning to live a better kind of life may be the very thing which will induce people to become more efficient or to seek new ways of increasing their incomes. The chief stimuli to a fuller and more satisfactory life come out of family, neighborhood, and community influences, that is, the way people are accustomed to live. Yet an increasing number of other influences have an important bearing upon a better rural life. In learning how to live a really satisfactory rural life, rural people must find out how to use most effectively the full range of social resources at their command; if they can learn this it will mean much to them, as well as to urban people.

Working Together in Primary Groups.—The most successful farm family is one which encourages and enjoys good family cooperation. This is equally true of good neighborhood and community life; the most desirable type of community life is that in which there is a high degree of cooperation. The best kind of cooperation is that which is done on a face-to-face or primary basis.

Primary association, in another sense, is characteristic of rural life. Living so close to nature, to his land and to its creative processes, the good farmer is a willing worker who takes great delight in helping the good earth bring forth good crops and in caring for his livestock. Hard work becomes second nature to such a farmer, for he knows how much depends on his skill and the sweat of his brow. Appreciation of the meaning of work has a distinctive value which is inherent in rural life.

Those who work with rural people will make progress only when they come to understand and appreciate these basic elements of rural culture. To fail to recognize, for example, that a particular rural group has the utmost respect for its particular form of religious belief and to speak lightly of it will jeopardize the chance of doing anything with or for the group.

The Family Ideal.—Rural families are important because they produce the surplus population which replenishes our urban areas. The reproduction of the race, the education of the child, and the transmission of wealth from generation to generation are fundamental processes in rural life. The family ideal, as it is expressed in most of rural life, involves also the recognition of the divine in man and the worth of the human soul.[1]

The family on the farm usually has a highly developed loyalty to the state, a love of peace, a belief in the protection of life and property, and a desire to promote public welfare. There is emphasis on the dignity of labor and a recognition of the necessity of some sacrifice: the present for the future, and the parents for the children, and

---

[1] O. E. Baker, Ralph Borsodi, and M. L. Wilson, *Agriculture in Modern Life,* New York: Harper & Bros., 1939, p. 181.

the citizen for the state.[2] These are the very roots of democracy itself, for truly voluntary groups are by their very nature democratic. It is in rural areas that such voluntary group action is most widespread. The various forms include the church, the farmers' organization, the community club, the parent-teacher association, the 4-H club, and similar groups.

Rural Life Objectives

Such social values are closely related to rural life objectives. Primary rural objectives would unquestionably include the following: (1) preservation of soil resources, (2) retention of the family-sized farm, (3) making farm tenancy a steppingstone to farm ownership, (4) strengthening the farm family as a social unit, (5) increasing and, where necessary, restoring rural neighborliness, (6) strengthening the cohesiveness of rural organizations, (7) improving, by adequate health measures, the quality of the human stock in rural areas, (8) reorganizing schools in rural areas, to enable them to contribute more fully to rural life, (9) strengthening and revitalizing rural churches, and (10) bringing the benefits of social security to rural people. Positive programs designed to realize these objectives will lead to a good kind of life in rural areas and a protection for urban areas against deterioration and decay.[3]

Cultural Adaptation

Great changes have occurred in the life of rural people. The most apparent changes have come through adaptation and adoption of better tools, plants, and animals. The most significant (but frequently very slow) changes have come, and will continue to come, from modifications in ideas, attitudes, customs, habits, traditions, mores, and institutions. Let us take brief note of some of the most important cultural adaptations.

1. Tools are perhaps the most dynamic means for cultural adaptation and advancement in recorded history. From the invention of the wheel to the present day of tractors, combines, and other modern

2 For a further discussion of these values, see *ibid.*, pp. 181-182.
3 See a discussion of rural values and their importance to the whole of society in Liberty Hyde Bailey, *The Holy Earth*, New York: Charles Scribner's Sons, 1915, reprinted by the Christian Rural Fellowship, 1943; Carl C. Taylor, *Rural Sociology* (rev. ed.), New York: Harper & Bros., 1933, Ch. I; Dwight Sanderson, *Rural Sociology and Rural Social Organization*, New York: John Wiley & Sons, Inc., 1942, pp. 35-40; David Edgar Lindstrom, *Rural Life and the Church*, Champaign, Ill.: Garrard Press, 1946, Ch. VIII; George Russell, *The National Being*, New York: The Macmillan Co., 1930.

machines, agriculture has been increasingly mechanized. Today, the American farmer is probably more dependent on machines than are the farmers of any other country. In fact, his efficient use of machines is the major factor which lies back of our increased food supply. Modern means of transportation have helped the farmer escape social isolation.

In some cases, as in the substitution of machine for horse and mule power, there have come serious economic and social consequences: many farmers buy tractors even though their land does not permit efficient use of a tractor, and thus impair rather than improve the living standards of their families.

2. The development of hardier and more productive crop plants and animals has had a profound effect on the way the farmer lives and functions today. Consider, for example, the tremendous improvements which have been brought about by rust-resistant wheat, by hybrid seed corn, or by the introduction of soybeans as an American farm crop.

3. Disease control and modern sanitation measures have had a profound effect on rural social life. The control of contagious diseases in man reduces death rates and makes possible such great population increases in some areas that it leads to real population pressures on the food supply. On the other hand, the better control of diseases in animals makes for increased food production. This cultural improvement, therefore, is of world-wide concern and is directly related to the activity of the United Nations Food and Agriculture Organization.

4. Some of the greatest changes in the life of man come, however, in the creation and group acceptance of new ideas. The established processes of behavior, the way people are accustomed to doing things, are very influential in conditioning the behavior of individuals.[4] Most important are the folkways, the ways in which we act when we are in a certain group or society of people; and the mores, the "sanctioned" modes of behavior which form most of the body of our ordinary moral code and which are, therefore, more powerful than the folkways, for their violation may bring censure, group disapproval, or social ostracism. Our folkways and mores reflect such ideologies as (a) that hard work is a blessing and play is a sin, (b) natural resources are inexhaustible, (c) farm land values will always advance, (d) woman's place is in the home, and (e) that the "old ways" are best. Attitudes against "book learning"

---

[4] L. L. Bernard, *Social Psychology*, New York: Henry Holt & Co., 1926, Ch. VI.

and new ways of doing things, such as planting crops on the contour rather than in straight rows, are often hard to overcome.

Rural people have accepted new ideas concerning the improvement of their material culture much more rapidly than they have accepted ideas for improving their rural group and institutional life. We find widespread use of tractors, combines, and automobiles in a culture in which our schools, churches, and health protection facilities are by no means modern. It is far easier to secure their acceptance of better machines, plants, and animals than it is to influence their social institutions such as our traditional forms of worship, our long-established systems of education, our accepted methods relating to land tenure. Rural people may belong to a certain church, or send their children to a certain school, or vote in elections for a certain party, and may have their behavior conditioned by the kinds of controls exercised by these institutions. Scientific developments, such as the control of tuberculosis in cattle, can be carried out through legal means only if the people, through their institutions and organizations, accept such control as desirable.

The growth of governmental service, especially state and Federal service, is profoundly affecting rural culture. The early forms of government service, such as the rural free delivery of mail, were at first not accepted, but they are now things which no one would think of stopping. Later services, such as extension service, farm credit, soil conservation, farm security, and rural electrification, have all helped to raise the level of living and the culture of rural people. As any new government service is developed, it will affect or become a part of rural culture only so far as it becomes a part of the institution already accepted and used by rural people.

———

A man's customs, beliefs, attitudes, traditions, folkways, mores, and institutions are rooted in and profoundly affect his behavior. These, in turn, affect and are affected by the behavior of other men with whom he comes into contact and to whom he adjusts himself in collective behavior. Hence, study and understanding of these group influences are essential to the improvement of life, either in rural or in urban areas. Sociology, in essence, is a study of human association; rural sociology is a study of human association in rural areas.

DISCUSSION

1. Discuss the importance of rural life: List the reasons for the importance of rural life. Why will rural life continue to be basically important to the rest of society?
2. Discuss the trend with respect to the interdependence of rural and urban people: What are the ways in which rural and urban people are becoming increasingly interdependent? What are some of the distinctively rural characteristics that tend to persist?
3. What do you consider the chief values necessary to a good kind of rural life? Which are most important to the nurturing of a rural type of life? Which are of basic importance to the whole of society?
4. Which of the means of cultural adaptation are of greatest importance to the improvement of rural life? Which of them affect the everyday behavior of rural people most? Which need more study and discussion to be understood and used more effectively in the improvement of human welfare? Support your position in each case.
5. What are the chief objectives for the study of rural life?

READINGS

Bailey, Liberty Hyde. *The Holy Earth.* New York: The Christian Rural Fellowship, 1943.

Baker, O. E., Borsodi, Ralph, and Wilson, M. L. *Agriculture in Modern Life.* New York: Harper & Bros., 1939, Ch. X.

Lindstrom, David Edgar. *Rural Life and the Church.* Champaign, Ill.: Garrard Press, 1946, Ch. VIII.

Sorokin, P., Zimmerman, Carl C., and Galpin, C. J. *Systematic Source Book in Rural Sociology.* Minneapolis: University of Minnesota Press, 1930, I, Chs. 1-2.

West, James. *Plainville, U. S. A.* New York: Columbia University Press, 1945, Chs. 1-2.

Chapter 2

THE STUDY OF RURAL LIFE

In studying rural society we determine the most common forms of association among people, and then determine how these forms of association are adjusted to each other and to the cultural environment in which they function. Our ultimate aim is to help improve the conditions under which rural people live. But to study rural life effectively we must first get the facts about rural group life which are more or less hidden from ordinary observation, and relate these facts to other facts, so that we may predict the behavior of different kinds of groups under given circumstances and conditions. This is the scientific approach to the study of rural society.

Rural Life in the History of Man

In one sense, the long history of man is a record of the growth of many forms of group life, each with characteristic and sometimes unique features. Various forms of group life have been studied by social scientists and many are graphically recorded in our museums and libraries. It is possible to study a primitive form of group life, such as was developed by the Cliff Dwellers of our Southwest (Figure 1), or one that exists today in a backward tribe or community such as the Coppermine Eskimos of far northern Canada. We can even see evidences of earlier ways of making a living and of living in some of the marginal rural communities in our own or other civilized countries. The following greatly simplified statement shows the changes from rural to urban group occupations:

1. The Collectors.—The most primitive peoples are those who depend for their livelihood on the collection of wild fruits, and on hunting and fishing. In their roving search for food, such peoples have usually found it necessary or very desirable to band together into clans, tribes, and into groups of tribes, for protection against wild animals and enemy tribes. A better chance for survival was, obviously, a prime benefit of group association.

2. The Settlers.—Human civilization was profoundly affected when man began the cultivation of plants and the domestication of animals, for tribal life became less mobile when crops were cultivated and animals were raised for use as beasts of burden and as sources of food. Nevertheless, many of these primitive farmers still carried on their hunting and fishing activities. Even today, in some of our rural communities, there are people who gain at least part of their livelihood from hunting, fishing, and the collection of wild fruits and plants.[1]

Planting and harvesting were the beginning of a new culture— agriculture. It has a long and venerable history. It is a basic and essential occupation and mode of life.

3. The Traders and Townsmen.—A further development leading to our present complex form of society was the growth of the trading group. Its origins are found in tribal life, the basic pattern out of which village life began, for village life developed when some members of the tribe began to carry on trade in agricultural and manufactured products. The systems of social control (or government) were part and parcel of life in the tribe, both nomadic and stationary. In fact, the basic pattern of rural life in most parts of the world today is rooted in tribal or village life. In some of the more developed countries the evolving pattern has been for farmers to live on the land and not in villages. The traders have helped to transmit culture traits from tribe to tribe, from village to village; then from town to town, from city to city, and from country to country.

Another change took place when some individuals spent more and more of their time in trade, thus developing a merchant-manufacturing class. Village "specializations" came into being, many being direct outgrowths of the basic industry—agriculture. The grinding of grain outgrew the home and brought forth the local mill, the ancestor of the modern flour mill. The weaving of cloth, another typical home industry, was the ancestor of the present vast clothing industry. In such ways the people who lived in villages, some of which grew into towns, took over more and more of the arts and crafts, except those relating directly to the growing of crops and the care of animals.

Many services—economic, educational, social—have developed with the advance of agriculture and the growth of towns. These

---

[1] See James West, *Plainville, U.S.A.*, New York: Columbia University Press, 1945, pp. 116 ff.

service functions not only provide farmers with more effective tools, but also in other ways effect improvements in living.

4. The Industrialists.—As communications improved, trade became easier and economic and cultural services more varied. New occupations arose. Most of the manufacturing functions were no longer performed in the home. Great metropolitan centers developed, where manufacturing was carried on through a massing of machines in a small space near sources of power. Such urban centers needed abundant sources of raw materials and manpower. The farms, the forests, and the mines have been and are still the chief sources of raw materials, and a great source of manpower has been and continues to be the farms and the rural communities. The emphasis in mass production was on efficiency, often at the expense of the worker, who was regarded merely as a source of energy for converting raw materials into goods for human use.

5. The Laborers and Professional Workers.—In agriculture, especially on family farms, the workers can be operators or owners, as well as hired laborers. But in almost all other occupations—in the forests, in the mines, in the factories, in the stores, and on trains, buses, and trucks—the human power has been supplied by those who work in return for wages or salaries, for some other individual or group. The workers for wages, including those hired on farms, form the most numerous economic group in our society.

Likewise, professional workers have formed a most important social group. Religious leaders, teachers, artists, lawyers, statesmen, and other professional workers have made almost immeasurable contributions in almost all periods of the development of our civilization. Modern rural communities need, and must have, well-trained professional people just as much as our urban communities.

This division of labor and of service is a basic feature of our civilization, and is particularly characteristic of the most technically advanced countries in the world. In all of these occupations there is association, i.e., group activity, and much of civilized society's progress comes as a result of improved human relationships and association.

It is natural for people to form themselves into groups; group life is found whenever human beings come into association with each other. Hence it is important that we study human association and group life, finding ways and means for their improvement. This is as true of rural as it is of urban life.[2]

---

[2] See Carl C. Taylor and associates, *Rural Life in the United States*, New York: Alfred A. Knopf, 1949, p. 5.

Recognition of Rural Social Problems.—It was not until the turn of the 20th century that a widespread recognition was given to an increasing number of deficiencies in rural life, not a few of which were social. The Theodore Roosevelt Country Life Commission was formed as a result of this increasing awareness of the existence of serious economic and social ills in rural areas in this country. This Commission held hearings among rural people all over the country and then published a report listing the chief problems, many of which were at the heart of the social problems of rural people. This report gave impetus to the first rural social studies.

The underlying problem of country life, as stated by the Commission, is "to develop and maintain on our farms a civilization in full harmony with the best American ideals. To build up and maintain this civilization means, first of all, that the business of agriculture must be made to yield a reasonable return to those who follow it intelligently; and life on the farm must be made permanently satisfying to intelligent, progressive people." [3]

Work is carried on in the colleges of agriculture and the USDA. The Theodore Roosevelt Country Life Commission made its studies from 1908 to 1911, the report being published for the first time in 1911. In the two decades from 1910 to 1930 several outstanding rural life studies were made: Galpin's classical study of what he called the "rurban community" was published in 1915; [4] Williams' case studies of rural attitudes and ideals were made in 1925-26; [5] Wilson's study of an early New England community, in 1923; and the notable works of Butterfield and of Morgan came out in this period.[6] During this time work in rural sociology had been started at Cornell, Wisconsin, and in a few other college and university centers of the country. In the decade 1920 to 1930 new Federal legislation was passed for the appropriation of funds to make scientific studies of rural life. These were called Purnell funds; they were allocated to the experiment stations for studies in agricultural economics and rural sociology.[7] They are still the chief source of funds for carrying on research in rural sociology.

[3] Reprinted from *Report of the Commission on Country Life*, by permission of the University of North Carolina Press. Copyright, 1945, by the University of North Carolina Press. See also the full report from which the above has been taken.

[4] C. J. Galpin, *The Social Anatomy of an Agricultural Community*, Research Bull. 34, Univ. of Wisconsin Agr. Exp. Sta., 1915.

[5] J. M. Williams, *Our Rural Heritage*, New York: Alfred A. Knopf, 1925; J. M. Williams, *The Expansion of Rural Life*, New York: Alfred A. Knopf, 1926.

[6] W. H. Wilson, *The Evolution of the Country Community* (2nd ed.), Boston: The Pilgrim Press, 1923; K. L. Butterfield, "League for Rural Progress," in L. H. Bailey's *Cyclopedia of American Agriculture*, New York: The Macmillan Co., 1909; E. L. Morgan, *Mobilizing the Rural Community*, Ext. Bull. 23, Massachusetts Agr. Coll., 1918; T. N. Carver, *The Organization of a Rural Community*, Yearbook Separate 632, USDA, 1914.

[7] See Theodore W. Schultz, *Training and Recruiting of Personnel in the Rural Social Studies*, American Council on Education, 1941, pp. 4, 5.

The Division of Farm Population and Rural Life was formed in the Bureau of Agricultural Economics of the U. S. Department of Agriculture in 1919; its name was later changed to the Division of Farm Population and Rural Welfare. The bulk of the research work in rural sociology is thus done by this Division and in the colleges of agriculture throughout the country.[8]

Rural sociology is now being offered in courses in most colleges of agriculture, as well as in numerous teachers' colleges.[9] Many denominational or church-related colleges and theological seminaries also have courses in rural sociology. Extension work in rural sociology is being carried on from many of the colleges of agriculture, each one of which has one or more specialists in rural sociology on its staff. This work is becoming increasingly needed and used by all group workers in rural areas.

Use of Scientific Methods in the Study of Rural Life

It is well for the student to recognize that there have been a number of approaches to the study of group problems of rural people. The sociologist endeavors to study rural life impartially, factually, and analytically, just as does the economist, political scientist, or any other social scientist. The rural sociologist approaches the subject from the angle of human association in rural areas; all forms of human association, be they concerned with economic, political, religious, educational, or other forms, are the object of his study.

Research workers in rural sociology have used scientific methods in carrying on their work, though it is difficult to use exact methods of measurement in the social sciences. This is true because (1) the scientist cannot gain and maintain control over the subjects being studied, for he must study people in the environment in which they live; and (2) the social scientist has the difficult task of retaining an objectivity when he is working with people, especially if he finds it necessary to live with the people whom he is studying.

Nevertheless, it is imperative that observation be as careful in the field of the social sciences as in that of the physical sciences if the results are to be reliable; for in order to have a science we must

8 See W. A. Anderson, "Rural Sociology in Agricultural Colleges," and Theodore B. Manny, "The Division of Farm Population and Rural Life, U. S. Department of Agriculture," both in *Rural America*, Vol. XIV, No. 2, February, 1936.

9 Judson T. Landis, "Rural Sociology in the Teachers' Colleges of the United States," *Rural Sociology*, Vol. X, No. 3, September, 1945, pp. 313-316.

Figure 1. Evidence of Primitive Group Life in the United States

Cliff Palace, Mesa Verde National Park. (Courtesy National Park Service)

develop an organized body of knowledge which has been tested for validity and reliability by the best known scientific methods.

Rural people live in close-knit groups: the family, the neighborhood, the community, and the various interest groups and institutions in rural life. It is through the study of their group life that we find many of the ways in which rural people are distinctive. It is through the study of their group life, moreover, that suggestions for many rural life improvements can be made. Group life and human relationships in rural areas compose the subject matter and field of the science of rural sociology.

Definition of the Group.—In order to study rural group life we must have clearly in mind what the rural sociologist means by a group. A social group is defined as follows:

1. A plurality, that is, it is made up of two or more persons.
2. A medium for psychic interaction, an interplay of the expressed thoughts of individuals.
3. An entity: members are conscious of being members of a group and others recognize it as a group.

In making a study of rural groups, we must recognize that they have the above characteristics. By testing them for these characteristics we can isolate them as groups and are then ready to analyze them.

Variations in Group Life.—Any student who starts to make a systematic study of group life can expect to find many kinds of groups. Most studies of rural life groups try to deal, therefore, with only one type of group, such as a rural neighborhood, a rural community, or a rural special-interest group. Even among these various types of groups there are, of course, great differences. But, as will be seen, there are basic patterns which can be discovered by studying large numbers of groups.

Rural groups may be temporary; a loafing group may form on town sidewalks on Saturday night. These temporary groups may be significant, for out of them may come individual or group decisions to take some action, such as to vote a certain way in a school election. Or rural groups may be relatively permanent, such as a school board or a church group. The nature of these various kinds of groups and what they can do to improve rural life are of vast importance to the student of rural sociology. They are an expression of democracy.

Rural groups can be viewed, also, from the standpoint of their simplicity or their complexity. Some rural groups, such as threshing rings or visiting groups, are simple in their organizational structure, but may be very important in the lives of the people. Other groups, such as a school system, can be very complex, operating under fixed rules of behavior, and changes in them can come but slowly.

Groups may also be made up of people who live close together, or they may be spread over a community, over a county, or even over an entire nation. The relations of local groups to each other and to more widespread groups are of increasing importance in rural life. The development of new forms of groups attached to the school, for example, can affect the groups already functioning in the church.

Differences Between Rural and Urban Life.—It is not too difficult to see the ordinary differences between rural and urban life. However, when one tries to define these differences and evaluate them he finds it a much more difficult task. A simple definition of "rural" is not possible, for, obviously, any description of rural life must take into account the traits wherein rural people differ from urban people. It is difficult indeed to assess these. More important, any definition of rural life must recognize that there are gradations of "rural," from the open country to the rural town near the city, both of which may depend in many ways on the people engaged in agriculture. We must recognize these gradations and must remember that the conditions which produce them are constantly changing.

Some of the most significant differences between rural and urban life are:

1. The chief characteristic of rural life is its dominant economic dependence on one occupation: agriculture. Farm people, particularly, are engaged in an occupation in which the whole family is primarily interested and in which most of them are engaged for most of the time. The mechanization of agriculture, the trend toward decentralization of urban industry, and the increase in part-time farming have, however, tended to narrow somewhat the gap between the types of rural and urban occupations.

2. The family life of rural, and especially farm, families is usually more closely knit because of their common occupation. Hence, they are more self-contained. Modern means of communication, however, and a lowering of the farm family size, as well as other influences, have tended to minimize the differences between rural and

urban families. Even so, the family is the important unit of rural society; whereas in urban society more social emphasis is placed upon the individual.

3. Rural communities are made up of people with firsthand knowledge of each other and common interests in similar pursuits and activities. Such communities are smaller, more compact, and less complex in organization than urban communities. However, the nearer they are to urban centers the less cohesiveness they have because the interests of many of their people become submerged in the interests of the urban center.

4. The rural church, the rural school, and other institutions are smaller than those in the city. They are made up of people who have more interests in common, and are more intimate and informal. Though many rural institutions take their patterns of action from urban life, they are nevertheless definitely influenced by the environment in which they function. For better or for worse, however, these differences are also becoming less marked as rural and town people join in the support of their institutions, especially their schools and churches.

5. Rural people are spread out. The American rural community is made up of those who live on scattered farmsteads and those who live in villages or towns. Even with this dispersed pattern of occupancy there is still more intimacy, more social contact, and more opportunity for mutual association among the same people, than there is among dwellers in urban areas. The social contacts of rural people are, it is true, more restricted than the contacts of urban people, but they are much less fleeting in nature.

6. This greater permanency of social contacts among rural people helps to explain why they think alike and are more alike than urban people. There is among farmers, of course, a general interest in the same occupation. This interest is also quite largely shared by the village and town people, many of whom have interests in farming or in farm people, through ownership of farms, through kinship, or by reason of trade, church, school, or other contacts.

7. Rural people do not move so much as city people, who seem always to be on the move. In the country, people tend to remain in one place for a longer time and when they do move it is usually within the same community or neighborhood. Many rural people spend their entire lives only a few miles from the place of their birth.

8. Because of their more stationary population, the groups formed by rural people are usually fairly stable and permanent, whereas groups in the city, with their fluctuating population, tend to

be temporary. For the same reason, groups in rural areas change less in membership than do groups in the city, which have a larger potential number to draw from.

The system of social contacts is different. There are fewer contacts per man and fewer contacts with different persons in rural areas than in urban areas. The contacts in rural areas are likely to be more permanent, more personal, more "human" than in urban areas.[10]

Though one can use the above criteria qualitatively to distinguish rural life from urban life, yet they are at best relative, for rural shades gradually into urban. There are, it is obvious, city people who live in the country and country people who live in the city. Moreover, the open country areas are not the only ones included in the term "rural," for the United States Bureau of the Census draws the line at places of 2,500 population. Though there are places larger than 2,500 which are primarily rural, yet for counting purposes it is necessary to draw the line somewhere and the best point seems to be a population of 2,500. Many townspeople do look upon themselves as having interests more closely related to those in the cities than to those who live on the farms. It is a fact, however, that people who live in villages and towns are increasingly dependent on, and have an increasing number of common interests with, those who live on the farms. If a rural community is to have a modern school system, for example, it must be a town-country school and give due attention to country or agricultural as well as other interests.

Relative Self-Sufficiency of Rural Groups.—People who engage in agriculture have traditionally formed many relatively self-sufficient groups. The early farmer's club, for example, was usually quite independent of other groups. The farm family, itself, is more self-sufficient than the family group in almost any other form of society. But with the increasing complexity of rural society, the farm family and other rural groups have become more and more interdependent. It is difficult for some groups in rural society to recognize this interdependence, however, and this is a definite deterrent to the most effective rural progress. Nevertheless, the village or small town is becoming more and more dependent upon the farming class for its economic and social welfare, and farm people are

---

[10] See the lengthier analyses of differences between rural and urban life in Pitirim Sorokin and Carl C. Zimmerman, *Principles of Rural-Urban Sociology*, New York: Henry Holt & Co., Inc., 1929, Chs. II, IV, and T. Lynn Smith, *The Sociology of Rural Life*, New York: Harper & Bros., 1947. Ch. II,

more and more dependent on town and city people for many economic, educational, and social services.

Structure and Function of Rural Groups

A basic, analytical approach to the study of any group can be made with respect to its structure: how it is put together, and its function: what it does. These two aspects may be analyzed as follows:

Structure.—Structure is partially defined in terms of means of identification: what limits the group or sets it apart from other groups. This is usually seen in the membership requirements or the conditions which make it a group, such as the locality in which it functions. Structure can also be studied from the standpoint of the composition of the group: the kinds of individuals who make up the group.

The group structure is also determined by the system of relationships existing between the members. Some have roles to play different from others within the group; these are its intragroup relations. Finally, its structure is determined by its relations to other groups: how it is affected or influenced by other groups. These are its intergroup relations.

Functions.—The functions of the group can be studied: (a) from the standpoint of what the group does for its members—its intragroup functions; (b) from the standpoint of what it does in relation to other groups—its intergroup functions; and (c) from the standpoint of the quality of the functions performed by the group—in terms of what happens to the individual as a result of contacts in the group, in terms of the character of the functioning of the group, and in terms of the influence of the group on the community or society in which it functions. Using the above as a frame of reference, studies can be made of all forms of group life in rural areas: the family, the community, the church, the school, the lodge, and the numerous organized and unorganized groups that can be found in all rural communities.

Primary and Secondary Groups.—"Primary" and "secondary" are terms used to distinguish types of group relations according to the degree of consensus and unanimity. Primary groups provide habitual personal, or face-to-face, contacts such as are provided in the family, play group, or closely knit neighborhood. Secondary groups supply less permanent and direct relationships. They fulfill fewer interests, and their bonds are more contractual and less sympathetic.

Forms of Interaction.—We have outlined briefly the characteristics of the group and have seen that the chief feature of group life is interaction, which leads to association or dissociation. A simple definition of the term interaction is "social contact resulting in modification of behavior." [11] Communication is the medium of social interaction, and attitudes and values are the forces which determine its nature and quality.

Forms of Rural Intragroup Interaction.—The chief forms of social interaction have been given the names "intragroup interaction" and "intergroup interaction." Intragroup interaction is that which takes place within a specified group, and intergroup interaction is that which takes place between groups. The type of interaction which takes place within a group depends on the relative intimacy and cohesiveness of the group.

1. Domestic interaction takes place in a family and is especially characteristic of farm family groups, for farming requires much more family cooperation than does any other kind of life. This form of interaction is carried over to some degree into neighborhood, fraternal, and similar groups; the more active the neighborhood the more likely there is to be domestic interaction, such as trading work or family visiting.

2. Obedience and submission are forms of interaction found in some rural groups, particularly family groups in which the father or head of the family exerts a paternal type of domination over other members of the family. These forms are found also in political groups, in church groups, and in other closely knit groups in rural life.

3. Neighboring is a valuable type of social interaction closely akin to domestic interaction. It is the sort of interaction which usually carries with it an unselfish concern for those in distress as well as interest in outstanding achievements.

4. Friendly competition is a very characteristic type of interaction in rural areas. It is regarded as essential to the full development of the school child. Friendly competition is found in fairs, games, and other forms of informal rural group life.

5. Leader and group interaction, in which there may be some form of parliamentary procedure in conducting group discussions,

---

[11] See Florian Znaniecki, *Social Action*, New York: Farrar & Rinehart, 1936, pp. 33-34, 71-77, for a discussion of the nature of social action.

is very characteristic of social interaction in rural areas. In some groups, such as those in school, it may take the form of teacher and learner interaction, in which there is considerable domination and submission.

6. Coordinated participation is a form of intragroup interaction which is best illustrated by a music group or an athletic team. It is any group in which each member is assigned to a specific role and then must play that role effectively if the group effort is to be successful.

7. Group discussion is recognized as a significant form of intragroup interaction in rural areas. The more common forms are conversation, gossip, "cracker-barrel," and similar rural discussion groups. In recent years considerable stimulation has been given to planned discussion groups in order to gain the participation of all members of the group in the solution of the problem.[12]

Forms of Rural Intergroup Interaction.—Interaction which takes place between groups is highly varied and depends for its nature on the types of groups involved and the circumstances surrounding the intergroup contacts.

The two fundamental forms of interaction are opposition and cooperation. The former is usually divided into competition and conflict. From opposition and cooperation spring differentiation, or the division of social labor in terms of role and status. Out of conflict comes accommodation or compromise, toleration, or some other truce which strikes a working balance between contending groups or individuals. From conflict and differentiation emerges the process closely related to accommodation called stratification, or the formation of society into castes, classes, or orders of status. Out of competition, conflict, and cooperation may arise assimilation, or the merging of divergent groups or persons into a new and homogeneous association.[13]

Let us examine these forms of interaction a little further:

1. Conflict is one of the most noted forms of intergroup interaction. Conflict may be restricted, as in conflicts over school consolidation, and result in the formation of two groups or in accommodation of one group to the other's wishes. Conflict which is absolute results in the attempted destruction of one group by the other or the exclusive possession by one of the value desired by both. It can result in the assimilation of one group and its values by the other.

12 See materials published by the Division of Program Study and Discussion, BAE, USDA.
13 Kimball Young, *Sociology*, New York: American Book Co., 1942, p. 642.

Class conflicts, race conflicts, or even conflicts over school consolidation are always recognized as such by those involved. If
conflicts are tactfully handled by the group leaders they can result
in some form of cooperation or accommodation. If, however, emotions predominate over efforts to find facts and to base action on
those facts, lifelong animosities may result.

2. Competition, also oppositional, is another form of intergroup
interaction which is indirect and involves some association, for competitors are usually seeking the same objective. Competition, of
course, may also take place within a group. It is usually interaction
without social contact in that there is not necessarily any direct contact between competitors. Direct competition may degenerate into
conflict. Hence, the various forms of competition range from the
completely indirect, such as the competition of the city for small
town trade, to direct, individual competition, such as that in athletic
contests. Competition is almost universal and among individuals can
be wholesome. On the other hand, as Young says, the strain of un-
satisfied competition may result in conflict or personal demoraliza-
tion.[14] Unrestrained or unregulated competition may well prove
injurious to an individual, to a group, or to the common welfare.

3. Cooperation is accommodational. It is a form of intergroup
interaction which, in its broadest sense, is fundamentally a group
process. Its earliest expression in civilized society was in the form
of mutual aid. Two types of interaction are involved in cooperation: (a) consensus, or the tacit agreement among members of a
group or between groups to do something together, as in helping
a sick neighbor gather in his crops; and (b) socialization, in which
a system or accepted manner of cooperation is worked out and used
to meet a need, or in which an individual learns to work together
with a group of his fellows.

Cooperation may grow out of recognition of the harmful effects
of competition. Church denominations, for example, can minimize
interchurch conflict through cooperation in planning weekday religious education programs.

Understanding Rural Society Processes

The change which comes in a group or a community from the
various forms of social interaction may be part of what is called a
social process. The change must occur over a period of time.
When, for example, a neighborhood changes through the years by

14 *Ibid.* See his discussion, ch. 24.

reason of people moving in or out, or if other influences bring about new forms of group behavior, we say this change has been a social process.

Causes of Social Changes.—No society is static, however much it may appear to be so. Rural society is constantly changing. The change may be due to physiological, technological, ideological, or to other forces. Soil erosion or depletion, droughts, dust storms or floods, the exhaustion of minerals or over-cutting of forests are all significant and potent causes of social change. The movement of people from place to place, with new ideas, methods, or philosophies which they weave into their new cultural environment, is another tremendously significant factor of social change.

Important discoveries, inventions, and innovations, such as the printing press, railroads, rural free delivery, hybrid seed corn, radio, electrification, cause social changes in the groups affected by them. New ideas or values such as the idea of religious liberty, the growing importance of social security, the spreading acceptance of the Rochdale idea of cooperation, and of group medical care, have caused social changes.

Most social changes take place slowly. When new things come along there is hesitancy on the part of rural people to accept them, for to them the old ways are good enough. The resistance to new ideas for material improvement is usually not as great as the resistance to new social relationships. Such resistance may in one way be a good thing, for it can be a sort of insurance against poorly tested techniques which, if accepted too rapidly, may do more harm than good. But if resistance to desirable or widely supported ideas becomes too great, conflict in the form of community feuds, revolution, or war, may result. The change can come gradually, however, as in the form of the farmers' movements for redress of wrongs, which have been in progress for the last 75 years.

Forms of Social Process.—Social processes may result in a variety of forms of group life, both associational and dissociational. These forms may be recognized under the following categories:

1. Accommodation, in which the individuals or groups are able to exist together, or in the temporary domination or suppression of one group by the other. Accommodation may also result in a stalemate, which may be a compromise, arbitration, conciliation, or armistice, and which may result in a state of toleration or tolerant participation.

2. Assimilation, which is the fusion of the social traits or culture of one group with that of another, results in common attitudes and values. This is a slow process and comes about through the gradual adoption by both groups of common customs, habits, folkways, mores, and laws. This form of social process may take the form, for example, of urbanization, wherein rural people take on the ways of urban people; or in acculturation, which is the acceptance of the culture traits of one society by the other.

3. Stratification, which is the splitting of one group into two or more competing or conflicting groups; or the natural grouping of a society into strata, such as the sharecropper class, which is set apart in some communities into a class by itself. Stratification is social process, and the social class is the result.

4. Institutionalization, which is the formalization or standardization of forms of human behavior. When a group goes through the process of making a practice a traditional and well-accepted part of the group life, that practice may be said to have become institutionalized.

Cultural lag is a result of lag between processes: the more rapid acceptance of certain ideas or modes of behavior than of others. Ideas relative to material things are usually more readily accepted than those which relate to individual or group welfare. For example, farmers quite readily use hybrid corn, but have been slow to· accept school consolidation.

Social Trends.—Our ability to see and measure the direction in which social changes are carrying us will help us to adjust ourselves to them. If we are able to study these changes and understand the form or forms of social processes going on, we may be able to make our plans to suit the situation in which we find ourselves.

An intelligent approach to the problems of discerning social trends is to find and chart the facts—facts about population changes, for example. Then we must relate these facts to the situations in the past and try to predict the future. In the economic field, to cite another example, farm people have found agricultural outlook reports to be of great value. In the same way, outlook reports on occupational changes, changes in size and composition of families, health conditions, school enrollments, church or other organizational membership, or similar subjects, can help the people of the community anticipate and prepare for future developments. An outlook service geared to human changes as well as to the trends in production and prices is needed if we are to look ahead intelligently.

Definition and Forms of Social Control.—The forces which cause persons to act collectively are the social controls exercised over them or accepted by them. They are the means whereby social order is established and maintained. The various forms of social control operate differently in different kinds of groups.[15] In a democratic society the people making up the group consciously determine the forms of social control; in a totalitarian society the controls are vested in the state.

In small or primary groups the controls are largely group controls or those exercised through the behavior of the group, whereas in large or secondary groups they are likely to be more legalistic or institutionalized. The chief types of these social controls are:

1. Prevailing attitudes, which grow out of the ways in which a people have become habituated to or accustomed to doing things. As long as a people hold the attitude, for example, that the traditional ways of doing things are the best, it will be difficult to get new and modern practices adopted.

2. Habits, fads, and customs, which are closely related. If an individual becomes accustomed to doing a thing in a certain way, it is not long until that becomes a habit for him. Fads, which are often forerunners of customs, grow out of the quick acceptance by members of a group of new "tricks," as of dress. Customs are simply the accepted, habitual way of the group. There is nothing compulsory about the customary way, but an individual will hesitate before he breaks away from it, for when he does, he becomes "different."

3. Folkways are the ways in which particular groups do different things. The habits of dress or of worship of certain religious groups may be said to be a part of their folkways. As with customs, folkways have no element of compulsion except that the person who behaves differently is set apart, and few members of a group like to be set apart.

4. Mores, which is a sociological term, are the group's folkways in which there are elements of threat or compulsion. They are closely related to the ingrained beliefs of the magical or superstitious practices of the group. Mores are a most important form of social control in rural areas. For instance, urban workers who come into rural areas and try to carry with them their city ways are likely to be criticized or not accepted by the group.

5. Institutions are established ways of doing things. They are organized sanctions which have been developed over long periods of

15 See Lowry Nelson, *Rural Sociology*, New York: American Book Company, 1948, p. 23.

time. Our methods of worship, of imparting knowledge through schools, of caring for the poor, are institutions, and the order they impose upon us is called institutional control.

6. Public opinion is also an important form of social control. There are those who dare not go against what the public believes is the right thing, though action in accordance with public opinion may greatly injure many innocent people. It may be formed through gossip, by means of whispering campaigns, or by radio, newspaper, or similar means of communication. There are numerous efforts to measure or test public opinion, and national politics have sometimes been guided by these tests.

7. Tradition is a form of social control which is closely related to the folkways of a people, and which is more likely to operate in long established communities in which families develop some form of ancestral worship. These types of groups are slow to abandon traditional methods of farming, even when better methods are urged on them.

8. Laws are forms of social control derived from the mores of the society. New laws come into being usually as a result of a desire to impose practices upon all of the group by legal means. They will be observed locally only if the group sanctions them.

9. Science, which can serve to release a people from a burdensome practice, is coming to exercise some degree of social control. Scientific developments such as the discovery of the means of controlling animal diseases can induce a group to secure legal means for the enforcement of control measures, as has been done in the case of tuberculosis in cattle.

Means of Social Control.—These forms of social control operate differently in different forms of groups, and different means of social control are used in different types of situations in which one or more of these forms operate. In all forms of social control the essence is the impact of one personality upon another. Some of the chief means of social control are:

1. Suggestion and imitation. The effectiveness of suggestion is determined by the impression made. This is often gained through the stirring of feelings and emotions and the use of such devices as ritual, music, and propaganda. Emotion often plays the major role, relegating reason to a secondary place.

2. Teaching and learning. We who live in a democracy believe that in an age of rapid progress the best means of control is through training people to evaluate and to discriminate between the estab-

lished social values and to judge and to be willing to try new ideas. It is through teaching and learning that we obtain many of the social ends desired.

3. Approval and disapproval. Flattery, praise, persuasion, and commendation are forms of approval. Derisive laughter, ridicule, satire, gossip, and blasphemy can be made expressions of disapproval. These means accompany attitudes of like and dislike. Conscious use of approval through systems of recognition often sets the individual apart from his group, and unless he has a strong personality which can overcome the desire to exploit such recognition, it can make living and working with one's fellows very difficult.

4. Coercion and submission. Coercion or the use of force, whether or not backed by rules or laws, is frequently resented. Any such means of social control has no permanent value unless the laws are adopted by the group and unless the individual can be induced to accept them rather than to suffer loss of his status in the group.

The forms and means of social control which are informal and which grow out of the group life are probably more effective in rural than in urban life. The closely knit nature of group life in rural communities—family, kinship, and neighborhood—makes them potent forces in maintaining social control.

Social Planning.—We have seen that in a democracy the people making up a group consciously determine the forms of social control, and that these forms develop gradually out of the slow change in values and attitudes. But with a rapidly changing social order, when rural people are increasingly dependent on other groups for their welfare, new forms of social control have been developed.

1. Farmers are more influenced today by state and national laws than they have ever been previously. Regulations relating to crops, prices, traffic, health, education, and welfare have developed rapidly in the last twenty years. Farmers are no longer primarily influenced by local regulations; they are coming more and more under the influence of state and national laws. These have come to be known as forms of social planning. They are desirable if the local people have had a real part in the planning process resulting in the regulation or laws.

2. Social planning can come as a result of discussion of needs in a group or community. People recognize a need, discuss the means

of meeting the need, decide upon a solution, and agree to abide by
the solution. Their agreement forms the basis for the exercise of
social control. They may agree, for example, to have all children
entering school for the first time given complete medical examinations. This is the basis for working out the means to be used in
carrying out the agreement. The first discussions may be held by
special groups, such as the schools, and final action taken by them
as well, or they can come through community councils, committees,
or organizations.

3. Social planning can come by means of a combination of local
discussions and organization and of assistance by community,
county, state, and Federal committees or agencies concerned with
agriculture, land use, nutrition, schools, or other matters of interest. The test of such forms of planning for securing new social
practices is the acceptance of them by the people.

To cite an example, we need to conserve our soils. In a democratic society we can form agencies of social control, such as soil
conservation districts, only by a majority vote of the landowners.
The chief means used to convince the landowners of the value of
these districts are suggestion, imitation, teaching, and learning. It
is conceivable, of course, that other means would have to be used
if soil erosion proceeded so far as to endanger the welfare of the
nation. This is why it is so important to carry on social planning by
means of a combination of local group discussion and action, with
county, state, and Federal assistance. Otherwise, rural society can
lose its unique freedom to accept new forms of social control and
might be placed in the position of accepting them by force of circumstances, national or even international in scope.

The Study of Rural Problems and Their Solutions

The student of rural life can approach his subject in two ways:
from the standpoint of finding facts about it and presenting those
facts and his interpretations of them for what they are worth; or
from the standpoint of consciously seeking the needs and problems
facing rural people and endeavoring to find solutions for them. The
one approach does not exclude the other, for in acquiring a body
of facts about rural life the student contributes materially to the
solution of problems facing rural people. If the primary interest
is to find solutions to needs and problems, the methods of study
may differ, and the student may feel the necessity for helping to set
social processes in motion.

Needs and Problems of Rural Life.—A full description of the needs and problems of rural life is impossible to prepare, for new problems are constantly arising. Furthermore, problems and needs are different for different peoples. The major problems and needs of rural life, however, and their suggested solutions so far as they are known, are discussed in the various chapters of this book. They may be stated as follows:

1. Population. The need for and problem of maintaining a virile type of people in the rural community.
2. The family. The need for and problem of nurturing a desirable type of family life in rural areas.
3. Security. The need for and problem of providing economic and social means for the development of a good kind of life in the rural community.
4. Organization. The need for and problem of devising neighborhoods, communities, and other rural groups which will contribute most to a desirable kind of rural life.
5. Institutions. The need for and problem of providing the best possible schools, churches, libraries, and other institutions in rural areas for education, health protection, recreation, and the provision of religious and cultural advancement in these areas.

We can, of course, recognize many other needs and problems. Rural people are becoming urbanized, many have drifted to the city, city ways have come to the country, and these have created sociological problems. Isolation has always been a part of rural life and still is a problem, though there are many means of overcoming it. Many farm people lack the cooperative spirit, and programs for effective and worthwhile cooperation are often thwarted because of this. The attainment of economic as well as social efficiency is a problem with which many agricultural economists and rural sociologists, as well as other leaders, are struggling.

The Role of Social Organization.—A measure of the value of the scientific findings of rural sociology is whether and to what extent conditions have been improved through their application. The chief means for the application of the science of rural sociology is through the techniques of rural social organization.

Social organization is simply the way in which people act together in securing desired ends. It involves formalized modes of acting together, making it possible to do things in groups better than they can be done otherwise; to accomplish ends otherwise impossible; to give the individual social experience; to get a group of individuals to form the habit or custom of acting together, thus saving time and effort and avoiding friction.

The effectiveness of social organization can be measured in a number of ways:

1. The effect on the individual. The personality—the self—is a *social* self: it is a self chiefly in terms of its reaction to its social environment.[16] The personality of the individual is therefore a product of group contact as well as of inheritance; the more the person takes part in group life, the broader is his personality. That does not mean that all group contacts make for the best kind of personality, for some groups such as gangs may produce highly antisocial personalities. One test of social organization, then, is the kind or quality of the personality that is developed. The development of personality through group contacts is called socialization: the "all-around participation in the thinking, the feeling, and the activities of the group."[17] In a group the individual learns what the group expects of him and what he can expect from the group.

2. The work of the group. The simplest measure of the value of a group is for its members to say "it is good." Each group may thus set up its own system of values, but these values must be tested in terms of the total culture of the society in which the group functions. The success of the group is therefore measured not only in terms of the extent to which it accomplishes its objectives but also in terms of the effectiveness with which it develops personality on the one hand, and by the degree to which it advances the community or social welfare on the other hand.

Groups which are not formally organized, such as families, cliques, and neighborhood or locality groups, can be evaluated only on the basis of whether or not they maintain approved values. One measure of effective social organization, then, is the degree to which it assists such groups to become conscious of their purposes and values, and to make them positive, voluntary objectives.

3. Community welfare. The most significant measure of the effectiveness of social organization lies in the degree to which it contributes to community welfare. The existence of desirable social organization depends upon the various groups in the community being

[16] Charles H. Cooley, *Human Nature and the Social Order,* New York: Chas. Scribner's Sons, 1902, p. 147.

[17] E. W. Burgess, *The Function of Socialization in Social Evolution,* Chicago: University of Chicago Press, 1916, pp. 236-237.

"so interrelated that the effectiveness of each is increased by its relation to the rest." [18] The integration of group activities is the heart
of social organization in so far as it is related to community welfare.

The effectiveness of social organization, then, can be measured
in terms of community betterment. The highest form of social organization will provide for some competition and allow for some
conflict, both of which cannot be entirely avoided. In doing so it
will endeavor to create social attitudes which recognize and tolerate
differences of opinion, and it will make use of these in the attainment of the highest degree of socialization possible on the part of
the individuals who make up the community.

Rural Community Organization.—The test of rural community
organization is its adequacy. [19] In striving for adequate community
organization, the people and their leaders will work for groups, organizations, and institutions sufficient to meet the needs of the people
within the limits of their ability to support them. They will try to
make these social organizations and social institutions adequate to the
needs of the people of the community.

The aim in a democratic society, whether in rural or in urban life,
is to give the fullest possible opportunity for development of personality and to advance the group and common welfare. One of
the best measures of the social organization of a community is the
degree to which all of its people participate in its organizations and
institutions, and the extent to which they make real contributions to
the community in which they live.

———

We have seen that rural sociology is the study of human association in rural areas. We recognize that the chief characteristic of
rural people is their nearness to and dependence on agriculture. The
ultimate aim of the study of rural society is to help rural people
achieve better living, which is as important as better farming and
better business. [20]

———

18 E. C. Hayes, *Introduction to the Study of Sociology*, New York: D. Appleton-Century
Co., Inc., 1919, p. 410.
19 For a fuller discussion of procedures in rural community organization, see Chapters
8, 9, and 10.
20 Horace Plunkett, an English social scientist working for the improvement of rural
conditions, coined the phrase "better farming, better business, better living," from which this
has been taken.

DISCUSSION

1. What are the aims of the science of rural sociology? Why is it difficult to use the scientific method in rural sociology? What is involved
in a scientific study of rural society?
2. Apply the definition of a group to the analysis of a rural group with
which you are intimately acquainted. Analyze the structure and functions of this group.
3. Describe the group situations in your experience that will illustrate
conflict, competition, and cooperation. Which were intergroup inter-
actions? which intragroup? What were the results of the operation
of these forces in the situations you have just described?
4. What are the chief causes of social change? When are such changes
called social processes? Describe one situation in your experience,
preferably taken from rural life, in which the various forms of social
process you have studied take place. What is the meaning of the
term "social trends"?
5. List the forms of social control studied, arranging them in order of
importance in causing immediate change. Which are most effective
in setting a social process in motion?
6. Make a list of the needs and problems in rural life. What is the role
of social organization in meeting these needs? What measures can be
used to show the effects of social organization? How would you test
the adequacy of social organization?

Readings

Albig, William. *Public Opinion.* New York: McGraw-Hill Book Co., Inc.,
1939, Ch. IV.
Gillette, J. M. *Rural Sociology.* New York: The Macmillan Co., 1936, Ch. I.
Hawthorne, H. B. *The Sociology of Rural Life.* New York: D. Appleton-
Century Co., Inc., 1926, Ch. I.
Hiller, E. T. *Principles of Sociology.* New York: Harper & Bros., 1933,
Chs. I, II.
Kolb, J. H., and Brunner, Edmund deS. *A Study of Rural Society.* New York:
Houghton Mifflin Co., 1946, Chs. I, II.
Landis, Paul H. *Rural Life in Process.* New York: McGraw-Hill Book Co.,
Inc., 1940, Ch. V.
Sanderson, Dwight W. *Rural Sociology and Rural Social Organization.* New
York: John Wiley & Sons, Inc., 1942, Chs. III, XXVI, XXVII.
Sims, N. L. *Elements of Rural Sociology.* New York: Thomas Y. Crowell Co.,
1940, Ch. I.
Smith, T. Lynn. *The Sociology of Rural Life.* New York: Harper & Bros.,
1946, Chs. I, II.

Chapter 3

ENVIRONMENT AND CULTURE PATTERNS

The land on which rural people live is society's basic resource. Unwarranted exploitation of the land, if long continued, can only lead to a nation's permanent impoverishment. Therefore, the proper use of our land resources is to the best long-time interests not only of the people on the land, but also to the interests of those who use the products of the land, and is therefore of utmost importance to all of society.

The natural environment in which rural people live must be studied because the factors of the physical environment—the climate, the topography, and the nature of the soil—no matter how favorable, directly influence the culture patterns which rural people have developed. Directly or indirectly, these factors limit the degree to which rural people can live the good life. Let us, then, first examine the physical environment in which rural people live, and then note the influence of diverse physical environment upon the settlement patterns and upon the ways in which the land is now used.

The Land on Which Rural People Live

The Influence of Rainfall.—The abundance or the lack of rainfall, and its seasonal distribution, determine whether or not people can farm, the kind of farming they can carry on, the distances they live from one another and, in some ways, the social organizations which they can develop. Rainfall conditions in the United States, when mapped, show ample rainfall in the eastern half of the nation; sparse rainfall in the Great Plains; very little rainfall in the western mountain regions and the Southwest; and abundant rainfall in the Pacific Northwest. In each of these regions crop adaptations form one of the bases for soil and crop areas.

Approximately three fifths of the 1,905,361,920 acres of land in the United States is in farms. (Table 1 and Figure 2.) Less than one fifth of this acreage, however, is in harvested cropland. Though most of the good farming land is in the Mississippi Valley, there are many fertile areas in other parts. The Plains Region, for example,

AMERICAN RURAL LIFE

TABLE 1. ACRES AND PERCENTAGE OF ALL LAND WHICH WAS IN FARMS AND IN HARVESTED CROP LAND IN THE UNITED STATES IN 1945 *

Item	Acres	Per Cent
Total	1,905,361,920	100.0
Farms	1,141,615,364	59.9
Harvested crops	352,865,765	18.5

Production Record of Farmers During World War II Shown by Agricultural Census, Dept. of Commerce, Bureau of the Census, mimeograph release, March, 1947, p. 5.

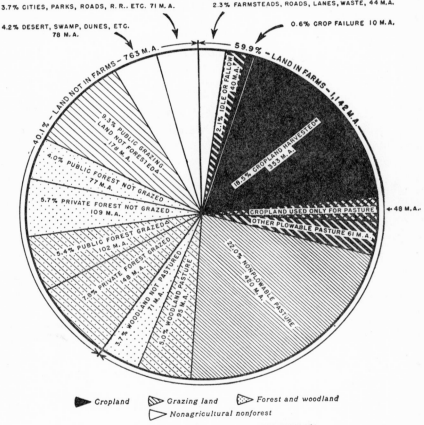

Figure 2. Major Uses of Land in the United States

Nearly three fifths is in farms or ranches; of this two fifths is cropland. (BAE, USDA)

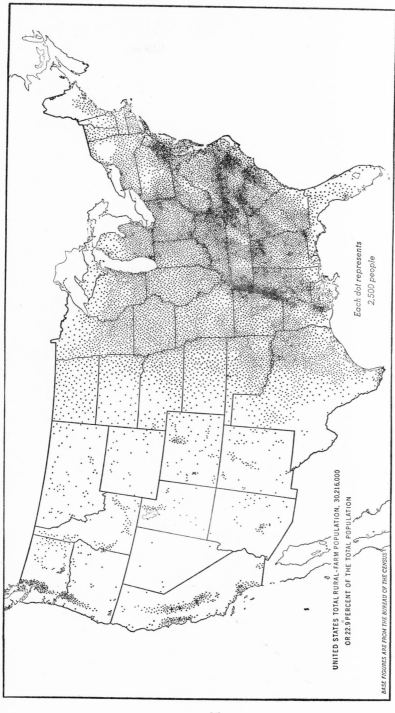

UNITED STATES TOTAL RURAL-FARM POPULATION, 30,216,000
OR 22.9 PERCENT OF THE TOTAL POPULATION

Each dot represents
2,500 people

BASE FIGURES ARE FROM THE BUREAU OF THE CENSUS

Figure 3. Distribution of the Rural-Farm Population, Census of 1940

Note heavy concentrations near cities, along the lower Mississippi, and in the poor-land areas of the Appalachians. (BAE, USDA)

would be very productive if it had ample rainfall. Therefore, because of ample rainfall, the most productive farming area lies in the humid region east of the Great Plains. As can be seen in Figure 3, the heavy concentration of rural farm population is in this eastern, relatively humid, section of the country. The north central and eastern areas, therefore, are in general the good land areas of the nation though there are in this region rocky hills, mountainous areas, and eroded soils. The Central Valley of California and some rich lands in the Columbia River Valley are being rapidly developed by irrigation.[1]

Where rainfall is consistently plentiful it ceases to be the critical limiting factor in agricultural production. The farmers living on the Atlantic seaboard, in the Mississippi Valley, and in the Pacific Northwest have long since broken up the most productive lands and have been using them for intertilled crops so long that programs of refertilization and of erosion control are generally necessary to keep their lands productive. The limiting factor in these regions is not rainfall but the quality of the soil.

In many agricultural areas, however, rainfall, because it is variable, is a critical factor in agriculture. Drought and dust storms came to the Great Plains in the depression years after 1930, causing as many as half of the rural-farm population in some areas to move out. The accompanying map (Figure 4) shows the high net out-migration from the Plains states and from some of the Rocky Mountain area, ranging from 5 to over 45 per cent of the rural-farm population. Even in normally well-watered states like Illinois, farmers in drought-stricken areas were given Federal aid. Much of the increase in agricultural production during World War II, on the other hand, was due to the return of favorable weather, including ample rainfall.

Controlling Physical Conditions.—Farm people generally have little control over certain physical forces. They are not able to make rain come when they need it, though some rainfall over limited areas has been produced experimentally; nor can they do much about the heat of the sun in summer nor the cold in winter; that is, they cannot change the weather. But they can make adaptations to take better advantage of these physical conditions. The change to tractor power, for example, has made it possible for farmers to put crops in quickly, and take advantage of fair weather.

---

[1] *Graphic Summary of Land Utilization in the United States,* Cooperative Report, U. S. Dept. of Commerce and USDA, Washington: U. S. Government Printing Office, 1947, pp. 2-5. Unless otherwise indicated, it is to be assumed that all government publications cited in this book may be secured from the Superintendent of Documents, Washington.

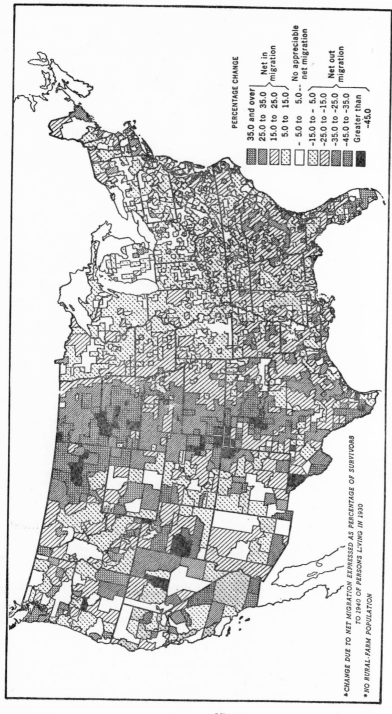

PERCENTAGE CHANGE

35.0 and over
25.0 to 35.0
15.0 to 25.0   } Net in migration
5.0 to 15.0

- 5.0 to 5.0 --   No appreciable net migration

-15.0 to - 5.0
-25.0 to -15.0
-35.0 to -25.0   } Net out migration
-45.0 to -35.0
Greater than -45.0

▲ CHANGE DUE TO NET MIGRATION EXPRESSED AS PERCENTAGE OF SURVIVORS
TO 1940 OF PERSONS LIVING IN 1930

* NO RURAL-FARM POPULATION

Figure 4. Gains and Losses in the Rural-Farm Population, 1930-1940

Greatest losses were from the plains and mountain states and from the southeastern part of the country. (BAE, USDA)

Various devices have been developed to combat the effects of too little or too much rainfall. Irrigation is probably the most notable of these devices; where irrigation is undertaken men cooperate in building the system and in establishing control over it. Crop insurance is a social invention designed to protect farmers against the financial effects of crop loss. The building of levees, the organization of drainage districts, and the development of soil conservation districts, are all social inventions intended to cope with adverse conditions arising out of too much or too little rainfall.

The Influence of Temperature.—One of the two essentials for crop growth is warmth. Only a very small proportion of the United States has summer temperatures too cool for the production of the hardier small grains, potatoes, and hay.[2] Yet no portion of our continental area is entirely free from frost. General farming, which usually includes the production of small grains, hay, and livestock, is possible almost everywhere in the United States except in the high altitudes and the arid regions, thus inducing the development of family or diversified farming as the major type of farming in the United States. Corn, for example, can be grown where the average summer temperature is not below 69 degrees F., and the growing or frost-free season is at least 90 days. Wheat, oats, barley, and rye will grow at still lower average summer temperatures, some being planted in the fall, going through the winter, and being harvested the next summer. But most fruits, especially citrus, and some vegetables are limited to those areas in which frost is light, such as along the coasts and in the South; and cotton is limited to areas in which temperatures are not below 77 degrees. Thus temperature affects or conditions the type of farming. To an extent, temperature directly affects the type of farm life, for cotton and fruit culture have demanded much greater seasonal labor than other types of farming, especially general or diversified farming. The result is a different social and cultural life in these areas, as compared with farming carried on by the labor of the operator and his family.

Topography.—The topography of an area has much to do with the development of group life. Topography can isolate whole areas as it has in the Ozarks and the Southern Appalachians, whose people have consequently developed a unique culture. Often settlements in

---

[2] O. E. Baker, "The World's Agricultural Resources," *Maryland,* Vol. IX, No. 1, December, 1947, p. 5.

little valleys surrounded by hills have become close-knit communities, many of which were settled by a single nationality or religious group. Streams have often divided neighborhoods, establishing divisions which have persisted even after the advent of modern communication. Settlements of hill or valley lands in the same community have been a major cause for the development of social classes in the community.[3] Topography has its positive as well as its negative effects. The great Central Valley of California is becoming one of the richest agricultural areas in the country. It is a region predominantly of interlocking, close knit, small communities. Contrasting forms of settlement due to topography (and rainfall) can be seen in western Oregon, with its small fruit farms, and in eastern Oregon, with its large wheat farms cultivated on the rolling hills of the area.

In modern times the automobile and all-weather roads have done much to break up the physical isolation of many remote communities, reducing distances in terms of time, and thus tending to weaken neighborhood and community ties. Nevertheless, topography still exerts an influence in rural communities.

Erosion of Soil and Culture.—The relative availability of water and the nature of the soil are two of the major determinants of the kind of agriculture which can be developed.[4] The way in which any kind of soil is used has much to do with the kind of life that will result.[5]

The dramatic dust storms of the 1930's caused a mass movement of impoverished people out of affected areas, and were the source of a multitude of serious social and economic problems. Yet the dust storms are less to be deplored than the widespread, gradual removal of topsoil or of soil minerals. At least 3,000,000,000 tons of soil are worked out of the fields and pastures of America each year,[6] a process which results not only in gullied hillsides and debris-buried valley lands, but also in low standards of living (Figure 8, page 48), poor schools and churches, lack of good health, and high relief rates. Note the look of forlorn hope on the face of the boy in the accompanying picture of a badly eroded tenant farm (Figure 9, page 48).[7] More will be said of this problem later in this chapter.

---

3 James West, *Plainville, U. S. A.*, New York: Columbia University Press, 1945, shows the close relation of topography and social stratification.
4 The general location of the various types of soils in the United States is shown in *Graphic Summary of Land Utilization, op. cit.*, p. 32.
5 See *Soils and Men*, 1938 Yearbook of Agriculture, USDA, p. 69.
6 H. H. Bennett, *The Land We Defend*, Soil Conservation Service, USDA, July, 1940.
7 See a study of the results of such processes in V. B. Fielder and D. E. Lindstrom, "Land Use and Family Welfare," Rural Sociology Mimeograph 10, Univ. of Illinois Agr. Exp. Sta., 1939.

It is probably true that more of our ambitious rural people will be found on the better farm lands. Yet the best lands have the highest percentage of tenancy, and high tenancy usually carries with it high mobility, which has adverse effects on soil as well as on family life, schools, churches, and other social institutions. Where most of the farmers are owners, on the other hand, there will be found better soil care, good homes, churches, schools, and neighborhood and community organizations. An effective program of soil conservation and a stable form of land tenure are usually essential elements of a good rural community life.[8]

It is of the utmost importance to have a system of social organization which will so control the use of soils and soil minerals as to provide the best possible level of living for the people on the land, as well as to protect the interests of future generations. Good cultural methods not only can conserve good lands, but can also improve poorer lands, if the system of social organization is such as to encourage these processes.

Out of the increasing possibilities of controlling or making adaptations to natural forces has come increased emphasis on the study of methods by which such changes can be made. Such studies are designed not only to find how to change the course of rivers or how to prevent the effects of soil erosion; they are also designed to determine desirable changes in the functions of the social organizations, to secure maximum benefit from new technological developments. The social organization of a given area, we must remember, depends not only on the geographic environment but also on man's purposes and ideals, and on his ability to devise methods of overcoming environmental handicaps.

Crop Regions and Culture Areas.—Climate, topography, and soils, taken together, are important determinants of major agricultural regions and socio-cultural areas. Both are of impelling interest and concern to the student of rural life.

Nine major crop areas of the nation are generally recognized by geographers. These areas are determined largely by the climatic conditions already described. The accompanying map (Figure 5) shows them: the cotton belt in the South, the corn belt in the Middle West, the grazing regions, the wheat areas, the hay areas—each region a definite agricultural adaptation to the limitations of climate and soil. In each of these major agricultural regions there are wide

---

[8] See, for example, P. A. Waring, *Teamwork to Save the Soil and Increase Production,* Misc. Pub. 486, USDA, 1942. A good illustration of neighborhood cooperation to conserve soil.

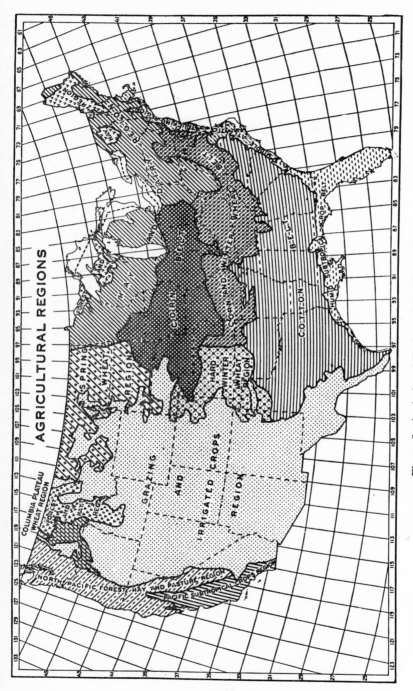

Figure 5. Agricultural Regions of the United States

Note the prominent corn belt, cotton belt, hay and dairy region, and the grazing and irrigated crops region. The plains area is the dominant wheat region of the country. (BAE, USDA)

41

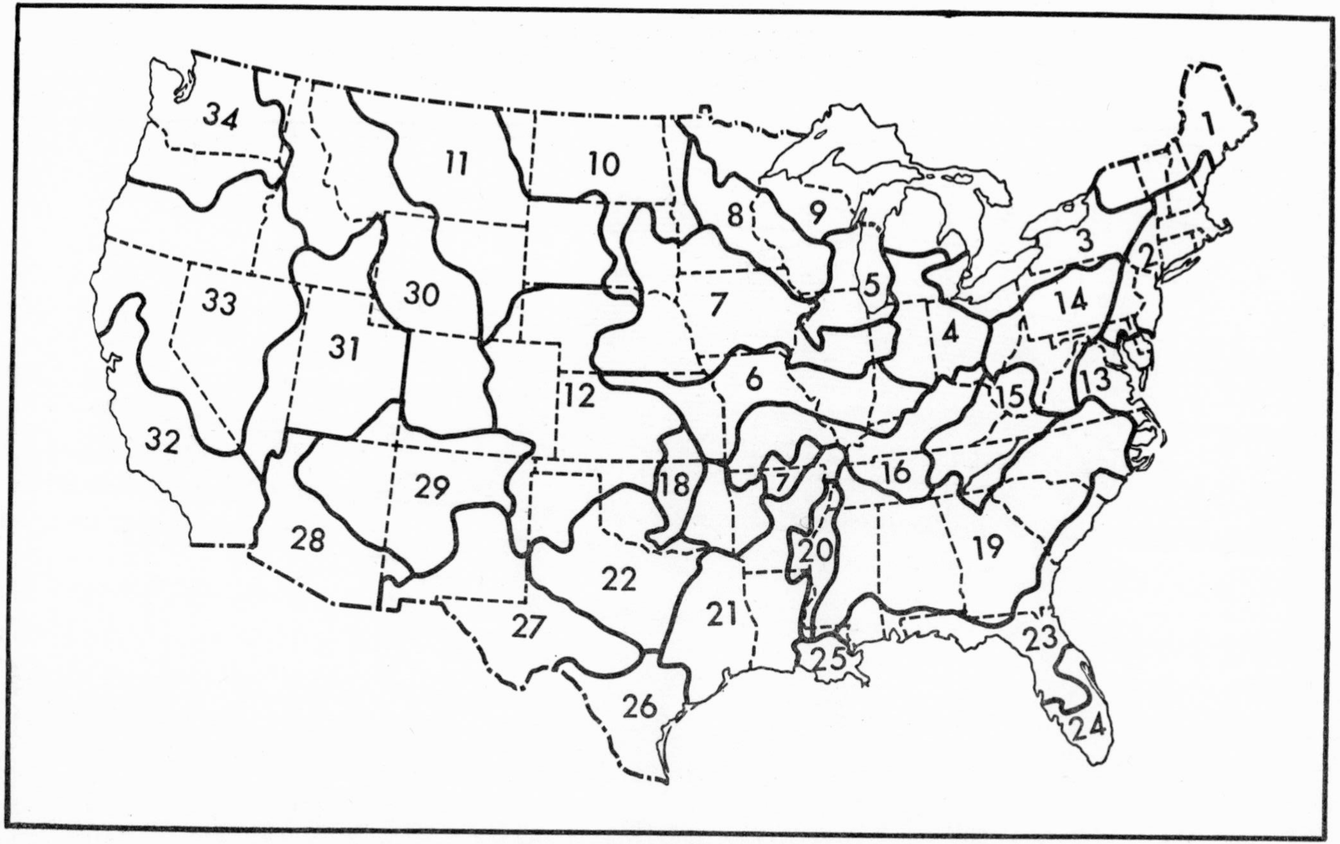

Figure 6. Rural Cultural Regions of the United States

(After A. R. Mangus, *Rural Regions of the United States*, USDA, 1940. This publication contains a detailed description of each cultural area.)

variations in the types of crops grown. Sociologists find that an analysis of the cropping systems of these agricultural regions is very helpful in understanding their widely divergent rural cultures. Crop areas have also been mapped for individual states. Illinois, for example, has been mapped into nine major farming type areas, ranging from cash-grain farming to orcharding, most of them being areas with more or less diversification in types of farming.

In addition to crop areas, rural sociologists use other factors to describe the manner of living of our rural people.[9] The density of settlement, the extent to which the area is predominantly rural, the extent to which the people are of native or of foreign-born stock, the principal source of income, the relative level of living, the birth rate, the percentage of tenancy, the relief rate, and similar factors have been used in outlining these cultural areas. Thirty-four such cultural areas in the United States have been delimited, and are shown in Figure 6. These culture areas range in nature from those originally settled chiefly by English and North European migrants, characterized by a dairying or diversified farming economy, low relief rates, low birth rates, advanced industrial development, high density of population, and relatively high levels of living, to the plantation areas, with a high percentage of Negro population with incomes chiefly from cotton and tobacco, relatively low levels of living, high tenancy rates (mostly sharecropper), and high relief rates.

The Spread of People on the Land

Forms of Settlements.—The outstanding development in rural America, so far as land occupancy is concerned, is the settlement of farm families on scattered farmsteads. In most countries of the world the predominant form of settlement is the hamlet or village, with homes of farmers grouped together in clusters. The development of the distinctive "scattered farmstead" type of settlement in America is an interesting study in social origins and processes.

---

9 See A. R. Mangus, *Rural Regions of the United States*, USDA, 1940, Maps 1 and 2, facing p. 4.

Explanation for Figure 6: 1. New England Upland. 2. Eastern Metropolitan. 3. Erie Canal-Lake Shore. 4. Buckeye-Hoosier. 5. Lake Shore Metropolitan. 6. Free Soiler's Territory. 7. Corn Belt. 8. Scandinavian America. 9. Lake Shore Cut-Over. 10. Northern Homestead. 11. Northwestern Homestead. 12. Southern Homestead. 13. Middle Colonial. 14. Allegheny. 15. Appalachian. 16. North-South Border. 17. Ozark-Ouachita. 18. Central Oklahoma-Kansas. 19. Southeastern Plantation. 20. Delta Plantation. 21. Cattle Trails. 23. Southern Colonial Flat-Woods. 24. Florida Semi-Tropical. 25. French Louisiana. 26. Gulf-Spanish American. 27. Central-Spanish American. 28. Desert Mexican-Indian. 29. Mexican-Navajo-Pueblo. 30. Rocky Mountain. 31. Mormon. 32. Factory Farm. 33. Pacific Forest Grazing. 34. Northwest Frontier.

This distinctive form of settlement did not begin to be important until after the Revolutionary War. The period from the first colonial settlement until the Revolutionary War spanned more than 150 years. In all that time the predominant settlement forms were the village-centered community in New England and the Middle Atlantic colonies, and the plantation in the South.[10]

The Village-Centered Community.—The village-centered communities of New England were carried over directly from England. The New England "farmers' villages" generally consisted of: (a) town lots of from 2 to 10 acres with house, barns, a garden spot, a meadow or lawn space, and often an orchard, (b) tillable lands out on the level part of the "open country" of which various families held portions, and (c) great meadows where all of the flocks and herds were grazed.

These village-centered New England rural communities were and probably still are America's foremost democratic communities, for in them can be found the town meeting type of government. All of the people—farmers and townsmen—are integral parts of the political, economic, religious, and social life of these rural communities.

This village-centered plan also characterized many of the communal settlements of 19th century America, such as Bishop Hill, Amana, New Harmony, and others.[11] It was carried west by the Mormons, who used the pattern as the basis for all of their settlements.

The Plantation South.—The dominant settlement pattern of the South was the plantation, each with its mansion and store and other control buildings, and the homes of croppers or workers scattered about on the plantation, not unlike the scattered farmstead type of settlement. Many planters, however, had their homes in towns and cities, and commuted to the plantations.

Line Settlements.—In some areas farmers would settle in strips along the base of the high lands overlooking their farms on the river bottoms because the lower land was subject to overflow. The early "line" villages, located on waterfronts and along highways, were an outgrowth of the peculiar geographic features of the site area. Such line settlements, said to be of French origin, can be seen in Kaskaskia, Prairie du Rocher, Cahokia, and Prairie du Chien on the upper Mississippi River.

---

[10] N. L. Sims, *Elements of Rural Sociology,* New York: Thomas Y. Crowell Co., 1940, pp. 60, 61.
[11] See William Alfred Hinds, *American Communities* (2nd rev. ed.), Chicago: Charles H. Kerr & Co., 1908.

Scattered Farmsteads.—England wished to keep her American colonies concentrated near the Atlantic coast, so as to retain control over them. Nevertheless, settlers began to move west, through the Cumberland Gap and over the Appalachian Plateau, even before the end of the Revolutionary War. Settlement of the western lands was encouraged by authorities in the colonies, for such settlement formed a possible barrier against Indian raids.

6	5	4	3	2	1
7	8	9	10	11	12
18	17	16	15	14	13
19	20	21	22	23	24
30	29	28	27	26	25
31	32	33	34	35	36

SCALE - 1/2 INCH EQUALS 1 MILE

Figure 7. The Basic Pattern for the Six-Mile-Square Township

The beginning of the spread of the scattered farmstead type of settlement can without question be traced to the Thomas Jefferson Act of 1785, creating the rectangular system of surveys in the United States. It provided for the establishment, in all newly opened lands of the public domain, of townships six miles square, each township to contain 36 sections of 640 acres each. (See page 46.) (See Figure 7.) It, says Smith, is "one of the simplest, most determinate, and permanent ways of dividing lands ever devised by man. But from the standpoint of the social and economic welfare of the population on the land it is one of the most vicious modes ever devised for dividing lands." [12]

---

[12] T. Lynn Smith, *The Sociology of Rural Life,* New York: Harper & Bros., 1946, p. 267.

Early Land Policies.—Farmers who own lands they operate usually have a deed describing the land's legal boundaries. These descriptions are based on land surveys which mark the legal boundaries of townships and sections.

In 1785 the first Federal land disposal act offered to the public tracts of 640 acres for one dollar an acre. The resulting fiasco is interestingly told by Brinser and Shepard:

> . . . At the first sale at government offices in Pittsburgh not 50,000 acres were sold, while at the Philadelphia land office not an acre was sold. One of the chief reasons for this failure was the fact that states were underselling the Federal government. Massachusetts was offering land at 50 cents an acre at the same time that the government was trying to sell its land at a dollar an acre in Ohio. The western states which had been given land to sell to pay for schools were also selling their land for considerably less than the prices fixed for Federal land. Later when Federal land grants were made to pay for roads and canals in the new states, Congress fixed the minimum price for sale on such land at $1.25 an acre. This was the first step taken by the Federal government to prevent underselling by the states. In addition to this cheap state land, ten million acres had been purchased by speculators, some honest, others dishonest. To keep the speculators from getting any more land the government raised its price to two dollars an acre in 1796. This was like locking the stable after the horse is stolen. With ten million cheap acres bought at from ten cents to two thirds of a dollar an acre, the speculators could afford to undersell the government whenever they chose. As a result, from 1798 to 1800 the Federal government got from its sale of land just about enough money to pay for an average farm in Ohio today.[13]

Many settlers had moved west down the Ohio River Valley in the early part of the 19th century simply to "squat" upon the land. Often, however, when titles were being cleared, conflicts arose between the "squatters" and the new owners, many of whom were regarded as "claim jumpers." These conflicts led to the agitation for a pre-emption law which would permit squatters to purchase the land upon which they had settled, on terms similar to those accorded people who bought land in the usual way. Much of the land east of the Mississippi River was settled in relatively small tracts. Availability of government land at $1.25 per acre was an important factor in settlement of this land.

As lands were settled on the basis of this rectangular system of surveys, they were patented in tracts in multiples of 40 acres, the 160-acre tract being most common. But the type of land description

---

[13] Ayers Brinser and Ward Shepard, *Our Use of the Land*, New York: Harper & Bros., 1939, pp. 34-35.

found in almost any abstract will show that the farms themselves have not followed the rectangular patterns. Rather, the farms are often elongated, or shaped like an "L," or like a "T." These shapes have arisen from the purchase or sale of additional tracts, such as the "forty" across the road, or the "eighty" lying just south of the present tract. In recent times, especially since the coming of rubber-tired farm machinery, 40- or 80-acre tracts, even several miles away, are rented or purchased so as to make a unit large enough for efficient use of machinery.

Free government land was made available to settlers through the Homestead and Timber Acts. Under the Homestead Act (1862) any American citizen could have 160 acres of land free if he would live upon it for five years. The Timber and Stone Act (1878) provided for the sale to any one person of 160 acres of land at a minimum of $2.50 per acre. The timber and stone could be removed for personal use. These Acts spurred the settlement of the grasslands of America, particularly those west of the Mississippi River. They placed a premium on the scattered farmstead type of settlement and on the small, or family, farm unit.

Grants of public land which could be sold at not more than $2.50 per acre were made to railroads to help pay the cost of construction. This caused many settlers to "follow" the railroads west.

Mexican land grants were respected by the terms of the cession of California to the United States. These grants, together with large acreages granted by the Government to the transcontinental railroads, and huge acreages sold to California and in turn wastefully managed, resulted in the present pattern of large-scale farms so frequently found in California.

The result of the early land policies was that settlers "came by the thousands, from Germany, from Ireland, from Scandinavia, from the eastern seaboard of the United States. Some of them were farm tenants who saw a chance for independence, while others were farmers who had exhausted their soil in the east. They included clerks, and small merchants, and factory workers who wanted to escape from the growing cities." [14]

Social Aspects of the Use of Land

Present-Day Nature of Land Holdings.—The limiting factor in the ability to become an owner of land in the United States is the amount of means with which to buy it. But many people who have

[14] *Op. cit.*, p. 45.

not had the means to buy land have nevertheless wanted to live on land and to work it. There have thus grown up four systems whereby people work land: full-owner operation, part-owner operation, tenancy, and sharecropping. A more complete discussion will be given later of each of these and of their social implications.

The distribution of land holdings in the United States reflects the unwritten land policy of the nation: ownership of land by small or family-type operators. This policy is the result of the low-priced and free-land policies of earlier decades. But the distribution of the people on the land in the above-described fashion, without a well-developed national conservation policy, has had its effects on the physical as well as the human resources of the nation. Widespread misuse of the soil, with adverse social effects, has resulted, especially in areas in which there has developed a high percentage of tenants.

The attitude toward land and its use in the United States has been different from that in other countries. In spite of the fact that many settlers came from countries in which land was looked upon almost as a sacred trust, in this country land seemed so abundant that exploitation set in soon after the process of settlement expanded. The attitude which spurred this exploitation was that the resources of the soil, as of the timber and minerals, were inexhaustible, and that there was always more land to be had, farther west.

Improving Soil Productivity.—From the time of the earliest settlements on the Atlantic seaboard there has been some interest in soil fertility. Early agricultural societies antedating the Revolutionary War discussed and wrote about good manures and composts, and the compositions of good native types of fertilizer were made subjects of prizes at local, county, and provincial agricultural fairs.[15]

One of the chief concerns of the U. S. Department of Agriculture, after it was organized in the 1860's, as well of the Land-Grant College Experiment Stations, was soil productivity. The earliest soil experiment plots showed the effect of crop rotation. Some of the early experiments such as those at the Morrow Plots at the University of Illinois (Figure 10) are still being carried on. These have had a very great influence on soil practices of farmers but soil fertility depletion still goes on.

---

15 Jonathan Periam, *The Groundswell*, Chicago: N. D. Thompson & Co., 1874, pp. 55-57.

Figure 8. Poverty Is the Grim Aftermath of the Loss of Surface Soil
(Soil Conservation Service, USDA)

Figure 9. The Future Is Forlorn for Youth on Land Like This
(Courtesy Farm Security Administration)

Figure 10. The Morrow Plots at the University of Illinois

Figure 11. The Effect of Wind Erosion: An Abandoned Farm Home
(Courtesy Extension Service, USDA)

More recent efforts have been aimed at getting farmers to test their soils for acidity and for phosphorus and potassium content. The Agricultural Extension Services in the various states have carried on demonstrations, held neighborhood testing meetings, and have encouraged the setting up of county soil testing laboratories in which the exact limestone, phosphorus, and potassium needs can be found for each acre of land.

Social Interest in Soil Conservation.—Soil conservation and fertility repletion are social problems whose fundamental importance has only recently been recognized. The Homestead Act was designed to get land settled quickly, irrespective of the consequences to the land, and the World War I policy was to plow up an additional 60,000,000 acres of grassland, because "food will win the war." It was not until President Theodore Roosevelt's time that we put a program of conservation of public lands into practice and only in President Franklin Roosevelt's administration were private lands purchased for reforestation.

The Progress of Erosion.—The exhaustion of soil minerals essential to plant growth, and wind and water erosion, have gone on, nevertheless, at such a rapid rate in this country, especially since World War I, that the situation is truly alarming. (See Figure 12.) H. H. Bennett, Chief of the U. S. Department of Agriculture Soil Conservation Service, estimates that 282,000,000 acres of crop and grazing land have been ruined for any further immediate practical use and that about 100,000,000 acres of this severely damaged area once constituted good crop land—as good as we had. The size of this depleted area, says Bennett, exceeds the combined extent of New York, Pennsylvania, New Jersey, Maryland, Delaware, and all of the New England states except Maine. Even before World War II, it was reported that farmers were taking out nine times as much essential plant food elements as they were putting back. The World War II period unquestionably accelerated the depletion.

According to authorities of the Department of Agriculture, a national policy with regard to soil and land use should assure

(1) secure farm homes, (2) adequate and stable incomes for farm people, and (3) continuous and abundant supplies of farm produce for all the people. Achievement of these purposes will save the soil, because soil conservation is an indispensable means for their full accomplishment; it is one of many inseparable aspects of the best permanent use of land. Land misuse consists of much more than permitting soil losses to occur. Its most serious manifestation is human misery; and the most serious soil losses are almost always

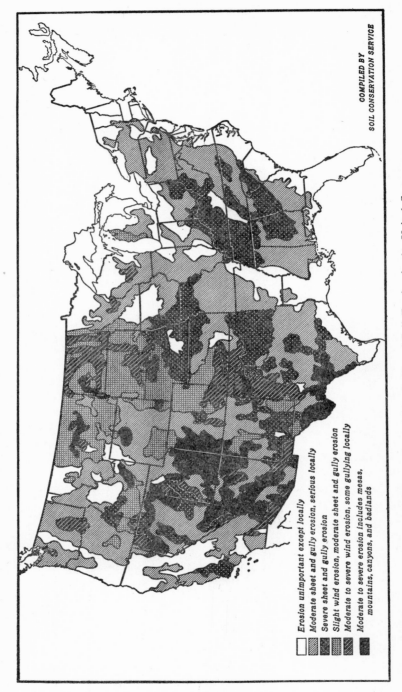

Figure 12. General Distribution of Soil Erosion in the United States

The areas where erosion is unimportant are relatively small, compared with areas of moderate to serious sheet and gully corrosion. (BAE, USDA)

COMPILED BY
SOIL CONSERVATION SERVICE

☐ Erosion unimportant except locally
▨ Moderate sheet and gully erosion, serious locally
▩ Severe sheet and gully erosion
▨ Slight wind erosion, moderate sheet and gully erosion
▩ Moderate to severe wind erosion, some gullying locally
▨ Moderate to severe erosion includes mesas,
   mountains, canyons, and badlands

either an effect of economic and social maladjustments or the result of a haphazard public land policy.[16]

Note in Figure 11 the result of wind erosion on land that, doubtless, should never have been plowed. This is land misuse with a vengeance!

Conserving Surface Soil.—On the other side of the picture—the physical maintenance of soils—efforts have likewise been made for many years to get farmers to fill up their gullies, plant grassed waterways, plow and seed on the contour, build terraces, and in other ways stop erosion. Note the effects in the following illustration, Figure 13. At the first extension service specialists and agents preached it. Then the Agricultural Adjustment Administration began to make payments for the right kinds of soil conservation practices. Then the Soil Conservation Service was organized.

So far, most measures used to secure the right use of land in the United States have been effective only to a limited extent. The dust storms of 1934, the floods of 1937 and 1945, and the gullies which appear almost everywhere in hillsides after heavy rain, all of them the result of continuing mistreatment of our soil resources, show that our soil conservation program in this country has not taken deep hold of the hearts and minds of our rural people. The desire for immediate returns, the feeling that it is too much bother to use proper practices, and the tendency to stick to the customary way of doing things in the community, are still potent forces.

Federal and state laws have now been set up to provide for the organization of soil conservation districts. These districts are set up by majority vote of the landowners, and range in size from a large community to a county. Soil technicians are employed by the Soil Conservation Service to aid farmers in the district in making an effective soil conservation farm plan. Group meetings are held to discuss such plans. An element of social control is thus introduced, for if one will cooperate, others are also likely to do so. Studies show that these "conservation" farmers actually have higher returns than their neighbors. A more direct force of social control is possible through ordinances to enforce conservation practices. By such ordinances, 75 per cent of the landowners can, by vote, enforce conservation practices upon all the operators of the district. Such control measures may be socially justified. The contrast between erosion

---

[16] Carl C. Taylor, Bushrod W. Allin, and O. E. Baker, "Public Purposes in Soil Use," in *Soils and Men,* 1938 Yearbook of Agriculture, USDA, p. 59.

and effect of control measures is apparent in the accompanying illustration (Figure 14).

Land-Use Planning.—Land-use planning was tried in the days immediately before World War II, in a large number of counties in the United States. The efforts were significant, for they called for a mapping of the best possible present and future land use by county, community, and neighborhood committees of farmers, bankers, merchants, teachers, pastors, and all interested community leaders. Upon the basis of present uses and the needs as discovered by the people in a neighborhood, the proper governmental agencies were called upon to help improve the situation. There are great possibilities in such a system of organization and it is hoped the system can now be fully tried.

In some states zoning laws have been enacted so that the people of a county can study their land-use situation and declare certain lands unfit for agriculture. The farmers who live in these areas are then aided in moving to farms in better agricultural areas. If they will not move they are denied state support for schools, roads, and other public facilities. But most of them move.

The TVA.—The Tennessee Valley Authority has shown that a significant degree of control can be exercised over natural forces. But the TVA has shown, also, that such adaptations require the development of a very intricate system of social organization. Much of the success of the TVA has been due to the effectiveness with which whole neighborhoods and communities were organized for soil conservation.

The development of the process whereby the resources of the U. S. Department of Agriculture, the agricultural colleges, and all the other agencies that were at hand could be used to attain the results desired by the TVA experts was a real challenge. Rather than approach the farmer from each agency's own point of view, whole farm demonstrations were held on thousands of dirt farms. "The farmers in a community," declares David E. Lilienthal, ". . . set up through farmers' associations community-wide demonstrations, with as many as eighty families in such a single little 'valley.' . . . These thousands of typical working farms are the schoolrooms of the valley. Here farmers, their wives and children, with their neighbors, learn and demonstrate the principle of grass-roots democracy. Here is brought to them the fruits of the technical man's skills." [17] The

---

[17] David E. Lilienthal, *TVA: Democracy on the March,* New York: Harper & Bros., 1944, pp. 79-80.

Figure 13. Soil-Saving Contour Farming at Its Best
Note terracing at lower left. (Courtesy Soil Conservation Service)

Figure 14. Good Land—Good Farms; Poor Land—Poor Farms
(Courtesy Extension Service, USDA)

same sort of regional development under a "Missouri Valley Authority" is being strongly advocated for the watershed of the Missouri River.

Interested Church Groups.—The churches, too, have recently taken a keen interest in the right use of land. The Catholic Rural Life Conference considers our land to be a sacred trust. The Protestant churches, through the Convocation of the Church in Town and Country, and through denominational channels, call for a use of land that will conserve its resources. A religious group called "Friends of the Soil" has been organized "to lead men to regard the earth as holy and man as a steward of the Eternal." [18]

———

In spite of all of the above-mentioned valiant efforts, we have by no means conquered our problem of soil erosion. What further steps are necessary? Nationalization of the land, say some. Adequate prices to enable farmers to keep up their soils, say others. A stable system of farm tenure, still others assert. In any case, it is hoped that the trend in this country can be changed from exploitation to conservation by democratic methods, with chief reliance on education. An effective, sustained program of proper land use will mean real stability and security for the people on the land they operate. Conversely, security must be assured if the right kind of land-use program is to be put into effect. Such a system will then insure greater stability of family life, schools, churches, and other rural institutions. This is a human welfare problem of the first magnitude.

DISCUSSION

1. Which of the physical features studied in this chapter have the greatest influence on the way of life of rural people? What are the most significant adaptations to physical conditions to improve rural life?
2. To what extent are neighborhood and community boundaries determined by topography? What effects have modern forms of communication had on these boundaries, especially as they affect natural groups such as neighborhoods? Describe the social conflicts that have come as a result of these new forms of communication. What social adaptations or adjustments have been made?

———

[18] Eugene Smathers, *A Primer for Friends of the Soil*, The Fellowship of Southern Churchmen, Big Lick, Tenn., undated.

3. What are the evidences of the misuse of soil? What relationships are there between the quality of soil and the kind of rural life to be found on the different kinds of soil? What effects do the different types of farming have on the social life of the people?

4. What is the chief pattern of settlement in the United States? Why did the people settle on the land in this fashion? What changes are taking place in this pattern of settlement with the advent, for example, of all-weather roads?

5. How was land first obtained from the government by the people who became the early settlers? What is the chief present method of land transfer and how does it affect the stability of people on the land? What changes need to be made to insure greater stability?

6. What are the present attitudes toward land use? What group methods have been used to check erosion? What additional measures are needed to insure the future fertility of soil and permanence of agriculture?

READINGS

Bennett, H. H. *The Land We Defend.* Soil Conservation Service, USDA, July, 1940.

Brinser, Ayers, and Shepard, Ward. *Our Use of the Land.* New York: Harper & Bros., 1939. Chs. I, II.

Graphic Summary of Land Utilization in the United States. Cooperative Report. U. S. Dept. of Commerce and USDA, 1947, pp. 3-7.

Lamartine Yates, P., and Warriner, D. *Food and Farming in Postwar Europe.* New York: Oxford University Press, 1943, Ch. I.

Lilienthal, David E. *TVA: Democracy on the March.* New York: Harper & Bros., 1944.

Loomis, Charles P. *Studies of Rural Social Organization.* East Lansing: State College Book Store, 1945.

McWilliams, Carey. *Factories in the Field.* Boston: Little, Brown & Co., 1939, Ch. II.

National Resources Planning Board. *Our Natural Resources.* Washington: 1940.

Sears, Paul B. *Deserts on the March.* Norman: Univ. of Oklahoma Press, 1935.

Sims, N. L. *Elements of Rural Sociology.* New York: Thomas Y. Crowell Co., 1940, Ch. VI.

Smith, T. Lynn. *The Sociology of Rural Life.* New York: Harper & Bros., 1946, Chs. X, XI.

Tabulations from the United States Census Regarding the Land and the People on the Land. (2nd ed.) BAE, USDA, October, 1941.

Waring, P. A. *Teamwork to Save the Soil and Increase Production.* Misc. Pub. 486, Soil Conservation Service, USDA, 1942.

Chapter 4

THE RURAL POPULATION

The most important element in the study of rural life is the people themselves. We usually think of the productivity of rural areas in terms of crops and livestock; it is startling, therefore, to realize that in the United States, as over the world, the most important rural crop is babies.

World Predominance of Rural Population.—About half of the people of the world, almost a billion souls, live in India, China, and adjacent countries. (See Figure 15.) More than three fourths of

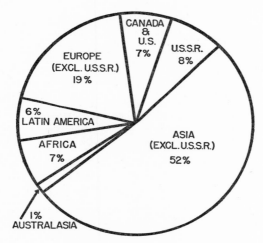

Figure 15. Distribution of the World's Population
(Courtesy O. E. Baker)

these people are rural, and most of them live on the land. Of the total population, more than two thirds are rural; in contrast, only two fifths of the population of the United States are rural, and less than half of our rural people live on the land.

The rural-farm population in the United States is not growing appreciably, due chiefly to the migration of rural youth to urban areas, where, in general, the birth rate is too low to reproduce the population. In Northwestern Europe and in the British dominions, the birth rate has been falling for many decades and is now so low as scarcely to reproduce the populations.

The situation is different in the Union of Soviet Socialist Republics and in the Orient. Though the birth rate is falling in the U.S.S.R., the death rate is falling much more rapidly, because of the progress of sanitation and the progressive conquest of poverty and disease. The result is a net, and rapid, increase in population. In Russia, as in the United States, the rural population is the most productive of babies.

In the Orient, the high birth rate produces a teeming population which presses most severely on the insufficient food supply. Poverty and disease are tragically dominant and result in a high death rate which tends to counterbalance the high birth rate. With the introduction of sanitation, however, and the transportation of food to drought-stricken areas, "the incidence of disease and famine may be greatly diminished, as occurred in India between 1931 and 1941. During these 10 years, population increased 50 million. This is an increase exceeding in number one third of the population of the United States, in a region with much less agricultural production." [1] China, moreover, "may well grow at a rate of 10-15 per cent in a decade for several decades." [2]

Let us recognize that these Oriental people, so largely rural, are carrying on a familistic culture, whose ideals and institutions will be slow to change, and whose birth rate, therefore, will decline only slowly. These Oriental peoples (who now make up half the world's population) need only an increasing food supply and the introduction of modern sanitation to double in population. Says Baker, "a people who do not care to have children will gradually cease to exist, and other peoples with greater love of life and children, with more thought to the future and a greater sense of responsibility cannot be blamed if they press into the partial vacuum." [3]

Classes of the Rural Population.—The rural population is subdivided by the Census Bureau as follows:

1. The farm population comprises all persons living on farms, without regard to occupation. The *rural-farm* population comprises those persons living on farms in rural areas. It forms the overwhelming proportion of our farm population. The *urban-farm*

---

[1] O. E. Baker, "The World's Agricultural Resources," *Maryland*, Vol. XIX, No. 1, December, 1947, pp. 7-9.
[2] Warren S. Thompson, *Plenty of People*, New York: The Ronald Press Co., 1948, p. 23.
[3] Baker, *op. cit.*

population comprises those persons living on farms located in urban areas. The urban-farm population, however, constitutes less than one half of 1 per cent of the total farm population.

2. The *rural-nonfarm* population comprises those persons living in incorporated villages and towns of less than 2,500, and those living in unincorporated areas and the open country, but not on farms.

A study of the rural population and its movement is of great value from a number of points of view, especially from the standpoint of (a) how many people can be supported by the land, (b) the effects of over-population, and (c) the relation of the welfare of the people on the land to the welfare of the people in the rest of society.

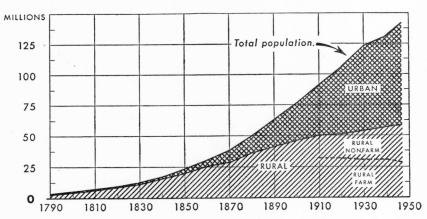

Figure 16. Population Growth in the United States, 1790 to 1947

Note the decline in the numbers of rural-farm people from 1920 to 1930 and from 1940 to 1945. (BAE, USDA)

The Rural Element in the United States Population.—Since 1920 the rural population has formed less than half of the total population. Previous to 1920, more than half of the population was rural. This is indeed a significant change. In 1850, less than a century ago, about 85 per cent of the population was rural and only 15 per cent urban. Note in the graph showing trends in the population since 1790 (Figure 16) that while both the rural and urban populations have increased, the urban increase has been much more rapid, especially in the years prior to 1910. It should be pointed out, of course, that part of this urban increase is accounted for by the fact that towns of less than 2,500, listed as rural by one Census, would be listed as urban by a subsequent Census if the town had increased to 2,500 and if it had been incorporated. Other reasons given for the rapid increase of the urban population are industrialization, especially in the north-eastern part of the country, and the net movement of rural people to urban areas, in search of better economic opportunities.

Regional Differences.—Though we look at the total population picture and conclude that our country is predominantly urban, yet when we examine the population of various parts of the country we find some very great differences. Over half our urban population lives within the area north of the Ohio River and east of the Mississippi River. The rest of the United States, constituting by far the larger part of its area, is still dominantly rural. Twenty-eight states, more than half the total, still have more rural than urban population.

Urban concentrations and areas of rural predominance can be seen in individual states. In Illinois, for example, where the total population is about 75 per cent urban, only one fourth of the counties have a population more than 50 per cent urban.

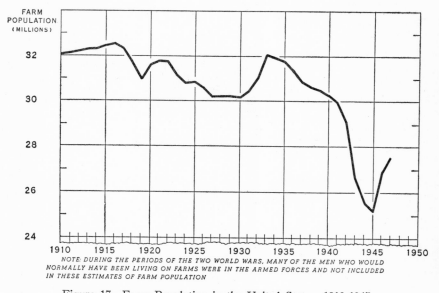

NOTE: DURING THE PERIODS OF THE TWO WORLD WARS, MANY OF THE MEN WHO WOULD NORMALLY HAVE BEEN LIVING ON FARMS WERE IN THE ARMED FORCES AND NOT INCLUDED IN THESE ESTIMATES OF FARM POPULATION

Figure 17. Farm Population in the United States, 1910-1947

Note the general downward trend, reversed only during the depression period and 1945 when the soldiers returned. (BAE, USDA)

Decline of the Rural-Farm Population.—Figure 17 shows a downward trend in the farm population of the United States from 1910 to 1947. Three periods of increase can be seen: following World War I, during the early depression years of the 1930's, and following World War II. The decline during this thirty-seven year period was from a high of 33,000,000 to a low of 25,000,000. This trend is indicative of the change of the character of our society from a rural or agricultural to an urban or industrial society. The trend is also indicative of the need for fewer workers in agriculture, or for fewer farmers, to produce the nation's needed food and fiber supply. It is indicative, also, of the "pull" of urban life in normally prosperous times, and of the "refuge" nature of farms following wars and in times of depression.

Growing Importance of the Rural-Nonfarm Population.—The part of the total population that has been growing most rapidly in the last two decades is the rural-nonfarm population. Look again at the trend of population growth in Figure 16, noting the relatively rapid increase in this group since 1920. In 1920, as we have noted, the rural proportion of the population dropped below the urban for the first time in our history. World War II ushered in a significant change in the proportions of the rural-farm and rural-nonfarm populations. Up to 1945 the rural-farm population was larger than the rural-nonfarm population; since that year the proportion of rural-nonfarm has been greater.

The chief reason for the rapid growth of the rural-nonfarm population doubtless is the desire of many city and town people to seek places to live in the open country, while remaining at their jobs in the cities. It is not unusual, as one travels beyond the limits of urban centers, to see the highway lined with dwellings on lots of a quarter or half acre.

Real Importance of the Rural Population.—Figure 16 is also a graphic demonstration of the fact that, numerically, the urban population now far exceeds the rural population, especially the rural-farm. Furthermore, since the rural-nonfarm population is more akin to the urban population in type of occupation and dominant social interests, the urban and rural-nonfarm population, taken together, make our nation urban-dominated. But, as will be seen later, the rural, and especially rural-farm, population, though outnumbered numerically, is of great importance as a major source of the population increases in urban areas. Studies have shown that as many as 60 per cent of all urban householders were rural-reared people.[4]

Concentrations of Rural Population.—When you look at a map of the United States showing the density of rural population per square mile, you will be impressed by the fact that the highest concentrations of rural people (50 or more per square mile) are in the

---

[4] Howard Beers and Catherine Heflin, *Rural People in the City*, Bull. 478, Univ. of Kentucky Agr. Exp. Sta., 1945, p. 48.

states of Pennsylvania, Ohio, West Virginia, Maryland, Delaware, New Jersey, Rhode Island, and Massachusetts. Yet, except for West Virginia, these states have low percentages of rural-farm population. The high density of rural population in these areas results from the large percentage of rural-nonfarm population, many of whom live in the large number of villages and towns under 2,500. Elsewhere in the United States, the density of the rural population is highest in the southeastern states, and the lowest in the Rocky Mountain states, Oregon, and the Dakotas, where there are fewer than ten rural people per square mile.

A study of the relative densities of the rural-farm population, however, presents a different picture (see Figure 3, p. 35). Here the highest concentrations are in the southeastern states, particularly Kentucky, Tennessee, Virginia, North Carolina, and South Carolina, which states also have a high proportion of the rural population (65 to 75 per cent). The heaviest densities of rural-farm population are along the Mississippi River below Cairo, Illinois, and in the mountain areas of the states mentioned above. Except for the rich bottom lands along the Mississippi River, these are the areas of relatively poor land, high birth rates, relatively small farms, and low living levels.

Of greater significance, however, is the fact that about half of the nation's school children are in rural areas. Moreover, of these rural children, 52 per cent are in the rural South. Of these school children in the rural South, two thirds live in farm areas, and one third live in rural-nonfarm areas. The rural South is obviously our greatest population reservoir.

The close relation between rural-farm population density, average size of farm, and low gross income per farm can be illustrated by a study of data for Illinois. In comparison with other sections of the state, southern Illinois, where the land is relatively poor, has more small farms, more large families, and the highest concentrations of rural-farm population.[5] A similar situation in Indiana has led to a study by its agricultural experiment station, which made specific recommendations relating to public policy which will, it is hoped, bring about a readjustment in the rural-farm populations of the state.[6] The report of the investigating body points out that in most of the counties in the southern third of Indiana a major decrease in the rural-farm population is desirable.

---

[5] See, for example, D. E. Lindstrom and R. F. Eshleman, *Indices of Human Welfare*, Rural Sociology Mimeograph 13, Univ. of Illinois Agr. Exp. Sta., 1943.
[6] As described in *Indiana: The Land and the People*, Bull. 496, Purdue Univ. Agr. Exp. Sta., 1944, Fig. 28, p. 54.

The matter of rural-farm population concentrations is of social concern, not only from the standpoint of encouraging adjustments that will provide a decent level of living, but also in relation to the provision of social services, such as schools, churches, roads, public utilities, health protection, etc. Where the population is sparse, the provision of these services becomes more difficult. State and Federal aid are essential if all areas are to have adequate social services.

Mobility of the Rural Population

Kinds of Mobility.—We cannot consider population as static, because people are always moving. The character of the rural population, as well as that of urban areas, is profoundly affected by the perpetual mobility of our population.

When we study the subject, we must recognize that migration— one type of movement of which we hear so much—is only one kind of population mobility. The various types may be classified as follows:

1. Horizontal mobility—the movement of people from place to place.
2. Vertical mobility—the change of a people from one social class to another.
3. Spatial mobility—the distance of the movement from place to place.
4. Temporal mobility—the frequency with which people move from place to place.
5. Migration—the general or mass movement of the population.
6. Continuous mobility—the movement of individuals or families from year to year within a neighborhood or community.
7. Fluidity—the movement of people back and forth to the same abode, such as the daily commutation of the suburban dweller between his home and the city.

Rural People a Minority Group.—We have already noted (Figure 16) significant changes in the numerical relation of the rural to the urban population from 1790 to 1940. The most obvious change, we have seen, is that the proportion of the rural-farm to the total population has become smaller and smaller as the years have gone by. The farm population of our country at one time made up nine tenths of the total; it has been changed to less than one fifth in the present day. Conversely, the rural-nonfarm and urban populations have gradually increased.

The migration to urban areas has been the inevitable result of (a) the invention of the steam engine and the development of factory production, (b) the invention of power machinery and the advances in agricultural technics, (c) a birth rate in the farm population still 40 to 50 per cent higher than needed to maintain the farm population, and (d) the completion of the agricultural conquest of the continent (there has been no real agricultural frontier since 1900). The time will come when the nation will need children as much as food.

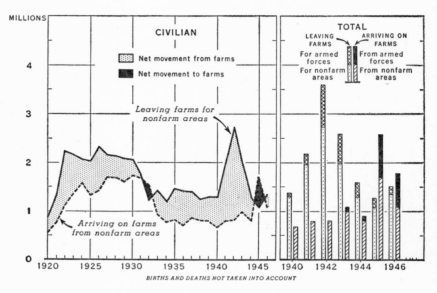

Figure 18. Movement to and from Farms, United States, 1920-1946
In only two periods was there a net movement to the farms. (BAE, USDA)

The total urbanward movement is impressive. In the prosperity decade, 1920-1929, over 19,300,000 people left the farms. (See Figure 18). During this period about 13,000,000 people returned to farms, many of them doubtless disillusioned with city life, indicating a net urbanward migration of 6,300,000. These were nearly all youth, for the middle-aged and old farmers found it difficult to change to other occupations. Moreover, farm people had already experienced one depression in 1921 and were feeling the pinch of the next depression as early as 1926.

But in the decade 1930 to 1940 the depression engulfed the rest of the people, many of whom began to move back to the land. This movement was especially evident in the first five years. Too often, the migrants back to the farm were forced to resume their rural life on the poor or marginal lands because they could not get a foothold on the good lands. Whereas the greatest net migration to the cities in the earlier decade was in the age group fifteen to nineteen years, the net migration to the farms in the 1932-1933 period was among persons of the ages thirty to thirty-four.[7] The beginning of improvement in urban prospects for work in 1933 led to the resumption of net outward movement from farms. During the decade 1930-1939 (depression years, mostly), some 14,000,000 left the farms and 10,700,000 returned to farms, indicating a net urbanward migration of about 3,300,000.

Then business conditions began to improve and the war started, so that from 1940 to 1945 urbanward migration increased sharply. There was a net loss of about 5,000,000 persons who either moved away from farms to cities, towns, or villages, or who were living on places which were no longer classified as farms because agricultural operations had ceased.

The excessive urbanward migration of the period 1940-1945 was due to employment opportunities in the cities and to military service demands. "A check-up of youth survey records in several corn belt counties indicates that about three fourths of the males eighteen to twenty-eight years of age had left the farms during the first two of these years . . . If this migration of youth proves permanent, and probably most of these young people will remain in the cities or return to the cities after a period of unemployment, if such occurs, it will involve a vast drift of wealth to the cities." [8]

The return of persons from military service and war industries in 1945 caused a sharp upturn in the numbers arriving on farms from nonfarm areas. The result was that by the end of the year the rural farm population had gone up again to over 27,000,000. It was a net farmward movement of short duration. By 1948 the net migration was again urbanward. This would indicate that as long as prosperity holds the net migration will be urbanward, and that if another depression comes there may again be a farmward movement of some proportions.

Rural Areas Adversely Affected by Out-Migration.—Since 1920 the rural-farm areas have lost over 15,000,000 people. In spite of this out-movement, the rural-farm population, until 1940, remained

[7] Eleanor H. Bernart, *Volume and Composition of Net Migration from the Rural-Farm Population, 1939-40, for the United States, Major Geographic Divisions and States*, BAE, USDA, January, 1944.

[8] O. E. Baker and Conrad Taeuber, "Some Trends in the Rural Population of Significance to Education," in *Rural Schools for Tomorrow*, Yearbook of the Dept. of Rural Education, NEA, 1945, p. 70.

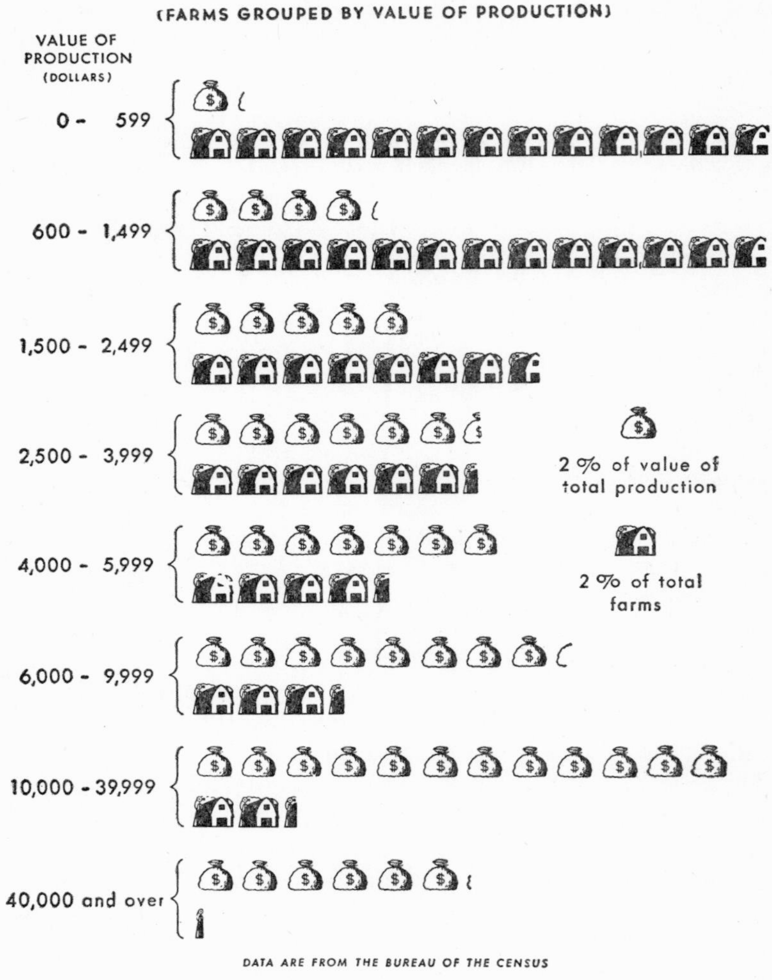

(FARMS GROUPED BY VALUE OF PRODUCTION)

Figure 19. Distribution of the 18 Billion Dollar Value of Farm Production, Produced by 5.8 Million Farms in 1944, a War Year

Over one fourth of the farms produced only slightly over 2 per cent of the products. (BAE, USDA)

relatively stable. This was due to the natural increase in the rural-farm population.

The major contribution of the less productive half of American farms to the national welfare consists of their youth, rather than food and fiber. We have noted that the chief urbanward movement is mostly among young people, especially girls, that it is from the poorer rather than the better lands, and that it attracts the best and the most qualified of the farm youth. Figure 19 shows that more than half of the farms in the United States produced less than $1,500 worth of products each in 1944; their sales of products constituted less than 10 per cent of the total from all farms in that year. Conversely, about a fifth of the farms which produced $4,000 or more worth of products had sales of products constituting two thirds of the total. We know that the better and larger farms having the highest sales of products have smaller families, many as small as the average city family. Hence, more than two thirds of the migrating youth come from farms producing less than a third of the products. By assuming that the annual income per migrant worker was about $1,000 after reaching the city, the value of the migrants from the low-income farms tremendously exceeds the value of their farm products.

Out-migration is a huge yearly cost to farmers. To assume, as does O. E. Baker, that the cost of food, clothing, medical care, and education for each farm child is $150 per year, would make the total cost of rearing and educating youth in the country about $2,000 per child up to fifteen years of age. The net migration since 1920 of about 15,000,000 persons from rural-farm areas, each of whom cost about $2,000 to rear, would mean a net movement of $30,000,000,-000—about $1,000,000,000 a year.

Farmers have had to draw heavily on their native resources, that is, to exploit the soil and use the unpaid labor of women and children, to make up the losses caused by the drain of this wealth. They have had to sacrifice many home comforts such as running water, electricity, and central heating, and many cultural advantages such as good schools, strong churches, and libraries, in order to pay this huge bill to the cities. The whole of society, therefore, should be deeply concerned about the quality of the human as well as of the animal and plant stock on the farms of America.

Nevertheless, as long as rural areas continue to produce a surplus of youth, their economic and social welfare will depend on out-migration. Otherwise, levels of living would decline, as in the over-populated rural areas of Europe, India, and China.

Interregional Migration.—The slogan "Go West, young man" had a meaning in 1936 entirely different from its meaning in 1836. Aided by the great land acts discussed in the last chapter, settlement was so rapid that after 1910 little good land was to be had. How-

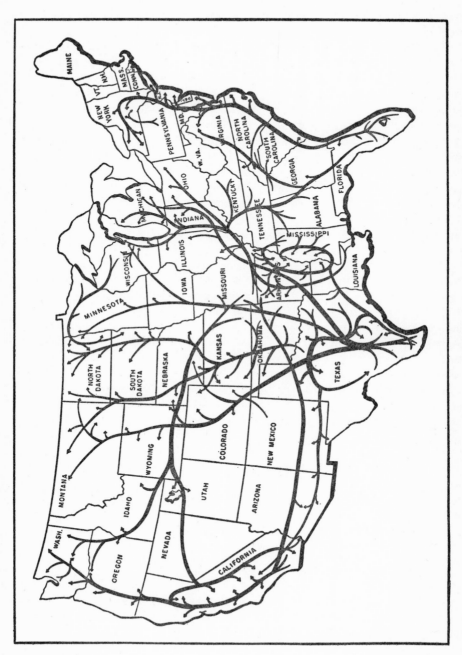

Figure 20. Travel Patterns of the Migratory Workers of the United States

They move to help harvest fruit, truck, berry, wheat, sugar beet, cotton, melon, pea, and beet crops. (Courtesy Extension Service, USDA)

ever, homesteading was permitted and took place in various sections as late as 1938, when the Homestead Act was repealed.

Another westward movement took place during and following the depression years of the 1930's. The interregional migrant of this period faced a situation different from that of the migrant of a hundred years before: he entered areas where the best opportunities in agriculture had been taken. This was, thus, primarily a movement of migrant workers.

The recent movements of migrant workers are graphically shown by Figure 20. The wheat migrants, although in decreasing numbers, still follow the wheat harvest from Texas into Canada. The California fruit pickers follow the orange and other fruit crops from section to section. An annual fruit-worker migration occurs from the strawberry farms of Louisiana to the cherry orchards of Michigan. Sugar-beet workers migrate from place to place in the Plains states. These seasonal migrants have been called the dispossessed citizens of America; their plight has been dramatically described by McWilliams, Steinbeck, and others, and some measures have been developed, in some areas, to alleviate their wretched living conditions.

These migrants present difficult problems of adjustment. They do not fit into the school systems; they are often not welcome in the churches; they crowd and "litter" the amusement places; and they find, too often, an unwelcome attitude toward them and their families on the part of the clubs and organizations of the community.

The social consequences of the movement of migrant workers have been summarized by Landis:

1. Culture shock—the difficulty of welcoming the newcomers into the life of the community.
2. Conflict—which arises from competition with the resident labor force.
3. Moral shock—when the migrants come in with a different, perhaps lower, standard of morals from that of the community.
4. Clash of family mores—migrant families may have different "work" or "life" codes than do the residents.
5. Housing adjustments—the local residents sometimes do not want to give decent space to the migrants, for a number of reasons.[9]

Accommodation of these migrants is vitally necessary. Although assimilation does sometimes take place, especially in cases where the migrants are of the same social and religious class as the people of the community, stratification too often takes place in that the new migrants are socially and physically segregated.

---

[9] Paul H. Landis, *Rural Life in Process*, New York: McGraw-Hill Book Co., Inc., 1940, pp. 266-268.

Most Rural People Move Within Their Community.—A number of studies show that most rural people, when they move to another farm, move only a short distance from the place of their birth.[10] In general, the movement is quite largely within the larger community. Even youth, when they move from one farm to another, tend to stay in the same community or county of their birth.[11]

This type of movement tends to provide stability and continuity of participation in the community, but for the smaller units of the community, such as one-room school districts, the moves may well result in maladjustments. Thus, families moving over school district lines disrupt the school program and retard their children, especially where there is little standardization as between schools. This is because the moves are generally made during the school term. Such moves, most of which are made by tenants or laborers who have large families, result in some schools having their attendance doubled, while others have their attendance cut in half.

Propertyless Move Most Often.—Much of the stability of farm families is related to tenure. Migrant farm laborers are more mobile than tenants, and tenants are more mobile than owners. Rural-nonfarm people are more mobile than the rural-farm population.

Tenants or laboring families who move once every two or three years, even though it is but a few miles, are therefore limited in their social and economic opportunities. In the South, for example, "the farmers who had moved most had the lowest socio-economic status and vice versa."[12] Such people cannot carry on a good farming program, their educational and religious life is not very satisfactory, and they do not get much out of, or contribute much in participation or leadership to the rural organizations and institutions.

Vertical Mobility.—The process whereby a farm boy is first a nonpaid laborer on his father's farm, then becomes a hired man, then a tenant, and finally an owner is usually called "climbing the agricultural ladder." Such a social process is desirable, but it fails to operate, or operates in reverse, at certain times and in many places. In the last depression period, for example, many owners lost their farms and became tenants, some on the farms they had previously owned. The process also operates in reverse when two adjacent farms are

10 "Spatial Mobility of the Rural Population with Respect to Local Areas," *American Journal of Sociology*, XLIII, No. 1, July, 1937, p. 92.
11 D. E. Lindstrom, E. G. Mosbacher, and R. B. McKenzie, *Rural Youth in Wartime Illinois*, Rural Sociology Mimeograph 10, Univ. of Illinois Agr. Exp. Sta., 1942.
12 B. O. Williams, *Occupational Mobility Among Farmers*, Bull. 296, South Carolina Agr. Exp. Sta., 1934, p. 73. See also Robert T. McMillan, *Migration and Status of Open-Country Families in Oklahoma*, Tech. Bull. T-19, Oklahoma Agr. Exp. Sta., 1943, p. 68.

bought by the same owner to make one larger unit. One, or perhaps both, of the former tenants become laborers for him. In such cases, not the least important result is what happens to the social status of these families. Their feeling of security may be undermined, their hope for cultural or educational advancement for themselves or their children may be dimmed, and they may feel ostracized from their neighborhood and community life. Many of them withdraw from all group activities and become socially isolated from their community associates.

Change in tenure status is only one form of vertical mobility, however. James West, in his *Plainville, U. S. A.*, describes the social classes in a typical marginal rural community, which exemplifies the resistances which operate to impede the movement of rural people from one social class to another. Rural people do not like to recognize these social classes, but some of them will admit there are differences due to geographic location, wealth, morals, use of traditional methods, income levels, and advancement or "manners."

The movement of rural people from one of these social classes to another is very difficult. "Movement across the line separating the upper from the lower class is virtually impossible, without leaving the community. It is not easy even by way of migration, because local manners, training, viewpoints, and the initial contacts . . . with the outside world are pretty apt to place them in a first job or social setting from which no very great 'rise' is likely." Moreover, it is more difficult to lower one's class than to lift it, "because the upper class is varied enough to retain anyone who retains its 'manners,' and because it is apparently almost impossible to lay upper-class manners aside, once they have been acquired." [13]

Age and Sex Distribution of the Rural Population

An analysis of the age and sex composition of the population shows clearly differentiated and significant patterns for rural and urban areas. These differences are important when considering the problems of supporting institutions such as schools and churches, and of economic and social services.

More Children in Rural Areas.—In 1940, children constituted approximately 28 per cent of the total population of the country, so distributed that they were almost 32 per cent of the total rural-farm population, 28 per cent of the total rural-nonfarm, and 26 per cent

[13] James West, *Plainville, U. S. A.*, New York: Columbia University Press, 1945, pp. 120-122, 134-141.

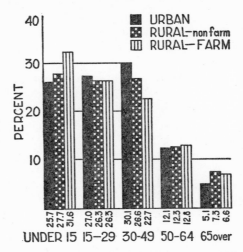

Figure 21. Percentages in Each Age-Group for Urban, Rural-Nonfarm, and Rural-Farm Populations in the United States, 1940

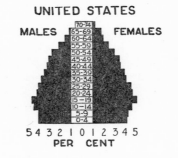

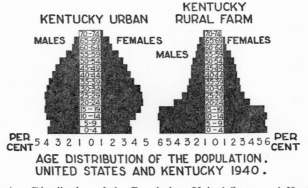

AGE DISTRIBUTION OF THE POPULATION.
UNITED STATES AND KENTUCKY 1940.

Figure 22. Age Distribution of the Population, United States and Kentucky, 1940

In Kentucky there were more infants under 5 than 5 to 9 years of age. (From Howard Beers and Robin M. Williams, *Age Structure of Kentucky Population, 1940*, Bull. 465, Univ. of Kentucky Agr. Exp. Sta., 1944)

of the total urban. Figure 21 shows distribution for the country by age groups. This situation is even more graphically shown by Figure 22, from a study of population in Kentucky. Note that the Kentucky urban population pyramid is very much like that of the United States, but that the pyramids for the rural-farm as well as the rural-nonfarm populations have unusually large proportions of those in the age groups under fifteen years.

Productive-Age People in Rural Areas.—Whereas the rural, and especially the rural-farm population, as shown by Figures 21 and 22, contain more children than do the urban areas, they have fewer people in the productive ages, from fifteen to forty-nine years. The cities, especially, draw very heavily on those from twenty to twenty-five years of age, this migration taking place earlier for the village youth, both boys and girls, than for other classes of the population. Girls tend to migrate from farms at an earlier age than boys.

More Old People in the Villages.—Reference once more to Figure 21 will show that the greater proportion of people sixty-five years of age or older are in the rural-nonfarm population. The villages of our country are, therefore, the "refuge" for old people. This is most marked in the Middle Atlantic and Middle Western states.

Two types of population movement contribute to this situation: the movement of farmers to villages when they retire, and the purchase by city people of homes in the villages. The characteristic "old age" situation in the villages has a real effect on the attitude of these people toward progressive movements. The older people are, the more reluctant they are to make changes.

Rural Population Growing Older.—The constant migration of youth from rural areas and the lowering of the birth rates in rural areas results in an increasing proportion of older people in rural areas. The median age of the rural-farm population in 1930 was 21.6 years; by 1940 it had advanced to 24.4 years. Even so, it was lower than the median age of the rural-nonfarm population, which was 27.7 years in 1940; and considerably lower than the urban population, with a median age of 31 in the same year.

The net migration of over 5 million from rural to urban areas from 1940 to 1945, as shown by Figure 18, probably further accentuated the trend toward a higher proportion of old-age groups in rural areas. Many farmers in the World War II period were over sixty years of age and would have retired had it not been for the need for man power on the farms during the war. Beginning with 1945 a net migration to rural areas became evident, due to the return of ex-service and war-industry personnel to rural life, resulting in a tendency for the rural population again to be of a younger character. However, this proved to be but a short-term movement; as shown by Figure 18, the net migration again became urbanward by 1946. The long-time trend of net migration to urban areas is reasserting itself even more strongly in the last years of the decade. Moreover, the size of farm family, which has been decreasing for several decades, is still moving downward.

More Men on Farms.—The measure used by the Census for the relation of number of males to number of females is the number of males per 100 females; it is referred to as the sex ratio. In 1940 there were 111.7 males to 100 females over fifteen years of age on farms, but only 95.5 males to 100 females in the cities. Table 2 shows the 1940 sex ratios of native and foreign-born, for the rural-farm, the rural-nonfarm, and the urban populations, according to racial composition. The proportion of white native-born was 94.5 males per 100 females in the cities whereas on the farms it was 112.2.

TABLE 2. URBAN, RURAL-NONFARM, AND RURAL-FARM MALES PER 100 FEMALES IN THE UNITED STATES, FOR 1940 *

Area and Nativity	Males per 100 Females		
	White	Negro	Other
Urban	96.1	88.1	191.4
Native	94.5	87.9	160.0
Foreign-born	106.8	109.2	287.2
Rural-nonfarm	103.9	99.8	118.6
Native	102.8	99.7	113.0
Foreign-born	124.4	157.8	245.6
Rural-farm	113.1	103.1	122.4
Native	112.2	103.1	118.8
Foreign-born	140.3	217.7	181.8

* U. S. Dept. of Commerce, Bureau of the Census, Sixteenth Census of the United States, *Population*, Vol. II, Part I, 1940, Table 5, p. 20.

Sex ratios are highest in each instance for foreign-born, which is to be expected in view of the fact that it is the males who have migrated here from other countries in greater numbers than females.

More Unmarried Men in the Country.—The 1940 Census shows 4.5 per cent of male heads of rural-farm families as single, compared with 3.3 per cent of the male heads of urban families who have not married. A recent Ohio study showed an exceedingly large number of bachelors and an unexpectedly large number of spinsters in the farm population, there evidently being "powerful factors in the farm environment that discourage marriage on the part of youth." [14]

Fewer Broken Families in the Country.—Family stability is greater in the country than in towns and cities. Table 3 shows that less than three fourths of the urban families have male heads and wives present, compared with more than four fifths of rural-farm families thus intact. Only 0.7 per cent of the rural-farm families have been broken by divorce, compared with 2 per cent for the urban areas.

TABLE 3. PROPORTIONS OF FAMILIES IN THE URBAN AND RURAL POPULA-
TIONS IN THE UNITED STATES WHOSE HEADS ARE MARRIED, SEPARATED,
WIDOWED, DIVORCED, AND SINGLE: 1940 *

Area	Per Cent Married, Wife Present	Per Cent Married, Wife or Husband Absent	Per Cent Widowed	Per Cent Divorced	Per Cent Single
All families	76.2	2.3	12.7	1.6	6.2
Urban	73.8	3.8	13.6	2.0	6.8
Rural-nonfarm ...	77.1	2.8	13.2	1.4	5.5
Rural-farm	82.3	2.0	9.8	0.7	5.2

* U. S. Dept. of Commerce, Bureau of the Census, Sixteenth Census of the United States, *Families, General Characteristics,* Table 11, p. 30.

These data do not show, of course, the complete divorce situation, for many who seek and obtain divorce are not counted by the Census. The rate of divorce is likely to be higher in cities because (1) restraints to divorce found in the country are lacking in the cities, (2) many of those residing in the country seek divorce in urban areas, and (3) the nature of farm family life, being a family business, is more conducive to family stability.

The rural-nonfarm and urban populations contain about a third more widowed people than are present in the rural-farm populations. When one of a married couple loses the other, for any reason, it is evident that farm life becomes more difficult for the family. Hence, relatively few widowers and widows can be found on farms, either in the households of others or as heads of families.

In 1940 there were more families with widowed female heads in the urban population than in either the rural-farm or the rural-

[14] A. R. Mangus, *Rural Children and Youth in Ohio,* Bull. 185, Ohio State Univ. Agr. Exp. Sta., 1945, p. 41 (mimeographed).

74 AMERICAN RURAL LIFE

nonfarm populations. Only 6 per cent of the rural-farm families had
widowed heads, compared with 9.6 per cent for the rural-nonfarm
and 10.7 per cent for the urban families. Most of the widowers and
widows were those in the older age groups, especially in the rural-
nonfarm population.

Rural Families Are Largest.—We have already noted the proportionately larger number of children in rural than in urban areas.
This difference in number of children is strikingly shown in Table 4.

TABLE 4. FAMILIES, BY NUMBER OF CHILDREN UNDER 18 YEARS OLD, FOR
THE UNITED STATES, URBAN AND RURAL: 1940 *

Area	No Children	Per Cent		
		1	2	3 or more
All areas	48.9	21.3	14.5	15.3
Urban	53.0	21.9	13.9	11.2
Rural-nonfarm	46.5	21.2	15.1	17.2
Rural-farm	39.4	19.6	15.5	25.6

* U. S. Dept. of Commerce, Bureau of the Census, Sixteenth Census of the United States,
Families, General Characteristics, Table 2, p. 10.

There is not much difference in the percentage of rural families and
urban families having but one child or two children; the great difference is in the families with three or more children. More than one
in four rural-farm families had three or more children less than
eighteen years old in 1940; approximately one in nine urban families
had three or more children under eighteen years old. Conversely,
more than half of the urban families had no children under eighteen
years old, whereas less than two fifths of the rural-farm families
had no children under 18 years of age.

Nationality and Race of Rural Population

First Rural Immigrants Were European.—Although the United
States has been looked upon as the melting pot for all the nationalities
and races of the world, we must not lose sight of the fact that most
of the people settling here came from Europe. The "old" migrants,
from northern and western Europe, came largely in the period before
1880, looking for opportunities on the new lands that were being
opened up on the American continent. The "new" migrations, which
reached their peak in 1914, came largely from eastern and southern
Europe and were attracted to the industrial areas. "With the

rapid industrial expansion which came with the recovery from the panic of 1873, it was apparent that a horde of cheap labor was necessary to hew our forests, mine our coal and minerals, lay the ribbons of steel across our far-flung continent, and tend the tireless wheels of industry." [15]

The evidence of the northern European nationality origins—German, Scandinavian, English, and French—can be seen clearly in many counties of many states. There was a tendency for the German immigrants, for example, to settle in groups and retain the customs of the homeland. They brought their culture with them—their religious beliefs, many of which were not tolerated by the state churches in the homeland, their agricultural methods, their habits of hard work and frugality, their independence. Many of these culture traits still cling to them and affect the life of the entire community. A knowledge of the nationality backgrounds of a particular rural people is therefore of importance as a basis for understanding their ways of doing things, especially in groups—families, neighborhoods, churches, etc.

TABLE 5. PERCENTAGE BY RACE OF THE POPULATION OF THE UNITED STATES, RURAL AND URBAN, 1940 *

Area and Nativity	White	Negro	Other
Urban	91.3	8.4	0.3
Native	90.3	9.5	0.2
Foreign-born	98.5	0.8	0.7
Rural-nonfarm	91.7	7.8	0.5
Native	91.3	8.2	0.5
Foreign-born	99.0	0.3	0.6
Rural-farm	84.3	14.9	0.8
Native	83.8	15.4	0.8
Foreign-born	97.9	0.2	2.0

* U. S. Dept. of Commerce, Bureau of the Census, Sixteenth Census of the United States, *Population*, Vol. II, Part I, Table 5, p. 20.

Non-Whites in Rural Areas.—Although the rural-farm population has proportionately more native-born than the urban (96.9 per cent for rural-farm; 87.5 per cent for urban), it contains, nevertheless, a greater proportion of non-white racial stocks, as can be seen by Table 5. By far the most important non-white race in the rural population is the Negro, the foreign-born of other races (chiefly

[15] Francis J. Brown and J. S. Roucek, *One America* (rev. ed.), New York: Prentice-Hall, Inc., 1945, pp. 5-6.

Orientals) forming only 2 per cent of the total rural-farm population.

The Negro rural-farm population is confined largely to the South, where it comprises about a third of the total rural-farm population. In Mississippi and South Carolina, Negroes form over half of the rural-farm population. There is no questioning the fact that the pressure of such large proportions of Negroes in the southern rural-farm population presents serious social and economic problems. Until World War II a large share of the farm labor supply of the South was Negro, but during the war many Negroes went into war industries and moved into other sections of the country. The shortage of farm labor in the South has hastened the perfection of the mechanical cotton picker. A return to prewar labor supply conditions may well cause unemployment, particularly among these new migrants, and create serious relief problems. This is a problem of nationwide significance.

The problem of providing economic and social opportunities for the Negro which will be on a par with those of others in this country is not so difficult in rural as it is in urban areas, for the Negro, like anyone else, can own and operate farms. Nevertheless, the evidence shows that the Negro in rural areas, especially in the South, is at a serious disadvantage, educationally, economically, and socially. According to the 1940 Census, more than two out of every three men who were heads of Negro farm families in the South had fewer than five years of schooling, compared with about one head out of every three for all farm family heads in the South, and less than one head out of every four, for the nation as a whole. This situation comes about not because the Negro is inferior intellectually, but rather because he lacks adequate educational opportunities.

Negro tenants of the South make up more than half of all farm tenants in the region. Over half the Negro tenants are croppers, who live in bitter poverty and dependence upon the rations system, by which they too often suffer rank exploitation. This is a system which thwarts ambition, inhibits thrift, and negates self-respect. We are often told that the poverty of Negro croppers of the South is born of their laziness. "But this is upside down, as their laziness is born of their poverty." [16]

The migrations of "dust bowl" laborers to California during the 1930's caused such serious social and economic maladjustment that a series of Congressional hearings was held on the matter. Careful

[16] Reprinted from *The Collapse of Cotton Tenancy* by Charles S. Johnson, Edwin R. Embree, and W. W. Alexander by permission of the University of North Carolina Press. Copyright, 1935, by the University of North Carolina Press.

planning will be necessary if we are to avoid similar conditions in the South, and quite possibly in other areas, in future times of stress. The rural South, which cannot satisfactorily employ all of the people it rears, must look to the industrial North and East for the employment of its surplus population.

Rural People and Their Employment

The total number of persons employed in the United States is about 60,000,000. (See Figure 23.) Of these, about one sixth are in agriculture, a labor force second only to the number employed in manufacturing. It includes farmers and farm managers, farm laborers and foremen, and unpaid family labor.

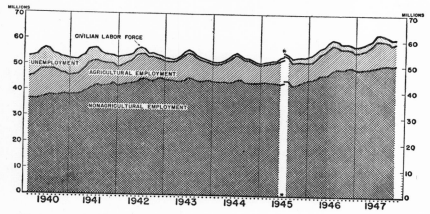

* Series on revised basis from July 1945.

Note: Excludes estimated number of persons in the armed forces and in institutions.

Figure 23. Civilian Labor Force, Employment and Unemployment for Persons 14 Years of Age and Over in the United States

Note the steady rise in the nonagriculturally employed contrasted with an approximately uniform number in agriculture. (Bureau of Labor Statistics, U. S. Dept. of Labor)

Rural-Farm Employment.—It is generally believed that most rural people are engaged in farming. This is true only of the male rural-farm population. Nine tenths of the rural-farm male population *are* engaged in farming. In numbers, they almost equal the number of males engaged in manufacturing. Manufacturing, the next most important occupation for rural-farm males, employs less than 5 per cent, and other occupations employ the remaining 5 per cent of the rural-farm males.

Even some of those engaged in farming, however, also work at other occupations. Almost a fourth of all farm operators work two months off the farm sometime during the year. The present-day "new" opportunities in agriculture thus seem to be for part-time farming.

The replacement opportunities for rural-farm males in farming are such that the available farms resulting from death or retirement due to old age will have been sufficient by 1950 to absorb only about three fourths of the rural-farm young men. The remainder will have to seek opportunities elsewhere. The extent to which part-time farming will develop in the United States, together with the extent to which manufacturing industries, especially those relating to agriculture, can be decentralized, will have considerable effect on the number of persons who can be employed in agriculture and in rural life occupations.

The Census Bureau classes housewives as engaged in home housework. Of the employed rural-farm women, two thirds are employed in agriculture and domestic service. A large proportion of these are southern Negroes, who work in the cotton fields. Many farm women in all parts of the country, however, especially in the war period, could be found working in hay, corn, wheat, and other harvest fields. These are not counted by the Census as employed in agriculture. Many girls from farms work as hired girls, but most of them go to towns and cities for such employment. A number of farm women teach school; in the World War II period many married women from farms taught country schools.

Rural-Nonfarm Employment.—When we turn to rural-nonfarm areas we find only one man in eight employed in agriculture, one in three in manufacturing, one in seven in trade and transportation, and one in ten in extraction of minerals. The man who lives in a town or village is not regarded as agriculturally engaged unless he retains an interest in a farm, and farms it, even though he lives in town. The female population of the rural-nonfarm areas is primarily employed in domestic and personal service, one third being so employed. Professional service and manufacturing occupy one fifth and trade one eighth of the rural-nonfarm women.

Changed Social Attitudes.—The war changed the farm and non-farm labor proportions considerably, for in the early years of the war large numbers of the youth, especially, went into other industries. The fact that so large a percentage of rural people have recently engaged in work other than agriculture cannot help but affect their social attitudes. Many of the rural-nonfarm people are now tied more closely to urban areas than to rural areas in their interests and loyalties, and even in their modes of thinking and behavior, despite the fact that their economic welfare depends largely on the economic welfare of the farmers. This situation creates a real problem in securing good town-country cooperation. There is a tendency to set up class lines between town and country people but these can be bridged by convincing the two groups that their social and economic welfare are interrelated.

How rural-urban relations can be improved will be dealt with in a later section. But there is one significant difference between town and country, and especially between urban and farm people, that should be noted in connection with an analysis of their occupations. In urban and town areas a large percentage of the people work for someone else. Most farmers, on the other hand, work for themselves. In Illinois, for example, about nine tenths of the urban workers are wage workers. On the other hand, more than two thirds of Illinois farmers are self-employed. The attitude and outlook of farm people is therefore quite likely to be different from that of the mass of town and city people. Farm people naturally think they are the makers of their own destinies—they run their own business. So their loyalties are tied more closely with the employer or self-employed groups in the cities than with the wage and salary workers. Yet their very economic welfare depends upon the buying power of these millions of wage and salary workers in the cities.

The Vitality of Rural People

We have already shown the importance of the rural to the urban population. Will it continue to be so? Much will depend upon the excess in births over deaths in rural areas and on the physical and mental stamina of the rural people.

The growth or decline of a population can be measured in terms of (1) birth rates—the ratio of births during an interval of time to the total number of population; (2) fertility ratios—the number of children under five years per 1,000 women fifteen to forty-four years of age; and (3) net reproduction rates—the measure of the reproductivity of the population, as shown by the potential mothers if birth and death rates remain constant.

Birth Rates Highest in Rural Areas.—Whereas in the urban population ten adults are rearing only about seven children, in the farm population ten adults are rearing fourteen children and, in the poor-land areas, fifteen or sixteen children. The rural regions of the Southeast and Southwest have the highest birth rates in the United States (New Mexico, with its high proportion of Mexicans, has the highest of all). The lowest birth rates are in the industrial states (notably New York, the lowest) and in Nebraska and Kansas, where dust-bowl migrations have brought down the rates.

If the present differential in the birth rate persists, future generations in the United States will come mostly from the farms and villages of

. . . the poor but proud and generally capable people of the Southern Appalachian Mountains, of the croppers and tenants of the cotton belt, or the hill folk that live along the Ohio River and its tributaries, of the Catholic farmers of Maryland and North Dakota, of the Mennonites scattered in groups in Indiana, Kansas, Pennsylvania, and Virginia, of the Mormons of Idaho and Utah, and of other people who, because of their geographic isolation or religious traditions have been more or less protected from the influences of modern culture.[17]

Rural-Farm Population Fertility Ratios.—It takes about 370 children under five years of age per 1,000 women fifteen to forty-four years of age to maintain the population at present birth and death rates. In 1940, our urban centers (except those with high percentages of foreign-born) had fertility ratios under 370. Most farm areas, except those in the good land areas, had ratios over 370. Some state averages were as high as 645. In Illinois, more than half of the counties in 1940 had average ratios of less than 370, most of these having in them relatively large cities and towns.

Rural Reproduction Rates.—The net reproduction rate in the urban areas of the United States in 1940 was 76 which, potentially, would bring about a decrease in urban populations of 25 per cent per generation, if there were no net migration to urban areas from rural areas. The net reproduction rate for rural-farm areas, on the other hand, was 136, and for the rural-nonfarm 116. In the long run, therefore, the population in rural areas will reproduce at a rate well above the replacement level. The difference in reproduction rates is graphically illustrated by Figure 24. Note the wide variation in rates for the urban, the rural-nonfarm, and the rural-farm areas, both for 1930 and for 1940.

Farm areas benefit by an increase in city populations, especially if those populations are kept employed at good incomes. A decline in

17 Baker and Taeuber, *op. cit.*, p. 68.

urban population can mean a decline in demand for farm products, unless consumption per capita should increase. Conversely, the urban demand for farm products will be intensified, so long as urban populations and incomes continue to increase.

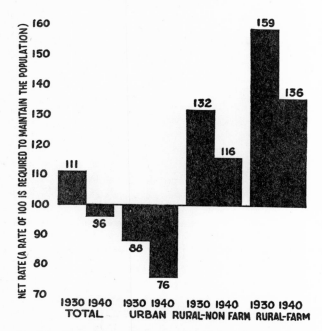

Figure 24. Net Reproduction Rates for the United States, 1930 and 1940

The Health of Rural People.—Rural people, and especially farm people, have traditionally felt that the country is the most healthful place in which to live. It is a shock to many of them to learn that rural boys, especially those from poor-land areas, failed to pass physical examinations for induction into the armed services in World War II in the ratio of 41 out of every 100, compared with but 25 rejections per 100 for other groups in the population. Rural people, as a class, are not as healthy as they have believed.

The fact that rural people get an abundance of good air, plenty of physical exercise, and are not so much exposed to the conditions leading to poor health, has nevertheless not prevented a relatively higher rate of sickness and higher infant and adult death rates in rural than in urban areas. Several reasons have been given for the existence of serious health problems in rural areas. One, for example, has been the indifference of rural people toward their problems. Because they take their good health for granted, provisions for protecting their health have been made more difficult. Rural people need more adequate health protection services, a need which will be more fully discussed in a later chapter.

Good health comes largely from eating good food. Rural people pride themselves on having plenty of good food. Again, a false impression has led to serious weaknesses in the physical stamina of rural people. Studies have shown that rural, and especially farm,

Figure 25. Hard Facts about Mental Disease in the United States
(Graphics Institute for This Week Magazine)

people do not eat enough of the right kinds of food. The resulting deficiencies in their diets lead to serious physical shortcomings and subject rural children, especially, to diseases which they could withstand if they had the right amounts of the right kinds of food.

The Mental Health of Rural People.—Very few studies have been made of the mental deficiencies of rural people and the result has been very little accurate knowledge as to the exact situation. Figure 25 shows the serious situation in the United States. There is a lack of adequate facilities to detect the presence of mental deficiencies in rural areas. This matter will be discussed at greater length in the chapter on health.

There is little material available as to the native intelligence of rural people. The result of the selective migration now going on is also problematical. Most students of rural life feel that the youth from the best and the poorest economic classes are being drawn to cities from rural areas, leaving a stable middle group. The fact that more and more of the surplus population is being drawn from poorer and poorer lands may mean that we in America will eventually suffer in the quality of our human stock. The study of this problem is at least just as important as the study of the problems of animal or plant breeding, but is nevertheless receiving little attention. We need to know more about what is happening to the quality of the human stock in rural areas.

Future Changes in the Rural Population

The future of the population in rural, and especially farm, areas will depend on a number of factors. Not the least important will be the extent to which rural people continue to have families large enough so that some of them will have to move into urban areas. But the forces which have caused a shrinkage in the size of urban families are unquestionably also at work in rural areas. Even now, on the best lands, there are only enough children reared to replace the population there. Higher economic and social standards of living, the emancipation of rural women, changed attitudes toward sex relations, and the knowledge and practice of modern birth control methods, have been some of the contributing causes. Nevertheless, there will doubtless continue to be more children born in rural areas than will be able to find lucrative occupations there.

There is a close relationship between the level of farm prices and the movement of the farm population. When farm prices are high farm population declines, and when they are low the farm population increases. "It is not *because* farm prices are low that farm population increases, but rather that low farm prices reflect low rates of employment in industry. Hence, it may be expected that if a high rate of employment can be maintained in the cities the farm population will remain the same or decrease." [18]

Moreover, as agricultural production per worker increases there is less need for employment on farms, unless the demand for farm products increases. The general trend upward in production per

[18] Lowry Nelson, *Minnesota's Farm Population Prospects,* Univ. of Minnesota Agr. Exp. Sta., 1944, p. 5 (see especially Fig. 1).

worker on farms can be seen in Figure 26. Agricultural production continues at a high rate; were it to decline when European demands are filled, the number employed in agriculture would not increase unless there were severe industrial unemployment.

The rural-farm population for 1950 and 1960 has been estimated by the Twentieth Century Fund: by 1950 it will decline to 29.4 millions and by 1960 to 28.4 millions. The family units on farms will be reduced from 7.1 million in 1940 to 6.6 million in 1950 and 6.1 million in 1960.[19] The decrease predicted by the Fund probably

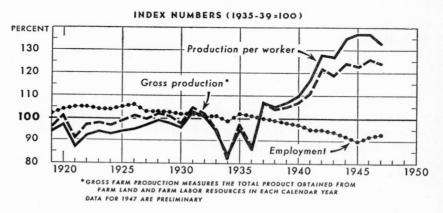

INDEX NUMBERS (1935-39 =100)

*GROSS FARM PRODUCTION MEASURES THE TOTAL PRODUCT OBTAINED FROM FARM LAND AND FARM LABOR RESOURCES IN EACH CALENDAR YEAR
DATA FOR 1947 ARE PRELIMINARY

Figure 26. Gross Farm Production, Farm Employment, and Gross Production per Worker in the United States, 1919-1947

Note the rapid rise in production per worker and gross production since 1936, and the gradual decline in farm employment to 1945. (BAE, USDA)

will occur, especially if a high level of employment is maintained in the cities. If unemployment increases in the cities there again may be a backing up of youth on the farms. Moreover, in periods of declining prices people tend to move to the country and thus increase the rural and farm population.[20]

In any case, the following conclusions may be drawn about the future of the rural population: (1) It will continue to supply the cities and must do so if rural youth are to find adequate opportunities for employment; (2) this surplus will probably come more and more from poorer and poorer lands; many good-land areas now produce only enough to replace their own population; and (3) the

[19] J. Frederick Dewhurst and Associates, *America's Needs and Resources,* New York: The Twentieth Century Fund, 1947, p. 43.
[20] See T. W. Schultz, *Agriculture in an Unstable Economy,* New York: McGraw-Hill Book Co., Inc., 1945, Ch. IV, for an excellent analysis of the effects of urban unemployment upon rural welfare.

population of cities would be static or in a state of decline if there were no migration from rural areas.

DISCUSSION

1. Why is it important to study the rural population, its characteristics and movements?
2. What are the reasons for the change in the relative proportions of rural and urban populations in the last 100 years? What are the present areas of highest concentrations of rural and farm populations? What is the characteristic type of life and level of living in these areas? Why are these areas of social concern?
3. What are the chief age and sex differences in the rural farm, nonfarm, and urban populations? Nationality and race differences? Discuss the social significance of these differences.
4. What are the chief effects of the cityward migration of rural people? What changes have come in the last three decades? What is likely to be the future trend? Of what social significance are these changes?
5. Describe the chief types of interregional migration in the United States. What are the social effects of these migrations on the migrating families? On the communities?
6. Discuss the effects of rural and urban differences in fertility and reproduction. Of what concern to society is the vitality of rural people? What factors will determine the trend in numbers of rural-farm people in the nation in the future?

READINGS

Baker, O. E., Borsodi, Ralph, and Wilson, M. L. *Agriculture in Modern Life.* New York: Harper & Bros., 1939, Ch. IV.

Brown, Francis J., and Roucek, J. S. *One America.* New York: Prentice-Hall, Inc., 1945, Ch. I.

Brunner, Edmund DeS., and Kolb, J. H. *Rural Social Trends.* New York: McGraw-Hill Book Co., Inc., 1933, Ch. I.

Dewhurst, J. Frederick, and Associates. *America's Needs and Resources.* New York: The Twentieth Century Fund, 1947, Ch. III.

Farm Population Estimates, 1910-1946. BAE, USDA, June, 1946.

Landis, Paul H. *Rural Life in Process.* New York: McGraw-Hill Book Co., Inc., 1940, pp. 183-279.

Releases on Farm Population Estimates. BAE, USDA, 1945.

Rural Schools for Tomorrow. Yearbook of the Department of Rural Education, NEA, 1945, Ch. V.

Sanderson, Dwight. *Rural Sociology and Rural Social Organization.* New York: John Wiley & Sons, Inc., 1942, Ch. V.

Schultz, T. W. *Agriculture in an Unstable Economy.* New York: McGraw-Hill Book Co., Inc., 1945, Ch. IV.

West, James. *Plainville, U. S. A.* New York: Columbia University Press, 1945, pp. 134-142.

Chapter 5

THE ECONOMIC BASIS FOR RURAL LIFE

Farming is both a means of earning a living and a mode of life. It may not always be a good way to earn a living, but it can be a wonderful way to live a life. The outstanding social characteristic of most farming enterprises is family participation; the most successful farmers, from a social as well as an economic point of view, are unquestionably those whose families cooperate fully in the success of the enterprise. The family, working and living **as a group,** is the basic social and economic unit in rural life.

Social and Economic Changes in American Rural Life

The present-day social fabric of America's rural life is the resultant of many changes. To understand the significance of the socio-economic evolution which has taken place since the Agrarian Revolution, it is necessary to continue the story of our westward expansion, which we began in Chapter 3.

The period from the founding of the Massachusetts Bay Colony until the end of the Revolutionary War—over 150 years—can be called the period of protection settlement along the Atlantic seaboard. The English had restrained settlement in the "West," and the Indian tribes had been a definite menace to any westward expansion. The signing of peace treaties quieted the fierce Iroquois and similar tribes and opened the plains for settlement. Released from the great danger of annihilation by Indians, more and more adventuresome people on the eastern coast began to move westward to new lands.

The religious and racial cast of the first migrants was of great importance. Both factors exerted a definite influence on the pattern of the life of many of the communities that came to be established in the Middle West and the Far West, such as the Zoar community of eastern Ohio, the New Harmony community in Indiana, the Bishop Hill Colony in Illinois, the Amana Society of Iowa, and the Mormon communities in the then virgin territory of Utah. Why these types of settlement with their communal and in some cases communistic systems of social organization did not spread, forms one of the most interesting studies in the development of our unique pattern of rural society in the United States.[1] The earlier migrations also included the Presbyterian, Baptist, Mennonite, and United Brethren. Each sect, because it had religious freedom, could form new groups.

Later migrants traveled overland—the Germans and Scandinavians coming directly from their homelands—to settle lands as much as possible like those they had known across the sea. The overland migrations included the Lutherans and the Mission groups. The Norwegians, Danish, and similar ethnic groups moved into Wisconsin, for example, to give many of its communities the solidarity that has characterized them ever since.

These settlements in the Middle West had just begun to take root when a new, almost wholesale, land-hungry westward movement took place. The Pre-emption Act (1841) and the Homestead Act (1864) gave it even greater impetus, and the broad plains of Iowa, Nebraska, and the Dakotas, and even of some of the Rocky Mountain states, became dotted with scattered farmstead settlements.[2] At first, these movements preceded the building of railroads, and towns and villages were built in the hope that the railroad would come. Some were disappointed (like the people of Urbana, when the Illinois Central was built to the west, giving opportunity for the growth of Champaign). Later settlers followed the railroads. Because of Government grants of alternate strips of land a mile wide and several miles back from the railroads, settlements could be encouraged.

The Agrarian Revolution

The Beginning.—After farmers had become established on the land they naturally began to seek a market for their products. At first, the nearest village center, which grew up at the most convenient crossroads, was the trading post for their products. Farmers' clubs, meeting regularly to discuss the crop and livestock outlook, were frequent. Meeting together regularly, farmers began to discover they had "grievances." At first the grievances were against the local merchants for charging too much for supplies, and because farmers were "told" what they could get for their products. Discriminatory freight rates, inflation and then deflation, usurious rates

[1] See N. L. Sims, *Elements of Rural Sociology*, New York: Thomas Y. Crowell Co., 1940, pp. 67-73, for a description of some of these early forms of settlement.
[2] See John D. Hicks, *The Populist Revolt*, Minneapolis: University of Minnesota Press, 1931, Ch. I and II.

of interest, increasingly heavy land taxes, and declining prices for farm products were the rallying points for farmers' indignation meetings, farmers' conventions, and farmers' movements for reform in the period following the Civil War.[3]

New and untried ventures based on mutual aid experiences, such as pooling purchases for flour, sugar, and other staples, led to setting up purchasing cooperatives and even farmers' stores. Many of these enterprises failed when farmers were unable to get credit, because of poor management, price-cutting by competing merchants, or dealers hostile to such ventures.

This was the period, also, of the establishment of land-grant colleges (1862), agricultural experiment stations (1887), and farmers' institutes to bring to farmers scientific facts about good soil, crop, and livestock practices. It was the period of rapid growth of towns and cities and of major agrarian efforts to break down the protective tariff policy.[4] Rural free delivery, which was started in 1896, helped to reduce the isolation of the farm family, and aided the development of a class consciousness among the farm people, which in turn helped lay the foundations of the "psychological wall" between farm and town people.

The Country Life Movement.—Up to the turn of the century the farmer and his family took their isolation for granted. He got along with his little school, his open-country church, and his lack of many of the conveniences of his town and city cousins. The first decade of the 20th century, however, saw the development of the Country Life Movement. Writers and teachers began to cry havoc, pointing out that the timberlands were being shorn off ruthlessly, that the soils were beginning to wash away, and that the rural church was declining, the rural school was inferior to that of the town, the roads were impassable for long periods in the year, the women and children on the farm had to work long hours and do without many good things, and that young men and women, the best in the country, were beginning to seek a better life in the cities.[5] At first, these warning voices went almost unheeded by other groups, each intent on its own problems. Finally, a spirit of helpfulness began to manifest itself.

---

[3] D. E. Lindstrom, *American Farmers' and Rural Organizations*, Champaign, Ill.: Garrard Press, 1948, Ch. VI.

[4] See the excellent chronology of American agricultural history in *Farmers in a Changing World*, Yearbook of the USDA, 1940, pp. 1184-1196. See also, O. M. Kile, *The Farm Bureau Movement*, New York: The Macmillan Co., 1921, pp. 62-68.

[5] See the *Report of the Commission on Country Life*, reprinted by The University of North Carolina Press, 1944.

A short period of agricultural prosperity, which began about 1910, somewhat blunted national interest in the woes of the farmers, but not before the efforts to alleviate the social and economic ills of agriculture had achieved some success. In 1914 the Smith-Lever Extension Act was passed, to provide a nation-wide system of agricultural and home economics education, largely for the adults, but also for the youth on farms. In 1917 came the Smith-Hughes Act to provide vocational education.

This period of prosperity continued and was enhanced by World War I. Slogans of "Food will win the war" led to the breaking up of pastures and new lands all over the country. Farmers "cast aside many policies of permanent farm organization, soil maintenance, of margins of cultivation [i.e., below which exploitation took place] which had shown indications of becoming established in the prewar period." [6] Wartime farm groups and agencies grew up, and 60 million acres of short-grass lands were plowed up. But measures for the alleviation of woman and child labor, improvement of home conditions, betterment of schools, revitalization of churches, health protection, and building of rural community life, were laid aside or forgotten in the heat of helping to win the war.

Agricultural Recession and Adjustment.—Farmers had built great hopes of a permanent high level of farm prices, following World War I. But they had not reckoned with our change from a debtor to a creditor nation, the decrease in our huge export trade in farm products, the building up of stockpiles of food and fiber in this country, the competition from the war-spawned crop lands in the west, the growing competition of food products from countries like Australia and Argentina, and the development of self-sufficiency in the war-torn European countries. American farmers experienced their first serious setback in the new century in 1920 and 1921.

Good prices returned by 1923, and prevailed until 1929. However, the effects of mechanization, which had been accentuated in the war period, began to be felt. The demand for feed grains decreased because of the widespread substitution of automobiles, trucks, and tractors for horses and mules. (See Figure 27.) Population increase in cities was not so rapid as it had been in the previous decade. Farmers who bought land at high prices had to pay for it after prices declined by one half or more, or lose their farms. Taxes remained high and in some instances increased. [7]

---

[6] Dwight Sanderson, *Rural Sociology and Rural Social Organization*, New York: John Wiley & Sons, Inc., 1942, p. 107.

[7] T. Swann Harding, *Some Landmarks in the History of the Department of Agriculture*, *Agricultural History Series No. 2*, Office of Information, USDA, 1942, p. 81.

The period of the 1920's was marked by efforts to secure relief measures for the economic pressures under which farmers found themselves living. This period was also marked by the constant public references to adverse conditions of living, the closing down of many open-country churches, the lack of high schools for rural children, the lack of adequate libraries, poor health protection facilities, and the seeming disintegration of rural neighborhood and community life. These conditions were shown by rural sociologists in numerous studies, made possible by grants of Federal funds to colleges of agriculture under the Purnell Act.

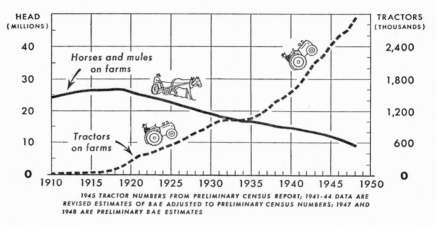

1945 TRACTOR NUMBERS FROM PRELIMINARY CENSUS REPORT; 1941-44 DATA ARE REVISED ESTIMATES OF BAE ADJUSTED TO PRELIMINARY CENSUS NUMBERS; 1947 AND 1948 ARE PRELIMINARY BAE ESTIMATES

Figure 27. Horses and Mules, and Tractors on Farms, United States, January 1, 1910-1948

The farms of America are becoming mechanized. (BAE, USDA)

When the depression began for all, in 1929, some groundwork had been laid for measures to meet the distressing situation of agriculture. The Federal Farm Loan Act had been passed in 1916, and the Capper-Volstead Act to exempt production cooperatives from the restrictions of the antitrust law in 1922. The Agricultural Credits Act, passed in 1923, had set up a Federal Intermediate Credit Bank in each Federal Land Bank District, for the purpose of making loans to farmers for periods intermediate between the usual long- and short-term loans; and the Federal Farm Board was established in 1929. The highly protective Smoot-Hawley Tariff Act was passed in 1930 in the hope that it would prevent imports of agricultural products from newer foreign agricultural regions, and the Stabilization Corporation, a part of the 1929 Agricultural Marketing Act, sought to buy up wheat and cotton surpluses.

Direct Action and Government Aid.—Two types of direct action grew up in the deep period of the depression during the early 1930's. The first direct action, taken by the farmers, was often violent. When a farmer was being forced to sell out to pay his debts, his neighbors attended the sale and prevented anyone from bidding more than a few cents. Then they turned the property back to the original owner, who consequently had his debts cleared and his property back at a very small percentage of its real worth. In milk strikes, men lined the roads to prevent milk from being marketed, dumping cans of milk on the side of the road and sometimes shooting holes into railroad milk tank cars.[8] These direct actions served to stir the country to some interest in the farmers' problems and made possible governmental direct action: the passage of emergency legislation. To relieve the situation, the Federal government established grants-in-aid to farmers in distress and set up committees to adjust mortgages downward.

The Agricultural Adjustment Act was the culmination of a long series of efforts to secure such legislation. The McNary-Haugen Equalization Fee Plan, the Debenture Plan, and the Allotment Plan, sponsored respectively by the American Farm Bureau Federation, the National Grange, and the Farmers' Union, had failed to pass in the 1920's. But elements from each plan went into the Agricultural Adjustment Act and all three organizations, as well as the land-grant colleges and the U. S. Department of Agriculture, had a part in the development of this first attempt at national social control of agriculture. The majority of farmers received payments for crop reduction, payments which not only helped to prevent complete ruin of many farmers but also had a salutary effect on merchants and other townspeople. Trade increased and bills were paid.

The first AAA, enacted in 1933, was only the first of a series of legislative acts. It had been in operation only a short time before the 1934 drought hit, resulting in a mass movement of people out of the "dust bowls" of Oklahoma, Kansas, and other plains states and the evacuation of farm after farm in the Dakotas and Montana. So widespread was the distress that as many as a third of the farm families of the nation were on relief at one time or another.[9]

This situation facilitated the passage of laws for relief of unemployment: The Civil Works Administration (CWA); the Federal Emergency Relief Administration (FERA); Works Progress

---

[8] Edmund deS. Brunner and Irving Lorge, *Rural Trends in Depression Years,* New York: Columbia University Press, 1937, pp. 41-44

[9] Carl C. Taylor, et al., *Disadvantaged Classes in American Agriculture,* Social Research Report, No. VIII, FSA and BAE, USDA. 1938.

Administration (WPA); and Public Works Administration (PWA). In rural areas the Resettlement Administration and similar agencies were later combined into the Farm Security Administration (FSA), now the Farmers' Home Administration (FHA). Federal credit agencies were consolidated into the Farm Credit Administration (FCA) to provide both long- and short-term credit, following the widespread movement to adjust farmers' debts. Other governmental direct action agencies which developed in this period were the Rural Electrification Administration (REA)[10] to extend electrification to farms; the Tennessee Valley Authority (TVA) to control floods and provide power and cheap fertilizer; and the crop insurance plans.

During this period cooperatives increased in activity, and new types of cooperatives, such as those controlling cold storage lockers or the hospital associations, for example, were formed. Whereas the trend in cooperation following the close of the last century had been toward producer and marketing cooperatives, the trend was now toward more consumer cooperatives. These were formed, in the main, to buy producer goods such as oil, seed, and fertilizer.

Prosperity Comes Again.—The depression was still on when the second World War broke out. Although prices for farm products had risen and farmers as a class were coming out of their distress, there were still about 8,000,000 people on relief in 1939. The World War II period was marked by a general increase in prices to farmers because of Lend-Lease and, after Pearl Harbor, because of the demands of a voracious war economy.

The war period was characterized by the setting of ceiling and floor prices sufficient to induce full production; by widespread educational efforts to get farmers to produce to the limit, such as campaigns conducted through the neighborhood leader system; and by the movement of large numbers of youth from rural areas. Farmers responded magnificently to the demand for increased production. In 1944, probably the peak year of our war efforts, and despite a loss of over 5,000,000 persons from the farms, production had increased 35 per cent over the 1935-1939 level and 50 per cent over the 1910-1914 level.

World War II left many countries impoverished, with huge national debts and millions of hungry and penniless people. Great hopes were kindled throughout the world by the organization of the

---

[10] See "Progress Report," *Rural Electrification News*, Vol. 12, No. 5, January, 1947, p. 6, for the growth of REA from 37,000 participants in 1937 to 1,675,000 participants in 1946.

United Nations, and its satellite organizations, including the Food and Agriculture Organization. The American farmer, blessed with good crops and stimulated by high prices, many of which were well above the parity figure established by government, became the chief producer of food needed by these destitute peoples. More than half

INDEX NUMBERS (1910-14=100)

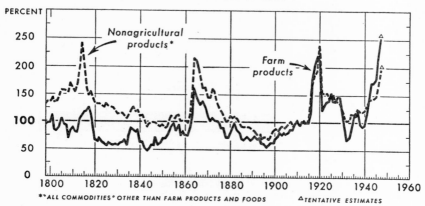

Figure 28. Wholesale Prices of Farm and Nonagricultural Products, United States, 1798-1947.

The farmers have been at a disadvantage for most of the period. (BAE, USDA)

of the world food exports in this period came from the United States. Wholesale farm prices, therefore, advanced more rapidly than non-farm prices, putting the farmer in a favored position for the first time since World War I. (See Figure 28.)

Family Farms and Family Welfare

Farmers in the United States have the highest capital investment (about 40 per cent of the total) and the second largest number employed (about 20 per cent of the total) of any industry in the country. In spite of the high investment, farm marketings represent only about one tenth of the national income. Except for the early depression period of lower prices and the present period of higher prices, the percentage of national income going to agriculture has changed but little, whereas that of manufacturing and trade has increased. The situation is of great social significance, for if farm people continue to be drained of their human and material wealth, the nation is doomed to impoverishment. Only by providing a system for an adequate replenishment of that wealth can we assure ourselves of national security.

Changes in Numbers and Size of Farms.—There was a general increase in the number of farms throughout the country from 1900 to 1940, though with a slight decrease from 1920 to 1925, and again

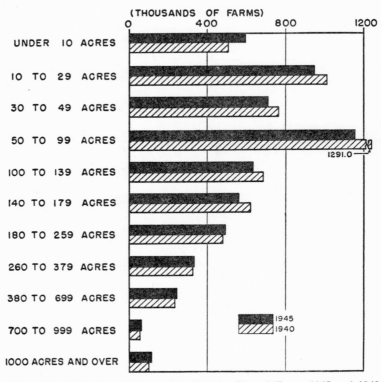

Figure 29a. Number of Farms Classified by Size of Farm, 1945 and 1940
Bureau of the Census, U. S. Census of Agriculture, 1945.

from 1925 to 1930, when the number of farms went slightly below the number in 1910. There was sharp increase in 1935, reflecting the movement of population from the cities during the depression period; the figure is 6,812,350 farms in 1935, the largest number ever reported by the Bureau of the Census. By 1940 the total number of farms had again declined sharply, to a quarter of a million below the 1910 figure.

The number of farms has decreased since 1935, especially in the better farming areas. The drop was especially marked from 1940 to 1945, chiefly because of the drainage of youth for war needs; but in good-land areas the change began with the increase in mechaniza-tion, making possible joining two or more adjacent farms under one operator. The influence of mechanization is brought out by the fact that the decrease in numbers of farms occurred chiefly in those over 50 acres and under 500 acres in size, yet there was a marked increase in the number of farms over 500 acres and particularly those over

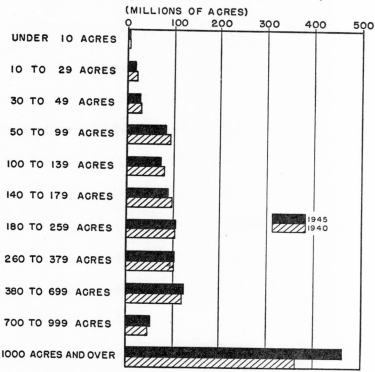

Figure 29b. Land in Farms Classified by Size of Farm, 1945 and 1940
Bureau of the Census, U. S. Census of Agriculture, 1945.

1,000 acres in size (Figure 29 a and b). This means that many small or medium-size farms, commonly referred to as "family-size farms" and commonly considered the backbone of the nation's agricultural and rural life, have been consolidated into larger farms. Such de-creases in "family farms" affect social conditions in rural communi-ties: fewer families on the land mean fewer children in school and fewer people in church. These changes call for different kinds and means of support of schools and churches in rural areas.

Our present national policy is to encourage the owner-operated, family-size farm. But when we work for that, we must know what we mean by the term. It was defined in the 1944 American Country Life Conference as "one on which the operator, devoting substantially full time to farming operations, with the help of other members of his family and without employing more than a moderate amount of outside labor, can produce needed farm products efficiently, make a satisfactory living, and maintain the farm plant. Such farms vary greatly in acreage, depending, among other factors, upon locality, kind of farming, size and composition of the family." The committee of the conference studying this problem stated that "any trend away from the family-type, owner-operated farm is detrimental to the future of American agriculture and to the nation." [11]

In general, there has been an increase in the average size of farms—an increase from 146 acres per farm in 1900 to about 195 acres at the present time. In New England, however, there was a decrease during this period from an average of 107 acres to 99 acres, because of the trend toward part-time farming in that area. In the Rocky Mountain area the increase has been from 458 acres per farm to 822 acres per farm because of mechanization.

In general, the largest farms are found on the best lands, and the increase in size has been most rapid in such good-land areas as central Illinois. In the South Atlantic, East South Central, and West South Central states the decrease in sharecropper units was accompanied by an increase in wage labor on larger units operated by owners and plantation managers.

Nearly two fifths of the farms in the country are under 50 acres in size and almost half are over 100 acres. Those over 100 acres, however, harvest nearly three fourths of the crops. Half of the farms produce about 90 per cent of the food and fiber needed for domestic consumption. But, as was shown in Chapter 4, it is the smaller farms, located in the poor-land areas, that produce the largest surplus of population for the cities.

Decrease in numbers and increase in size of farms in the last decade and a half have resulted in serious inroads on the family farm in America. This trend has meant the closing of many small schools, the abandonment of churches, the increase of transient farm labor, and the disruption of neighborhood and community life, especially in areas in which owner-operators have been replaced by tenants. Such changes call for careful study in the formulation of a national policy for the conservation of family farming in America.

---

[11] *Proceedings of the American Country Life Association,* 1944, p. 48. See also recommendations in *Improving Farm Tenure in the Midwest,* Bull. 502, Univ. of Illinois Agri. Exp. Station, 1944.

It is fully as important as the formulation of a national policy for the conservation of soil.

Types of Farm Tenure.—As we have seen, the nearly six million farm units in the United States vary widely in size. They also vary widely in type of tenure.

1. Most of the farms in the United States are family farms, that is, farms operated by families. The dominant type is the *commercial farm* from which the bulk of products grown is marketed and on which, as on other family farms, most of the labor is furnished by the family. Other types of family farms are the *part-time farm,* whose operators work 50 days or more off the farm and whose location is usually near cities and larger towns; and the *subsistence farm,* whose products are primarily for family use and whose location is in the poor-land areas of the country.

2. Large-scale farms, which involve a number of laborers, are not numerous. Nevertheless, they embrace almost a third of the farm land in the country. "A meager 1.6 per cent of the farmers of the United States, those with farms of 1,000 acres or more, now operate 34.3 per cent of all lands in farms." [12] (See Figure 29a.) They include *factory farms,* which are especially characteristic of the West,[13] and *cotton plantations,* which are smaller and more numerous than the factory-type large-scale farms. From the social point of view, however, they are the same, for they use hired workers who are under close control of management, similar to that of a manufacturing industry. Some large-scale cooperative farm ventures have been tried in the United States, though not by government ownership of large-scale farms, as in Russia and Mexico.[14]

Social Implications of Changes in Size and Type of Farms.— What is a good-sized farm? Most of the world's agriculture is done on the subsistence-farm basis. In the United States recent economic developments have encouraged both the small- and the large-scale types of farm. Many believe that the commercial family farm is still the type of farm most desirable in America because "a nation of subsistence farms is of necessity a nation with a low standard of living —a nation of large-scale farms is a nation with definite social distinctions and one in which there are wide differences in economic

---

[12] Edgar Schmiedeler, "Will History Repeat Itself in Rural America?" *Rural Sociology,* VI, No. 4, December, 1941, p. 295.

[13] Carey McWilliams, *Factories in the Field,* New York: Little, Brown & Co., 1939, Ch. V.

[14] Stanley W. Warren, *Making Agriculture Pay,* Yearbook of the Department of Rural Education, NEA, 1945, p. 48.

well-being; commercial family farms can provide more efficiently than most large-scale farms because of more effective use of labor." [15] In any case, for the best rural community welfare the family-sized owner-operated farm is much to be preferred to the large-scale farm.[16] The following reasons are given in support of this claim:

1. The small-farm community generally supports almost twice as many separate businesses as does the large-farm community. The volume of trade is correspondingly greater, and the expenditures for household supplies and building equipment over three times as great in the small- as in the large-farm community.

2. The small farm in the community supports a larger number of people per dollar volume of agricultural production. The people have a better average standard of living, more than three times as many of them are independently employed, and less than half as many are hired laborers. They have better facilities—schools and parks—and more of them take part in church and other organizations than is true in the large-farm community. The greater stability, homogeneity, interest in social life, and cooperative attitudes in the small farm community make it evident that small farms have a very definite relation to the character of American rural society.

There is a widespread interest in the kinds of farms that place primary emphasis upon farming as a way of life. Economists have been criticized for giving too much attention to the problem of increasing the prosperity of farmers engaged in commercialized agriculture.[17] We know that both production per worker and the size of farms are increasing. Yet to formulate a national policy tending to limit farm operation to the so-called commercial farm—the economic-sized unit—would mean that farms must be made larger on the poorer lands and that as many as half of the farmers in the United States would be taken out of farming. Perhaps, through education, the middle ground of increasing the efficiency of farms (especially that of small-sized farms) to secure greater production for the home as well as for market, could be reached without sacrifice of living standards—a trend toward modern agrarianism in America. New studies being made, moreover, show that family owner-operator

---

[15] *Ibid.*, p. 49.

[16] See Walter R. Goldschmidt, *"Large Farms or Small: The Social Side,"* BAE, USDA, June, 1944. Also by the same author, *"Small Business and the Community,"* Washington: Senate Committee Print No. 13, 1946, pp. 5-7. See also *Rural Life in a Changing World,* Proceedings of the American Country Life Assn., 1946, Champaign, Ill.: Garrard Press, p. 38.

[17] O. E. Baker, Ralph Borsodi, and M. L. Wilson, *Agriculture in Modern Life,* New York: Harper & Bros., 1939, pp. 207-208. See also L. G. Ligutti and J. C. Rawe, *Rural Roads to Security,* Milwaukee: Bruce Publishing Co., 1942; and Louis Bromfield, *Pleasant Valley,* New York: Harper & Bros., 1945.

farms are the most productive, are doing the best job of soil conservation, keep more people in the community, and provide better living levels. Legislation, therefore, may be desirable to *encourage* family farms and *discourage* large-scale types.

Land Tenure and Rural Life

Increasing Farm Tenancy.—Farm tenancy is more than a matter of verbal or written leases. It is a matter of human relationships, and it may be that the human or social aspects will outweigh the purely economic aspects in providing a solution to these major problems.

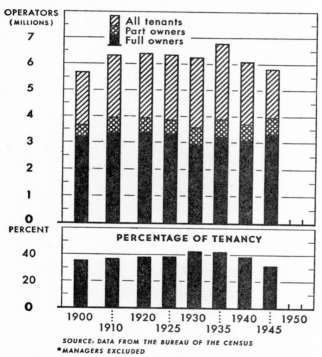

Figure 30. Number of Farms by Tenure of Operator, and Percentage of Tenancy, United States, 1900-1945

The percentage of tenancy has decreased since 1935, due largely to the change in the situation in the South. (BAE, USDA)

Why have we moved from an operator-landholding type of farm tenure to one in which an increasing percentage of the land is owned by nonoperators? Baker declares that the principal cause for tenancy is our aging population. Old world immigrants who settled the land have increasingly been moving to town and renting their farms. Whereas in 1880, the first year when figures were available, a little over one fourth of America's farms were operated by tenants, 60 years later almost two fifths of the farms were tenant-operated. (See Figure 30.) Moreover, the farm land under lease by the operator, for which rent had to be paid, increased from one third of all farm land in 1910 to more than two fifths at present.

A recent decrease in tenancy must be noted. Most of this decrease, however, occurred in the South, which has about half of the farms of the nation. Tenancy has continued to increase in most other sections of the country. The decrease in the South has come largely through a decrease in sharecroppers and share-tenants, many of whom moved out to more lucrative employment in the war years. Without question, the long-time trend is for an increase in tenancy in the United States.

Relationship Between High Tenancy and Good Land.—A high proportion of farms operated by tenants is generally associated with the richest soils, with cash crops, and with a highly commercial agriculture. In the Cotton Belt the highest proportion of tenancy— over 70 per cent of all farms and holdings—is found in the bottom lands of the Mississippi Delta and on the black prairies of Alabama and Texas. Be it noted, however, that land values have fallen greatly in the black prairie of Alabama, as soil fertility has declined. These lands are or have been areas of intensive cotton production and of high value per acre. In the Corn Belt the highest proportions of tenancy—over 60 per cent—are in north-central Illinois and northwestern Iowa, both being areas of intensive corn production and of the high land values in the United States.

Social Effects of Tenure Arrangements.—The most common form of tenancy, called the crop-share form of tenancy, is one under which the tenant shares the crops with the landlord. The size of the share due the landlord varies from region to region. In some regions the share is one third of all crops, or one third of the grain; in other areas, such as central Illinois, it is one half of the grain. A variation of the share crop lease is the livestock-share lease, in which the landlord owns a share of the livestock.

A second fairly common form of lease is the cash lease, under which the tenant pays a stipulated sum for the use of the land—in some areas $6 to $10 per acre. A variation of this lease is that in which the tenant pays cash rent for the hay and pasture and shares the grain or cash crops. The share crop or livestock-share and the cash rent systems are most prevalent in the Corn Belt.

The Tenant Farmer and Insecurity.—Most of the leases for share crop or cash rent are verbal leases; that is, the tenant verbally agrees to the terms, commonly those accepted in the community. Thus community usage or custom plays an important role in determining what the lease arrangements are to be. Also, most leases are for one year only, although the tenants hope they can stay longer.

Tenancy, wherever it may be found, is associated with a certain amount of insecurity. The greatest relative stability in tenancy is found in the best lands in the United States. From one fifth to two fifths of the tenants on the good lands of Illinois and Iowa reported less than two years' occupancy of the farms they were operating. It is obvious that two fifths of the farmers living on farms but one or two years is not conducive to great security or stability. Yet in most areas of the country more than two fifths, and in some areas more than three fifths, of the tenants reported less than two years' occupancy. (See Figure 31.)

The movement of tenants from farm to farm every year or two brings about several conditions which are socially significant. The tenant feels insecure: he hesitates to follow a system of farming which he can develop successfully over a period of years, such as is required if a good soil conservation program is to be carried out. He hesitates to take part in or become a leader of various groups in his community, for he does not want to get involved in something if he cannot see it through. He does not do much to improve conditions on the farm or in the home, for he knows that when he leaves he will not be able to take along the improvements he may have made—for example, the limestone he put on the soil, or the electric wiring he installed in the house. Though he wants a modern house and conveniences for his family, he cannot get them. He knows that he must own good equipment to meet competition for good farms; therefore he must put all of his spare cash into modern machinery.

There is a tendency, then, for the tenant who moves frequently to sacrifice many of those things which go to make up a satisfactory farm life. His children, seeing the situation, often take a vow that they will not be trapped as their parents were—instead, they determine to go to town.

This feeling of insecurity on the part of the highly mobile tenant is reflected in the instability of rural organizations and institutions. The tenant family is itself not a secure institution and is only poorly integrated into neighborhood life, especially when it moves often

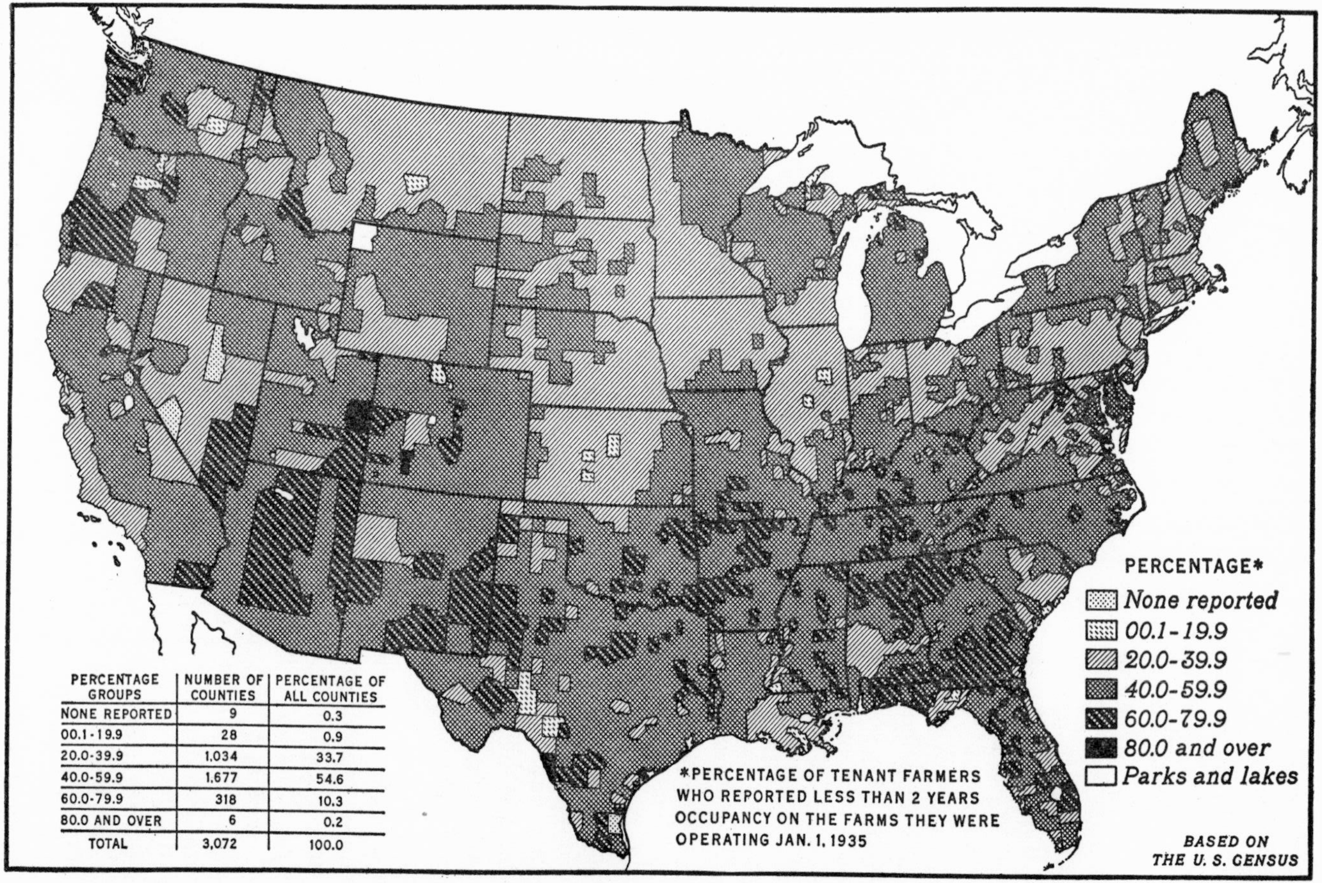

PERCENTAGE GROUPS	NUMBER OF COUNTIES	PERCENTAGE OF ALL COUNTIES
NONE REPORTED	9	0.3
00.1-19.9	28	0.9
20.0-39.9	1,034	33.7
40.0-59.9	1,677	54.6
60.0-79.9	318	10.3
80.0 AND OVER	6	0.2
TOTAL	3,072	100.0

Figure 31. Instability and Insecurity of Tenant Farmers

from one neighborhood to another. The school is insecure and upset almost yearly, for new children come in and old ones must leave, usually on March 1, which is moving day for many tenants. The country church also suffers because it may lose good church families. These are only a few of the social consequences of a mobile type of farm tenancy in a rural community.

The Sharecropper and Insecurity.—The sharecropper system, prevalent in the South, presents equally baffling social problems. The sharecropper does not own his own tools and work stock, these being furnished by the landlord under whose direct supervision he works. If he works for a share of the crop he is a sharecropper. The price situation from year to year may make it more advantageous, however, for the landlord to hire him, and so he becomes a laborer.[18] Thus the sharecropper's status is constantly changing, hampering his opportunities to become a constructive member of society.

Half of the tenants in the South are sharecroppers, separated from the owners by sharp lines of class and caste. Their dependent position has been aggravated by the "furnish" system, a system of advancing supplies to the tenant by the plantation commissary or by local merchants, with loans on the crops at exorbitant rate of interest, often as high as 40 per cent. Many tenants are rarely out of debt and exist in a state of modified serfdom.[19] They usually live in shacks, have many children, and take it for granted that they must do without the decencies of life. They have a high incidence of disease and infant deaths and a greater amount of illiteracy than almost any other group.

Though it may seem to the economic and social advantage of the plantation owners to maintain such a system, certainly it is not conducive to the best interests of society. Many of these sharecroppers move easily to relief rolls and in other ways contribute to a high relief load. A large percentage of the youth from this class was rejected for military service, because of both physical and educational unfitness.

The Social Status of Farm Laborers

That the farm labor problem in the United States is primarily a problem of labor supply for large farm enterprises is vividly brought out by the fact that more than two thirds of the cash wages in agri-

[18] T. Lynn Smith, *The Sociology of Rural Life*, New York: Harper & Bros., 1947, pp. 279, 280.
[19] See Arthur F. Raper and Ira DeA. Reid, *Sharecroppers All*, Chapel Hill: The University of North Carolina Press, 1941, Ch. V, especially p. 63.

culture are paid on only 9 per cent of the farms.[20] Most farms in the country are family enterprises; before World War II fewer than one out of six farms in the United States employed more than two workers.

World War II, however, almost reversed the situation relative to our farm labor. Previous to the war there was a surplus of farm labor and monthly wages had been as low as $15 to $25. Under wartime conditions of a scarcity of labor and high farm incomes, competition both from farmers and others led to a situation in which farm laborers received wages as high as $100 and $150 a month and keep.

Normally we have several kinds of farm laborers: the hired man or the hired girl who shares in the life of the operator family; the resident seasonal worker who is the "pick-up job man" of the community and who is usually the first to go on relief; the casual farm worker who quits his job in town to follow the harvests during the summer; the hobo or "bindlestiff," a migratory single worker; and the migratory farm family worker, who seeks jobs at which the whole family can work.

In normal times the farm labor problem is one of considerable social consequence, the most serious question being how to provide adequate living wages and conditions for these workers. The most acute problems are caused by the migrant labor family. Such families, whose children are out of school for much of the year, have inadequate medical services, rarely participate in church life, and in other ways find it hard to establish a stable family life in the community. For most farm labor families there is a lack of adequate housing, proper diets, participation in the life of the community, and the enjoyment of modern conveniences and facilities.

The good farm land of the nation is now occupied. More acreage may well be added by irrigation or drainage, but the total will be insignificant in comparison with the present total land in farms. The family farm is still the predominant type of farm in America, but it is increasing in size and its numbers are decreasing in favor of large-scale farms on the one hand and part-time farms on the other hand. Tenancy has been increasing, and there are still a large number of farm laborers, with the migrant element becoming increasingly important. If we believe that a national policy should be formed to encourage family size, owner-operated farms—farms which will be

---

[20] Louis J. Ducoff, *Wages of Agricultural Labor in the United States*, Tech. Bull. 895, USDA, 1945.

operated by intelligent people who are given some assurance of security, and who will assure our nation of an adequate food and fiber supply—then we must be interested in the means for attaining these ends.

DISCUSSION

1. What are the chief social characteristics of the various periods of development in American agriculture?
2. What are the trends in the numbers and sizes of farms in the United States? What changes are coming in the types of farms? What are the social implications of these changes?
3. Discuss the trends in tenancy and their relation to good land and stability of tenure. What are the causes for change in tenure? Discuss the chief social effects of various tenure arrangements.
4. What are the chief purposes of taxation? Discuss the real estate tax as a fair means of taxation. What are the means suggested for alleviating the burden of local taxation, yet retaining local control? (See Chapter 6 for further discussion of this problem.)
5. Discuss the social situation of the sharecropper and the farm laborer. Discuss the extent to which these groups are set apart in social classes of their own. What are the merits and the unfavorable results of such a process?

READINGS

Brunner, Edmund deS., and Lorge, Irving. *Rural Trends in Depression Years.* New York: Columbia University Press, 1937, pp. 41-44.

Farm and Rural Life After the War. Proceedings of the American Country Life Association, 1944.

Goldschmidt, Walter R. *Large Farms or Small: The Social Side.* BAE, USDA, June, 1944, entire study.

Harding, T. Swann. *Some Landmarks in the History of the Department of Agriculture.* Agricultural History Service, No. 2, Office of Information, USDA, 1942, especially introduction.

Hedrick, Ulysses P. *History of Agriculture in the State of New York.* Geneva: N. Y. State Agr. Exp. Sta., 1933.

Hicks, John D. *The Populist Revolt.* Minneapolis: University of Minnesota Press, 1931, Chs. I, II.

Lindstrom, D. E. *American Farmers' and Rural Organizations,* Champaign, Ill.: Garrard Press, 1948, Ch. IV.

Raper, Arthur F., and Reid, Ira DeA. *Sharecroppers All.* Chapel Hill: The University of North Carolina Press, 1941, Ch. I.

Smith, T. Lynn. *The Sociology of Rural Life.* New York: Harper & Bros., 1947, Ch. XI.

Taylor, Carl C. *Disadvantaged Classes in American Agriculture.* Social Research Report No. VIII, FSA and BAE, USDA, 1938.

Warren, Stanley W. *Making Agriculture Pay.* Yearbook of the Department of Rural Education, NEA, 1945, pp. 48 ff.

Chapter 6

ECONOMIC MEANS TO IMPROVE RURAL LIFE

Fluctuating prices of farm products and supplies have been a major factor causing distress in rural areas. To stabilize farm prices on a level of parity with nonagricultural prices has been a major concern of rural sociologists, agricultural economists, farmers' organization leaders, representatives in Congress, and farmers themselves throughout the history of our country, but especially in the last three and a half decades.

Other economic problems, however, have beset the farmer. As indicated in Chapter 5, the farmer wants security on the land. Good management is an important factor. The reduction of farm tenancy, the raising of farm labor living standards, working for equitable taxation—these are being studied. The formation of cooperatives, the conservation of the soil, and the right use of land have commanded increasing attention. The formulation of policies that will assure the farmer parity and security is of widespread national and even international concern. Only brief attention can be given in this chapter to these means of improving rural life and their social implications.

Good Farm Management to Provide Security and Stability.— Much of success in farming rests with the farmer and his family. The difference between good management and poor management shows up in earnings. Management has its human relations or social aspects.

The differences in Illinois farm earnings, due largely to differences in management, have been studied by Mosher.[1] Figure 32 shows the differences in earnings on about 200 Illinois farms between the one fifth most profitable and the one fifth least profitable. On most of these farms accounts have been kept continuously for a period of years, some for as many as 30 years. The differences in earnings, according to Mosher, can be attributed largely to fifteen factors, most of which have social implications (the social implications are the author's) :

[1] M. L. Mosher, "Good Management Pays in Farming," *Capper's Farmer*, Vol. 59, No. 1, January, 1948.

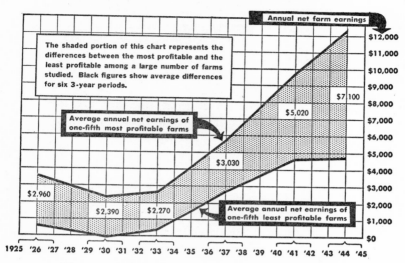

Figure 32. The Human Factor in Farm Management
(Chart by *Capper's Farmer*)

1. Sound land use and soil conservation. To carry out such a program requires remaining on the same farm over a period of time; stability of tenure is essential.

2. Good crop rotation and field arrangement. Merely to start good rotation schemes requires several years, and a farmer who would change his line fences to enlarge fields must be assured occupancy of the same farm for a period of years.

3. Suitable kinds and amount of livestock. Livestock farming at its best calls for stability of tenure.

4. High crop yields. Application of fertilizer, use of legumes, careful use of manure, timeliness, and other recommended practices require that the family remain on the same farm long enough to be assured of returns from the application of these practices.

5. Efficient livestock. It takes time to build up a good breeding herd, provide sanitation, and to carry out other desirable livestock practices. Care of livestock with kindliness and gentleness is a trait that can be learned through family cooperation and in which all members must take part.

6. Carefully planned use of labor. Here family labor plays a part; family cooperation in getting jobs done on time enhances success of other recommended practices.

7. Effective use of power and machinery. To purchase and use the right kind of machinery for the farm in question, and to keep it

in good condition, require family cooperation; its best use, too, is adaptation to a particular farm, which takes time. A good balance of labor saving devices must be maintained between the farm and the home.

8. Conservative buildings and fences. Too many farmers build barns for show, rather than for efficiency. Costly buildings can be economic liabilities, sacrificing efficiency and other living amenities. Ramshackle or poorly kept buildings and fences, on the other hand, can also be an economic and social liability, or even a hazard.

9. Attention to prices of products sold. The farmer with security of tenure can plan on a long time basis; short tenure often induces sales at a sacrifice of business and family welfare.

10. Large enough business for a good living. Families differ in their ability to use income effectively for living purposes; good management—family cooperation—is needed especially with respect to use of income.

11. Constant study of the farm business. The cooperation of family members, the use of community and service agency resources, and the feeling of stability on the land will help induce the desire to study.

12. Timeliness and regularity. Planning the time of family members cooperatively to do needed jobs and still have time for family and community affairs is important.

13. Kindliness, cleanliness, and thoroughness. These, too, come out of the pattern of habit and culture growing out of family and community life.

14. Will to do a good job. Such an attitude is largely a matter of childhood training at home, in school, and through other social contacts in the community.

15. Love of farm work and farm life. This comes chiefly from a vision of what farm life can be. The attitudes relating to the desirability of farming and farm life taught in school, church, group, and community life, as well as in the family, have much to do with the development of a love for farm work and farm life.

Proposals to Improve the Tenure Situation.—What is the remedy for the tenancy situation described in Chapter 5? A revision of the tenancy system would be conducive to what is now generally accepted as a desirable national goal: family-sized farms operated by the owner and his family.

1. Tenancy as a step to farm ownership. Any proposals for the revision of the tenancy system must not lose sight of the fact that tenancy is one step in the process toward ownership of a good family-sized farm. It is quite generally recognized that the process of advancement from laborer on the home farm, to farm laborer for hire, to farm tenant, to part owner, to full owner is a desirable type of social and economic process.

. . . Regardless of what is done to promote farm ownership, a considerable proportion of farms will continue to be operated by tenants. Many young men need to gain experience as operators in that way until they can accumulate enough resources to buy farms. But a young man should not have to sacrifice many of the accustomed and desirable amenities of living for his family—a modern house, advanced educational opportunities for his children, and opportunities for social-cultural and recreational advantages.[2]

If the desirable function of tenancy is to be protected, it must be by written leases which are fair to both parties, by state laws for minimum housing standards, compensation for disturbance without cause, and reimbursement to tenants for unexpended improvements made by them. Protection should also be afforded owners against misuse of their property.

2. Measures to discourage large-scale operation. The Midwest Regional Committee on Farm Tenure calls specific attention to needed measures for curbing large-scale operation; they recommend appropriate measures to discourage corporations whose major interest is not farming from purchasing land for farming purposes. Moreover, they insist that Federal and state laws should be enacted to prohibit private corporations from investing in farm land as a means of avoiding taxes on corporate earnings. Land taken in satisfaction of debt by a lender should be returned to farm family ownership as promptly as practicable. Consideration should be given to the possibility of levying graduated land taxes that will discourage the extension of large scale absentee ownership of farms.[3] The retention of such legislation as the 160-acre limitation of irrigation water to reclaimed lands might well have been stressed.

3. Protection for the heir remaining on the land. From one third to one half of the tenants on farms are sons or other relatives of the owners. Often the heirs on the land must buy out the absentee heirs, usually at the highest prevailing prices and on the most strin-

---

[2] From *Report* of the Postwar Committee of the Association of Land Grant Colleges and Universities, 1944.
[3] *Improving Farm Tenure in the Midwest,* Bull. 502, Univ. of Illinois Agr. Exp. Sta., 1944, p. 150.

gent terms. Thus from one half to four fifths of the value of the
land must be paid to nonresident heirs. The solution to this problem
is difficult. Perhaps an arrangement could be made whereby the
operating heir, by keeping accounts, could pay the nonoperating heir
or heirs only out of net profits, after all costs including labor and
management wage have been paid.

Other measures to improve farm tenure include the provision of
adequate credit facilities; providing a high level of urban employment; giving more stability to the general economy; developing conservative land appraisals; preventing through education the purchase
of farms at inflated land values by those who expect to live a life on
the farm; improvement of farm land, equipment, and buildings, and
aid to owner-operators in such improvements; encouraging farm
families to give up inadequate farms through zoning and similar
means; and the development of a national part-time farming policy.
Church bodies are giving increased attention to church-financed
farms on which they seek to place young married couples of the
church. The Catholic Rural Life Conference has been fostering a
move for establishing urban families on the land, which they term
rural homesteading. The following sections survey some of these
proposals.

Farm Credit and Rural Stability.—As free land became scarce in
this country farmers gained possession by purchase, paying cash in
part and mortgaging the balance. The system of mortgage credit
became widespread in the country. At the present time, more than
40 per cent of the acreage in farms and nearly 50 per cent of the
value of farm real estate are represented in mortgaged farms. The
accompanying chart (Figure 33) shows how the mortgage debt
increased steadily from 1890 until 1940. In general owner-operated
and especially part-owner-operated farms are more heavily mortgaged
than farms operated by tenants.

Farm operators find it easiest to buy farms in periods of high
prices. Too often in these periods they pay from 25 per cent to 75
per cent more than the land is worth from the long-time standpoint.
Young farmers, particularly, often mortgage a farm for as much as
three fourths of these inflated land values. Then, when prices decline, they find that their land is worth no more than the amount of
the mortgage. Decent living standards are thus sacrificed to pay
for land purchased at the wrong time.

High incomes during the war resulted in a drastic reduction in
mortgage debt. Whereas, in the World War I period the total mort-

gage debt had increased more than $2,000,000,000, in the four years of World War II the debt decreased more than $950,000,000. Farmers, seemingly, had learned something from their first experience. Decreases came principally in the Middle West and Far West, except in three states, New Mexico, Nevada, and Oregon. Yet by 1947 the total of farm real estate debt had again increased. Many farmers, especially on the best land, still prefer to rent rather than

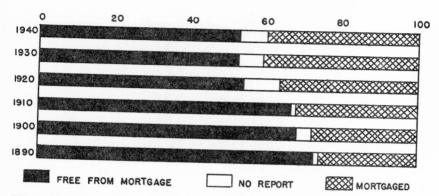

Figure 33. Mortgage Status of Farms Operated by Owners: Percentage Distribution for the United States, 1890-1940

One half of the part-owner operated farms in the United States were mortgaged, compared with less than two fifths for farms of full owners.

to risk ownership and thus, with but limited resources, to become heavily encumbered by mortgage. Yet the best chances of "paying out" are on the best lands.

Most authorities encourage farmers to buy land on the basis of its long-time productive capacity, to work out a payment plan that will protect against foreclosures as long as the farm is competently operated, and to pay a reasonable share of the available income on the principal and interest, with "standstill" payment agreements in case of arrested income due to drought, floods, or conditions not within the control of the borrower. These measures, if fully effective, will do much to stabilize the farm family on the land.

Credit on land has been used not only to secure land to operate but also as a means of speculation. From the social point of view, a good mortgage system is one which enables the operator progressively to improve his land and provide his family with a good level of living, and protects the operator from hazards beyond his control which might involve his "social status" and cause him to lose his farm after he and his family have put years of labor and love into it.

Interest rates can materially affect the burden of debt. Farmers' groups have fought many years to reduce interest rates. This fight is bearing fruit. In 1919 the interest rate on mortgage debt was, roughly, about 7 per cent of the estimated cash farm income from mortgaged farms; today it is about 5 per cent. But in some areas, particularly in the South and West, high interest rates still prevail. In these areas, farms encumbered with high mortgage debt in relation to value have high interest charges in relation to cash farm income.[4] Much of the mortgage debt is now held by federally sponsored and large central lending institutions such as insurance companies, although some local country banks still do a good farm loan business. The chief interest of the private lending agencies is the safe investment of surplus funds. The Federal agencies are cooperative in nature, localized, and administered by farmer-representatives; their chief interest is in serving the farmer.

The Farm Credit Administration.—The Farm Credit Administration provides loans

1. Through the farm loan associations for 20 to 40 years. The mortgage interest rate was set by law in 1946 at 5 per cent.[5]
2. Through production credit associations, to enable farmers to borrow, at reasonable rates, to pay for seed, fertilizer, tools, and other needs for the production of a crop in the current year.
3. To farmers' cooperatives, to enable them to get started in business.
4. To farmers having no available source of credit, for the emergency financing of crop and livestock enterprises.

All local credit associations are cooperative; the farmers who borrow must buy stock in the lending cooperative. The objective is to make it possible for farmers eventually to own their own cooperative credit systems. At the present time they have moved far in this direction. One of the chief problems, which is as much social as economic, is to make farmers feel the real responsibility of membership in their credit cooperatives.

The Farmers' Home Administration.—This Federal agency finances the operation or purchase of farms by those who cannot get credit from any other source. (See Figure 35.) The FHA loans are really rehabilitation loans to help make borrowers self-supporting.

---

4 See *The Balance Sheet of Agriculture*, Misc. Pub. No. 260, BAE, USDA, 1946, pp. 5, 10.
5 *The Thirteenth Annual Report of the Farm Credit Administration*, Washington, 1947, p. 28.

The borrower must have a farm and home plan which definitely looks to eventual repayment. Professional workers check periodically with each client to help him work toward a satisfactory system of farming, a good home life, and repayment that will free the family from debt without undue strain on farm and family resources. Thus, the FHA exercises a high degree of social control.

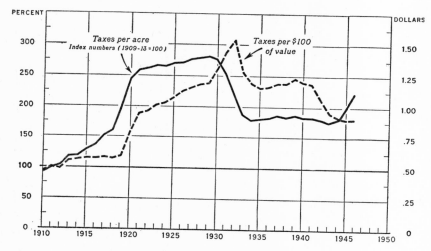

Figure 34. Farm Real Estate Taxes per Acre and per $100 of Value, United States, 1910-1946

Note that "taxes per $100 value" exceeded "taxes per acre" during the depression and until 1944. (BAE, USDA)

It may be argued that for this class of people such control is essential. It may also be argued that the basic credit philosophy is wrong—that such credit encourages the least efficient to remain in agriculture. The FHA claims that the policy leads to the kind of family-farm operation that is not only efficient but desirable in our form of society—that it produces a family which learns to use its own human and natural resources in becoming self-supporting.

Taxation and Rural Welfare.—We tax ourselves for two chief purposes: to afford protection and to provide services. The proportion of taxes to provide services is increasing; our people seem to be moving increasingly in the direction of more services paid by taxation. Taxes on farm real estate rose drastically following World War I and are again swinging upward; they are now a third higher than they were in 1910. (See Figure 34.)

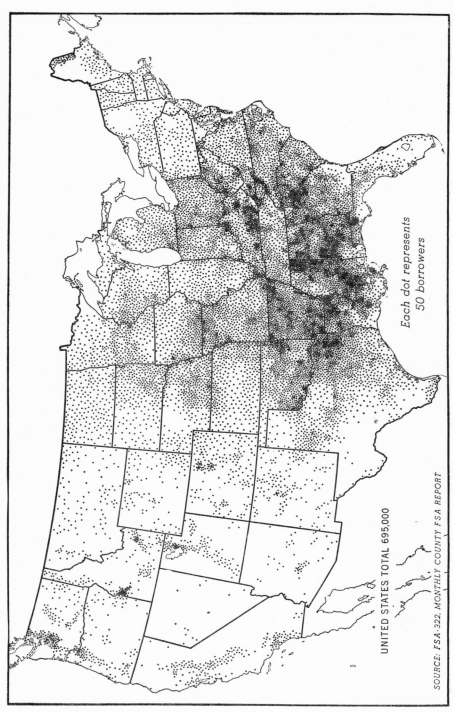

UNITED STATES TOTAL 695,000

Each dot represents
50 borrowers

SOURCE: FSA-322, MONTHLY COUNTY FSA REPORT

Figure 35. Standard Rural Rehabilitation Borrowers Through September 30, 1943

114

The manner in which taxes are raised is also changing. At one time expenses for most governmental functions were paid out of property taxes. Today, most of the taxes on property go to support local institutions: schools, roads, local government, etc. Some of these burdens have been relieved by licenses and fees. Recently an increasing amount of revenue for government has come from income and sales taxes. But taxes on real estate are of chief concern to farmers.

Farmers' property can be appraised more easily than that of city people. Therefore, farmers have worked for a system of assessment more equitably balanced between town and country property, and for greater dependence on other forms of taxation for local, state, and Federal revenues. Because property in itself may not represent earning power or income, there is even a desire to relieve real estate of all taxation and place the tax on incomes, which really determine a person's ability to pay taxes. In some areas over nine tenths of the local support for schools and other local services come from the property tax. The real question is whether rural, and especially farm, people should be expected to bear the full burden of such services since they contribute so much to the rest of society, particularly through the migration of youth.

Taxes can be levied for a wide variety of services and by a large number of taxing bodies. Most of the taxing bodies providing funds for these purposes are small, with a wide range in valuations and a wide variety of tax rates. In some school districts, for example, the tax rates are as low as 3 cents on each $100 valuation; in others they are as high as $1.50 per $100 valuation. Furthermore, the valuations themselves vary. In a single county in Illinois, for example, one school district had a valuation of over $7,000,000; another nearby district had a valuation of less than $26,000, a ratio of over 265 to 1.[6] Thus an unbalanced situation arises in which one area bears a far greater burden of taxation than another area only because the latter is lucky enough to have property other than farm lands on which to base values.

These situations have caused demands for a single county levy for schools, for example, or for a higher percentage of the funds for local purposes to come from state funds. In some states, over half of the needed funds for the support of schools comes from the state revenue. The demand for Federal funds is now increasing, so that states with low valuations may have more equitable educational and other advantages.

Suggested Remedies for Tax Inequities.—How can we remedy our system of taxation? One suggestion is to cut down on the number and kinds of services. But society is moving in the other direction, towards more educational facilities, more public health protection, more social security, etc. The question which must be answered is, Will the mass of people be given such needed services at a lower total cost than at present? Is a good education for every child a good investment for our society? Will the cost of providing medical service for everybody be less than the present cost of inadequate service to the family and to society? We shall discuss these problems at greater length in later sections.

Measures to Improve Farm Labor Conditions.—We have noted the importance of the farm labor group in America, in Chapter 5. We have seen, too, how production per man has increased over the years. Figure 36 shows the significant increase in production per acre. Yet the need for year-round seasonal or transient labor on farms will continue. The welfare of these people—for they have the largest families of any class in our society, rural or urban—is of national concern. It is something which must be considered in establishing any national policy relating to rural life. "Any statement of national agricultural policy may well incorporate the principle that such policy is directed toward furthering the welfare of all the people engaged in agriculture . . . those who till the soil for hire as well as those who cultivate it as tenants or owners." [7] Objectives for farmers of real parity with nonfarm people—parity of income, of public services, of housing, of health facilities, of security—must also embrace the principle of parity for hired farm workers. The extension of social security legislation to farmers and farm workers and of unemployment insurance to farm wage workers are important objectives. Other suggested objectives include more widespread tenant-purchase opportunities for the farm laborer; the breaking up of large holdings so that more farmers can gain foothold on the land; provision of year-round work so that the farm labor family can have a stable residence in the community; cooperative farming; and the unionization of farm labor. [8]

---

[7] Louis J. Ducoff, *Ways of Agricultural Labor in the United States,* Tech. Bull. 895, USDA, 1945, p. 124.

[8] See the Congressional Reports of the work of the Tolan Committee, especially House Report No. 369, pp. 81-148; and Carey McWilliams, *Ill Fares the Land,* Boston: Little, Brown & Co., 1942, Chs. I-III.

"An adequate system of farm placement services can help to lessen the periods of unemployment of hired workers and of underemployment among some groups of farm operators. Similarly, guidance offered prospective migrants from farms, and assistance to some groups in relocating in promising areas and occupations would help

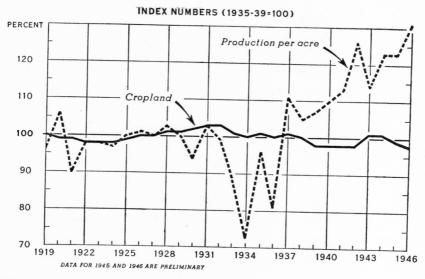

Figure 36. A Total Cropland and Crop Production per Acre, United States, 1919-1946.

The U. S. Department of Agriculture defines crop land as the sum of the estimated acreage of land from which one or more crops were harvested, plus estimated crop failure and summer fallow acreage. (BAE, USDA)

in achieving a better balance between rural population and resources." [9]

Economic Cooperation and Farm Stability.—The formation of economic cooperatives has been a social development of the first magnitude. At first, economic cooperatives were neighborhood and community groups, operating more or less independently of each other. Then, to meet "old line" competition more effectively, they were formed into district, state, regional, and sometimes national associations. Thus, farmers operating many small units can bargain more effectively with the industrialists operating fewer large units. It gives the farmer greater control in processing, marketing, and purchasing. The cooperative way is therefore of great social signifi-

[9] Ducoff, *op. cit.*, p. 123.

cance; it is an important means for helping farmers attain a greater degree of security. The types of cooperatives, their systems of organization, and principles guiding their operation will be discussed in a later chapter.

Agricultural Policies and Their Social Implications

When we speak of agricultural policies we usually mean governmental policies which affect agriculture. We are concerned not only with the effect on rural people of the policies already established but also with the manner in which these policies are made and administered. Already in force are significant policies affecting agriculture, such as those to provide special educational services to farmers, to help adjust production to demand, to help dispossessed farmers secure a foothold on the land, to remove marginal land from cultivation, to assist and protect cooperative efforts, to encourage the family-sized owner-operated farm, and to extend needed services and new forms of protection to farm people. Most of these policies have come after long discussion and considerable agitation by farm groups, and some only when the nation was faced with a serious emergency.

Most of the recent policies have been administered on the basis of "rulings" or interpretations of the law made by administrators. Conceivably, Federal authorities can to an increasing extent take over the interpretation of the attitudes of farm people and, on the strength of such interpretations, assume considerable authority in the making of new rulings. Indeed, this was the rule rather than the exception in the World War II period. It is highly questionable whether such procedures should ever be permitted in peacetime.

Demands for Parity Price and Production Control.—The farmer has been at a disadvantage in securing a just share of the national income most of the time since the Civil War. Since 1921, and until 1941, prices paid by farmers for commodities bought have been considerably above prices received for farm goods, when 1910-1914 relationships are taken as a standard. Thus there came a demand for farm prices on a parity with nonfarm prices.

Since the Civil War agricultural production has increased steadily. Even in depression periods, as in 1921 and 1932-1933, farmers maintained their production, and even after the enactment of the Agricultural Adjustment Act (AAA) in 1933 there was no appreciable reduction in total agricultural production. Industrial production, on the other hand, decreased sharply in depression periods, especially in the years following 1930. (See Figure 37.) In periods of good demand, as during the recent war, industrial production increased sharply. There is a close relationship between industrial employment and farm prosperity. Many industrial employees were laid off in the 1930-1935 depression period, not a few of whom moved

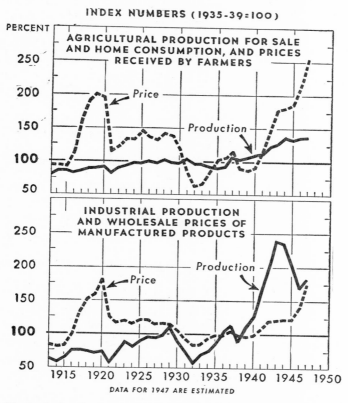

INDEX NUMBERS (1935-39=100)

Figure 37. Agricultural and Industrial Production, and Prices, United States, 1913-1947

Farmers maintained production and suffered price decline; industry cut production in depression times. (BAE, USDA)

into agricultural areas. Industry endeavored to maintain prices at the expense of employment, whereas agriculture kept up production and suffered serious decreases in prices in the depression.

The AAA was enacted into law to provide farmers with a "parity" price for farm products which would have the same relative purchasing power as they had from 1909 to 1914, while at the same time exercising control over production. Farmers were led to reduce production by payments for decreased acreages of cotton, wheat, tobacco, field corn, rice, decreased supplies of hogs, and milk and its products. The money for benefit payments in the 1933 AAA came out of processing taxes on food; this Act, however, was declared unconstitutional because "one group in society was being taxed to benefit another."

Two other acts soon followed the demise of the first AAA. A new feature was added in the Soil Conservation and Domestic Allotment Act of 1936, namely, to pay farmers to conserve soil. The Agricultural Adjustment Act of 1938 provided for payments to be made to farmers from the Federal treasury. The Act had as its objectives:

1. To conserve the soil;
2. To produce enough for domestic consumption, for export, and for reserve supplies;
3. To store up supplies in years of bumper crops to meet needs in lean years;
4. To make possible the control of surpluses of cotton, wheat, corn, tobacco, and rice by marketing quotas when voted by two-thirds of the producers and enforced by the Secretary of Agriculture;
5. To release supplies as and where needed to meet any shortage; and
6. To provide insurance against crop loss (in wheat) through crop failure or other means.

The AAA is a socially significant step forward: it provides protection against disaster to the farmer, the producer of our basic necessities, and protects other segments of our society against a scarcity of food and fiber.

Administration of the Act.—The system of organization for the AAA has been democratic. Farmers are signed up voluntarily, there being no compulsion except that voted by the farmers, and then only when a price-depressing surplus was threatened. Community sign-up elections and educational meetings were held several times a year. County and community committees elected by the farmers to administer the act were paid for the time they spent in administration out of the benefit payments due the farmers. Some efforts were made by politically minded leaders to use this system of organization, which reached into every rural community of the nation, for other purposes. Some sought to found a new farm organization, while others were charged with exerting influence on the voters to retain the existing administration. One can see danger in such procedures.

The AAA system of social control is compatible with our ideas of democratic procedures. An effective system of adult education not under the supervision of this system of social control is highly necessary, however, to prevent the development of a centralized form of absolute control over production or over any other fundamental function.

Changing Ideas Regarding Parity.—Price and income relations that existed in 1910-1914 have become obsolete; "any set of prices representing some past period is always out of date when applied to current production."[10] If the parity principle is retained—and it should be retained—it must be applied to two other fields: parity of income and parity of public services. The nation should undertake to assure to farmers an income per person, or per family, that will provide the members of the family an opportunity for satisfactory living equivalent to the opportunity of those who live elsewhere.

We are now beginning to give equal prominence in our thinking and planning to the equitable distribution between rural and urban areas of adequate schools, good health and medical service, electric power, good roads, public recreation, education, and other social benefits. They are of as great significance as production.

Desirable elements in a national farm program have been outlined by Norton.[11]

A single objective for a general course of action . . . involves a number of objectives:

(1) Encourage high-level production of farm products.
(2) Provide adequate food for our own people.
(3) Furnish our fair share of food for other people.
(4) Preserve and improve the productivity of our soil.
(5) Maintain a sound rural population.
(6) Provide for a good rural life.
(7) Allow farmers to receive their fair share of the national income.
(8) Provide freedom in production and marketing.

Norton points out that such a program would eliminate the commodity approach to parity and provide for government payments to farmers in periods of depression. Farm leaders are objecting to this proposal. It would require a good export outlet for surpluses and a high level of consumer income. A high level of production would

---

[10] See T. W. Schultz, *Redirecting Farm Policy*, p. 15. Copyright 1943 by The Macmillan Company, New York, and used with their permission.
[11] From L. J. Norton, "The Objective for a Sound National Farm Program," *Proceedings of the American Country Life Association*, 1947.

make possible better rural diets, better schools and health conditions. A good rural culture, however, must grow out of the wishes, needs, and aspirations of local people. These Norton recognizes; he also recognizes that the best chance for professional leadership is among those who live and work in rural areas. Of such is a democratic program made.

Expansion of Government Service.—One of the national policies is to protect land against exploitation and to increase its productivity. The Soil Conservation Service has been organized specifically to carry out this policy. Laws in the various states have been enacted to make possible the organization of soil conservation districts in which the owners of land can vote ordinances upon themselves, and thus establish social control over land use in the district.

It is always to the interest of the individual farmer to produce efficiently. Society, also, is interested in efficient production. But the long-time interest of both the individual and society is to conserve and improve human and material resources. Only in that direction lies real security. Hence, controls must be exercised by society to do that which the individual cannot do alone, not only to encourage economic efficiency but also to insure a program of conservation, family security on the land, and thus a source of better human beings.

A national policy to insure this kind of security must include a number of points. (a) Land which can no longer produce agricultural products efficiently must be put to other uses. The Government is now doing this by buying so-called submarginal farm land. (b) Land so run down as to bankrupt any individual who tried to build it up is now being restored by government aid. (c) Farmers who have lost everything through no fault of their own should be helped to get back on their feet again. (d) Farmers do not have the time or facilities to experiment with new crops, breeds, or implements. Experimentation is the task of government. (e) Farmers find that their interests and those of society are advanced through cooperative, nonprofit activities. Government has not only exempted such nonprofit activities from taxation, but it has also made provision for loans to help them get started and keep going.

These services are now accepted by farm people, who once feared the encroachment of government on the rights of the individual. Much of this is service, not by local government, but by state and especially by Federal government. It represents government planning for agriculture hitherto undreamed of in the country.

The Maintenance of Democracy in Agriculture.—"Farmers Like Less Liberty" is the challenging title of an article in the *Rural Co-operator,* Toronto, Canada.[12] A nationwide forum reaching 327 Canadian groups showed that while these groups admitted that marketing control infringes on the freedom of farmers they felt that the farmer is only giving up one freedom to acquire a greater one, that he is only delegating his freedom to another; and that marketing control hurts only the producer of poor quality material and the "chiseler." An English publication states that "we now realize that there is no room on the land for large numbers of inefficient people. The land is too valuable to be wasted like that and if the state takes up the responsibility of creating favorable conditions for agriculture, the industry must in return guarantee standards of efficiency to the state." [13] What about the United States, where democratic processes are believed to be at their best?

Many years ago, Dr. Liberty Hyde Bailey asserted that "if agriculture cannot be democratic, then there is no democracy." [14] The most important processes of democracy are those which go on in the home, the neighborhood, and the community. Our future national agricultural policies must be formed very largely on the basis of the effectiveness of the rural family, neighborhood, and community. Every effort should be made, therefore, to strengthen the democratic processes in these fundamental groups, and to relate them to state and national policy making.

DISCUSSION

1. What human and social factors are important in the management of a farm?
2. Discuss proposals for increasing farm owner operation. What is a good size of farm from a social point of view? What would do most to bring about a stable form of farm tenure, a form that would contribute to a good kind of community life? What would be a desirable national policy relative to land tenure?
3. Discuss the social situation of the farm laborer, especially the transient laborer. Weigh the relative merits of various proposals for meeting the needs of farm laborers, from the standpoint of the employer and of the laborer.

---

[12] Vol. IX, No. 13, March 13, 1945.
[13] Lawrence E. Easterbrook, *British Agriculture*, New York: Longmans, Green & Co., Inc., 1943, p. 46.
[14] *The Holy Earth*, New York: Chas. Scribner's Sons, 1915, p. 149.

4. What meaning can be given to the concept of parity? Discuss the proposals for attaining these goals of agriculture. Which are most likely to attain the greatest degree of farm stability, national security, and social welfare?

5. What are the chief issues in the maintenance of democracy in agriculture? What are the best ways to nurture the democratic processes in rural life?

READINGS

Agricultural Co-operatives. Publication of the Inter-bureau Commission on Postwar Programs, USDA, 1945.

Improving Farm Tenure in the Midwest. Bull. 502, Univ. of Illinois Agr. Exp. Sta., 1944.

McWilliams, Carey. *Factories in the Field.* Boston: Little, Brown & Co., 1939, Ch. V.

Mosher, M. L. "Good Management Pays in Farming." *Capper's Farmer,* Vol. 59, No. 1, January, 1948.

Schultz, T. W. *Redirecting Farm Policy.* Chicago: University of Chicago Press, 1943, Ch. I.

The Balance Sheet of Agriculture. Misc. Pub. 620, BAE, USDA, 1946.

Zelomek, A. W., and Mark, Irving. "Historical Perspective for Postwar Agricultural Forecasts: 1870-1940." *Rural Sociology,* Vol. X, No. 1, March, 1945, pp. 60-69.

Chapter 7

THE RURAL FAMILY AND HOME

The family is the most important group in rural life. The family —like the neighborhood, village, governmental, or community group—is a locality group. We become a member of a family by reason of circumstance and not by choice. Therefore, the family has been called the basic or primary group in rural life. It is basic because it is the chief group out of which comes our knowledge and training in group living and getting along with others. It is primary because it provides frequent, intimate, face-to-face, social contacts out of which the basic nature of our personality develops.

The Social Organization of the Family Group

Because we are all a part of a family group we fail to look upon it as having a form of organization. But, like all other groups, it has structure and function. Children are essential structural elements of the family group. A husband and wife without children form only a marriage partnership; it is only when a child is born or adopted into a family that one can say a family is a complete group.

Structure of the Family.—The basic structure of the family is the parents and children. It may also include what is termed the "great family"—grandparents, uncles, aunts, and cousins. The great family in rural life often shows its ties in the loyalty of one member to another, even in the face of great danger. There are rural communities in which a kinship group spreads itself over the land, acquiring farm after farm until few except relatives of that "clan" live there.

The rural family is marked by other structural characteristics. It usually has a *head,* who influences the forms of behavior of its members, and in some close-knit groups is responsible to society for the behavior of the individual. This is especially true in those groups in which the father, or "head," exercises dominant control. It is reflected, for example, in a refusal to let children go beyond a certain grade in school.

The rural family has a system of *assignment of roles* to its members. In the farm family group, the members share in both the work and the benefits of farm life. That is why we say **farming is** a family business, in which business, in the course of time, the nature of the role that each plays undergoes a change. As the children grow up, for example, they are given more difficult tasks.

A rural family also has its *ritualisms* or *systems of social control*. In some families certain folkways are followed in marriage, the birth of children, deaths in the family, etc. These observances are usually dictated by the customs of the community. In some rural communities a marriage which takes place outside the family church may mean that the young couple will be forever ostracized by the family group.

Functions of the Family.—The family group in rural areas has several distinctive functions which are socially significant and important to its welfare, and to that of society in general:

1. Procreation. The rural family looks upon the production and rearing of children as an important function. In some family groups the birth of boys brings greater joy than that of girls because boys are regarded as being more helpful on the farm. But in the American farm family this attitude toward offspring is gradually disappearing. Boys and girls alike share in the family inheritance.

2. Training of members in individual and social responsibility. The farm child learns individual and social responsibility at an early age. There are always chores to do, and each must do his share. In some farm families there is an excellent spirit of sharing, not only of work and responsibility, but also of the fruits of labor. Many farm children are taken in as partners at an early age, or are given enterprises of their own. They know that when they marry the family group will help them get started farming for themselves.

3. Provision of security and emotional stability. The members of a farm family, especially one which owns a home relatively free of debt, has an emotional stability, a sense of security, which comes out of sharing, hard work, and a realization that "we can always raise what we need to eat." But there are youth in farm families who share the emotional instability of their parents, especially those who have only an insecure status on the land. Some of these, also, fail to find a sense of security in other groups, which affects their whole future.

4. Acquiring of social status. The social role played by a member in a farm family and in other groups is conditioned to a great extent by the kind of family of which he is a member. If the parents have the attitude that work is the only important activity and that play is sinful, the young people are likely to seek other forms of

occupation. If the parents make it apparent that they want their children to grow up to be something other than farmers, the young people will inevitably develop an attitude of inferiority when in the presence of other youth. If, on the other hand, farming is held up as an essential industry requiring the best that one has, then young people on farms will feel that they are just as important and essential as anyone else.

How the Rural Family Is Different

The rural family group is different from other family and social groups in that it is relatively more permanent; the leaders in the group (the parents) create more followers, i.e., more children; the members are more closely tied in with the welfare of the family in rural than in urban areas, and the form of interaction is more domestic, that is, of a basic and primary nature. The family has more to do with personality development, both in rural and urban areas, than has any other group.

The Farm Family.—The farm family is different [1] because it ordinarily has more members than have other family groups; because farm family members have more in common, with diverse phases of a common occupation as a basic interest; because they live more to themselves than do others and therefore learn to be more self-contained and self-reliant; because the children often are more under the domination either of one or of both parents, which may mean either that the children truly learn the meaning of authority and order, or that they get so much direction that they do not adjust themselves as well to new situations as do children in city families; and because they work in the neighborhood and community as family groups except where this pattern is interfered with by outside influences.

It is the natural thing for farm families to participate as a group in such things as family gatherings, visits to relatives, and church activities, and to seek to educate children in accordance with the family's idea of what an education should be. Even farmers' organizations such as the Grange have been supported and stabilized because of family-group participation.

Forces tending to break into this family pattern of participation are attendance at schools, where child training suffers from the in-

---

[1] See Harvey Locke, "Contemporary American Farm Families," *Rural Sociology*, Vol. No. 2, June, 1945, pp. 143-144.

ability of most rural teachers to project school work into community life; other diverse outside activities in the community; and the development by outside organizations of individualized approaches to the solution of economic and social problems in rural life. These approaches, by providing programs of activities for some members of the family which may conflict with the interests of other members of the family, exercise a divisive influence.

Thus, the very agencies which work for unification of the family group may tend, by their types of appeal, to tear the farm family apart, and in some cases to set one member against the other. When the family group, which should form the warp of the fabric of rural society, is being thus torn by these diversified interests, it is not surprising to see the same kind of disintegrating process going on in rural areas that one finds in city life.

The Village Family.—What is true of the farm family may not be true of the village family. Though many village families come from farms, they are more definitely under the influence of the city. They are nearer the city family in size, and their types of occupations more closely resemble those found in the cities. Village families tend to ape the ways of city families, and the fads and fashions flow out from the city to the village and the farm, rather than the reverse. Also, the interests of the village family are divided more like those of the city than of the farm family.

On the other hand, the village family is in closer contact with the business of the village than is the city family with city business. It eats more of its meals together. It probably engages in more collective activities. It may produce some of its own food. And the kinship group is likely to have greater influence. The larger the village, the more likely its families are to become like those of a city.

Social Causes and Effects of Differences.—The differences between farm and city families result chiefly from their different environments. These differences, in turn, affect the kind of family life which results. A study of the differences is significant chiefly in showing the characteristics of the family which are most conducive to a good kind of family life.

1. Marriage. We have seen that more householders in rural areas, and especially on farms, are married than are householders in villages or towns. Since a satisfactory life on the farm depends so much on a good family life, young single men seek to find mates as soon as they can. Because the ratio of single men to single

women is much higher in the rural than in the urban world, a rural girl's opportunities for marriage are more numerous. More couples on farms stay married than in towns or cities because success in farming requires the most effective family cooperation possible. Each member of the family has a stake in the enterprise and is less likely to want to quit.

Youth on farms who expect to farm tend to marry at an earlier age, for if they are going to get ahead they feel they need to get started as soon as possible. Some may sacrifice educational or other advantages because of this tradition or custom. In accordance with this tradition, a young couple, when they move to their own rented farm, are often helped to get started by kinfolk. Most rural youth now depend upon the parental home for whatever guidance they get in preparation for farm family life. They also need the help that is now available through some extension services and in a few school programs. Education for family life should form a part of their general education.

2. Size. Probably the most significant difference between farm and city families is size. More than three fourths of the rural-farm families have children, whereas only two thirds of the urban families have children. Table 6 shows that, in 1940, less than two fifths of the urban families with children had four or more members, but more than half of the rural-farm families had four or more. Note in this Table that a tenth of the Southern nonwhite rural-farm families had nine or more members.

TABLE 6. PERCENTAGE OF FAMILIES IN THE UNITED STATES, RURAL AND URBAN, WITH SPECIFIED NUMBER OF MEMBERS; AND PERCENTAGES FOR RURAL-FARM FAMILIES, BY REGIONS: 1940 *

Area or Region	Percentage of Families Having Specified Number of Members:								
	1	2	3	4	5	6	7	8	9 or more
Urban	11.1	27.5	22.9	17.7	10.0	5.3	2.7	1.4	1.5
Rural-nonfarm	11.1	25.5	21.8	17.2	10.5	6.2	3.5	2.0	2.3
Rural-farm	6.3	20.7	19.4	17.4	12.8	8.8	5.8	3.8	5.1

Rural-Farm Percentages, by Regions:

	1	2	3	4	5	6	7	8	9 or more
Northeastern	8.6	23.0	19.6	16.8	12.2	7.9	5.1	3.0	3.7
North Central	6.4	22.9	20.8	18.4	12.7	8.0	4.7	2.8	3.3
South (total)	4.8	18.6	18.6	17.0	13.1	9.7	6.9	4.7	6.7
South (nonwhite)	7.4	20.2	16.5	13.2	10.8	8.8	7.2	5.6	10.2
West	12.4	22.7	18.9	17.1	11.7	7.3	4.4	2.5	3.0

* U. S. Dept. of Commerce, Bureau of the Census, Sixteenth Census of the United States, *Population and Housing—Families—General Characteristics*, Table 8, p. 24.

We have learned that urban families in general have too few children to maintain the population, and that rural-farm families, in general, have a considerable surplus of children who are not needed to work the farm. We have also seen that there must be an increasing and constant flow of youth from rural to urban centers. This fact is very important to the whole of society, for if rural areas are to continue to send their youth to become useful members of urban areas, it is important that the family group in rural areas be such as to inspire its members with the will to work, the desire to learn, with a love and some understanding of the democratic process, with integrity of purpose, and with a high degree of interest in the common welfare. These differences in family size raise significant questions not only about the quality of life in the rural family but also of the adequate organization of all groups and institutions in rural areas.

Family Standards of Living

The five chief factors that go to make up a farm-family standard of living are food, shelter, clothing, medical care, and advancement. The first four are basic living items of families everywhere. Advancement includes the benefits of all social facilities for leisure, recreation, and self-improvement. We may justifiably include in living levels the basic values, freedoms, and beliefs of a people; and that some degree of security or assurance that goods and services and all rights will continue to be enjoyed in spite of illness, adversity, or old age.[2]

The standard set by a particular society is that which most adequately conforms to the cultural norms and which meets "biological needs and social goals of individuals."[3] The level of living may be measured by how much money is available for each of these things, but the standards set by or for a family are socially determined. A tremendous influence is brought to bear on what we want for ourselves by what we see and know other people have. The role that a family plays in the social group determines to a large extent the standard of life to which a group aspires. "What is finally considered necessary or proper—that is, 'desirable'—emerges as regular and recognized. This is the social process of building up a social institution."[4]

---

[2] Edgar A. Schuler and Rachel Rowe Swiger, *Trends in Farm Family Levels and Standards of Living*, BAE Mimeograph, USDA, 1947, pp. 1-2.

[3] A. R. Mangus and Howard Cottam, *Level of Living, Social Participation, and Adjustment of Ohio Farm People*, Bull. 624, Ohio Agr. Exp. Sta., 1941, p. 4.

[4] J. H. Kolb and Edmund deS. Brunner, *A Study of Rural Society*, Boston: Houghton Mifflin Co., 1946, pp. 390-391.

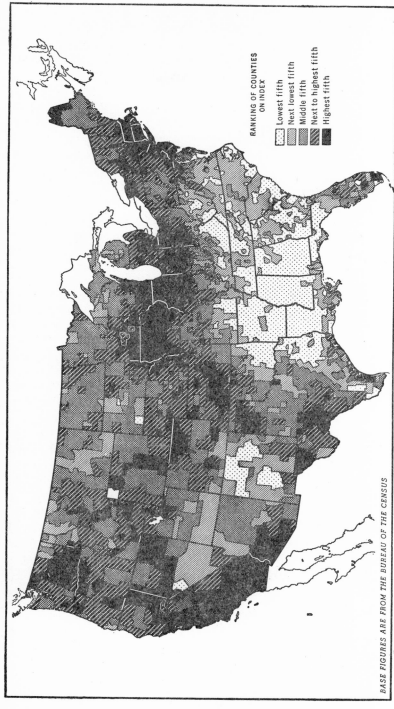

RANKING OF COUNTIES ON INDEX

Lowest fifth
Next lowest fifth
Middle fifth
Next to highest fifth
Highest fifth

Figure 38. Farm Operator Family Level of Living Indexes, 1945

Note the concentration of the lowest fifth in the South and Southwest, from which come the largest number of children. (BAE, USDA)

Rural-Farm Levels of Living.—Rural levels of living have been measured for every county in the nation, using data from the Bureau of the Census. The areas of lowest living levels are in the Southeastern states and bordering parts of Maryland, Ohio, Indiana, Illinois, Missouri, Oklahoma, and Texas; in Arizona and New Mexico; and the Lake States cutover area. Significantly, our largest surpluses of population come from these areas. (See Figure 38.)

Within the framework of social control over family living standards, there still remain wide opportunities for choice as to how money shall be spent, whether for food, clothing, or other things, for example. Because most studies of living standards have centered upon money expenditures, information on the forces leading to the choices made by the family is lacking. Some studies, however, show the influence of the community or the social group upon the kind of food consumed or clothing purchased by a family.[5] To change the diet of a family, for example, the customs in the social group must often be changed. Even more effective may be the influence of the "great" family, for though a young woman who marries into a family clan wishes to improve the diet of the family, she finds she cannot do it because of the greater influence of the mother-in-law or grandmother, who insists that the old ways are best.

The Farm Home as a Consuming Center.—To a great extent the home is a consuming center. Leaders in industry have not recognized as well as they might the great consuming potential of farm homes. Farmers, too, have neglected opportunities to produce or process for their own needs. This nearsightedness is partly responsible for the large percentage of farm homes without modern conveniences; farmers have felt they must spend first for production needs.

The situation, however, is changing. Electric power, for example, is coming into the home (Figure 39), and with it home freezer lockers and other modern aids to make home life on the farm more attractive. Farm-family demands for modern conveniences are growing steadily. More emphasis needs to be given to farm-family consumption if "the family is to be fed for nutrition and positive health, clothed and housed for protection and social respect, and trained to be at ease in any situation to which its desires and capabilities may lead." [6]

---

[5] See for example, Alice Bowie and Dorothy Dickens, *Clothing Supplies of Socially Participating White Farm Families of Mississippi*, Tech. Bull. 30, State College Agr. Exp. Sta., 1942, pp. 43-45.

[6] *Farm and Rural Life After the War*, Proceedings of the American Country Life Association, 1944, Champaign, Ill.: Garrard Press, p. 59.

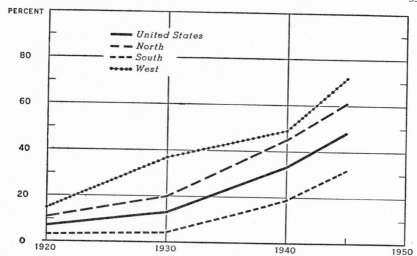

Figure 39. Percentage of Farm Operators Reporting Dwelling Lighted by Electricity, United States, 1920-1945

Note the recent rapid increase for all regions. Even so, only a fourth of the farm dwellings in the South have electricity. (BAE, USDA)

Studies in Living Standards.—The study of how rural people live in families is not new. Gregory King made comparisons for the years 1688 and 1699 in England, France, and Holland. A Parisian professor, Le Play, started his studies in 1830 and carried them on for half a century. His studies were case analyses, secured by living with rural families; and he concluded that there was a close connection between the consumption habits of families and the social policy of a nation. If in times of prosperity, such as exist in wartime, habits of waste and unwarranted expansion were allowed, suffering followed later. Suffering caused by wars, industrial crises, and famine could be avoided and the lowering of living standards averted if national action were taken to prevent such things as inflation. Le Play recommended that a good course for any nation to follow in any war and postwar period is to make real efforts to get debts paid, to avoid going into debt at high prices, and to hold prices at a decent level after the war in order to help assure better living standards later.

Expenditures as a Measure of Living.—In Belgium in 1886 and 1891, another important student, Engel, made studies of expenditures which enabled him to show relationships between the distribution of items in the budget and the rise of the family in the social scale. He formulated "laws" of consumption:

1. That the importance of food in the budget was the best single index of the social position of the family;
2. That an increase in income was associated (a) with declining proportions of the budget spent for food; (b) with about the same proportions spent for clothing, fuel, rent, and light; and (c) with increasing proportions spent for education, health, recreation, and amusements.

These laws hold true in general today, though some modifications have been made on the basis of more recent studies. One report, based on a nationwide study, shows that with increased incomes expenditures for food increase least; those for "other" and medical care increase most.

In 1945 it was estimated that half the farm homes in America needed major repairs. The United States Census for 1940 showed many rural-farm homes without modern conveniences:

90 per cent had no central heating.
82 per cent had no running water.
69 per cent had no electric lights.
63 per cent had no refrigerating equipment.
40 per cent had no radio.
 9 per cent had no inside or outside toilet.

Trends in farm family levels and standards of living which have been charted from Census figures and from other data show an upward swing for most items in the budget. Of especial significance since 1940 has been the increase in numbers of homes on all-weather roads, with electricity, running water, radios, daily newspapers, sewing machines, power-driven washing machines, and other conveniences. (See Figure 40.)

The fact that families with low living levels must spend so much of their income for food means that they must sacrifice advancement, that is, adequate health protection, good schooling, and the many amenities which make life worth while. (See Figure 41.) Because a large percentage of the rural families normally live on incomes below $1,000—one third were actually on relief in the depression years—it is not difficult to see why we are so much concerned with more adequate systems of public education, health protection, social security, rural electrification, and similar measures. An improvement

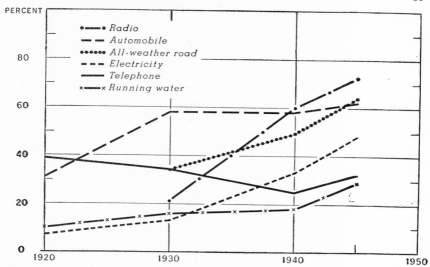

Figure 40. Percentage of Farm Operators Reporting Specified Family Living Items, United States, 1920-1945

Note the advance in all items except telephone to 1940, and of all items after 1940. (BAE, USDA)

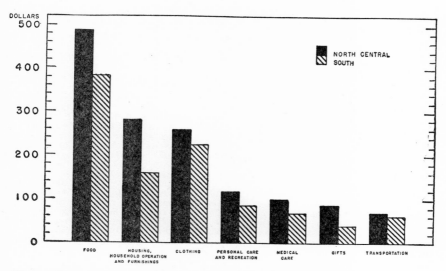

Figure 41. Spending for Family Living by Farm Families in North Central and Southern Regions, 1945

(Bur. of Human Nutrition and Home Economics, USDA)

in the living levels of people on the lowest economic levels can mean an improvement in living levels all along the line.

Rural sociologists have played an important role in studies of levels of living, especially from 1920 to 1940. Home economists have also made significant studies, one of the most comprehensive being the Consumer Purchases Studies of families in 66 farm counties, 140 villages, 29 cities, 14 medium-sized cities, and 6 large cities by the Bureau of Home Economics, the Bureau of Labor Statistics, the Central Statistical Board, and the Works Progress Administration, in 1935 and 1936. The Farm Security Administration and the Bureau of Agricultural Economics, cooperating, carried on a series of standards of living studies published in a series of monographs during the years 1938 to 1940.[7] The Division of Farm Population and Rural Welfare of the U. S. Department of Agriculture is now engaged in setting up a nationwide study of rural living levels which, it is hoped, will go beyond a statistical enumeration of the family expenditures.[8]

Expenditures for Living.—A general pattern of the expenditures of farm families for various purposes is shown by the Consumer Purchases Studies referred to above. A pattern of family living which persists in all parts of the country [9] was typified by the income of a selected group of Pennsylvania and Ohio farm families, a group of middle-income families with an average net income of $1,127. The family unit had an average of 4.17 persons. Half of the husbands were over forty-seven years of age. About two thirds owned the farms they operated.

---

7 Schuler and Swiger, *op. cit.*, p. 15.

8 See E. L. Kirkpatrick, *The Farmer's Standard of Living*, Bull. 1466, USDA, 1926; Carl C. Zimmerman, *Incomes and Expenditures of Village and Town Families in Minnesota,* Minnesota Bull. 253, University Farm, 1929; W. A. Anderson, *Farm Family Living Among White Owner and Tenant Operators in Wake County,* North Carolina State College Agr. Exp. Sta., 1929; Randall C. Hill, et al., *Social, Economic and Homemaking Factors in Farm Living,* Research Bull. 148, Univ. of Missouri Agr. Exp. Sta., 1930; T. C. McCormick, *Farm Standards of Living in Faulkner County, Arkansas,* Bull. 279, Univ. of Missouri Agr. Exp. Sta., 1932; E. L. Kirkpatrick, *Farm Family Living in Wisconsin,* Research Bull. 114, Univ. of Wisconsin Agr. Exp. Sta., 1933; W. V. Dennis, *Social Activities of the Families in the Unionville District,* Bull. 286, Pennsylvania State College Agr. Exp. Sta., 1933; J. K. Geddes, *Farm Versus Village Living in Utah,* Bull. 269, Utah State College Agr. Exp. Sta., 1936; C. R. Hoffer, *Some Characteristics of Rural Families in Three Michigan Communities,* Special Bull. 283, Michigan State College Agr. Exp. Sta., 1937; Dorothy Dickens, *Family Living on Poorer and Better Soil,* Bull. 320, Mississippi State College Agr. Exp. Sta., 1937; Eben Mumford and J. F. Thaden, *The Standard of Living of Farm Families in Selected Michigan Communities,* Michigan State College Agr. Exp. Sta., 1937. See also the series of *Consumer Purchases Studies* published by the BAE, USDA, in cooperation with the Works Progress Administration; O. D. Durreau, "Contemporary Sociological Research in Farm Family Living," *Rural Sociology,* Vol. 6, No. 4, December, 1941, pp. 300-310; and Social Research Reports Nos. X, XI, XIII, XIV, XV.

9 *Family Income and Expenditures,* Five Regions, Part II, "Family Expenditures," Farm Series, Misc. Publ. 465, USDA, in cooperation with WPA, 1940.

1. Expenditures for necessities. Food, clothing, housing, household operation, and medical care account for more than 80 per cent of the farm family's total value of consumption. The use of the car for the family took another 7 per cent, leaving about 13 per cent for personal care, education, reading, recreation, travel other than by automobile, tobacco, gifts, welfare, poll and income taxes, furnishings and equipment, and other items of family living. It has been shown that families with smaller incomes made smaller expenditures for all items and had but a very small amount left for net surplus.

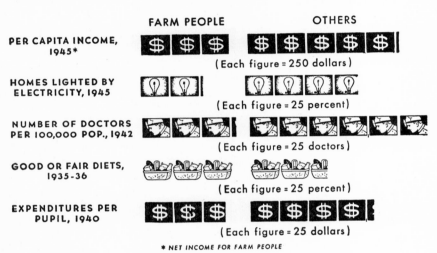

Figure 42. Some Significant Farm and Nonfarm Comparisons
(BAE, USDA)

2. Farm furnished goods. Of especial significance is the percentage of goods furnished by the farm: it furnishes housing, food, fuel, ice, and other products. For a middle-income group of Pennsylvania-Ohio farm families included in the study, "more than two fifths of the average value of consumption at most income levels was obtained directly from the farm." Many good farm families get as much or more of their living from their farms.

3. Relation of incomes to savings and health. The average middle-income farm family has a net surplus of around $1,000, whereas the low-income group has less than $50 to lay away. About half of the farmers of the nation have incomes under $1,500. (See Figure 19, page 64.) Medical care costs alone, for the entire group, average only $45 per family, less than half of the $100 esti-

mated as the cost of adequate medical care. It is startling to realize how large a proportion of our farm families use up all their earnings currently.

Farm Family and Labor Incomes.—Incomes and expenditures for living of wage earners and farm families are the lowest of any group in the country; average disbursements for all consumption items for a typical group of middle-income farm families was $1,101, according to the Consumer Purchases Study.[10] In 1940 the average net income per worker in agriculture was $531 compared with a wage income per employed industrial worker of $1,273. In 1944 the comparable figures were $1,456 and $2,360. The absolute amount of disparity had increased by $162, although the farm worker received 62 per cent as much as the industrial worker in 1944 compared with 42 per cent in 1940. (See Figure 42.)

Family Incomes and Size of Family

There are wide variations in the levels of living among rural people, even in a single rural community. In general, however, the gap is not as wide between the lowest and the highest levels of living in rural areas as it is in urban areas.

TABLE 7. MEDIAN SIZE OF FAMILY IN THE UNITED STATES, URBAN AND RURAL: 1940 *

Region	Urban Families	Rural-Nonfarm Families	Rural-Farm Families
All regions	3.00	3.12	3.71
Northeastern	3.17	3.32	3.44
North Central	2.99	2.93	3.49
Southern	2.98	3.32	3.97
Western	2.55	2.86	3.29

* U. S. Dept. of Commerce, Bureau of the Census, Sixteenth Census of the United States, 1940, *Population and Housing—Families,* Table III, p. 5.

Number of Children.—Of considerable social significance is the relation between family income and number of children. In normal times almost one third of all children, rural and urban, are in families with unit incomes [11] of $150 to $229; about 70 per cent are in families whose unit incomes are below the national median of $474.

---

[10] Family Income and Expenditures, Farm Series, *Consumer Purchases Study, op. cit.,* Misc. Pub. No. 465, p. 2, Table 33.

[11] See P. J. Woofter, "Children and Family Income," *Social Security Bulletin,* Vol. VIII, No. 1, January, 1945.

(A family unit income is the wage or salary income of a family divided by the number of family units, with median income of a group of families divided by the average number of family units in the group.) Farm incomes are even smaller than those of non-farm families, and farm families are larger. The median size of farm families of the southern region of the United States was 3.97 for 1940 compared with under 3.5 for other parts of the country (Table 7).

Regional Variations.—The regional variations in living levels in the United States are also significant. (See Figures 38 and 41.) Families in the South and the Mountain and the Plains regions have the lowest incomes; and those in the New England, North Central, and Pacific regions, the highest. New England and Pacific families have the highest total value of goods used, though the average size of families is lowest. Farm families are largest in the low-income South.

Regional differences persist. By 1945, for example, the South Atlantic, East South Central, and West South Central divisions of the United States had indexes of farm operator level of living ranging from 48 to 81 with 66 for the Southern region. The index for the West was 125, for the North Central 128, and for the Northeast region 139, the Pacific division having an index of 150.[12] In prosperous and depression times these differences cause folk migrations.

Farm Family Security.—The close relation between large size of family and low income has led to considerable agitation for various types of social security plans for farm people, especially those in the lower income brackets. It is now quite generally conceded that social security benefits should be extended at least to farm labor families, and there are proposals for broadening the base of social security to include medical care and protection against disaster.

Family Changes in the Rural Home

Rural families go through several periods in their growth, periods which affect their family and home life. These periods can be based on the school life of the children, as has been done by Brunner and Kolb. It must of course be recognized that rural, and especially farm, families often have children in various stages of growth in all of the periods described below. In the South, especially, a farm

---

[12] Margaret Jarman Hagood, *Farm Operator Family Level of Living Indexes for Counties of the United States, 1940 and 1945*, BAE, USDA, 1947, Table 1.

family may have children in preschool, elementary school, and high school stages of growth.

The Family with Preschool Children.—The chief characteristic of the family with most of the children not yet in school is that the mother is tied closely to the home and her children. During this period she needs considerable help in prenatal and infant care, which too few of our rural mothers receive. Families in this stage often do without many of the most elementary home conveniences, and their lack of these conveniences, especially running hot and cold water and toilets in the house, contributes to a needlessly high infant death rate.

The Family with Grade School Children.—The family with children in grade school still makes considerable sacrifice to give them a basic education. Too many families, especially tenant families, are frustrated in this desire, because they are forced to send their children to a school in which there may be but one child per grade.

In this period parents should be extremely interested in information from agricultural colleges and other sources. Many, however, feel themselves too tied down to farm work to take much interest in new developments. The dominant influences on the young couple are the kinfolk, the neighbors, the merchants, the banker from whom they must often seek "favors"; the landlord whose only interest, too often, is in returns; and possibly the pastor of their church, whose teachings depend on how well they are adapted to the needs of their growing family.

The Family with High School Children.—By the time children are in high school the family is far enough along so that the older children can help on the farm. Family conflicts, however, may result when a son who wants to take part in the extracurricular events in the town high school is needed to do chores. Wise community leaders will ease these conflicts by developing a calendar of activities acceptable to the parents, especially if those parents can see that the activities aid in the physical, mental, and spiritual development of the child.

The family with children in high school is also the target for the special-interest group demands of the community, for different members of the family are often drawn to many different fields of interest. A coordinated approach to programs for the advancement of family living by the various organizations of the community builds the social solidarity of the family, the basic rural social group.

Most youth fail to realize that farm family contributions to their advancement are more than the youth themselves contribute. Costs have been computed showing that each farm child costs at least $140 per year to rear and educate to the age of fifteen. Costs are highest for youth in the high school period—almost double those of the grade school period. The successful family group faces these facts in the family cycle and makes plans to meet them without unduly sacrificing either the parents' or the children's welfare.

The Family with Children Beyond High School.—By the time the children are grown the family is faced with "inheritance" problems.[13] Fortunate is the family that has worked out a family philosophy regarding succession. If this has been done, the son who wishes to take over can be given a start through a father-son partnership, satisfactory arrangements be made with all heirs so that those remaining on the land will be protected, and the "old folks" can remain on the land, possibly in another modern home in the vicinity.

Means of Raising and Protecting Living Levels

Concern for the welfare of the rural, and especially the farm, family has become nation wide. The rural family, as has been pointed out, produces not only the essential raw materials for food and clothing but also the surplus population. We have shown the close relation between living levels and quality of living, and the large proportion of rural families who still lack the elements that make for a good kind of life.[14] It is, therefore, important to consider means of raising and protecting living levels in rural areas.

Encouragement of Ownership Relatively Free of Debt.—A primary approach, closely related to higher farm incomes, is to provide farm families with the means to own their farms. Owners generally have higher standards of living than do tenants, even in the best land areas in the country. The exceptions are for those owner-operators who are unduly burdened with debt. Any national policy which looks to the encouragement of a farm family owning, relatively free of debt, the land it operates, is a highly desirable social policy.

Provision of Better Educational Opportunities.—Education, or the lack of it, is closely related to living levels. In general, farm operators and homemakers whose schooling has been neglected, or

---

[13] See discussion in connection with section on land tenure, pp. 108-110.
[14] See especially the studies on satisfactions derived from rural life, p. 130, footnote 3.

who fail to take advantage of adult educational opportunities, have a low level of living. Usually, those families with a good education have the best incomes and the most money available for advanced living.

Protection in Times of Stress.—Living levels should be protected in times of depression. Farm families tend to brace themselves against rainy days better than do city families. They will substitute food produced on the farm for purchased food, spend no money for house repairs, cut down in the use of the telephone and automobile, buy very little new equipment, make their own clothing, sacrifice on health expenditures, and reduce their contributions to education, recreation, church, and social organizations.

In times of stress rural people do not "lay up" surpluses. They use them in expenditures for service goods, the manufacture and sale of which affect the employment of many urban people. But more important is the effect of times of stress on the health and stamina of the people on the land and of those who migrate to the cities.

Changing Community Customs and Habits.—Another important development is the evident determination of rural America to improve its family as well as its community standards of living. A rural community, through its schools, churches, social organizations, and other groups, can do much to give pace and direction to improvement of diets, as well as other good health practices; to secure the adoption of sensible credit measures; to promote cooperative activities; to insure the cooperation of its families in utilizing local resources to good advantage; and to promote a careful budgeting of time so that its citizens may benefit fully from the educational and cultural opportunities offered by the community.[15]

Usually those families with low living levels do not attend community meetings. From this class, in cities, towns, and villages, as well as in the country, come many of the delinquents and dependents upon public welfare. Families which take responsibility for the social conduct of their members contribute relatively few inmates to our correctional institutions. A family participating in church, school, and similar activities is usually one which has a good living level and a good house. School and church leaders, especially, should be challenged by this situation to devise community programs of action in which all classes can and will participate.

---

15 See *The White House Conference on Rural Education*, NEA, 1945, pp. 131-134, for the responsibilities of the schools for economic welfare and good family life.

The Help of Government.—Government agencies have endeavored in many ways to advance family living levels. The valuable work being done by such agencies and services as the U. S. Department

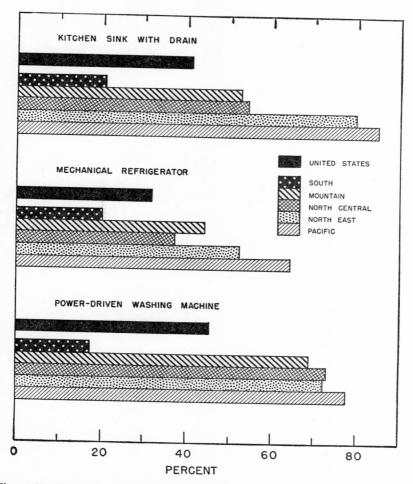

Figure 43. Percentage of Farm Operators Having Specified Household Facilities, by Region, 1945

(Bur. of Human Nutrition and Home Ec., USDA)

of Agriculture, especially its Bureau of Human Nutrition and Home Economics, the state and county agricultural and home economics extension services, the vocational agricultural and home economics courses in high schools, and nutrition classes—all contribute to advancing living levels.

Another class of governmental efforts, exemplified by the work of the Farmers Home Administration (FHA), has been directed at helping low-income families. Here a semblance of social control is exercised, as has been indicated, for home supervisors help families to make home plans and to carry out the approved practices. The success of such measures depends to a large extent on the approach made to the family. Often the chief factor preventing a family from advancing its living level is lack of appreciation, proper attitude, or understanding. Supervisors need to know both case-work techniques and the characteristics of farm people—their pride in their independence and their satisfaction with their present ways of doing things. A "family counseling" approach is usually more successful than an authoritarian approach.

Several other governmental measures to improve rural living have been used, such as drawing up low-cost, modern housing plans, developing landscaping demonstrations, and encouraging home gardens on a widespread scale. The nation expects certain performances in the use of the additional income given in the form of these and other social services, performances which will serve the general interest. Hence, "supplementary income is most appropriately granted in kind, in the form of specific services, such as food, houses, medical services, education. Distributing public service in this way is likely to give the greatest help to low-income families, and the low-income families will have to receive major attention because they are bearing a wholly disproportionate share in the cost of rearing the nation's children." [16]

Family and Group Pressure.—These measures depend primarily upon educational processes and group acceptance of practices which will improve local conditions. Such group acceptance is closely akin to the transmission of culture traits in a society. The more close-knit the group, the more likely it will be to adopt a new practice, if the new practice has been accepted by the group's natural leaders. But if only one family—especially if it is a family that is "out" with other people of the community—takes up the practice, then others may scorn it. Thus, group acceptance in a democratic form of society can have much to do with advancing living levels.

---

[16] T. W. Schultz, *Redirecting Farm Policy*, p. 67. Copyright 1943 by The Macmillan Company, New York, and used with their permission.

The Future Security of Rural Family Life

Greater farm family security is of national concern because (a) society will benefit or suffer according to whether farmers conserve or abuse natural resources; (b) society will be affected constructively or adversely according to how well farm families live; and (c) society will benefit or be injured in accordance with how much food and fiber are produced and how they are used. Farm families must receive a fair share of the national income, and they must use the income wisely.

The real effects of the second world war and of this postwar period on the security of the farm family are, of course, still to be determined. The farmer wants to produce; the world needs more food than is now produced. The farmer's security can be enhanced by getting food to needy peoples and by prices for farm products that will pay him to continue to produce.[17]

Agricultural production in 1945 was about one third greater than it was in 1935-1939 and more than 50 per cent greater than it was in 1910-1914. No more farms are needed to produce what is necessary for domestic consumption; the present farms can produce about all the markets will take. However, technical improvements, as well as added acres to be developed through irrigation, drainage, and land clearing, are likely to mean that by 1950 the agricultural output will be from 35 to 45 per cent larger than the 1935-1939 level. Unless this surplus can be absorbed by greater domestic consumption and by broadened foreign markets, it will inevitably create anew the farm insecurity experienced in the 1930-1940 decade.

Security Through Economic and Social Means.—Family security on farms cannot come solely through economic measures such as increasing and stabilizing the ownership of family farms (including legal enactments to encourage them), and assistance to families on poor lands to secure a foothold on better land. These measures are certainly needed, but they cannot, of themselves, accomplish family security on farms. Even such valuable efforts as those to stabilize prices at levels high enough to provide adequate incomes and to employ large numbers of workers in cities at good year-round wages will not assure family security on farms. Farm security must also be induced by a feeling of the worthwhileness of the occupation; by an acceptance of the rural family into a social status comparable to that hoped for in city life, and by strengthening all rural institutions

[17] See L. J. Norton, *The Objective for a Sound National Farm Program*, Proceedings of the American Country Life Association, 1947, in manuscript.

which work for the betterment of family life on the farm and in the rural community.

The Stability of the Family.—The permanence of the family as a basic and essential institution of rural life is rarely questioned. Yet the same deteriorating influences attacking the city family are at work on the rural family, especially as it comes more and more under urban influences. Some examples will illustrate what is meant here.

The restraints which rural family and community life put on sexual promiscuity, and the rural group's natural hostility to divorce, tend to be minimized as rural areas become urbanized. If lenience with respect to such things as divorce is harmful to the family group,[18] then efforts to maintain a wholesome relation between sex and family life are essential. Perhaps more than ever before, the life of a modern farm family requires emphasis on companionship. And it is hardly arguable that opportunities for such companionship are greater in rural families than in urban families.

A well-secured civilization shows its strength through the quality of family life that it has brought forth and protects. The future of the family, therefore, will be determined by the future of the civilization in which it is imbedded . . . The proper functioning of the home, however, demands that parental intelligence improve since chiefly from the home must come the discipline and motivation necessary for a wise use of the resources provided by our rapid material progress. From no quarter will our political and social leadership get larger returns than from investment of thought and endeavor in matters that concern the family. The social functions that belong to the family give it the key position in the program of social adaptation which decides the survival of each civilization just as the physical and psychic adjustment determines the life career of each individual.[19]

DISCUSSION

1. Why is the family called the basic and primary group in rural life? Discuss the farm family in relation to its effectiveness in performing the functions of a family. In what ways does the average farm family fail to perform these functions in the interest of family welfare? in the interests of the society of which it is a part? What is meant by "familism" and of what significance is it?
2. Outline the ways in which the farm and village family are alike and the ways in which they differ. What are the social implications of these differences? What can be done to overcome them?

---

18 See Ernest R. Groves, *The Family and Its Social Functions*, Philadephia: J. B. Lippincott Co., 1940, p. 568.
19 *Ibid.*, p. 594.

3. What are the chief factors that make up a family's standard of living? What influences are most important in the formation of a standard of living of a rural family? Analyse the Le Play and Engel studies in terms of their application to present-day rural and farm family standards of living. What is the difference between a standard and a level of living? How do levels of living compare in various parts of the United States?

4. Analyse the stages in the living cycle of rural families: What are the reasons for the differences in the various stages? What measures can be taken to plan more effectively to meet the needs of the family as it goes through these stages of growth?

5. Discuss the relative merits of the various methods for raising living levels. If you were placed in a rural community as a professional leader which of these methods would you employ and how would you use each? How different would be your approach if you were a voluntary or nonprofessional leader?

6. Discuss the national policies needed to assure rural people a greater degree of economic and social security. Why must we be concerned about farm family security?

READINGS

Anderson, W. A. *The Composition of Rural Households.* Bull. 713, Cornell Univ. Agr. Exp. Sta., Ithaca, 1939.

Bowie, Alice, and Dickens, Dorothy. *Clothing Supplies of Socially Participating White Farm Families of Mississippi.* Mississippi Agr. Exp. Sta., State College, 1942.

Farm and Rural Life After the War. Proceedings of the American Country Life Association, 1944. Champaign, Ill.: Garrard Press, 1944, pp. 59-71.

Hoffer, Charles R. "The Impact of War on the Farm Family." *Rural Sociology,* Vol. X, No. 2, June, 1945, pp. 151-156.

Kirkpatrick, E. L. *How Farm Families Meet the Emergency.* Research Bull. 126, Wisconsin Agr. Exp. Sta., Madison, January, 1935.

Kolb, J. H., and Brunner, Edmund deS. *A Study of Rural Society.* Boston: Houghton Mifflin Co., 1946, Chs. 11, 17.

Locke, Harvey J. "Contemporary American Farm Families." *Rural Sociology,* Vol. X, No. 2, June, 1945, pp. 140 ff.

Mangus, A. R., and Cottam, Howard R. *Level of Living, Social Participation, and Adjustment of Ohio Farm People.* Bull. 624, Ohio Agr. Exp. Sta., Wooster, September, 1941.

McVoy, Edgar C., and Nelson, Lowry. *Satisfactions in Living: Farm versus Village.* Bull. 370, Minnesota Agr. Exp. Sta., St. Paul, 1943.

Schuler, Edgar A. "Some Regional Variations in Levels and Standards of Living." *Rural Sociology,* Vol. IX, No. 2, June, 1944, pp. 122-141.

Schuler, Edgar A., and Swiger, Rachel Rowe. "Trends in Farm Family Living." BAE Mimeo., USDA, 1947.

Zimmerman, Carl C. *Family and Civilization.* New York: Harper & Bros., 1947.

Chapter 8

THE NEIGHBORHOOD AND VILLAGE IN RURAL LIFE

The basic locality groups, in addition to the family group, are the neighborhood and the village. A knowledge of their structure and functions is fundamental to an understanding of the way in which rural society is made up.

The Neighborhood as a Primary Group

Next to the family, the most important group in rural life is the neighborhood. Like the family, it is a primary group, for it provides intimate, face to face contacts and has much to do with the formation of personality and character. The locality characteristic of the neighborhood is important, for it often indicates social status; one thing which people ask about when they plan to move is "What kind of neighborhood is it?" As a primary group, the locality in which a neighborhood functions is quite small, usually about the size of a one-room school district, though not necessarily having the same boundaries. The smallness of the neighborhood makes close contact possible. Usually everyone in the locality "belongs," though all do not take part in neighborhood activities. You recognize a neighborhood by its name, its social ties, and its group relations.

Significance of Neighborhood Name.—The open-country neighborhood is made up of those families in a given locality who are bound together by ties of religious affinity, by nationality, by topography, or by similar ties. All of the people live on the land; their farmsteads are not clustered together, as in the villages of other countries, but are dispersed over the land, each on a separate farm.

A country neighborhood is usually, but not always, identified by a local name. Almost anyone having lived in a neighborhood for a time can usually give its name. The name is often the same as the New England town, or perhaps the German or Scandinavian village from which the early settlers came. Many small neighborhoods are made up of people having the same nationality or religious belief. Other neighborhoods take their names from peculiar characteristics of the locality, or from the name of an early settler.

148

Neighborhood-Making Contacts.—Association patterns, of course, change over a period of time, but most rural neighborhoods continue to perform a variety of personal functions such as family visiting, exchanging work, participating in local church affairs, attending the country school, patronizing the local cheese factory or creamery, trading or talking at the local store or garage, and mingling in social clubs or local farmers' organizations.

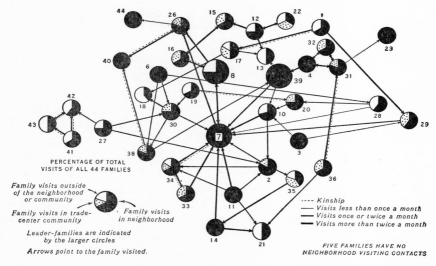

Figure 44. Visiting among Families in a Neighborhood

For most people there is more visiting among those of the neighborhood than with those outside. Yet this neighborhood is split by community lines. (From Linden S. Dodson and Jane Wooley, *Community Organization in Charles County, Maryland,* Bull. A21, Univ. of Maryland Agr. Exp. Sta., January, 1943)

1. Visiting. The simplest and perhaps most influential type of activity in a neighborhood is visiting. Note the visiting patterns in Figure 44. The intimate details of family life are frequently discussed. Out of visiting with neighbors comes an exchange of ideas ranging from care of babies and marketing of hogs to world peace.

2. Mutual aid. A second significant activity is mutual aid, which may take the form of trading work (which played so important a part in keeping up farm production in the World War II period), or helping with planting or harvesting the crops of a sick, injured, or widowed neighbor. The neighbors coming in with their equipment are able to do in one day what it would take the farmer a week or two to do by himself. (See Figure 45, page 158.)

3. Formal activities. Neighbors can take part in formalized activities, such as organizing a neighborhood club, building a local church, improving the roads in the neighborhood, or consolidating their schools. Such things characterize an active neighborhood; the people who live there do things together.

There are also certain other factors involved in the activities of neighborhoods. These include the length of residence of families in the locality, nationality, religious backgrounds, and tenure arrangements with respect to the land.[1] In an Alabama study the following were the "chief reasons people give for sticking together as a neighborhood":[2]

Reason	Only Reason Given	Given with Others	Total Times Mentioned
Just always have	25	20	45
Belong to same church	12	16	28
Kinship	2	17	19
Loyalty to school	7	5	12
Economic ties	4	8	12

Neighborhood Relations to Other Groups.—Rural neighborhoods, whether of the open-country or hamlet-centered type, are not isolated, nor are they the only locality groups in rural society. Families in neighborhoods find themselves in contact with a number of community and rural-urban groups all the time. They do not belong exclusively to a visiting circle, to a neighborhood, to a community, or to a town group. Rather, they take part in several or all of these and groups also go to town, and take part in activities outside the neighborhood. Some families, in fact, may have more contacts outside than within the neighborhood.

The neighborhood is recognized as a distinctive group by those who live both in and outside of it. People in neighborhoods are conscious of their own identity, especially if the neighborhood is an active one. Hence it is possible to determine the members of a neighborhood and its geographical boundaries.

Neighborhood Area and Size.—The area of a neighborhood is determined by the "neighboring" families who visit, trade work, take part in church activities, or in other ways are active together. Sometimes the topography of the land determines the boundaries of the neighborhood. Neighborhoods may, but do not necessarily, follow

---

[1] John H. Kolb and Douglas G. Marshall, *Neighborhood-Community Relationships in Rural Society*, Research Bull. 154, Univ. of Wisconsin Agr. Exp. Sta., 1944.
[2] Irwin T. Sanders and Douglas Ensminger, *Alabama Rural Communities*, Bull. XXXIII, Alabama College, Montevallo, 1940, p. 20. See also Frank Winchester, *Rural Neighborhoods and Communities in Thirteen Kentucky Communities, 1941*, Bull. 450, Univ. of Kentucky Agr. Exp. Sta., 1943, p. 12.

local school district or similar rigid lines. Usually, where a school district forms the basis for the neighborhood, it includes families across the line.

The boundaries of a neighborhood can be determined by a number of methods. One simple method to determine such boundaries is (1) to make a list of the families in a locality who look upon themselves as neighbors and (2) to draw lines on a plat map of the area which includes all of the farms occupied by families which look upon themselves as neighbors. A map has been made of the neighborhoods of Fayette County, Illinois, as determined by this method. The boundary lines are the outside legal boundaries of the farms of families living on the boundaries of the neighborhood. In such studies it was usually found that a neighborhood consisted of from 15 to 25 families. Because people "neighbor" across neighborhood lines, to visit relatives, for example, a check was usually made by asking two or three local people to bound the neighborhood in which they live.

A second and comparable method used in Alabama,[3] Maryland,[4] and other states was to ask people who had lived in a neighborhood for a long time, to draw boundaries of the neighborhood, based on their knowledge of how people grouped together to trade work, attend church, or perform similar functions. A third method, used by Kolb and his associates, identified the neighborhood by the activities or interests—religious, educational, economic, and social—held in common by the families in various localities of the community. Questionnaires were sent out ahead of field schedules to discover and check on active and inactive neighborhoods.[5] This is an intensive and more difficult, but more accurate, method of determining neighborhood lines.

Neighborhoods usually do not have a formal structure, though there may be organized groups within the neighborhood or in which the people of the neighborhood take part, such as a Grange or a local school club. But membership in a neighborhood is by family rather than on an individual basis,—the important characteristic of rural society.

Persistence and Inclusiveness of the Neighborhood.—These analyses have enabled rural social scientists to discover, bound, and describe neighborhoods. They show two significant results: (1) that neighborhoods persist in rural life in spite of modern changes

---

[3] Sanders and Ensminger, *op. cit.*
[4] Linden S. Dodson and Jane Wooley, *Community Organization in Charles County, Maryland*, Bull. A21, Univ. of Maryland Agr. Exp. Sta., 1943.
[5] Kolb and Marshall, *op. cit.*, p. 35.

such as those caused by the automobile, radio, etc., and are, therefore, an important primary group in rural society, and (2) that the neighborhood is about the only group beyond the family which includes and provides social interaction on the part of every person in the locality, in a personal and intimate way.

Trends in Neighborhood Functions.—In general, there are four major functions of the neighborhood which persist through the years: religious, educational, economic, and social. As will be seen in Table 8, the highest ranking function in certain Wisconsin neigh-

TABLE 8. RANKING FUNCTIONS FOR ACTIVE NEIGHBORHOODS *

Function	1941	1931	1921
Religious	1	3	1
Educational	2	1	2
Economic	3	4	4
Social	4	2	3

* From Kolb and Marshall, *Neighborhood-Community Relationships in Rural Society, op. cit.,* p. 5.

borhoods in 1921 and again in 1941 was the religious one, with the educational function ranking second in these two years and first in 1931. "Functions or activities are found in combinations. The most frequent combination was educational, economic, and social; religious, educational, and social was second; and religious, educational, and economic, third."[6] In 1941 all of these neighborhoods had educational functions with either public or parochial school, adult educational classes, and 4-H clubs. In more than four fifths there were social activities: clubs or social organizations, parties, and visiting. In three fourths there were economic activities such as stores, garages, filling stations, creameries, and cooperatives. Almost three fifths had religious activities, such as church services, religious education, and church societies.[7]

Relationship to the Community.—In the South a collection of neighborhoods is said to make up the rural community.[8] Elsewhere, the neighborhood is usually, but not always, a part of a rural community.

A neighborhood is part of a particular community only if the people feel that they belong to it. If it develops near the community boundary, it may find itself divided between two or more com-

6 Kolb and Marshall, *op. cit.*
7 *Ibid.,* p. 5.
8 Sanders and Ensminger, *op. cit.*

munities. On the other hand, neighborhoods too near a community center may be affected adversely by the center. A church or school within the neighborhood can strengthen it, but a church or school outside the neighborhood has a disintegrating effect.

Changes in Rural Neighborhoods.—Like any form of group life, neighborhoods change. Neighborhoods near towns and cities seem to suffer the most, their activities becoming more and more related to, or a part of, the town center's activities.

Neighborhoods undergo change when special interest groups or institutional forms of activity develop, such as a town club or school. Neighborhood outsiders begin to take part in the activity, whereupon some of the less active neighbor-members drop out, or associate with groups elsewhere. They also become inactive when a local church or school closes, or when a nationality group becomes scattered. In times of economic stress, however, neighborhood activities become intensified. New ones appear and old ones become active again. The types of groups which seem to increase most in numbers are the characteristic trade-work groups.

The outstanding fact about neighborhoods is that they change no more than they do and that they persist in spite of modern forms of communication.

Problems of Organization.—Lay and professional leaders need to recognize the inherent value of the neighborhood as a common interest group in which democratic processes can work. Mutual aid, moreover, will doubtless remain a feature of rural life, in spite of the changes coming with mechanization, modern schools, churches, and town- and city-centered trade and service interests.

The chief problem of neighborhood social organization is how neighbors make contacts with each other and how they act together for their mutual benefit. Groups may form within the neighborhood for numerous purposes. These will function or fail in the degree to which the neighborhood is a close-knit, active group. If there is lack of unity, if there are personal or family conflicts, resulting in social isolation, or if other disintegrating influences are at work, little can be done except on a selective basis to interest families in such special projects. But if the neighborhood is closely knit by a common religion or nationality, or simply by ordinary contacts, almost any project or activity appealing to the group will succeed. If the appeal is strong enough (as, for example, to buy bonds, save scrap paper, etc.), there can be effective neighborhood action even in a disintegrating neighborhood.

In the close-knit neighborhood, the leader, that is, the person or family to whom the people look for leadership, is all-important. If he or she approves and will take action, the thing will be done. The natural neighborhood leader assumes the role by reason of what he does for the group and at the behest of the group. There is no better kind of leadership. Outsiders seeking to get things done in an active neighborhood must know how to find such natural leaders and how to get their confidence and support.

Modern Role of the Neighborhood.—Both World War I and World War II demonstrated what could be done through neighborhood organization. The system worked in areas in which the processes of neighborhood leader selection and of group activity were understood. It usually did not work where "leaders" were selected by those on the outside who knew little about natural leaders in the neighborhood. Sometimes those selected were by chance the natural leaders; too often they were persons who had the least influence because they were of the group socially somewhat ostracized, who went outside for many of their activities.

The neighborhood has a place in our modern life. In all its activities it is important to the continuation of the most effective kind of democratic society. Whether it will be used to improve and stabilize rural life and to make more effective use of programs of rural life improvement will depend somewhat upon the importance attached to it by administrators and rural leaders. A wider recognition of its functions is needed by those seeking to establish programs of rural improvement through family contact.

The Agricultural Village

The agricultural village has been called the capital of rural America and the farmers' service center. The trend is probably more toward the latter. Either designation makes imperative an analysis of the village in an agricultural community as a trade, religious, educational, and social center.

Importance.—The usual agricultural village has farm land on all sides; a population ranging from 250 to 2,500; "a bank, 30 or 40 stores, and the social, religious, and educational agencies to meet the needs of both the village and the farm people in the 80 to 100 square miles of open country that constitute the community area." [9] Villages of this nature are the homes of about one sixth of the nation's

---

[9] David R. Jenkins, *Growth and Decline of Agricultural Villages*, New York: Bureau of Publications, Teachers College, Columbia University, 1940. p. 3.

population. Although such villages include resort, mining, lumber, and suburban centers, most of them are primarily agricultural service centers.

Social Origins.—The agricultural village in America was the only available source of farm supplies and services for the farm population until hard-surface roads and the automobile "emancipated" many farm people, enabling them to travel to larger trade centers. It developed in a pattern different from that in Europe or in other parts of the world. In Europe farmers lived in the villages and were a real part of the village life. They had grazing lands in common, and went back and forth each day to farm their "strips" of land.

It was only the exceptional village in the United States which provided this pattern of social life. Most of our villages grew up at the crossroads of a scattered farmstead community. At first there was just a grocery store or a blacksmith shop, perhaps a post office. Later came the mill, the grain elevator, the bank, the dry-goods store, the hardware store, and still later the railroad, the hotel, and other establishments. At first some of the farm folks spent part of their time taking care of the store, but later the "professional" merchant came in. Originally established to serve the needs of the farm people, merchandising later became a matter of business. In the former case there was a close relationship with the farm people; in the latter, there arose cleavages and friction, for some merchants took advantage of the farmers through "hidden" charges, secret price labels, and exorbitant prices.

This sort of exploitation led in part to the agrarian revolt, which started in the middle of the 19th century and culminated in a widespread system of general and cooperative farmers' organizations. Gradually, the village merchants had come to feel that they were the only ones who had a right to carry on the merchandising function, that the business of farmers was to farm and not to "meddle" in the business of banking or storekeeping. Thus the line of demarcation between the town and country was originally drawn because of economic reasons and was later extended into the social life. Whether justified or not there gradually grew up a feeling that townspeople considered themselves just a little better than country people, a feeling that was partly responsible for the maintenance of the psychological barrier between town and country.

Structure and Functions.—An agricultural village can be defined by making an analysis of its structure and functions. Its economic welfare is primarily dependent upon the welfare of the farmers in the area it serves. When farmers of the area are prosperous the village people prosper; conversely, when hard times come for farmers the villagers suffer, too. Also, the village depends somewhat on the country people for the support of its social institutions. Many of those who are reared in the country later live in the village, attend church there, or send their children to the village school.

The village is made up of people who live close together but who are engaged in a diversity of occupations. However, like the country neighborhood, the village is also a locality group; the smaller the village the more like a neighborhood it is.

1. Population size. Most people probably think of a village as having a population of not more than 500. But we have seen that the rural social scientist looks upon settlements up to 2,500 as villages. Jenkins, in his study of growing and declining villages, excludes places under 250 people, which he calls hamlets, and all places over 2,500.[10]

2. Incorporation as a measure of size. Incorporated villages have definite boundaries, which are legally determined. To be incorporated, a village must have enough people to support the services for which incorporation is intended: improved streets, sewage systems, lighting systems, water systems, parks, etc. Incorporated places under 2,500 population are regarded as villages. This is not true of unincorporated places, which include many small hamlets and also some larger places. Only by the study of an area can we determine which unincorporated places can be called villages. Studies have shown that the area of an unincorporated village can be determined by including within the village all occupied dwellings which are less than one tenth of a mile apart, or on the basis of a dwelling density of thirty or more per mile of street.[11]

Service Aspect of Village Occupations.—The chief occupations in the average village are service occupations. The banker is there to serve the credit needs of the town and country people, the storekeeper is there to provide a stock of consumer supplies for both village and farm, the garageman depends for his livelihood on the service he can perform for both the town and country people. The service aspect of the village extends, also, to religious, educational, and social, as well as to economic affairs. Schools and churches, doctors, dentists, health centers, and similar services can be centered there and are available to all of the people—both town and country.

10 *Ibid.,* p. 5.
11 N. L. Sims, *Elements of Rural Sociology,* New York: Thomas Y. Crowell Co., 1940, p. 6.

Organizations, both village and farm, can meet in the schools, churches, or halls located in the village. Thus, the village can be the farmers' service center for religious, educational, and social, as well as economic purposes.

Types of Villages.—The layout of the village and its relative size often determine the kind of social organization found within it. The smaller, hamlet type of unincorporated villages—the primary service centers—are often "run" by the storekeeper, or by some similar natural leader. These typical hamlets often have a hall for local social or educational organizations. They may have but one or two stores, a garage, and a filling station or two.

The village of medium size—from 500 to 1,200 population—is more diversified and better stocked. It is the center to which farmers come for most of their day-to-day trade needs. A good elementary school is usually located in the medium-sized village; often the school district's boundaries are the same as those of the incorporated boundaries of the village. A high school may also be there, but is usually a township or "community" high school which serves, and receives support from, farms adjacent to the village.

Some of these villages are strung along the railroad or highway. Others have at their center a square which may be a park, and about which are lined the business houses. Back of these stores can be found the residential section—the "good" on one side and the "poor" on the other. This medium-sized village has also its governmental and political structure, with political parties or groups to elect the mayor and other officials. It has its social organizations, most of which limit their membership to the families of the village, though some take in a few representative farmers.

The larger country town villages are usually county seats, and are relatively self-sufficient, with their hardware, drug, dry goods, and other stores, and their movies, pool halls, banks, hotels, schools, lodges, and several doctors and dentists. They are usually large enough to support one or two weekly newspapers. As communication centers they have access to railroads, bus lines, telephones, telegraph, and postal service. The nature and extent of many of these services depends on the size and location of the village.

Economic Competition.—These larger centers are always in competition with the small- and medium-sized villages. The retail stores and dealers in agricultural produce and supplies form the main core of village life. When farmers were able to get good roads and automobiles they began to pass up the smaller centers to trade in the larger center, where they could usually get better service and better quality. The extent to which a village can perform its marketing, banking, and other professional services in modern days in the face of large-center competition determines whether its people will earn a good living or be able merely to struggle along.[12]

Midway between the country and city is the small town, which tries to be a counterpart of the city and whose function has come to be that of "gateway" for the flow of many services. It is more and more dependent, as we have seen, upon its country hinterland for its economic and social well-being.

Some larger villages and towns provide craft and manufacturing services. The opportunities of expansion in these fields, which can include processing on a greater scale than heretofore conceived of, are only now being realized.

Social Competition.—The larger country towns also compete with the smaller villages with respect to their provisions for education, religious services, and social and recreational activities. The better high schools of the larger centers aggravate the problems of maintaining the dwindling high schools in the smaller villages. The smaller village may well become the attendance center for elementary pupils, and the larger village the junior and senior high school center. The competition between the small rural church and the better village church has been a major factor in the decline of the former. If the village church can manage to keep the close-knit characteristics of the open-country church, the village can well become an increasingly important church center.

Smaller villages are now centers for farm family social and recreational activities, but the larger centers are still too aloof. About the only recreational opportunities available to farm families in most of the larger villages are school entertainments and the commercial amusements: the taverns, pool halls, movies, and dance halls.

Changes in Villages.—In his study of agricultural villages, Jenkins shows that small villages, especially those which are unincorporated, have suffered, although they are by no means doomed to extinction; and that farmers are more closely attached to larger centers than formerly, for high prices in World War II gave rise to finer, larger, and more luxurious services in these centers.[13] However, although the number of rural incorporated centers in 1940 was

---

12 See T. Lynn Smith, "The Role of the Village," *Rural Sociology*, Vol. VII, No. 1, March, 1943, pp. 16-20.
13 Jenkins, *op. cit.*, pp. 5, 6.

Figure 45. Mechanization Need Not Hamper Neighborhood Cooperation
Neighbors help each other get in the crops. (Courtesy Farm Security Administration)

smaller than the number in 1930, their total population increased from 9,183,453 in 1930 to 9,343,910 in 1940. The estimates for the unincorporated villages vary, with the number probably exceeding 43,000.[14]

TABLE 9. PERCENTAGES OF SMALL INCORPORATED PLACES WHICH LOST POPULATION FROM 1930 TO 1940 *

Population	Percentages That Lost Population
All places	34.1
1,000—2,499	20.0
500— 999	29.7
250— 499	39.3
1— 250	52.0
1— 499	44.7

* From S. C. Ratcliffe, "Population of Hamlets and Villages," *Rural Sociology,* Vol. VII, No. 3, September, 1942, pp. 319-328.

Table 9 shows the 1930-1940 population changes in small incorporated rural places. Population changes are also shown in Figure 46. Note the loss for places under 500, and the great decrease in places under 250 population. This number may have been affected by an increase in population during the decade, so that more were counted in the next larger size-of-place bracket. Though the small places did decrease most in numbers during the decade, yet they still represent a significant factor in rural life. Some of the significant conclusions from Jenkins' study are that (a) changes in population size of agricultural villages are due to migrations and not to changes in birth and death rates, (b) the most important factor influencing population size is trade with the open country, (c) in depression times village populations increase because of a movement of "relief" families into town, where they can more easily get relief, and (d) the size of the village is not an important factor in determining whether it will grow or decline.

A growing village has a larger proportion of people in the age groups under ten years of age and from twenty to thirty years. A declining village has a larger proportion of people in the older age groups, which means not only a preponderance of old people but also a weeding out of leaders in the middle-aged group and an exodus of those seeking jobs.

Growing villages, also, have a small proportion of unmarried women, more children, larger families, fewer widowed and divorced

[14] Smith, *op. cit.,* p. 15. See also T. Lynn Smith and Edmund deS. Brunner, "Village Growth and Decline," *Rural Sociology,* Vol. IX, No. 2, Sept., 1944, pp. 103-115.

people, and more jobs for women. Consolidated schools are more likely to be found in growing villages, which retain more of their students, and send more of them to college, whereas declining villages send more to work elsewhere, either on the farm or in other occupations.[15]

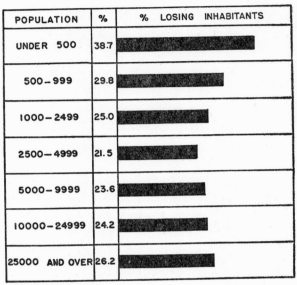

POPULATION	%	% LOSING INHABITANTS
UNDER 500	38.7	
500 – 999	29.8	
1000 – 2499	25.0	
2500 – 4999	21.5	
5000 – 9999	23.6	
10000 – 24999	24.2	
25000 AND OVER	26.2	

Figure 46. Percentage of Incorporated Places in the United States, Exclusive of New England, Which Lost Population in the Decade 1930-1940

(After J. M. Gillette, "Some Population Shifts in the United States, 1930-1940," *Am. Soc. Rev.*, Vol. 6, No. 5, October, 1945)

Village-Country Relations

The fact that present-day farmers have a much greater ease of communication and travel than did their fathers and grandfathers is of great sociological significance. Good roads, automobiles, telephones, radios, newspapers, and now even airplanes, have so shortened the distances between country and town that one finds it difficult, if not impossible, to draw the line between the two.

Increasing Social Interaction.—Social distances, too, have been reduced, for there is an increasing number of social contacts between town and country people.[16] The modern farm dweller is in almost

---

15 Jenkins, *op. cit.* See summary.
16 See D. E. Lindstrom, *Forces Affecting Participation of Farm People in Rural Organizations*, Bull. 423, Univ. of Illinois Agr. Exp. Sta., 1936.

immediate touch with community, county, state, national, and international affairs, through his radio. Ease of travel makes it possible for him and his leaders to meet in conferences, discussions, or conventions with his fellow farmers from all over the nation. Because of his new sense of independence, the farmer feels freer to discuss issues, openly and frankly. This will open the way to increasing town-country cooperation if only the leaders can overcome inertia and the firmly established town-country psychological wall.

Some of the results, with respect to village-farm interaction, are significant. Freed from the necessity of trading in the nearby village, the positions of the farmer and the town merchant are reversed. The town merchant must now cater to the farmer. Sometimes his attitude has been one of resentfulness because farmers sometimes go to larger towns for some of their purchases. However, efforts on the part of townsmen to attract farm people to their village center are sometimes narrowly self-centered, e.g., showing free movies to attract trade. The more intelligent and effective approach is an effort to match the quality of services of larger towns. Other things being equal, farmers still prefer to trade in their own or nearest trade center.

Increase in Farmer Cooperatives.—The expansion of the cooperative movement to deal in gasoline, oil, and other farm supplies has caused anxiety on the part of many small-town merchants. Every time a new cooperative is formed they see a new threat to their security as merchants. Farmers, it must be remembered, formed cooperatives to secure better service, better prices, and more control over the marketing processes. If economic services are effectively performed by the independent merchant, the farmer is inclined to be loyal to him. However, the development of processing plants and cold storage lockers may mean that some village merchants will in the future find more security as managers of cooperatives than as independent merchants. With the coming of medical cooperation the doctor in the small town may find himself in the same position— with greater security and a finer opportunity for service through the cooperative.

Release from Dependence on Local Credit.—The country bank, organized from local funds and manned by local people, must now recognize the importance of government credit. Farmers can get a variety of forms of credit at low rates of interest—as low as 3 per cent for Farmers Home Administration loans—from governmental agencies. Though most of the credit for farmers still comes from private sources, the Farm Credit Administration agencies provide a control element, not only on forms of credit and interest rates but, by their insistence on scientific appraisals, they also exert some control over land values.

From Opposition to Cooperation in Education.—Schools supported by village people alone are often too costly. Villagers must have the help of the farm areas contiguous to their villages if they are to modernize their schools. Yet to mention consolidation to some farm people is like waving a red flag in the face of a mad bull. Though farmers can retain their one-room schools and support them on a relatively low tax rate, especially in good land areas, they are beginning to realize that the resulting poor schools are a terrific social cost, not only to themselves but to town areas as well. More and more, farmers are sending their children to village schools. Where farmers and townsmen have worked out cooperative plans for education they vow they never will go back to the old system. A consolidation project can not only overcome long-time grudges between neighbors, but can also bring cooperation between elementary and high school boards in the use of the same buses, buildings, and other facilities. Town and country people mingle freely and wholesomely in the activities sponsored by the new consolidated school.

The Trend Toward Industrial Decentralization.—More and more, farmers are coming to trade in the larger towns and small cities. The movement of large manufacturing and trade establishments to these larger towns and small cities makes them industrial and trade centers in their own right. The farther they are from metropolitan centers the more complete they are in such services. Nearness to metropolitan centers places them in a position of secondary influence. Nevertheless, they are increasingly important as wholesale trade and service centers for small town and country areas. With the population movements tending to converge on the smaller cities (movements from metropolitan areas as well as from rural areas to such places) the smaller cities are benefited. They can have the facilities and opportunities for the modern stores, schools, churches, and other social services without so many of the serious slum and housing problems of the great cities.

Until the World War II period there was not much of a move to decentralize industry. Now, with the vulnerability of larger population centers to dangers of the atomic bomb and similar hazards, there may be a real move in this direction. Small industries related to agriculture and sections for making specialized parts for large industries are being located in smaller areas. Many of the smaller places have the power, raw materials, transportation facilities, and labor supply for such decentralization. Such industrial decentralization can mean new life to many rural communities.

Relations of City to Village and Country Life

The great human, economic, and social nerve centers of the world are the large cities. The modern city is often only a half-day's drive from many farm and village homes. Yet to most rural people the city is judged by the remembrances of fleeting visits, or through the movies and magazines, the newspaper or the radio. Perhaps the chief impression of a first visit to a large town or city is its impersonality. It is the home of many strangers.

With their powerful radio stations and big newspapers, large cities have become significant centers of control over public opinion. The cities have, moreover, attracted the central offices of state and national farmers' organizations. They are hosts for state and national farmers' meetings and exhibitions, and as such provide one form of important contact between city and country people. Yet to the farmer cities are undoubtedly most interesting because they are centers of control for grocery, dry goods, and other "chains," and are the major markets for grain, livestock, and other products of his farm.

Rural-Urban Interaction.—We know that cities are becoming progressively dependent for population growth upon country areas. If the movement from rural areas were to stop, the largest cities would soon suffer serious decreases in population. Rural areas must depend upon urban areas for their absorption of their population surpluses, which move in largest numbers to the nearest urban centers.

The contacts between country, village, and city people are increasing and are becoming more important in a number of ways.[17] We have noted the competition of larger places with smaller villages for the farmers' trade. The growth of the impersonal but more efficient services in larger centers has also led the farmer to feel more free to develop his own cooperatives in his own way, and he has expanded most of them beyond the neighborhood and community level. We have also emphasized the transfer of wealth from country

---

[17] See E. T. Hiller, "Extension of Urban Characteristics into Rural Areas," *Rural Sociology*, Vol. VI, No. 3, September, 1941, pp. 242-257.

to city areas. These changes have resulted in a sort of regional concentration, so that the larger cities have more and more become the control centers of wealth. The city has always had an attraction for rural people because of its variety of recreational opportunities. Urban types of recreational activities have tended to spread to the rural areas, chiefly in the form of movies.

The city is a more healthful place in which to live than the country because the city has developed better health facilities. Most of the best hospital facilities are there. The best specialists are in the largest cities. To obtain their services the country dweller must bear the expense of going to the city.

Public health regulations relative to food are essential to the control of disease in the city, but many of these regulations are disregarded by farmers. Hence there has been an effort, as we have seen, to extend these regulations and services to rural areas.

There has also been a growth of urban concern for the rural church. The urban church membership is more than three fourths of the total in the United States. This fact and the fact that the largest church memberships are in urban areas has led to the dominance of the city in the making of policies and in administration. Theological seminaries have long concentrated on training their students for urban churches. It was only after a campaign on the part of zealous rural church leaders that some of the seminaries developed programs of rural training; only recently have Protestant denominations recognized their dependence upon rural areas for the recruitment of future members and leaders in the church.

Yet the average rural minister is said to be still thirty years behind the times, as far as knowledge of scientific developments in agriculture is concerned. Nationwide programs are being developed by some of the more rural denominations such as the Church of the Brethren, and by such major groups as the Catholics, Methodists, and Presbyterians.

The interdependence of agricultural and industrial groups was dramatically shown by the necessities of the recent war. Before the outbreak of the war a number of agricultural-industrial and rural-urban conferences had been held. These conferences have been continued, most of them through cooperation of Chambers of Commerce and farmers' organizations. Some efforts have been made to include labor. This is very desirable, because agriculture, labor, and industry have many interests in common. Such conferences, which provide face to face contacts, often lead to tolerance and understanding when other means fail.

Traits and Processes of Rural-Urban Interaction.—A brief review of the social aspects of rural-urban relations will show how the above trends are of social significance. We have seen that primary group contacts are characteristic of rural life, and that the most definitely rural areas—the open-country areas—provide opportunities for direct community organization. Such primary contacts lead to more emphasis and attention upon the individual—he counts for more in the group of which he is a part. Family participation, provincialism, and conservation are part and parcel of rural life.

The cities, with their emphasis on manufacturing and commerce, can be called areas of commercialization. This leads to a complex form of social and economic organization and emphasis on personal affairs, rather than on family and community affairs.

Reconciling Extreme Ruralism and Extreme Urbanism.—The development of town-country cooperation provides a medium for "rurbanism," in which the finest values of both town and country can be nurtured. Rurbanism recognizes that farm life is essential and worthy of modernization, and that town life is equally essential as a catalytic agent between city and country.

We have seen that the rural-nonfarm element in the population has grown more rapidly than any other. We must recognize a problem arising out of this movement,[18] namely, that when city people move to adjacent small towns to live and commute to work, they may eventually outnumber the native residents. When that happens, conflicts over problems such as the provision of modern public services can easily arise. The people who have always lived in the community have become so accustomed to what they have that they resent moves on the part of the newcomers to provide additional public services. Strife over these problems is latent and may flare up at any time. But as the ex-city people send their children to the local schools, and attend the local churches, they gradually begin to find a common ground on which to work for the things desired.

———

In summary, the neighborhood and the village are the basic locality groups beyond the family which form the basis for the rural community. The neighborhood provides the simplest forms of social contacts, which are important in forming attitudes, influencing be-

———

[18] See W. R. Gordon, *Satellite Acres*, Bull. 282, Rhode Island State College Agr. Exp. Sta., 1942

havior, and developing leadership. The small village or hamlet has the characteristics of the neighborhood in providing close-knit social relationships, but the larger village and the town have within them a number of neighborhoods. These, and the interest groups to be discussed in a later chapter, form the woof and warp of the fabric of the rural community. The nature and organization of the rural community is the subject of the next chapter.

DISCUSSION

1. Analyze a country neighborhood for its typical activities and social bonds. What changes have come in the last 20 years? What are the factors contributing to neighborhood social solidarity? Disintegration? What are the modern possibilities of the neighborhood?

2. What reasons can be given for nurturing the agricultural village? What does incorporation do for town-country relations? How can these influences be minimized? What are the social implications of the occupational characteristics of the agricultural village or town?

3. What are the chief causes for conflicts between country and town people? What are some of the most significant forms of cooperation? What are desirable approaches to the improvement of town and country cooperation?

4. Discuss the fields of rural-urban interaction and movements to improve relations between agriculture, industry, and labor.

5. What are the characteristics of urbanization? Ruralization? How reconcile extreme ruralism and extreme urbanism? What measures such as the introduction of small industries can be taken to revitalize a rural community? Discuss the economic and social effects of such a program on the rural community.

READINGS

Arvold, Alfred G. *Neighborhood Activities in Country Communities.* Circular 171, Ext. Service of the College of Agr., Univ. of North Dakota, 1940.

Brunner, Edmund deS., and Lorge, Irving. *Rural Trends in Depression Years.* New York: Columbia University Press, 1937, Ch. IV.

Gillette, John M. "Some Population Shifts in the United States, 1939-40." *American Sociological Review,* Vol. VI, No. 5, October, 1941, pp. 619-628.

Hiller, E. T. "Extension of Urban Characteristics into Rural Areas." *Rural Sociology,* Vol. VI, No. 3, September, 1941, pp. 242, 257.

Jenkins, David R. *Growth and Decline of Agricultural Villages.* New York: Teachers College, Bureau of Publications, Columbia University, 1940, especially Ch. X.

Kolb, J. H., and Marshall, Douglas. *Neighborhood-Community Relationships in Rural Society.* Research Bull. 154, Wisconsin Agr. Exp. Sta., 1944.

Landis, Paul H. *Rural Life in Process.* New York: McGraw-Hill Book Co., Inc., 1940, Ch. II.

Ratcliffe, S. C., *Population Changes in Hamlets and Villages,* Rural Sociology, Vol. VII, No. 3, September 1942, pp. 318-328.

Rusk, H. P., and Shoemaker, Warren W. *Postwar Problems Facing Agriculture and Business.* Circular 582, Ext. Service in Agr. and Home Ec., Univ. of Illinois, 1944.

Tylor, W. Russell. "The Process of Change from Neighborhood to Regional Organization and Its Effect on Rural Life." *Social Forces,* Vol. XVI, No. 4, May, 1938, pp. 530-541.

Chapter 9

THE RURAL COMMUNITY AS A FUNCTIONAL AREA

"In modern times the small community has played the part of an orphan in an unfriendly world. . . . Yet the small community has supplied the lifeblood of civilization, and neglect of it has been one of the primary reasons for the slowness and interrupted course of human progress." [1] In recent years, however, the rural community has come to be looked on as a basic unit of organization for rural society. More and more the rural community, in contrast to the neighborhood, is thought of as the area in which rural people "live, move, and have their being." Moreover, it is being integrated more and more with the larger society of which it is a part.[2]

The distinction between a neighborhood and a community is a matter of degree. It is difficult to tell when a village is a neighborhood center and when it becomes a community center. Many farm people look upon their neighborhood as a community, especially when they have an active farmers' club or similar organization which draws from three or more localities or normal neighborhoods. If the people of their group come from the larger areas, if the meetings of the organization provide the chief contact for these people, and if most of them regard themselves as a part of the group, then they make up a primary or small community.

How the Community Idea Developed

The community originated in village-centered agricultural life, a way of life characteristic of agriculture almost everywhere except in the United States. This type of village probably started with the kinship group—a "great" family—which became a clan. When roving bands became sedentary and agricultural they fixed their abodes in a group for protection, grazing their cattle on the commons, and allotting fields to families to farm. These villages had their systems of social organization. For example, in the English manor the various classes were made up of the lords; the yeomen or freemen;

---

[1] Arthur E. Morgan, *The Small Community*, New York: Harper & Bros., 1942, p. 3.
[2] See W. Russell Tylor, "Community and Neighborhood," *Social Forces*, Vol. XVI, No. 4, May, 1938.

the villeins, or land workers bound to the lord; the cottagers, the lord's tenants; the slaves or servant class; and other people in the community.[3]

Early Types in America.—Two types of community life were transplanted by colonization to America: the manorial system which developed into the plantation system of the South, and the settlements by the yeoman class in New England. Only the manorial or plantation system took deep root; it now remains as a significant form of rural life in the South. The village-centered New England system, with its town meetings, has persisted there but did not spread westward, except with certain religious or other close-knit groups, the Mormon settlements being the most outstanding present-day examples.[4]

The Major Type.—The major type of settlement in America, as pointed out before, was the scattered farmstead type, settlements being on the basis of the mile-square sections and 6-mile-square townships. These resulted in the checkerboard pattern of land division that prevails in the United States and which nears the maximum possible in separation or isolation of farm families.[5] Hence it is not surprising that it was the fashion to speak of the American farmer as a man without a community. "Living outside of compact districts, the farmer seemed altogether devoid of any community." [6] Though he seemed to belong to no population group, nor be designated by reference to any social unit, as Sims puts it, yet as time went on two legal units were recognized, namely, the open-country school district and the township or precinct. The boundaries of these units are usually definitely known by most farm folks and have been used not only for population determinations by the Census Bureau and for school records, but for social-group purposes as well, as in the formation of school district community clubs and township farm organization units. But such boundaries are arbitrary at best and can usually be used only for population enumeration or for delineating boundaries of local government units. (See Figure 47.)

Early Studies of the Rural Community.—The difficulty of "assigning" a farm family to a specific community has led to numerous method studies. Wilson defined the country community by the terri-

---

[3] N. L. Sims, *Elements of Rural Sociology*, New York: Thomas Y. Crowell Co., 1940, pp. 35-37.

[4] See Lowry Nelson, *A Social Survey of Escalante, Utah,* Brigham Young Univ. Studies, Provo, Utah, 1925; and William Alfred Hinds, *American Communities,* Chicago: Charles H. Kerr & Co., 1908.

[5] T. Lynn Smith, *The Sociology of Rural Life,* New York: Harper & Bros., 1947, p. 267.

[6] Sims, *op. cit.,* p. 75.

tory which lay within the "team haul" of a given center—this being the radius of social intercourse. "Within this radius," reported Wilson, "all the affairs of any individual are known in minute detail . . . it is a man's home town." [7] Galpin made the first important study of areas from which farmers came to a certain center

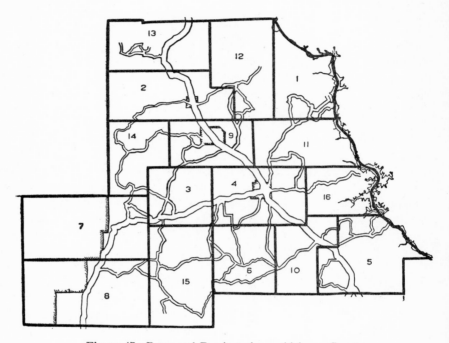

Figure 47. Beats and Precincts in an Alabama County

Political boundaries are artificial. (From Irwin T. Sanders and Douglas Ensminger, *Alabama Rural Communities,* Ala. Coll. Bull. Vol. 33, No. 1A, July, 1940)

to buy and sell, and to seek other services. He found that "comparatively determinable and fixed areas of land" surrounded each center "whose inhabitants, averaging about the same number of families as in the center itself, were served by the center with precisely the same character of service as it rendered to the people within its corporate limits." [8] He thus made popular the idea that a rural community was made up of the people in the village service center and the people in the country who were served by that village.

_____

[7] Warren H. Wilson, *The Evolution of the Country Community,* Boston: Pilgrim Press, 1923, p. 112.

[8] See C. J. Galpin, *The Social Anatomy of an Agricultural Community,* Research Bull. 34, Univ. of Wisconsin Agr. Exp. Sta., 1915, pp. 3-19.

Galpin called it a "rurban" community, made up of rural and urban people.

Trade Areas and the School Community.—Rural sociologists have since endeavored to delimit the rural community by determining a composite of the areas served by grocery stores, banks, hardware stores, high schools, and similar agencies. (See Figure 49, page 174.) When the areas served by these institutions are mapped, a composite line of the different boundary lines separating these centers will usually approximate the boundaries of the communities. It seems evident, however, that the area served by the consolidated school or the high school is tending to become more important and definitive than the economic area. This latter conclusion is borne out by recent studies, which show a wide variation in trade-area patterns. Groceries and hardware may be purchased in the near-by village, for example, whereas banking may be done and "store clothes" bought in the county seat centers. Note the importance of the county seat town for trade as shown in the banking and trade service areas of McDonough County, Illinois (Figure 48). Moreover, farmers may sell their grain through the nearby open-country elevators, but they are likely to truck their livestock to a distant city market or other concentration point.[9] Hence, the attendance at consolidated schools or at high schools seems to be one of the most effective means of identifying the community area.

The Rural Community Defined

A community cannot be determined merely by the center where people trade, go to church, or send their children to school. Nor can it be defined by the legal or political limits of an area. It is, rather, a grouping of people around a core of interests, not all of which are coterminous.

Identity.—The definition of a rural community accepted by most rural sociologists is that of Dwight Sanderson: "A rural community consists of the social interaction of the people and their institutions in the local area in which they live on dispersed farmsteads and in a hamlet or village which forms the center of their common activities." [10] This definition (a) places the elements of social interaction as the determining characteristics of a rural community, and recog-

---

[9] See D. E. Lindstrom, *Forces Affecting Participation of Farm People in Rural Organization*, Bull. 423, Univ. of Illinois Agr. Exp. Sta., 1936, pp. 94-96.
[10] Dwight Sanderson, *Rural Sociology and Rural Social Organization*, New York: John Wiley & Sons, Inc., 1942, pp. 278-279.

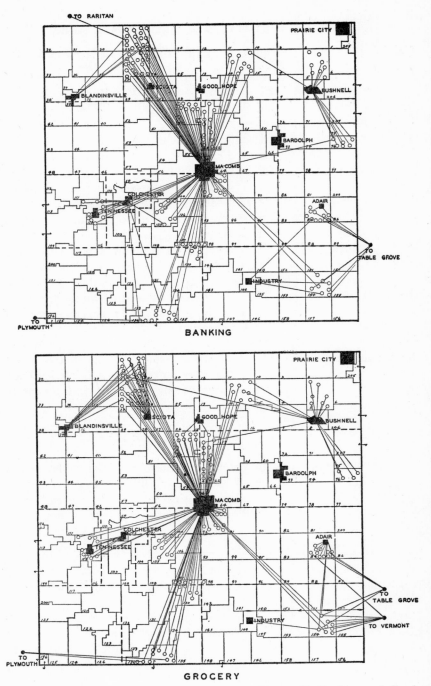

BANKING

GROCERY

Figure 48. Banking and Trade

Note the dominance of the county seat town for supplies but not for livestock sales.
McDonough County, Illinois, Rural Sociology Mimeograph 11, Univ. of Illinois Agr. Exp.

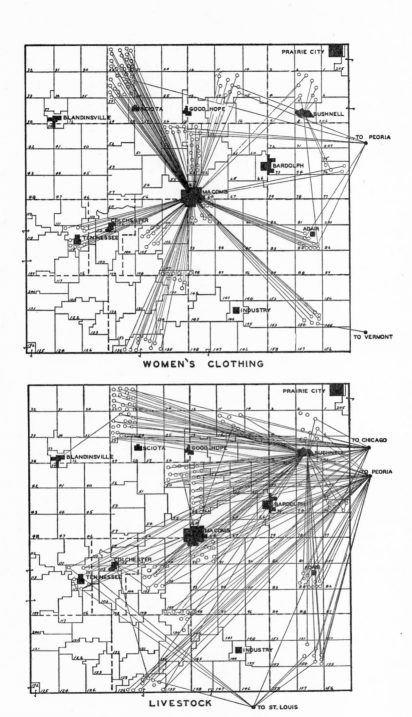

WOMEN'S CLOTHING

LIVESTOCK

Areas, McDonough County, Illinois

(From D. E. Lindstrom, *The Need for and Possibility of Rural School Reorganization in* Sta., April, 1943)

nizes that a rural community is made up of a village as a center of interests of the people in it and of the surrounding territory; (b) places importance upon the psychic element: a consciousness of belonging to this or that community; and (c) emphasizes the locality aspect of the rural community, placing it in the category of a locality group.

Secondary group contacts are the hallmark of the larger rural community, especially those with a town center of a thousand or more people. This means that there are intergroup as well as intragroup activities within the rural community. Its contacts are the personal, intimate, face-to-face contacts provided in its families, neighborhoods, interest groups, and institutions. It is thus made up of primary, locality, and special interest groups which provide a complex matrix of social relationships, all of which go to make up the modern rural community.

Boundaries.—If we accept the fact that the larger rural community is a secondary group, made up of numerous other types of groups, and that the village center forms its nucleus, we are given a starting point for locating or geographically describing the rural community. The classical method for mapping a rural community is to make inquiry of merchants and businessmen as to farm families farthest from the village who habitually trade there, and check these families on a map. The location of the "boundary" families attending church, sending children to school, taking part in farm organization or similar meetings held in the village, is also checked on the map. Visits to families living along the boundary lines thus drawn make it possible to determine more exactly to which community these people feel they belong. As you travel out to these boundaries you find a lack of use of the unimproved dirt roads on the "divide" between two community areas.[11] Lines drawn on the map through the points thus indicated (or along the outside boundaries of the farms thus located) form the composite boundary of the community. Figure 51 shows the larger communities of a South Dakota community, informally determined by the residence location of the farm families who patronize the institutional and business services of the village.

Another method of determining rural community areas, called the neighborhood cluster method, has been worked out for the South by Ensminger and Holt. Close-knit neighborhoods are first mapped

---

[11] F. Howard Forsyth, "Use of Road Turnings in Community Research," *Rural Sociology*, Vol. IX, No. 4, December, 1944.

Figure 49. Airplane View of a Central Illinois Rural Community

Note the scattered farmsteads which are a natural part of this community. (Courtesy "Bloomington Pantagraph," Bloomington, Illinois)

Figure 50. Planning for a Community Self-Survey

A community's frank facing of its shortcomings, needs, and possibilities can do much to start it on a program of improvement. (Courtesy "Bloomington Pantagraph," Bloomington, Illinois)

according to the method described above. These are then grouped around and identified with the cluster of neighborhood service centers used most by their people. It is claimed that more interests in common can be found in this than in any other way.

The consolidated school can be the predominant factor in creating a "larger community" feeling on the part of farm families. Where the high school has become a community school the area from which

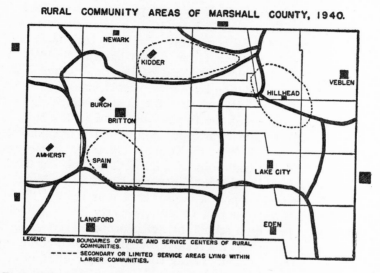

RURAL COMMUNITY AREAS OF MARSHALL COUNTY, 1940.

LEGEND: ▬▬▬ BOUNDARIES OF TRADE AND SERVICE CENTERS OF RURAL COMMUNITIES.

‒ ‒ ‒ ‒ SECONDARY OR LIMITED SERVICE AREAS LYING WITHIN LARGER COMMUNITIES.

Figure 51. The Rural Community Boundaries of a South Dakota County

(From W. F. Kumlien, *Basic Trends of Social Change in South Dakota: Series III, Community Organization,* South Dakota State Coll. Agr. Exp. Sta., December, 1941)

it draws its students comes as near being the community area as any single area which can be found.[12]

A combination of three factors seems essential to delimit most community areas: (1) what farm people themselves consider to be their community center, (2) where they actually go for trading, school, church, and to attend meetings, and (3) the community center used by most of the people in the neighborhood. If only one of the factors is used, it will reveal communities of varying sizes and shapes, some with only open-country centers such as a school or a

[12] See I. I. Sanders and Douglas Ensminger, *Alabama Rural Communities—A Study of Chilton County,* Alabama Coll. Bull. XXXIII, 1940, p. 80; J. B. Holt, *Rural Neighborhoods and Communities of Lee County, Alabama,* BAE, USDA, 1941; *Report of a Reconnaissance Survey of Neighborhoods and Communities of Caswell County, North Carolina,* BAE, USDA, 1940; and Harold Hoffsomer and Herbert Pryor, *Neighborhoods and Communities in Covington County, Mississippi,* BAE, USDA, 1941.

church, yet serving a larger area, and others approximating a smaller county in area, if the county has one dominating trade and service center. The best single index seems to be the center to which children are naturally sent for high school.[13]

Relative Proportions of Town and Country Populations.—If we assume that every rural community has a village center, then the basic composition of the community is the village population and the adjacent farm population which uses the village as a service center. Because there are differences in interests, the proportions of village to country people in a rural community can be of real concern.

In general, the urban town (over 2,500) has two or three times the population found in the rural part of its community. Villages of more than 1,000 population have somewhat over half of the total population of the community, whereas the smaller villages have only one third or one fourth of the total. The trend in the country is toward larger units of service area, since in these larger communities the villages and towns do have the voting advantage. For example, the one-room school is traditionally a farmer's school, but the high school is a townsman's school. When the property in town lacks sufficient valuation to support a high school it is natural that consideration be given to including country property in the school district. If, then, a new high school district is proposed including both town and country property, the relative size of the town and country population is of real concern. If the country people outnumber the townspeople they can prevent the organization of the new district, but if the town has the most voters the country districts can be voted in whether they wish it or not. Some very serious cleavages can thus arise between town and country. In some states, therefore, the country people, through their organizations, are asking that the town and country votes be counted separately for such things as school reorganization.[14] Settling some issues of concern to both by counting votes separately may be a better method than enforcing the will of the townspeople upon the country folks.

Multi-Group Nature of the Community.—The average rural community is made up of a variety of groups and institutions. (See Figure 52.) In the first place, the area covered by a rural community usually takes in a number of neighborhoods. These neighborhoods can be discovered in the town center itself, as well as in

[13] See J. F. Thaden and Eben Mumford, *High School Communities in Michigan*, Special Bull. 298, Michigan State College Agr. Exp. Sta., 1938.
[14] A community unit school law passed by the Legislature in Illinois in 1947 provides for counting town and country votes separately.

the open-country areas. Within the community, also, and often extending beyond its boundaries, one can find "interest" groups—groups organized around special interests and thus being selective in their membership. Not everyone in the community belongs; some group members may come from one neighborhood and some from another. These interest groups provide a means of participation in

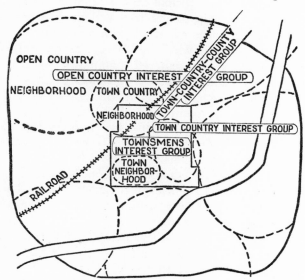

Figure 52. Schematic Diagram of the Interrelationships Between Neighborhood and Interest Groups in a Rural Community

Neighborhoods include everyone, whereas interest groups are selective.

the life of the community. What they—the service club, the woman's club, or the farmer's club—may do can vitally affect the life of the community.

It is significant also that some members of the community, often as many as one fourth to one half, do not belong to any of these interest groups. In general, more people in the town or village belong to some special-interest organization than do the people in the country part of the community. Thus the benefits that may accrue to all of the people of the community through the activities of special-interest groups must be indirect.

The best measure of socialization of the community is the degree of membership and participation in its various organizations. Likewise, the social control of the community is largely determined by the strength, influence, and cooperativeness of the individual groups composing it; that is, whether they have common standards and work together for community solidarity or are divisive in their influence.

Extent of Formal Organization.—Rural communities, of course, may vary greatly in the nature and extent of their functional organization. Some have no formal organization but depend on individual or group leadership to get things done in the community. The smaller (especially open-country) primary community may have a community organization which holds regular monthly meetings. In some of the larger village-centered communities service clubs and commercial clubs which include farmer members, and "ruritan" clubs, or groups going by the name of "community association," serve as the organization for the community. In others, the only functions performed on a community basis may be those carried out by high school boards, fire departments, or township or village boards. These are limited to specified functions.

A few communities have community councils which represent the various organizations and agencies in the community. They are too often limited by what the least willing or least cooperative group will allow for community improvement.

In most rural communities, therefore, any progress toward improvement is carried out on a functional basis; that is, when something is desired, such as a youth center, the matter is discussed informally and in groups. Committees are then set up to investigate and make plans, after which a campaign is put on to obtain general acceptance and support. The final step is to see the project through to completion.

The Complete-Service Rural Community.—To be complete, a community that provides essential services—trade, educational, religious, social, public utility and communication, and professional— for its families must be big enough to care adequately for all these interests. Yet it must be small enough to make it possible for community members to have personal contacts with those who locally administer the services, in order that they can have a voice in the way things are run. For such other services as health protection, hospital and medical care, library service, and care of the needy, it may be necessary for the community to cooperate with neighboring communities in setting up county or district systems of organization.

There are many smaller communities, of course, that provide some of these services: the village neighborhood may have its elementary school, a church, a general store, and a repair shop. The larger or intermediate service centers—those serving primarily agricultural areas—may have a few stores, an elementary or junior high school, a church or two, a meeting place, a bus stop or railroad station, and possibly a doctor. These neighborhoods and smaller communities are really a part of a larger complete-service community; the people use this larger community to satisfy many of their needs.

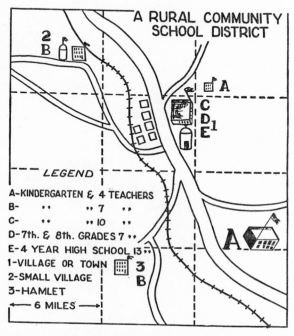

Figure 53. A Complete-Service Educational Organization for a Rural Community
(From *Schools for Wisconsin's Tomorrow,* Wisconsin State Department of Education, 1946)

The size of the complete-service community can be judged from an educational point of view, or from the point of view of several of the other services. Using education as an example, to be a complete-service community both elementary and high school services are needed. (See Figure 53.) The high school provides the key, but it must be considered only a part of a community school system in which the kindergarten, the elementary schools, and the high school are a part of a unified system. Its program to develop future citizens, prepare them for occupations, develop civic competence, and prepare for community life, must be related to community needs.

A four-year high school whose program is adequately related to community needs will require the services of from 12 to 14 teachers in addition to a principal or superintendent.[15] To offer such a program at reasonable cost requires a minimum of 20 pupils per teacher. Thus the four-year high school of our modern complete-service community should have at least 240 pupils. For rural areas little is gained if such a school exceeds 350 pupils, and many rural values would be lost if enrollments were greater than 500 pupils.

In a community of 240 pupils there would be about twice as many elementary pupils, or about 480 all told, making a total pupil population for the community of around 720. The average modern rural family would have about two children in school; if each family had a total of four persons, the complete-service rural community—town and country—would need a minimum population of 2,800 to 3,000 to provide for a good school system. In it there would be open-country, village, and smaller community centers for elementary and junior schools.

The town population of a rural community of this size usually makes up somewhat more than half the town-country community population. Consequently, the school community would have to have a town center of about 1,500 to 2,000 population, depending on the density of the farm population. If there is more than one town in the community, these, together with the open-country population, need a minimum of 2,800 people upon whom they can draw to provide adequate educational services. Such a community will also provide some specialization in trade. It will have a doctor and a dentist; it will support two or three churches; and it can be on good roads, with railroad and bus line outlets. It may have a library with some branches in the smaller villages, forming a part of a county or district system of library organization. Health protection can be provided for it by cooperating with other communities in the county for a county department of public health. Its needy should be taken care of by workers from a county department of public welfare. But wherever it cooperates with neighboring communities to provide these services, it should always have representation on policy-making bodies. Of such is the complete-service community in a democracy.

Rural Community Organization

Unifying Community Interests.—The increasing interdependence of town and country makes possible and desirable some attempt to work out principles of cooperation that will more clearly bind the in-

[15] *Education for Rural Wisconsin's Tomorrow,* Madison: State Dept. of Public Instruction, 1946.

terests of the two and unify life in the rural community. We have seen how the rural community serves as an area for the functioning of many types of rural organizations, agencies, and institutions. If the rural village-centered community is to be a social unit there must be better integration of country and village interests. We have already outlined the trend, and have shown that the village-centered community can be an effective unit for education, religion, trade, socialization, and recreation. In many communities these functions are performed by different groups having little relation to one another.

We have noted, also, how neighborhoods which are not near a village center tend to persist and remain active, and that those near or adjacent to a village tend to be assimilated into its life. A system of social organization which makes use of the neighborhood structure of the community can provide the kind of "full coverage" not possible otherwise. A good illustration of the use of the neighborhood structure of the community was the wartime neighborhood-community organization for carrying out various drives.[16]

Accommodation and Integration of Community Institutions.—It is possible to provide more closely-knit community life through its institutions.[17] For example, the schools of a community can be organized into a unified and integrated unit. Reorganization into larger administrative units is a step in that direction. To set up a unit system providing for a continuous program including elementary, secondary, and adult education will supply the basis for real community organization for education. Similar moves to secure co-operation or integration of religious functions can be carried on. The simplest procedure is to form a community interchurch council. More advanced systems are larger parishes and community churches.

The numerous interest organizations can be called together in some communities to help plan and carry out special enterprises, such as community festivals. A number of communities have successfully formed community councils to conduct programs of community improvement.

16 See the following studies by the BAE, USDA: Nat T. Frame, *Rushmore-Village-Centered Community in the Corn Belt in Wartime,* 1945; H. Otto Dahlke, *A Rural Community in Time of War,* 1945; A. H. Anderson, *The Rural Community and the War,* 1945; T. Wilson Longmore, *Watson, Arkansas,* 1945; Lawrence B. Ryall, *The Rural Community and the War,* 1945; E. J. Niederfrank, *The Massachusetts Hill Towns in Wartime,* 1945; Herbert Pryor and Theodore L. Vaughn, *A Rural Community in Wartime,* 1945; and *Wartime Influences in Jasper County, Illinois,* 1947.

17 See W. Russell Tylor, "The Process of Change from Neighborhood to Regional Organization and Its Effect on Rural Life," *Social Forces,* Vol. XVI, No. 4, May, 1938.

Frequently, intercommunity interaction is essential. For example, any successful plan of school district reorganization requires a certain degree of intercommunity cooperation. Too often there is conflict between communities over such things as bus routes or school district territory. The sensible plan is for adjacent communities to work together to provide the kind of accommodations that will insure all children in all communities a good education. This may mean in some cases that two or more communities will share one system of administration. State and Federal aid to rural areas make possible social facilities in the poorer areas on a par with those in the more fortunate areas. By removing conflicts over financial support, such aid induces people in neighboring communities to work together and furthers the process of accommodation.

Procedures in Community Organization

If the rural community is indeed the basic unit of social organization for rural life, then its concern must be to strive for adequacy of the services it provides. Because of its organizational structure—neighborhoods, interest groups, and basic institutions—there is the possibility of healthful interplay of professional leadership. Expansion can come in more effective integration and cooperation among the groups in the community and in more effective use of service agencies and organizations. Rural people can get almost anything they want if they have the wisdom and foresight to use their own leadership and the services of county, state, and national agencies in the interest of real community development. It is the feeling of those who have studied rural communities that they can become what the people in them are led to *want* them to become; the emphasis is placed both upon leadership and desire, for without either nothing much can be accomplished.

Functions.—The community can be made the modern unit for getting needed things done in rural life. Through integration and collective action, using the voluntary association of the people, many important functions can be performed. Some of the things that the people of a community, working together, can get done include:

1. Discover, develop, and train leadership under which the community can act.
2. Map the trade and social service area of the community and thus give it a visual identity in the minds of the people.

3. Analyze the needs of the community and work out plans to meet them.

4. Provide a way in which peoples' ideas can be used constructively in improving the life of the community.

5. Obtain social control by encouraging collective action for the common good and preserving the community from undesirable influences or conditions such as roadhouses, taverns, and other places of questionable amusement.

6. Get groups and organizations to work together to promote efficiency and avoid conflict and competition.

7. Cooperate with other communities to secure needed services.

Principles of Procedure.—One necessity in community organization is to recognize principles of procedure. If there are persons ready and anxious to improve conditions, recognition of operational principles will insure better results and prevent unwise efforts:

1. The people in the area, with the help of outside agencies, should determine local unit requirements in terms of population, finances needed, and area to be covered.

2. They then should take responsibility for support of the enterprise, seeking, if necessary, a wider equalization base, for there are needed services for which rural people require and merit county, state, and Federal support.

3. The people of the community must also take responsibility for, and ownership of, the enterprise.

Securing Community Action.—The next thing is to get action. The first essential is to awaken a recognition of the need, for a need may exist unrecognized and nothing be done about it. The matter may be discussed on street or road corners, or in meeting places of the community. Such preliminary discussion is desirable, but some individual or group must eventually take action. Discussion leading to action often takes place after studies have been made of the situation, and recommendations formulated for a course of action.

If the recommendations are for enterprises that command general public interest and afford enjoyment, they will arouse little conflict and are likely to succeed. Success will instill a sense of pride in common achievement and will likely result in a desire to take another step. But some projects may not be acceptable at first. To gain acceptance of these it is best to go slowly, provide widespread discussion, even make personal visits to secure better understanding and support, and finally obtain action through vote of the people or by common consent. In all of these steps constant, effective contact with service agencies—county, state, and Federal—is essential.

Importance of Community Leadership.—The leadership in any community enterprise is a decidedly important factor. Often the person who proposes a new idea must be willing to stay with it until it is accepted or rejected. He must secure the help of his own friends with whom he can discuss the idea, the help of other leaders in the community, and the help of outsiders such as county agents, from whom he can obtain inspiration and guidance.

If the new project arises in a group and no leader seems available to carry on, it may be desirable to choose one, and the final success of a venture may depend upon the wisdom of the choice. It may well be that the person who believes in the need for doing something about the matter is the one to select. The process of selection of leadership in a community must be a "group" process—names of prospective leaders can be proposed by a small group knowing the qualifications needed, and their judgment can be passed upon by the group initiating the project.

The role of the outside or professional leader is likewise important. If he is guided by the sentiment or "cautions" of the local leaders he can furnish excellent guidance and direction, possibly bringing with him a fund of techniques and factual materials. But a professional leader or outsider can "gum up the works" by assuming too much initiative or by hurrying the process. It is important that such leaders be accepted and that they inspire faith and confidence in what they bring to the group. Thus schoolmen, ministers, doctors, and lawyers, as well as county agents or state specialists, can be of great benefit in helping solve community problems. The local professional leaders in whom the people have confidence are in an excellent position to help bring outside leaders in and use them wisely and effectively in the local situation.

Criteria of a Community.—The rural community is an area in which people live together in association close enough to enable them to do *together* many things for themselves which will make their lives more wholesome and enjoyable. The effectiveness of the community arises not only from what it has or does for its individual or its family, but also from the part that the individual or the family takes in community life. If the individual's or the family's only participation is in the kinds of activities in which benefits or pleasures are received and nothing is given in return, this individual or family is a community liability. The same principle holds true for the special-interest and other groups in the community. A community in which but few people take part in its groups and organizations does not measure up to its possibilities.

The problem of measuring objectively the effectiveness of the community can be solved by the use of a system of scoring, in which scores are given at a particular time for the various services provided. Then later, perhaps at the end of the year, another scoring is made to check progress during the year. The effort in itself stimulates widespread participation, and thus helps to achieve the desired objectives.[18] The most commonly used method, however, is to study the effectiveness of particular services from time to time. A church survey may be carried on, for example, to find out who attend and participate regularly. Such a check up can be the basis for programs of improvement; without a follow up the chief value of the survey is lost.

Rural Community Self-Analysis.—Rural communities can improve if they will devise means for getting needs recognized, study these needs, make wise use of local and outside leadership and service agencies, and press for action by getting as many people and groups as possible to take part in solving the problems that arise. Practical demonstrations of community self-analysis have been and are being carried on in various parts of the country. A case in point is the project started in Illinois by the Bloomington *Daily Pantagraph,* in cooperation with the University of Illinois. This progressive newspaper recognized that "you cannot have a good social environment unless the business of the community is on a sound basis. Nor can the community prosper in a business way if the social facilities—those that have to do with education, religion, health, social welfare, and recreation—are not satisfactory." [19]

Recognizing, also, that rural communities are now going through great changes, particularly in standards of living and the need for specialized services, the project leaders asked this important question of the people in five central Illinois rural communities: "What do

18 See, for example, W. H. Stacy, *Tomorrow's Community,* Extension Service Circular 251, Iowa State College, 1940; Dwight Sanderson, *Locating the Rural Community,* Bull. 413, Cornell Extension Series, 1939; *Rural Communities of Wisconsin,* Circular 353, Extension Service of the College of Agr., Univ. of Wisconsin, 1945; and D. E. Lindstrom, *Knowing Your Community,* Rural Sociology Extension 81, Univ. of Illinois Ext. Service in Agr. and Home Econ., 1941.

19 *Your Community—Which Way?* Bloomington, Ill.: The Bloomington *Daily Pantagraph,* 1947.

you think your community needs to survive and prosper?" Steps in the program for the community betterment in these five communities were:

1. Arousing interest. Those in the community must be convinced of the need of a community betterment program. The first step is to appoint a community committee, usually called the Community Council. Such a committee is needed because no existing organization is likely to represent completely the various interests in the community.

2. Getting the facts. The next step is to find out what the present situation is in the community. What are the resources, both physical and human, of the community? What do local people think of the facilities and services now available to them? What about the labor supply? How well does the town satisfy the community's social needs? What additional services are needed?

3. Putting the program into action. The final test of any community-betterment program is action that will produce results. All the information is only a means to this end. The entire community should be behind this action.

The Community Council needs at least three separate committees: one to study local economic enterprises and how they may be expanded; another to examine the social facilities and services and see how they can be improved; and a third to deal with civic affairs and public activities.[20]

The project called first for an opinion survey of the communities. Three questionnaires, each with three questions, were sent to a representative sample of the families of the five communities. The first questionnaire covered economic interests, the second social interests, and the third civic interests. The questions asked on each questionnaire were (a) What criticisms do you have of present conditions? (b) What do you think needs to be done to improve them? and (c) What new enterprises or programs need to be brought into the community? The questionnaires were accompanied by a descriptive folder and were sent out by the community councils set up in each community. They were summarized by workers at the University of Illinois, and formed the basis for programs of action in the community.

Though this initial survey was considered to be only a beginning, almost immediate results were apparent in the five communities. Supervised summer playground programs, new businesses and industries, improvement in the administration of civic affairs, more

---

20 *Ibid.*, pp. 2-3.

adequate sewage disposal, the extension of fire protection to farm homes, expansion in the educational program with teachers hired for twelve months, illustrate the suggestions offered for consideration. Store fronts were painted, parks were cleared of rubbish, community recreation programs were worked out, new businesses were set up out of the resources of the community; many other advances are all concrete results of this initial survey. Two other communities have asked to be helped with the same sort of project, and one has already carried out the questionnaire program, adding a fourth section, that of improvement of agricultural relations.

The study and action that have followed through the community councils and committees have stimulated the various organizations of the communities to renewed action, and led to the formation of community clubs in two of them. (See Figure 50, page 175.) The people of these communities have found that they can organize, and can do something concrete, to make their home localities better places in which to live. The initiative or prime motivation must come from the communities, but they do need guidance and direction from outside sources. Universities and colleges of agriculture need to give more attention to helping rural communities take action to make their communities better places in which to live.

The Modern Role of the Rural Community

The bulk of the productive population of this country lives in rural communities. They are places of great potential employment possibilities, and are characterized by a greater predominance of the small owner-operator than can be found in the larger places. Modern, small communities can offer incomes and living attractions to those who wish to find pleasant places in which to live, superior in many respects to the larger centers.

Life in a rural community can be made, and should be made, as profitable, as delightful, and as worth-while, as life anywhere. The rural community is a most important area for the focusing of efforts to get action in the improvement of social and economic conditions of the people. Such action can be related to family, neighborhood, community, state, national, and even to international affairs.[21]

---

[21] *Rural Life in a Changing World,* Proceedings of the American Country Life Association, 1946, pp. 1, 2.

DISCUSSION

1. What does the term "rural community" mean to you? What developments have taken place to change the nature of the rural community from its original concept? Define the modern community; what elements determine community identity?
2. Discuss the nature of the social organization of the rural community. What types of groups are involved? What functions can be performed by rural community organization? Discuss the principles of procedure to get functions performed; how would they work out with respect to education?
3. What are the characteristics of a complete-service rural community? What roles in education are played by the smaller communities and neighborhoods within the complete-service community boundaries?
4. What is the process for securing community action? What must be the role of the initiator? Where does the outsider or professional leader fit in?
5. How can you measure the results of community action? What are the procedures for community self-analysis? What should be the various roles of the community council; what approach must be made to the groups already active and what part should they play in getting the job done?

READINGS

Brunner, Edmund deS., and Lorge, Irving. *Rural Trends in Depression Years.* New York: Columbia University Press, 1937, Ch. XIV.

Clark, Frederick P. *Your Home Town.* New Hampshire Planning and Development Commission, Concord, 1939.

Frame, Nat T. *Rushmore—Village-Centered Community in the Corn Belt in Wartime.* BAE, USDA, 1945.

Lindstrom, D. E. *Forces Affecting Participation of Farm People in Rural Organizations.* Bull. 423, Univ. of Illinois Agr. Exp. Sta., 1936.

Loomis, Clarence B. *The Principles of Community Organization.* Clayton, Georgia: The Rabun Press, 1944, Ch. V.

Morgan, Arthur E. *The Small Community.* New York: Harper & Bros., 1942, Ch. I and Part II.

Roberts, Roy W. "The Co-ordination of Community Activities for Educational Purposes." *Rural Schools for Tomorrow.* Yearbook of the Dept. of Rural Education. Washington: NEA, 1945.

Rural Communities of Wisconsin. Circular 353, Ext. Service of the College of Agr., Univ. of Wisconsin, 1945.

Sanderson, Dwight, and Polson, Robert A. *Rural Community Organizations.* New York: John Wiley & Sons, Inc., 1939, Chs. III, IV, VIII.

Should My Community Organize? Publication 241, Agr. Ext. Service, Univ. of Tennessee, 1940.

Your Community—Which Way? Bloomington, Ill.: *The Daily Pantagraph,* 1947.

Chapter 10

RURAL INTEREST GROUPS

We have seen rural group life as it is organized on a locality basis into neighborhoods and villages. Now let us look at the interest groups which affect the life of people in rural areas. These groups, in contrast to locality groups such as neighborhoods, are characterized by the interests they represent. Because they arise out of deliberate efforts on the part of like-minded individuals to get together, they are indeed selective, and cut across locality group lines. This was clearly shown by Figure 52, in the previous chapter. When people are brought together on the basis of congenial interests the tendency is for them to hold together and form a sort of "in-group" which keeps the group largely to its original members and excludes outsiders.

Rural interest groups may be roughly divided into common-interest groups which appeal to a variety of interests, such as a community club; and special-interest groups which appeal to a single, or at best two or three, interests, such as a women's or homemakers' club. Due to improved communication, special-interest groups have formed rapidly in rural areas, making it possible for people to seek their satisfactions in group arrangements of their own choice or design. The formation of such groups tends to break down neighborhood and even family group solidarity. They may take the leadership out of a neighborhood, leaving it relatively inactive. They may often divide the family group into segments with relatively unrelated interests.

Common-interest groups, on the other hand, often have a reintegrating influence. By their very nature they include everyone interested, and thus tend to minimize class differences. They may be said to be the result of a conscious effort to bring the people of a locality together, around common interests. But common-interest groups can have some of the characteristics of special-interest groups in that only the most socially inclined belong and take part. Common-interest groups, moreover, can be selective, such as a service club in a town. A service club does appeal to common interests, but only includes a select few in its membership.

AMERICAN RURAL LIFE

Characteristics of Rural Interest Groups

Formal Groups.—Interest groups in rural areas may be studied by name, affiliation, purpose, structure, interest, function, type of membership, and area served.

1. Name. Simply to count the different kinds of active interest groups in a community will reveal an astounding variety. One recent study, which merely listed the groups active in 622 Illinois townships, revealed 12,336 groups, an average of 19.8 groups per township. Among them were parent-teacher associations, farmers' clubs, 4-H clubs, homemakers' clubs, community clubs, cooperatives, spray rings, cow testing associations, shipping associations, and literary societies. The range in number was from a half dozen to over 75 per locality.[1]

2. Affiliation. More than half of the local groups in the Illinois study were affiliated with some parent group. Those affiliated with a parent group, for example, were local units of county, state, and national farmers' organizations.

3. Structure. Most interest groups have some form of officer and committee setup, although there are some which come into being under voluntary leadership, to do a special job. The more formal groups usually have an organizational framework providing for (a) administration, (b) record keeping, (c) care of finances, (d) program planning, and (e) care of special duties. Highly formalized groups have boards of directors and executive committees, who, elected by the members, sometimes assume policy-making duties. In some cases much of the work of the local group is administered by county, state, and national leaders.

4. Interests. The general interests which give rise to rural groups are chiefly social, educational, religious, or economic in nature. A composite classification of group interests, based on various studies,[2] follows:

Aesthetic: art, drama, music
Civic: community improvement, patriotic

---

[1] D. E. Lindstrom, "Changes in Rural Organizations in Illinois," Bull. 84, Univ. of Illinois, Dept. of Agr. Econ., 1942, pp. 288-291. See also *An Inventory of Voluntary Groups Participated in by Farm People in Illinois*, Rural Sociology Mimeograph 1, Univ. of Illinois Agr. Exp. Sta., 1931.

[2] J. H. Kolb and A. F. Wileden, *Special Interest Groups in Rural Society*, Research Bull. 84, Univ. of Wisconsin Agr. Exp. Sta., 1927; Edmund deS. Brunner and J. H. Kolb, *Rural Social Trends*, New York: McGraw-Hill Book Co., Inc., 1933, p. 242; Edmund deS. Brunner and Irving Lorge, *Rural Trends in Depression Years*, New York: Columbia University Press, 1937, Ch. IX; N. L. Sims, *Elements of Rural Sociology*, New York: Thomas Y. Crowell Co., 1940, p. 488.

Fraternal: lodge

Health: tuberculosis associations, medical societies

Home improvement: home demonstration, household science

Intergroup cooperation: councils, federations

Recreation: athletic, playground, dancing

Social enjoyment: card, fraternal, visiting

Social welfare: aid to needy, children's aid

Socio-economic: farm and business groups

Socio-educational: school improvement, library improvement, farmers' clubs, discussion groups

Socio-religious: church congregation, church clubs, church societies

Youth serving: 4-H, rural youth, Future Farmers of America, Scouts, etc.

Sometimes several of these interests were served by one group. Granges, for example, served fraternal, socio-educational, economic, and in a sense, religious interests.

5. Functions. The function of a group is best revealed by what it accomplishes. Some groups disseminate information, others carry on special projects, and still others provide social enjoyment. In general, interest groups in rural communities provide for civic improvement, economic improvement, educational advancement, health protection, religious improvement, and social enjoyment.[3] The functions often overlap. Many groups try to perform too great a variety of functions, and conflicts arise. It also happens, at times, that too few people are benefited and "ingroupism" results. A real task for leaders in community organization is to develop cooperative planning and to avoid such conflicts.

6. Types of membership. Most interest groups have membership requirements, the simplest of which is the payment of dues. Common-interest groups, such as community clubs, endeavor to get everyone interested in attending or taking part. But special-interest groups consciously or unconsciously set up membership qualifications which a prospective member must meet before he or she is asked to join. The common-interest groups are more democratic, but generally suffer more from lack of support. They are usually most successful in open-country areas; the larger the population center, the greater the tendency is to form special-interest groups.[4]

---

[3] See Sims, *op. cit.*, pp. 482-483, for his analysis of the functions of rural organizations.

[4] Dwight Sanderson and Robert A. Polson, *Rural Community Organization*, New York: John Wiley & Sons, Inc., 1939, Ch. VII; E. A. Wilson, *Community Clubs—Factors Essential for Success*, Circular 107, North Dakota Agr. Coll. Ext. Service, 1931; Fred Boyd, Merton Oyler, and W. D. Nichols, *Factors in the Success of Rural Organizations*, Bull. 364, Univ. of Kentucky Agr. Exp. Sta., 1936.

People's attitudes toward organizations vary with their experience. Those who take part in a number and variety of organizations generally have favorable attitudes toward them; those who take part in few or no organizations generally have unfavorable attitudes toward them. This relationship is graphically shown by Figure 54.

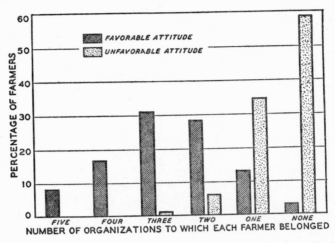

Figure 54. The Attitude of Members and Nonmembers Toward Business and Educational Organizations

(From D. E. Lindstrom, *Forces Affecting Participation of Farm People in Rural Organizations,* Bull. 423, Univ. of Illinois Agr. Exp. Sta., 1936)

7. Area. Many rural-interest groups—farmers' clubs, mothers' clubs, school community clubs, soil conservation discussion groups, etc.,—still function on a *neighborhood* basis. On this basis they usually coincide with the locality group because everyone is included. Such groups are very important in a democratic form of society.

The *community,* however, is the most important area of service. Except in the small, open-country community most groups which function in the community are selective. To find adequate leadership and to serve the members, farmers' organizations usually set up their local groups on a community rather than on a neighborhood basis.

County organizations seem to be developing rapidly, some on the basis of federations of locals, others on an individual membership basis such as rural youth groups or county farm bureaus. They can often depend on professional leadership, and most of them are tied to some overhead organization.

A few groups, like *regional* cooperatives, serve areas comprising two or three counties. Most are service organizations, as are the state or Federal organizations such as the Farm Bureau, the Grange, or Farmers' Union.

Some *state* and *national* organizations like the American Country Life Association have individual memberships, that is, any individual may become a member. Most state and national groups, however, are federations or associations of local groups.

Informal Groups.—Many interest groups have no formal organization; some of the most influential are the neighborhood visiting circles, birthday parties, political or social cliques, and gangs. Studies have shown that

> . . . (1) in the everyday life of a community, informal activities are more numerous and more frequent than the formal ones; (2) by reason of their number and frequency within classes of similar characteristics, they are of paramount importance in developing a feeling of fellowship and creating social bonds; (3) they not only operate within groups of similar characteristics, but cut across and connect the tough strands in the fabric of community life, permit joint action, and encourage enthusiasm for things of mutual interest; (4) as patterns of informality crystallize into customs they exert a tremendous influence on both group and individual behavior; and (5) patterns of informality tend to weaken or strengthen formal community life and thereby to determine the real character of a community.[5]

These patterns of informality may be nurtured in the community through frequent visiting—on the street corner, in stores, at amusement places, and wherever people gather and talk. Out of such visiting, cliques may form, which induce the formation of other cliques. In some instances cliques of young people may degenerate into youthful gangs.

Sometimes these informal groups are formed on the basis of social classes,[6] but more frequently they give rise to the formation of social classes in the community.[7] They provide intimate contacts which permit frequent visiting and interfamily rituals, such as having meals together or even in connection with intermarrying.[8] They profoundly affect the functioning of interest groups and community organizations. They are natural and inevitable. Their influence

---

[5] Leland B. Tate, "The Role of Informal Activities in Community Life," *American Sociological Review*, Vol. X, No. 2, April, 1945, pp. 159-160.

[6] See James West, *Plainville, U. S. A.*, New York: Columbia University Press, 1945, pp. 133-134.

[7] See Allison Davis and John Dollard, *Children of Bondage*, American Council on Education, 1940, p. 13.

[8] Dwight Sanderson, *Rural Sociology and Rural Social Organization*, New York: John Wiley & Sons, Inc., 1942, p. 553.

should be capitalized upon, perhaps by the formation of common-interest groups or community-wide functions such as the organization of a community school.

Organization Participation

Normally, four fifths of the heads of farm families take part in some type of organization. The opportunities to take part vary, of course, from community to community and from region to region

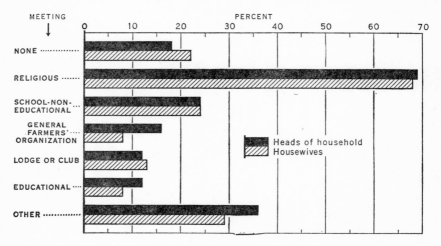

Figure 55. Percentage of Housewives and Heads of Farm Operator-House Operator Households Reporting Attendance at One or More Meetings of Specified Organizations During the Preceding Year, United States, April, 1945

Only religious meetings attracted more than one fourth of the farm people. (BAE, USDA)

in the United States.[9] The most frequent type of participation is in church activities; the second most frequent is in school functions such as athletic events, plays, and programs. (See Figure 55.) Fewer than one in six rural persons takes part in farm organizations activities, and fewer than one in eight is active in lodge or club functions.

Based on participation studies, Anderson has formulated some participation principles which are of significance to those who are interested in the effective functioning of a democratic society.[10]

[9] Edgar A. Schuler and Rachel Rowe Swiger, *Trends in Farm Family Levels and Standards of Living*, BAE, USDA, 1947, p. 21.
[10] W. A. Anderson, *Some Participation Principles*, Cornell Ext. Bull. 731, New York State Coll. of Agr., 1947.

1. It is axiomatic that successful organizations are those in which there is extensive participation by the members. People must first be given the opportunity to take part, and must then embrace the opportunity. This is the foundation principle of any successfully operating democratic group.

2. The limits of participation are seldom reached by rural people; a total of three organizations seems to be the practical upper limit for most people.

3. The individuals most likely to take part are members of families in which there is a high degree of participation. If wives take part, husbands usually do too, but not necessarily in the same organizations. If husbands take part, so do children. To secure individual participation, therefore, it is desirable to get family trust and support.

4. The first approach to family support is best made through wives and mothers. Wives, mothers, and daughters participate more than do sons, husbands, and fathers, in the order named.

5. Few families participate to the fullest possible extent. Full participation means taking leadership in community affairs, taking part in community organizations, and participating in informal social affairs of the community. Only one in ten rural families participates fully. (See Table 10.) Rural Community workers must seek to discover who are the nonparticipators, and direct group activities so that as many as possible potential participants can take part. Too much dependance can be put on the aggressive few.

TABLE 10. SELF-RATINGS OF 344 FARM FAMILIES IN OTSEGO COUNTY, NEW YORK, AS TO THEIR POSITION IN THE COMMUNITY RELATIVE TO SOCIAL PARTICIPATION *

Participation Factors	Per Cent Rating Selves in:			
	First Group	Second Group	Third Group	Fourth Group
Leadership in community affairs	6	8	17	69
Participation in community organizations	9	10	22	59
Participation in informal social affairs	9	29	36	26

* From W. A. Anderson, *Some Participating Principles,* Ithaca: Cornell Ext. Bull. 731, New York State Coll. of Agr., 1947.

6. Participation is related to social status. The groups to which a person belongs and the way in which he takes part in them help to determine his social status. The first effort, therefore, should be

directed toward getting people to take part in their own accepted group—the group in which they "feel at home."

'7. Participation is also related to feelings of inferiority and superiority. The opinion which a family has of its position in the community affects its cooperation. Hence respected leaders should encourage nonparticipating members to accept responsibilities which they can carry out successfully.

8. Participation in one organization stimulates participation in others. Nonparticipators who are brought to take part in one activity have taken the first step toward participation in other groups. The active participation by all families in some form of activity in the community should be the objective in order to approach the ideal in the operation of a democracy.

Principles of Interest Group Action

Any attempt to determine what it takes to make a common- or special-interest group function effectively must recognize, first of all, that every group has its ups and downs and is affected by changing conditions. A few basic principles, however, can be stated.

Most rural groups go through life cycles. The first stage is a period of stimulation, which is followed by a rapid rise in membership due to the popularity of the group. Then interest begins to wane and there is a rather long carry-on period. After a carry-on period there may be a period of decline when the original leadership lets go somewhat, which may lead to complete inactivity. Sometimes, however, the group gains new leadership and starts a gradual upward climb in popularity.

The principles guiding the operation of most organized interest groups can be stated. Observance of these principles will assure the successful operation of any organized group. Failure to observe one or more of them may mean the mediocre functioning of the group, or its possible failure.

1. Objectives or purposes. A clearly defined objective is, of course, the first essential for a successful organization. A group with a specific goal produces more and gives more satisfaction than the organization that drifts along on a haphazard course. The people concerned must feel the need of the organization and be willing to contribute to its operation. There must be a felt need for the organization; this felt need must be expressed in the aims or objectives.

2. Leadership. The officer and committee setup should be adequate. The leaders in a formally organized interest group are

usually responsible for (a) administration, (b) record keeping, (c) care of finances, (d) program planning, and (e) care of special duties. In some groups all of these functions are performed by two or three elected officers who may appoint committees from time to time to take over special duties. The most successful local organization is the one in which the leadership provides for a division of labor among the leaders and members. Effective executive officers are those who seek to train and to place responsibility on the membership. They appoint committees, outline their duties, aid them in their work, and secure reports from them on recommended action.

3. Program planning. The success or failure of an organization is often determined by the quality of its program and activities. The program should be planned to carry out the aims and purposes of the organization. Programs for meetings should be planned in advance and should have variety and balance to meet the varied needs and interests of members and potential members. The projects and activities are often the means by which the influence of the organization is felt in the community. They should be planned not only in terms of the membership needs but also in terms of what they contribute to community welfare.

4. Membership. The people enrolled as members should feel themselves a part of the organization, not only by receiving special benefits, but also by being given some responsibility in the organization. If members are to participate, a definite plan or policy of encouragement or of member assignment to roles or duties must be worked out. New members can be given simple tasks at first; as they take more responsibility they can share in the management of the organization. To permit a few leaders to monopolize the leadership and management functions will block opportunities for leadership development in the organization. All members should be given leadership opportunities and responsibilities.

5. Intergroup cooperation. The organization should always endeavor to cooperate with other groups and organizations working on common problems, or on problems of related needs. Basic to such intergroup cooperation is an awareness of local needs and how the various groups are meeting these needs. Overlapping memberships can be a means of helping bring better understanding and working relationships between groups.

6. Sensitivity to change. The organization and its leaders must be aware of social and economic changes and adapt the organization to those changes, even if this means a change in the purposes or objectives of the organization, or the merging of the work of the

organization into that of a new or different type of organization. Organizations can stand in the way of social progress by carrying on functions which have become outmoded or ineffective.

7. Use of service agencies. A system of secondary contacts assuring local groups of the benefit of service organizations and agencies is essential to the most successful functioning of these organizations. The system can take the form either of becoming a part of a larger organizational system, such as a national farmers' organization, or voluntary participation in conferences and services available from county, state, national, and international agencies, such as the Extension Service in Agriculture and Home Economics or the Food and Agriculture Organization of the United Nations.

The Leadership of Rural Groups

All forms of rural organizations, especially those operating on a voluntary basis, are primarily dependent for their success on the availability, type, and nature of local leadership. Churches, farmers' organizations, interest groups—all kinds of rural group life—are effective quite largely to the extent to which local leaders are available and are willing to support these groups.

Professional leaders are coming into rural areas in increasing numbers, especially on the county level. With the enlargement of the rural community to perform needed functions, other leaders than the pastor, the teacher, the doctor, and the lawyer, may appear at the community level. The effectiveness of the work of professional leaders, however, is largely dependent on the number and quality of local, volunteer leaders that they can get to work with them.

Definition of a Local Leader.—Leadership comes from group action or the need for group action. The leader's functions are to carry out specific duties in bringing needed information to the group, or to act administratively in the interest of the group. A leader is thought of, also, as one who develops new ideas for the use of the group. New ideas are generally a combination of old ideas, but persons who can form new ones are social inventors. Just as there are few true inventors in the physical field, so are there few true inventors in the social field. The ideas of social inventors are more slowly accepted than are those of inventors, say, of new machines. Social inventors must work against established social usage, which is even more deeply ingrained and more closely related to motives and prejudices than is resistance to new devices.

Primary reliance in a rural community is placed on the leader who is willing to do something for a group. Almost everyone in a rural group can at one time or another perform as a leader. An endeavor on the part of a group or community to spread its leadership functions to as many members as possible develops an excellent system of leadership training. To center leadership functions in the hands of a few will often mean that when those leaders leave the group it will cease functioning.

Functions of a Leader.—When a person becomes a group leader he must accept certain leadership roles. He becomes the group spokesman, who represents their ideas or decisions. Sometimes he must be the group harmonizer, who helps overcome frictions and differences of opinion. He is looked to as the group planner, who expresses that which he knows the group wants to do. By being chosen leader he is the group executive, and carries out policies and plans. If he is to be a leader he must be a group educator who, by keeping the group abreast of new developments and by urging acceptance of new ideas, brings about some form of group agreement. Such a leader is careful not to move faster in furtherance of the new idea than the group is willing to move.[11]

Leadership Development.—A true leader needs and must have the approval of the group; he cannot be a good leader without group sanction and support. It is often difficult to find a rural person who will take the responsibilities of leadership. To get him to accept, it is necessary to find an effective motivating force, such as satisfaction of personal needs, perception of common needs, personal initiative based on inspiration from an outside source, or a desire for recognition. The acceptance of a leadership function is usually tied to an emotional drive, a desire to keep a thing going, or to get a thing done.

The chief and probably most effective type of leadership training is by acquiring understanding of group processes and taking part in a group. In youth groups, more experienced youth and adult leaders can give help and guidance to group members who are keen to advance into leadership roles. A good leader should have the fundamental facts necessary to aid the interests of a particular group, plus the ability to handle the group and lead it in thinking through its own problems.[12] Many potential leaders are hesitant or reluctant

---

[11] Dwight Sanderson, *Leadership for Rural Life*, New York: Association Press, 1940, pp. 31-34.

[12] See D. E. Lindstrom, *Let's Talk It Over*, Circular 581, Univ. of Illinois Ext. Service in Agr. and Home Econ., 1944.

to assume leadership. That is why it is so important for schools, churches, and all youth groups to give widespread opportunities for leadership experience.

Opportunities for Training.—Numerous leader-training opportunities are now available. Public schools are holding night or part-time classes. Extension agents hold leader-training schools for a variety of purposes. County, district, and state training schools, conferences, and camps are numerous.

Much depends on the individual and his attitude. If he seeks training merely to benefit himself, the results will not be of much service to his group. But if he really wishes to train himself to be of value to his group and to his community he will have the interest of the group foremost in mind when securing training.

The Professional Leader.—In the rural community, professional leaders such as the pastor or the teacher can also play the role of volunteer leader. To do so is almost essential to being a good professional leader. However, a good professional leader will never deprive others who are really willing to assume responsibilities of leadership of a chance to gain the needed experience. A professional leader's most effective approach is through stimulating others to be leaders—to be a "leader behind the scenes." Working with and through his volunteer leaders, the professional leader can be a significant factor in the acceptance of new ideas and practices.

Professional leaders should endeavor to gain and hold a community point of view, and then be ever alert to possibilities of intergroup cooperation. Great things could come to rural communities if all pastors and teachers were to meet frequently to discuss matters of concern to the community. These local professional leaders should keep in close and cooperative touch with all county, state, and national service agencies; they can be of great help. The basic needs of the community can be served by these agencies if they are "discovered" by local people; and professional leaders can do much to bring their people to a realization of these needs.

Cooperation in the Community

Interest groups find their greatest field of usefulness in the rural community. Their influence in the community is greatly enhanced through their effective cooperation with other groups and institutions in the community. We have seen that church and school groups are the types in which most rural people participate. Much of the initiative for intergroup cooperation can come from the church and school leaders in the community.

Inventorying the Leadership.—The church has traditionally depended upon voluntary leaders. Most other voluntary groups in the community—farm organizations, lodges, women's clubs, farmers' clubs, etc.—also depend upon voluntary leaders. In some cases there is overlapping leadership, but usually each organization develops its own leaders. Too often the leaders in the various groups know each other only in a cursory fashion. If there is to be intergroup action some individual or group must take the initiative. The first practical step in securing intergroup cooperation is to develop a fellowship among the leaders of the interest groups.

Initiating Action.—The simplest approach to intergroup cooperation is for one group to initiate a project and then invite other groups to cooperate. For instance, the parent-teacher associations in many communities take responsibility for a health clinic. The project will be even more successful, however, if other groups are urged to cooperate so that all children are given attention. The task is not so much getting the examinations made as to follow through to see that corrections are made. Noncooperating groups can stand in the way of an effective follow-up.

Securing Council Action.—Interest groups do not provide full coverage in many communities. If full-fledged community action is desired, the approach must include locality groups as well as interest groups. The formation of a community council, formal or informal, would then require representation from both interest and locality groups. In taking action the council could pursue one of two courses: (a) operate through the existing organizations, if there are those willing and in position to take action; (b) take responsibility for carrying on the project. If no group is in position to take the initiative, the council may have to carry it on. Council groups in many communities have been responsible, for example, for initiating and carrying out projects for European relief.

Community councils are effective systems of intergroup cooperation if for no other reason than to provide a clearing house for the work of the various interest groups in the community. Councils in a number of rural communities take responsibility for organizing community calendars, so as to prevent conflict in dates and events in the community. They function, also, as a means of getting widespread discussion of issues of common concern, and thus to help crystallize public opinion.

DISCUSSION

1. What influence do the various types of interest groups have on the attitudes and activities of their members? Are they more, or less, cooperative in carrying on community activities? Discuss reasons for these attitudes and activities and how to improve them.
2. Select an interest group and analyze it to determine which principles of group action apply to it. In what ways is it ineffective? How can it be improved?
3. Examine the leadership of this group. To what extent do the leaders fulfill the functions of a leader? What types of leadership training are needed to make the work of these leaders more effective?
4. What is the procedure for getting the cooperation of the interest groups in the community in order to get needed jobs done, such as to improve the school system or to organize for the more adequate protection of the health of the people?

READINGS

Anderson, W. A. *Some Participation Principles.* Cornell Ext. Bull. 731, New York State Coll. of Agr., 1947.

Brunner, Edmund deS., and Lorge, Irving. *Rural Trends in Depression Years.* New York: Columbia University Press, 1937.

Kolb, J. H., and Wileden, A. F. *Special Interest Groups in Rural Society.* Res. Bull. 84, Univ. of Wisconsin Agr. Exp. Sta., 1937.

Lindstrom, D. E. *American Farmers' and Rural Organizations.* Champaign, Ill.: Garrard Press, 1948, Ch. III.

Sanderson, Dwight, and Polson, Robert A. *Rural Community Organization.* New York: John Wiley & Sons, 1939, Ch. VII.

West, James. *Plainville, U. S. A.* New York: Columbia University Press, 1945.

Chapter 11

FARMERS' ORGANIZATIONS

We have seen rural group life as it is organized on a locality and an interest basis in neighborhoods, villages, and communities. Now let us look at the county, state, and national organizations in which rural and especially farm people take part.[1]

General Service Organizations

In general, two types of farmers' organizations have developed: farmers' general organizations and farmers' cooperatives. Almost every rural community has been influenced by or is aware of the work of organizations such as the Grange, the Farm Bureau, and the Farmers' Union. Their origin and development are rooted deeply in the social and economic experience of farm people. Not so much is known of other forms, such as agricultural societies, fairs, and farmers' clubs, though these too have their influence on many rural communities.

Agricultural Societies and Fairs.—The modern agricultural society has developed into a breeders' association, a crop improvement association, or some similar semi-scientific group.[2] The first agricultural societies in this country, however, were patterned after the old English bodies, most of which were made up of gentlemen farmers. These societies held annual meetings and distributed scientific or descriptive papers on new agricultural practices. Because of their interest in new agricultural methods they were instrumental in the formation of state boards of agriculture, which later developed into state departments of agriculture. These influenced the organization of the U. S. Department of Agriculture.

Agricultural societies also sponsored local, county, state, and even national agricultural fairs, in which agricultural produce and stock were shown and through which some purchasing and selling of bred

---

[1] For a more extended discussion of the topics in this section see D. E. Lindstrom, *American Farmers' and Rural Organizations*, Champaign, Ill.: Garrard Press, 1948, Chs. 11-13.

[2] See *Farmers in a Changing World*, Yearbook of Agriculture, USDA, 1940, pp. 114-115.

stock took place. Two significant developments which resulted from these efforts were the widespread development of county and state fairs, and the organization, on a state and national basis, of specialized societies of horticulturists, breeders, seed improvement enthusiasts, beekeepers, etc. Even so, there are still many active local societies, especially in the eastern part of the United States.

Farmers' Clubs.—In many a neighborhood, on the other hand, farmers' clubs were formed to provide social and educational opportunities for the isolated farm families. They, too, were patterned after the local farmers' clubs of England, having regular meetings, officers, and a program.[3] Out of these clubs, where farmers could come together to discuss their mutual problems, came movements for redress of wrongs. Farmers' clubs in the Middle West, for example, were formed as early as 1846, and representatives from them came together in conventions, such as the Centralia, Illinois, Convention in 1858, which set forth a "Farmers Platform." [4] This platform called for more attention by organized farm groups to the superior importance of production, declared that secret cost marks should not be tolerated, asserted that agriculture and commerce can be considered identical only when each has a share in regulating trade, and asked for a national bureau to make an annual census of all national products and to collect and disseminate valuable seeds, plants, and facts.

Following the Civil War, conventions met to protest against unfair prices and railroad rates, to work for better market and transportation facilities, and to urge the formation of farmers' cooperatives. They were held through the years 1853 to 1873, mostly in the Middle West. They formed the nucleus out of which developed several farmers' movements of the period.[5]

The Grange.—The Grange, known by its members as the Patrons of Husbandry, is the oldest and most venerable of farmers' organizations in America. It was organized in 1867, soon after the Civil War, under the leadership of Oliver Hudson Kelly.[6] The first Grange was a group made up of officials and clerks in the various governmental departments at Washington who saw the need for an organization which could help farmers to break their isolation, make possible a concerted discussion of issues, provide a means of helping

---

[3] According to Jonathan Periam in *The Groundswell*, Chicago: N. D. Thompson & Co., 1874, p. 108.
[4] See *American Farmers' and Rural Organizations*, *op. cit.*, p. 73.
[5] Periam, *op. cit.*, p. 223.
[6] See *Farmers in a Changing World*, pp. 945-954.

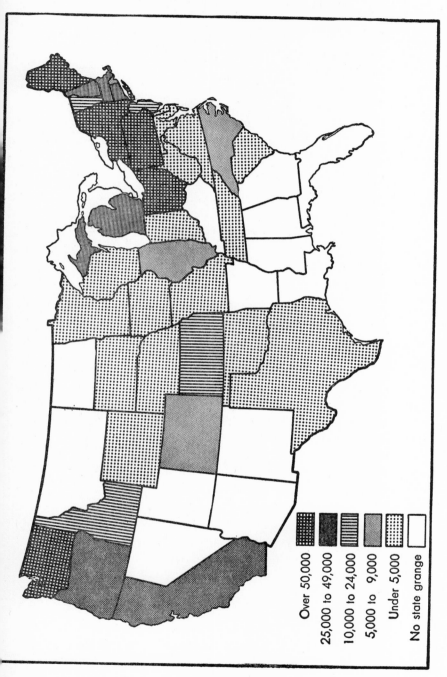

Figure 56. Grange Membership in the United States

Note the heavy concentration of membership in the Northeast and Northwest. (From D. E. Lindstrom, *American Farmers' and Rural Organizations*, p. 163)

Over 50,000
25,000 to 49,000
10,000 to 24,000
5,000 to 9,000
Under 5,000
No state grange

to reunite the North and South through an agricultural organization, and supply better opportunities for mutual aid among farmers. Kelly's group decided that the organization should be a secret, fraternal group, and patterned its ritual on that of the Masonic order.

The Grange soon spread to Ohio, Indiana, Illinois, Minnesota, and Iowa. Some Granges were organized in California, Oregon, and Washington. Today there are state Granges in thirty-seven states and in the District of Columbia. The bulk of its membership, about 800,000, is in New York, Ohio, Pennsylvania, Oregon, Washington, and the New England states.[7] (See Figure 56.)

1. Organization. The Grange has a uniform system of organization throughout the country. The basic unit is the subordinate Grange, which is a neighborhood or community group. Many of these subordinate Granges meet in their own halls. Each has its set of officers, including the master, overseer, secretary, lecturer, steward, chaplain, treasurer, and gatekeeper. The same general system of organization is used by the county, state, and national Granges. Opportunity is provided for participation by all members of the family through the ritual, the hour for discussions, talks, or entertainments, and the social hour.

Prospective members of local Granges are recommended by active members and are voted on in secret. In some groups one "black ball," or vote against a prospective member, will keep him out. Members of local Granges are carried through "degrees," as in any fraternal order, and may become members of the county, state, or national Grange by taking advanced degrees.

2. Functions. Throughout the years the Grange has supported agricultural experiment stations, rural free delivery of mail, agricultural extension service, vocational agriculture, agricultural adjustment but no "regimentation," as well as many other needs and programs. The work of the Grange is carried on through committees and in programs of the meetings. Resolutions can be framed by any member and submitted to the local, county, state, or national Grange. The Master's address constitutes the stand of the Grange on issues—local, state, and national.

The Farmers' Union.—The Farmers' Educational and Cooperative Union was organized at Point, Texas, in 1902. It followed in the wake of the Alliance Movement, which was most virile in the South, but which faded out with the failure of the Populist Revolt.

---

[7] *Journal of Proceedings*, National Grange, Springfield, Mass., 1947.

The Farmers' Union patterned its early organization somewhat on that of the Grange.[8]

1. History. The history of the Farmers' Union has been checkered. At one time (1907) it was reported to have a membership of 937,837, largely concentrated in the South and Southwest. But by the end of World War I, membership in the Farmers' Union had declined to its lowest point. In the 1920's and early 1930's the Union regained some strength by championing the McNary-Haugen Bill and the Domestic Allotment Act. In the Middle West direct action groups were formed out of some of the state groups "to strive against low prices by holding goods off the market," to incite farmers to carry on "penny sales," milk strikes, and marches on courthouses to prevent farm foreclosure sales. In other areas the Farmers' Union championed measures to scale down mortgages, to refinance indebtedness, to lower interest rates, and to set up moratoriums during the depression. Recent activities have included working for more family-size, owner-operated farms, the development of a modernized AAA with farmer-elected local, county, state, and national committees, supporting the United Nations Food and Agriculture Organization, and encouraging the organization of cooperatives on the Rochdale plan.

2. Organization. The Farmers' Union organization comprises local, county, state, and national units. A local must have ten or more male members; five or more locals may form a county union. Each local with ten or more members may have one delegate at the state convention. Youths between the ages of sixteen and twenty-one may belong if they are members of a dues-paying family. A national junior department holds camps and institutes for youth, conducts courses of instruction by mail, puts on national radio programs, and develops cooperatives among the youth.

3. Objectives. The Farmers' Union, always the most militant of the great farmers' organizations, has its own educational service to train its members in economics, production, and cooperatives. It favors farmer-owned cooperatives to carry each product through the processing stage to the ultimate consumer. It champions the cause of the low-income farmer. It has sponsored the formation of cooperative medical societies, and is sympathetic to organized labor and its program. The chief strength of the Farmers' Union is in the Plains states; its present membership is about 150,000. The membership in

---

[8] Gladys Talbott Edwards, *The Farmers' Union Triangle,* Farmers' Union Educational Service, Jamestown, N. D., 1941, pp. 18-21, 23.

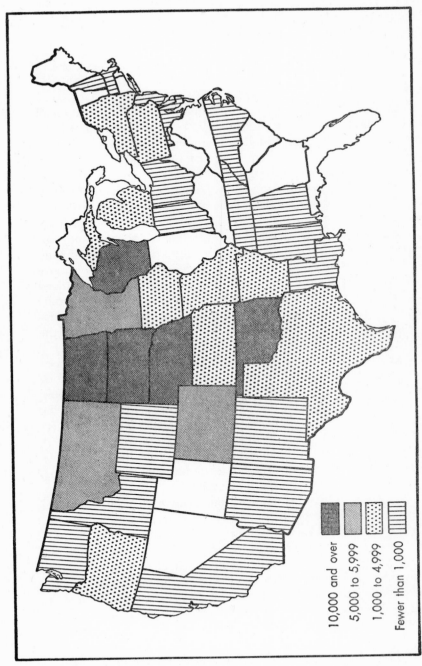

Figure 57. Farmers Union Members in 1946. (From D. E. Lindstrom, *American Farmers' and Rural Organizations*, p. 205)

The heaviest membership is in the Great Plains states.

10,000 and over

5,000 to 5,999

1,000 to 4,999

Fewer than 1,000

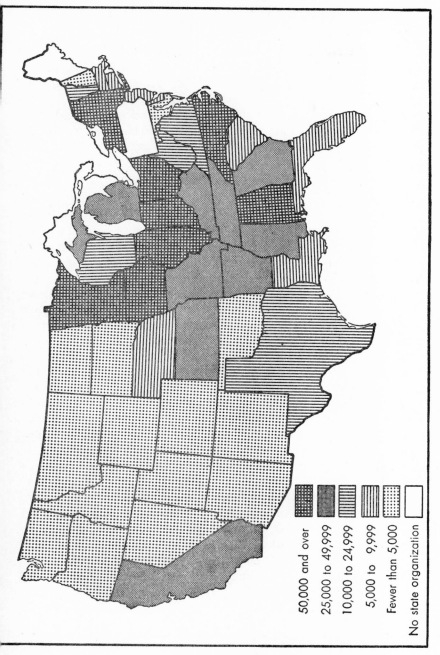

Figure 58. Membership in the American Farm Bureau Federation in 1946

The Midwest, California, and New York state have the bulk of the membership. (From D. E. Lindstrom, *American Farmers' and Rural Organizations*, p. 180)

50,000 and over

25,000 to 49,999

10,000 to 24,999

5,000 to 9,999

Fewer than 5,000

No state organization

its various sponsored cooperatives numbers approximately 300,000. (See Figure 57.)

The Farm Bureau.—The largest and most recently organized farmers' organization is the American Farm Bureau Federation, whose membership is now over 1,275,000. Membership usually includes but one member of the family, hence the Farm Bureau probably represents more than 1,000,000 farm families. (See Figure 58.) There are state Farm Bureau organizations in all states but Maine, Rhode Island, and Pennsylvania, and there is also an organization in Puerto Rico.

1. Origins. Unlike the other two national farmers' organizations, the Farm Bureau was organized in relatively prosperous times. County farm bureaus were first organized in 1911 and 1912, in the middle of the "golden age for agriculture," and the national organization was formed in 1919, in the prosperous times immediately following World War I. The chief membership strength of the AFBF is found in the rich Mississippi Valley.

County farm bureaus grew up with the extension service in the period 1914 to 1919. The first farm bureau organized was in Broome County, New York, in 1911, as a bureau of the local chamber of commerce. A county agent was hired to work for the farmers, on the theory that "farm and factory must prosper together." It was not until 1913, however, that the farmers of Broome County felt they must have a hand in directing the county agent's work, and formed a County Farm Bureau Association.[9] In the meantime, in 1912, county crop and soil associations were formed in Kankakee and DeKalb counties, Illinois, which later became Farm Bureaus. From that time on county farm bureaus in several states were organized with the help of extension workers to provide an organized means of carrying to farmers the results of experimentation. By 1915, two, and by 1917, four, state federations had been formed.

2. Objectives. The Farm Bureau has been called a middle-ground organization. Though this view has been refuted by its leaders, most people consider the Farm Bureau to be made up of the most prosperous farmers. Because of its emphasis upon economic matters, especially production and marketing, the Farm Bureau takes on the character of a man's organization, and tends to neglect the social and community phases of agriculture. Since it is geared to economic

---

[9] See O. M. Kile, *The Farm Bureau Movement*, New York: The Macmillan Co., 1921, pp. 60-93.

needs, it is sensitive to economic changes, and its membership totals fluctuate with changing economic conditions.

3. State and national organization. Unlike the other two groups, the Farm Bureau shows little uniformity in organization from state to state, or even from county to county. The basic unit of organization work is the county, though in many counties there are community or township units which have regular meetings.[10] Most state organizations are federations of county organizations. The national organization is a federation of state organizations. A state organization must have 500 members to become a member of the national organization. One voting and one nonvoting delegate to the national annual meeting can be selected by each county farm bureau which has at least 200 members or 20 per cent of the eligible farmers as members. There are also affiliate members of the AFBF, such as the Associated Women of the American Farm Bureau Federation. (See pages 217 ff.)

The great variation in organizational procedures from county to county and from state to state makes it difficult to describe the Farm Bureau's system of organization. In some counties the organization is run by a county board elected at the annual meeting of members from each township. In other counties all board members are elected at local meetings, the member of the board becoming the director of the local unit. Probably the greatest weakness of the Farm Bureau is its lack of uniformity in organization, especially on the community level.

4. Program. The Farm Bureau has given effective support to the work of experiment stations, has championed the cause of the extension service, and recently has made concerted efforts to improve relations between industry, labor, and agriculture. It has been a strong supporter of the AAA, international trade agreements, the United Nations Food and Agriculture Organization, the International Federation of Agricultural Producers, agricultural research, rural electrification, farm-to-market roads, etc. It has opposed the resettlement projects of the FSA, compulsory military training in peacetime, and extensive development of new lands.

For a number of years the national Farm Bureau maintained a Home and Community Department which encouraged the organization of local or community farm bureaus. A change was made by the formation of the Associated Women of the American Farm

---

[10] See abridgment of Clifford Gregory's "The Good Old Days," in *Farmers in a Changing World*, 1940 Yearbook of Agriculture, USDA, pp. 960-972.

Bureau, made up of state associations of farm and home bureaus, home demonstration councils, and societies of farm women, which had previously worked closely with the Farm Bureau. Although this organization meets annually with the men's organization, it formulates its own program and resolutions, dealing with the American home, the church, education, libraries, health, nutrition, safety, youth activities, military training, reconversion, and peace. The implementation of these programs lies in the hands of the various affiliated groups and in most states is carried on through county and township or community committees of the respective county and township or community Farm Bureaus.

Farm Bureaus are giving increasing attention to youth. In states in which formal agreements exist between the Farm Bureau and the Agricultural Extension Service the Farm Bureau sponsors 4-H club and older youth work. In other states the Farm Bureau has set up its own youth program and organization, chiefly to work with the youths who have finished school but who are not yet married.

Farm Bureaus in most states conduct or sponsor cooperatives. In some states the Farm Bureau encourages cooperative organizations, but sees to it that they have their own organization. In Illinois, for example, separate or affiliated cooperatives are formed, whose boards of directors interlock with those of the Farm Bureau. Only Farm Bureau members who become members of some of the cooperatives can get patronage dividends.

Of the three great farmers' organizations, the Farm Bureau seems to have been most active in encouraging cooperation among farmers' organizations, often taking the leadership in calling farm organization leaders together. Its policy seems to be to avoid conflicts with other farm groups, preferring to advertise and advance its own program rather than to disparage those of other groups.

The Inclusiveness of Farmers' Organizations.—A glance at Figure 59 will reveal that in many areas only a small percentage of farmers belong to any farmers' organization. A rough estimate of the total membership of all three major farmers' organizations shows that about 2,250,000 farm families are members, or approximately one family out of three. Except in a few areas, this percentage can be considered good. It is principally in those areas in which there is an active local unit that one finds the majority of farmers in the neighborhood or community are members of a farm organization.

Nevertheless, the three great farmers' organizations consider themselves the chief national and state organized voice of the farmer.

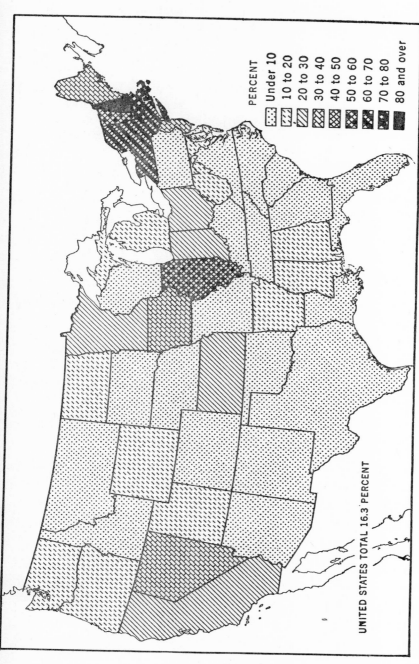

Figure 59. Percentage of the Rural-Farm Population Fourteen Years and Over (1940 Census) Who Were Members of Farmers' Organizations in 1943

The areas of greatest social and economic need are those with 10 per cent or less membership. (BAE, USDA)

The wishes of the members of these organizations are made known
in legislatures and in public by representatives of these organized
groups, and many decisions relative to national and state policies
affecting rural life have been guided by the attitudes and official
actions of these groups.

A farmer who is not a member of one of these organizations
obviously has little influence. Until the majority of farmers in a
county find a better means of exerting influence, these organizations
will continue to be the voice of agriculture. However, their effectiveness might well be increased in two ways:

1. Since the three farmers' organizations are somewhat regional
in membership, a form of comity can perhaps be worked out whereby
each is given the right of way in its own territory. This could be
accomplished by the formation of a strong national council.

2. Each organization could well strive for more complete membership, community by community, so that the majority rather than
the minority of farmers in the community would belong. Major
efforts would be necessary on the part of all three organizations to
develop active *community* organizations in their respective areas of
influence—if most farmers are to be reached.

Farmers' organizations are often most ineffective on the community level; other groups, such as the church and school, reach
more people. Hence, dependence for changes in rural life must be
placed on those social organizations and institutions which function
in every rural community and reach the majority of the people.

Farmers' Cooperative Organizations

The development of farmers' cooperatives is closely linked with
that of farmers' general organizations. Lest students and leaders
overlook the importance of the social and organizational aspects of
cooperatives, it is well to point out that economic cooperatives are
social organizations, for they function as groups and depend for
success largely on the loyalty and understanding of the cooperating
groups.[11]

From Mutual Aid to Marketing.—The earliest cooperatives in
Europe were formed for mutual aid and to help alleviate distress, and
in early pioneer America as trade work groups. Unlike European

---

[11] John Barton, *Co-operation: Principles, Philosophy, and History,* Univ. of Illinois,
Dept. of Agr. Econ., 1936 (mimeographed).

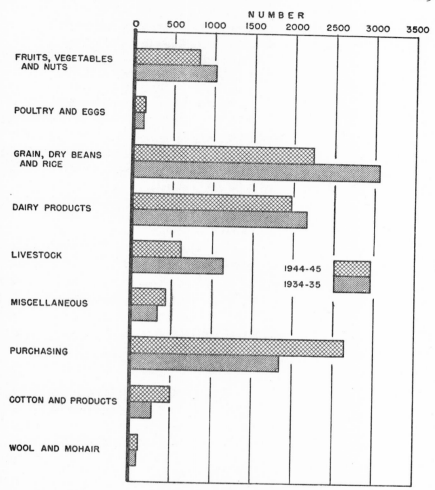

Figure 60. Number of Local Associations, by Specified Crops, for 1934-1935 and 1944-1945 Marketing Seasons

Greatest gains were for purchasing associations; greatest losses for marketing groups. (FCA, USDA)

cooperatives, which had considerable support from church leaders, farmers' cooperatives in America grew largely out of economic necessity. The first farmers' cooperatives which went beyond the trade work stage were designed to pool purchases of supplies, such as twine, sugar, etc. Eventually, some were expanded into farmers' stores. Most of these efforts failed because of poor management and bitter competition from private merchants. A few succeeded, however,

such as the Farmers' Union Cooperative Wholesale Society at Omaha,
Nebraska. Despite the advent of the marketing cooperatives, beginning with the fruitgrowers' cooperatives in the 1890's, by 1900
there were only 500 associations of all sorts.

Beginning in 1900, however, the number of grain, fruit, vegetable,
livestock, cotton, and tobacco marketing cooperatives began to grow.
With the development in the next three decades of favorable legislation, culminating in the Agricultural Marketing Act, the number of
associations grew to 12,000, with a membership of over 3,000,000.
In recent years the number of associations has dropped somewhat,
but the membership continues to grow, and now is said to exceed
4,500,000 members.

A significant change came again in the period 1930-1940 with
the increase in the number of production associations. Note in
Figure 60 the very large number of these associations, many of
which were sponsored by the Farm Security Administration.

From Folk Movement to Economic Enterprise.—Two trends
have marked the development of cooperatives: (1) a decline in the
number of marketing associations, and (2) an increase in the number of purchasing associations. The most numerous type, however,
is for marketing cotton, dairy products, fruits and vegetables, grain,
livestock, etc., though in recent years numerous "group service"
cooperatives have developed under the sponsorship of the Farm Security Administration.

In addition to marketing, purchasing, and machinery cooperatives,
there are an increasing number of service cooperatives, which provide for processing, warehouses, insurance, generating and distributing electricity, insurance and credit, medical and hospital service,
cold storage of foods, etc. Most cooperatives are now federated
and have expanded from neighborhood and community service groups
to county and regional associations. They are, therefore, much more
highly selective—the member usually looks upon the cooperative as
just another economic enterprise. Cooperation among farmers,
therefore, has grown in America from a folk movement to an economic enterprise.

Principles of Cooperative Organization.—The cooperative has
been recognized as an important way for farmers to meet their economic problems. The traditional principles guiding the cooperative
have been:

  1. Democratic control. A member has only one vote, irrespective
     of the number of shares he holds.

2. Limited returns on capital, and a limitation of the capital stock which one person can own.
3. Sharing benefits and savings in direct proportion to patronage.[12]

To these principles have been added others: unlimited membership; cash business; use of part of the savings for educational purposes; nonparticipation in political and religious affairs; union with other societies if necessary; producing goods and services that members need; and securing access to raw materials.

Some Limitations to Cooperation.—About 80 per cent of the farmers' cooperatives in the United States observe the one-man-one-vote principle. Most of them limit returns on capital, and most of them pay patronage dividends. Most of them, also, now suffer from indifference on the part of the individual member. Unless a big ballyhoo program is put on, only a few attend the annual meetings. Hence, increased attention is being given to the educational program to "keep the member sold on his cooperative." [13] Neighborhood and community discussion meetings on the cooperative have brought significant results. Perhaps in this way cooperation can again become a folk movement.

Rural Women's Organizations

Previous to the 20th century the conditions of women on the farm were given little concern by farmers' organizations, though the Grange included women in its membership on a par with men from its start in 1867. The first national concern for farm women's welfare came with the Theodore Roosevelt Country Life Commission, which in 1911 pointed out the various inconveniences farm women had to contend with and the need for educational systems to help them remedy these conditions.

When the Smith-Lever Act was passed in 1914, setting up the Agricultural Extension Service, it recognized the need for improving home as well as farm practices. By 1918 the movement for setting up organizations for rural women was well under way. The period 1918 to 1920 was one of great stimulus to the organization of farm women's groups because of World War I food needs.

---

[12] Ward E. Fetrow, *Three Principles of Agricultural Co-operation*, Circular E-24, Farm Credit Administration, 1940. See also Benson Y. Landis, *A Co-operative Economy*, New York: Association Press, 1943, p. 5.
[13] Homer L. Brinkley, *Problems of Educational Assistance Needed in Co-operative Marketing and Purchasing*, Official Yearbook, 1944, Vol. II, Washington: National Council of Farmers' Co-operatives, 1944.

Organizations for farm women have been developed (1) in connection with farmers' general organizations, (2) through adult educational agencies, such as the extension service, (3) by state or national women's organizations, and (4) as independent groups in the community. The most widespread forms are those arising out of farmers' organizations and through adult educational agencies, although women's clubs, garden or sewing clubs, and similar groups are the only types found in many rural communities.

Women's Groups in Farmers' Organizations.—No separate organization for women has been set up by the Grange. Within each Grange—local, state, or national—there is a home economics department or committee, which carries on projects such as securing finances to build or remodel Grange halls, developing student funds, exhibiting at fairs, aiding the sick and needy, giving canning and baking lessons and demonstrations, compiling cook books, serving hot lunches at schools, promoting music groups, aiding girls' 4-H club work, developing health centers, and sponsoring numerous community and social welfare projects. Women in Granges also carry on important "degree" work. They frequently have charge of juvenile Granges, and are represented on most of the functioning committees of the Grange.

The work of the Associated Women of the American Farm Bureau has already been mentioned. In addition to representation at the annual AFBF meeting, the association conducts public speaking contests, furnishes advisory service to the national Children's Bureau, provides material for local meetings, sponsors rural-urban conferences, develops support for adequate medical and hospital service for rural areas, etc. In some states the local Farm Bureaus, especially on the community level, are set up with women taking part and often assuming responsibility for carrying on the work.

The Farmers' Union has no separate organization for women. The women of a member's family who are over twenty-one years of age are referred to as honorary members. They vote, hold office, and take part in all of the work, especially in the local unions.

Women's Organizations Formed by the Extension Service.— Two types of organization have developed in connection with Home Economics Extension Service in the United States. One is an organization closely related to but independent of the Farm Bureau, called the Home Bureau. The other has relationship only to the Extension Service. Home Bureau groups have developed on much the same pattern in two states: Illinois and New York. In these states the women's extension groups were set up separately and as distinct from men's groups. In their early development they were organized with membership dues and responsibilities.

The educational work of the Extension Service is under the direction of a state Home Economics Extension representative and is accomplished through home advisers or home demonstration agents in each county. Local units are formed of from ten to forty farm and rural women in any county which signs up 300 or more members. Each unit president is a member of the county advisory committee. The county officers and executive committee or board members are elected at the annual county meeting. The county groups are organized into a state federation which meets annually, usually during farm and home week at the college of agriculture.[14] Details of organization vary from state to state.[15]

Home demonstration clubs are encouraged by the home demonstration agent in the county, so as to enable the agent to contact as large a number of rural women as possible. Most groups number from fifteen to twenty-five women, although some have as many as 150 women as members. Each group elects its officers and plans its programs. Committees are appointed as needed. There are no dues except as desired by the local group. With the community and neighborhood as the accepted unit of organization, all women interested are urged to take part. Countywide committees are set up and in some states countywide federations have developed. Some states have a state federation of home demonstration clubs. A very active national Home Demonstration Council has been organized, which holds national meetings fairly regularly. At one time these meetings were held in connection with those of the American Country Life Association.

Vocational home economics teachers in rural communities are now beginning to have group meetings with rural women. Out of some of these are growing local homemakers' clubs, which often bring together mother and daughter in a mutual project of value to the home. Sometimes these groups are part of, or cooperate with, groups developed in connection with agricultural vocational work, the two groups coming together in the same evening and devoting part of the evening to a joint session. Since the vocational teachers

---

[14] See Lita Bane, *The County Home Bureau in Illinois*, Circular 253, Ext. Serv. in Home Econ., Univ. of Illinois, 1940.
[15] See W. A. Anderson, *Farm Women in the Home Bureau*, Mimeographed Bull. 3, Cornell Univ. Agr. Exp. Sta., 1941.

are on the ground floor, so to speak, in the community, the possibilities of such groups are limited only by the vision of the teachers
and the leaders working with them.

International Organization.—Rural women's groups in America
have an international point of view. Joining with rural women's
organizations from other parts of the world, they have formed the
Associated Country Women of the World. This association was
made up of sixty-nine national, provincial, and state country women's
organizations from twenty-seven countries in 1937. The 1947 meeting was held in the Netherlands, and was attended by representatives
from more than 30 countries.

Rural women's groups have often been social emancipators; they,
more than the men's groups, have given a definite human and family
emphasis to work and life in the country. There is a tendency for
farm women's groups to be separated from men's organizations and
to become merely tolerated or to be relegated to second place. Where
women are on a par with men in rural organizations they should
participate equally in all discussions, even those allegedly of concern
only to men, for on the farm everything is of concern to all members
of the family.

Organization for Rural Youth

Youth organizations have always been important in rural life—as
a part of rural church programs, in the Grange as juvenile Granges,
in rural public schools, and in the Scout and Hi-Y movements, which,
though mostly town-centered, have been significant. But probably
the most extensive rural youth organization is the 4-H club, which
developed with the Agricultural Extension movement. More recently so-called "older youth" groups, usually going by the name
Rural Youth, have developed. Another national youth group of
significance is the youth section of the American Country Life Association, now named the Rural Youth of the United States. At
first, this organization drew together the rural youth or rural life club
representatives from colleges, especially teachers' colleges,[16] but it
later attracted other youth groups as well. 4-H club work has had
a phenomenal growth since its inception. More than 1,600,000 members in more than 75,000 clubs have been organized in all parts of
the United States and in a number of foreign countries.

---

[16] See Nelson Antrim Crawford, "Doc Smith and the Appleblossom Club," condensed
from *Household* in *Readers Digest*, May, 1945, pp. 45-48.

4-H Club Work.—The chief characteristics of 4-H club work are that (1) it is voluntary, for any youth between ten and twenty years of age can join; (2) it is educational—members "learn by doing" project work; and (3) it provides for social or group experience. The youthful members have their own organization, select their officers, and conduct their programs.

The work is conducted through voluntary adult local leaders. The group activities—club meetings, leader-training meetings, rally day meetings, achievement meetings, tours, and camps—are an essential part of 4-H club work. Figure 61 (page 222) illustrates the type of meetings in which leaders and members take part.

The core of 4-H club work is the project, which each youth must carry on. A member learns by doing things himself, under trained supervision. He or she not only learns the new practice but also demonstrates it to others, including his parents. The boys and girls, especially those liking farm work and life, have their belief in its worth strengthened, and their attitudes definitely improved toward the possibilities of farm life.[17]

Future Farmers.—The national Future Farmers organization was set up in 1928; in 20 years it has spread to 47 states, Hawaii, Puerto Rico, and to several foreign countries.[18] During World War II many departments were closed and the membership fell, but the postwar years have seen a renewal of its growth.

Future Farmers has many objectives. Perhaps the most important are (1) providing vocational education in agriculture in the public schools, (2) increasing interest in the intelligent choice of farming occupations, (3) nurturing a love of country life, (4) encouraging recreational and educational activities among students of vocational agriculture, (5) stimulating thrift, (6) encouraging cooperative efforts among students of vocational agriculture, (7) strengthening the confidence of the farm boy in himself and his work, (8) promoting scholarship among students of vocational agriculture, and (9) developing rural leadership.[19]

The national system of organization is made up of chartered state and local chapters in high schools having departments of vocational agriculture. Besides the regular membership of students enrolled in

---

[17] D. E. Lindstrom and W. M. Dawson, *Selectivity of 4-H Club Work*, and *Effects on Capability and Personal Character*, Bull. 426 and Bull. 451, Univ. of Illinois Agr. Exp. Sta., 1936 and 1939. See also, Mary Eva Duthie, *4-H Club Work in the Life of Rural Youth*, Committee on Boys' and Girls' Club Work, Chicago, 1935; Gertrude Warren, *Organization of 4-H Club Work*, Misc. Pub. 320, USDA, 1938.

[18] *Official Manual for Future Farmers of America*, Baltimore: The French-Bray Printing Co., 1945, p. 6.

[19] See D. E. Lindstrom, *American Farmers' and Rural Organizations, op. cit.*, p. 233.

the department's course, associate and honorary membership may
include young men out of school or taking part-time school work.
Their vocational teachers act as advisers, and state and national advisory members and boards are provided.

Programs are designed to supplement regular class work in helping
boys become established in farming. Regular meetings are held in
which the ritual is recited, business conducted, educational programs
are presented, and a social and recreational program is provided. In
addition, club activities include father-son banquets, community fairs,
sports, music, drama, and public speaking. State camps and conferences, and local, state, and national annual meetings are held.

Rural Youth.—Rural youth leaders, including those in the extension service, recognize that 4-H club work generally fails to keep
the interest of youths over sixteen. Leaders in the 4-H movement
recognize that the problems of the older youth are different from
those of youth in the younger ages, and recommend that special
provision be made for older youth.

Different systems of administration in various states have been
developed. Some states carry the work as part of rural sociology
extension; other states carry it as an extension of 4-H club work;
and still other states have appointed specialists in rural youth work.
Various names have been used: Utopia clubs, 4-H extension clubs,
rural life associations, older young people's groups, senior extension
clubs, young adult clubs, country life clubs, and rural youth groups.
Most groups have been set up on a countywide basis, having monthly
meetings, carrying on special projects, taking trips or tours, and
conducting drama, music, or sports festivals. Some were organized
on a larger community basis, with quarterly or annual county
meetings.

Chief emphasis at first was on programs built by the youth themselves with the help of an extension specialist. Some educational
programs deal with farm and home problems, personal adjustment,
problems of community life, and others with marketing, consumption,
and similar fields. Entertainment and recreation, providing for group
participation on the part of both sexes, are almost always included.
Folk games and dances, music and drama festivals, trips, tours, and
sports activities appeal particularly to these youth.

Collegiate Rural Youth.—The first Collegiate Rural Youth group
was organized by A. W. Nolan at the University of Illinois in 1913.
By 1922 an estimated 150 to 200 clubs were active at colleges and
normal schools of the country. They go by various names, including

Figure 61. A Club Leader Takes Over

Training of rural youth in the arts and techniques of leadership is an important part of 4-H club work.

Collegiate 4-H clubs, Student Granges, Campus Future Farmers, Rural Life clubs, Agricultural clubs, and by such designations as "Appleblossom," "Blue Shield," "Trailblazer," etc. Clubs are usually sponsored by the college rural education, rural sociology, or extension division.

Activities include regular meetings, special programs, extension trips to put on programs for rural groups, special studies, tours, maintenance of student loan funds, and delegations to state and national conferences. They aim to dignify rural life, promote an interest in it, and create the right attitude toward it.

Youth in Farmers' Organizations.—Each of the three farmers' organizations has programs for youth. The Grange has its Juvenile Grange for youth aged six to sixteen. In some areas it has youth committees to give young people over sixteen an important place in the program. The Farmers' Union has a very active youth program, as has been indicated. Farm Bureaus in some states have developed their programs in connection with the Agricultural Extension Service. In other states, as in Michigan, the State Farm Bureau has its own rural youth program.

Most farmers' organizations, moreover, cooperate with the Extension Service or other agencies in encouraging 4-H clubs, Future Farmers chapters, Boy Scouts, Campfire Girls, and similar youth groups.

Rural Youth Prospects.—Rural youth groups and programs can best be stimulated and maintained through adult group sponsorship, for the rural youth are a mobile group. Rarely do you find a rural youth member in the same organization more than two years. They move frequently from place to place and soon grow into adult work and marriage.

Numerous studies have been made of rural youth and their prospects. Brunner's study, for example, set forth five findings: (1) youth groups need adult interest and sponsorship, (2) youth are often able, once started, to take care of their own needs, especially social and recreational, (3) youth resources are largely an unused resource in rural communities, (4) cooperation and coordination between youth-serving and other agencies are essential, and (5) the local unit of any youth program should be the true neighborhood or community.[20] Beginning in 1940 a series of rural youth studies was made through the cooperation of the Division of Farm Population and

[20] Edmund deS. Brunner, *Working with Rural Youth*, Washington: American Council on Education, 1942, pp. 101-108.

Rural Welfare of the U. S. Department of Agriculture, the state colleges of agriculture, and local rural youth groups. These studies dealt with the present situation and the chief problems of rural youth.[21]

Among other findings, these studies showed a pattern of land operation by father and son whereby two or more supplementary tracts were operated several miles distant from the home place, a development made possible by rubber-tired equipment. Also, though their schooling for the most part did not go beyond the eighth grade, it was shown that young farmers and rural youth were eager for additional training but saw little opportunity for it in their localities. Moreover, most of them were interested in social and recreational opportunities but had few facilities for them in their communities. Finally, these studies indicated that though most of the youth were held to the status of farm helper or laborer on their home farms, they would grasp at an opportunity for their own farm enterprises or for partnerships with their parents.

Rural youth need better educational and social opportunities. They need educational opportunities which will more effectively fit them for modern agriculture and for group life in the country, and social opportunities which will enable them not only to come together in the community as out-of-school youth, but also to participate as young adults in adult groups. There is need for more effective programs for the young married couples, like those now provided by some rural church programs, designed to help such youth become established on farms in the community. Then, too, youth interests should have a larger place in rural community life. Most youth do not know how to work with and in groups, and too few amusements and programs, other than commercial ones, are available to them in the rural community.

Rural Organizations and the Community.—Although it would seem that rural people have enough voluntary organizations to do almost anything they desire, rural life still has many deficiencies. More intergroup cooperation is needed, and more rural people should

---

21 See, for example, *The Rural Youth of Ross County of Ohio,* Mimeographed Bull. 140, 141, 142, Ohio State Univ. Agr. Exp. Sta., 1941; Lynn Roberston, H. F. Ainsworth, W. V. Rusk, O. E. Baker, and Nat. T. Frame, *Rural Youth—Blackford County, Indiana.* The Agr. Exp. Station of Purdue and U.S.D.A., BAE, Cooperating, Lafayette, Ind., Dec. 1940. D. E. Lindstrom, et al., *Rural Youth in Wartime Illinois,* RSM-10, Univ. of Illinois Agr. Exp. Sta., 1942; Nat. T. Frame and Warren Schmidt, *Whither Rural Youth?,* Ohio State Univ. Agr. Exp. Sta., 1942; A. R. Mangus and Christopher E. Sower, *War and Migration of Rural Youth,* Mimeographed Bull. 149, Ohio State Univ. Agr. Exp. Sta., 1942; D. E. Lindstrom, *Wartime Movement of Rural Youth,* RSM-12, Univ. of Illinois Agr. Exp. Sta., 1943; D. E. Lindstrom, Nat. T. Frame and R. F. Eshleman, *Rural Youth War and Postwar Adjustments,* RSM-15, Univ. of Illinois Agr. Exp. Sta., 1944.

be included in the groups. More, not less, attention needs to be paid to the social as well as the economic needs of rural people.

The next few chapters will deal with the most significant rural community institutions—the church, the school, the library—and with the current programs for meeting basic needs of rural people. These institutions, like the groups already studied, are a part of rural community life, each group serving its purpose as best it can. All rural organizations, institutions, and service agencies, by working together more effectively, can better meet the basic social and economic needs of rural people. We must study these institutions in the light of what has already gone before if we are to understand how each can better play its part in the effort to improve life in the average rural community.

DISCUSSION

1. Compare the systems of organization of the Grange, the Farm Bureau, and the Farmers Union. What is the distinguishing mark of each? Compare the effectiveness of each in making contacts with the people of the rural community.
2. What have been the chief developments in cooperative marketing? What changes have come in the principles of operation of cooperative associations and in the extent to which they keep in contact with their members and the people of the community? How can present limitations of cooperative organization be overcome?
3. Discuss the work of the various farm women's organizations. Which seem most effective in serving the rank and file of farm women? What can be done to increase the effectiveness of their work?
4. Compare the organizational methods of 4-H clubs, Future Farmer organizations, and rural youth groups. In what ways can their work be made complementary? What significant role does each play for youth in the rural community?
5. Discuss the outlook for the work of interest groups in the rural community. Will they become more divisive, or are there evidences of their work being integrated in the interest of community welfare? How do farmers' organizations fit into the picture? How can their programs be more effectively integrated for community improvement?

READINGS

Bakken, H. H., and Schaars, M. A. *The Economics of Co-operative Marketing.* New York: McGraw-Hill Book Co., Inc., 1937, Ch. I.
Brunner, Edmund deS. *Working With Rural Youth.* Washington: American Council on Education, 1942.

Buck, S. J. *The Granger Movement.* Cambridge: Harvard University Press, 1913.

Edwards, Gladys Talbott. *The Farmers' Union Triangle.* Jamestown, N. D.: Farmers' Union Educational Service, 1941.

Hamlin, H. M. *The Community Program of Adult Education.* Champaign, Ill.: Stipes Publishing Co., 1943, pp. 95-97.

Hedges, Harold, et al. *Agricultural Co-operatives in the Postwar Period.* Inter-bureau Committee, USDA, July, 1945.

Hicks, John D. *The Populist Revolt.* Minneapolis: University of Minnesota Press, 1931, Ch. III.

Kile, O. M. *The Farm Bureau Movement.* New York: The Macmillan Co., 1921.

Landis, Benson Y. *A Co-operative Economy.* New York: Association Press, 1943, pp. 1-55.

Lindstrom, D. E. *American Farmers' and Rural Organizations.* Champaign, Ill.: Garrard Press, 1948, Chs. XI-XVIII.

Warren, Gertrude. *Organization of 4-H Club Work.* Misc. Pub. 320, USDA, 1938.

Chapter 12

THE RURAL CHURCH AND ITS SOCIAL PROBLEMS

The home and church are the two most important institutions in rural life. Home life in rural America has always been vitally affected by the church, its leadership and program, and by the kinds of social control exerted by them. Indeed, the rural church and its program are of concern to the entire church world.[1]

The Church as a Social Institution

A people's mode of religious worship can become an institution. You will recall we defined an institution as a people's accepted way of doing things. Hence, the church buildings and church activities are but symbols of the institution.

Obviously, because people are different, because they live in different environments and have different historical backgrounds, there are different kinds of religion, and therefore different institutions of worship. Wherever people go they either retain their mode of worship or develop new modes of worship. Hence, almost the first organization to appear in a new settlement is a church. Indeed, in the early period of our nation's history church bodies were frequently the instigators of new colonizations.

The New World Ideology Regarding the Church.—Many divisions have occurred in the Church since 100 A.D. One outstanding characteristic of American colonial settlement was the number of colonists who came here to gain freedom to worship in their own way, unhampered by state or other domination. When this nation was formed after the Revolutionary War that essential element of human freedom was preserved. Today we zealously guard our right to freedom of worship and insist upon complete organic separation of church and state. Because of this insistence upon complete separation of church and state and upon the freedom of any individual or

---

[1] See Patrick T. Quinlan, *Cities Must Look to the Land*, published by the National Catholic Rural Life Conference, undated, to show why the Catholic Church is concerned about rural welfare. See also D. E. Lindstrom, *Rural Life and the Church*, Champaign, Ill.: Garrard Press, 1946, for a more complete discussion of the social role of the church in rural life.

group to worship as he or it chooses, our national history has seen
a widespread growth of church bodies, denominations, and sects.
More than 250 sects and divisions have grown up. Of recent years
there has been some consolidation, as with the union of Northern
and Southern Methodists and the Methodist Protestants into one
church body. As we shall see, we can continue to have complete
separation of church and state and still cooperate on matters of concern to both.[2]

Rural areas in America were settled primarily by people of Protestant denominations, many of which were offshoots of groups which
had rebelled against the mother church in Europe. Others, such as
the Mormon church, grew up in the American environment. There
are great differences in creeds and practices among the various denominations of the Protestant churches.

The Roman Catholic Church has had its greatest strength in cities,
yet it has also had a remarkable growth in the rural, more sparsely
settled sections. However far apart these Catholic churches may be
located, they are all subject to the central authority in Rome and are
alike in their beliefs, teaching, observance, and practice.

Group Characteristics of the Rural Church

We can look upon the church as a local group of people coming
together more or less regularly for worship and to carry on other activities, as a particular denomination or sect which carries on a
specific form of worship and organization. We can also look upon
it as the institution in the matrix of our lives which stands for
spiritual values: the church universal.

Need for Common Objectives.—Never in history has there been
a time when cooperation among church groups everywhere has been
more needed than now. Cooperation is needed to bring their influences to bear, for example, upon the establishment of a world
order that will preserve peace. The primary role that can be played
by cooperating churches is to convince all men that our lives must
be lived in brotherliness, and that the undramatic production or
creation of good things for man's use accomplishes infinitely more, in
the long run, than the bitterness, destruction, and chaos of war.

Church Group Characteristics.—The local church has certain distinctive group characteristics.

---

2 See Arthur Morgan, *The Small Community*, New York: Harper & Bros., 1942, Ch.
XXIV.

1. In the first place, it is a voluntary organization; anyone who subscribes to its tenets may become a member.

2. Secondly, a local church is selective. Most churches will accept anyone who will subscribe to their beliefs and regulations. This makes the church, as a group, a selective influence to the extent that it bars those individuals who do not subscribe to its tenets. But there are other factors which make the church group a selective one. Some churches do not encourage racial groups to attend, and others are made up of only the socially elite. Most devout church leaders try to overcome such barriers, but nevertheless these conditions do characterize churches in many rural communities, especially the old, established Protestant churches.

3. Every church has its own membership requirements. When one becomes a member of a church he makes certain commitments which accord with its traditional beliefs or creed. Most churches do not have distinguishing marks for their members, though a few, such as certain of the Church of the Brethren or the Amish, require their people to dress in a certain way.

4. Each church has its own system of social control in its ritualism or observances, such as the form of baptism or the manner of taking communion. These forms may have great meaning for those who observe them, but they can be and often are barriers against inter-church cooperation, for they are sometimes of such significance that those of a particular creed feel "right" about participating in them, or even being present when the observances take place, only in the presence of their fellow-believers.

5. The members of a church group in rural, and especially open-country areas, are usually relatively homogeneous because most of them belong to the same social class even though they follow various occupations in the community. As the membership of the church enlarges, it becomes more heterogeneous and the less immediate is the responsibility of each individual member. The small church must rely on widespread membership participation to keep it going; those not coming or taking part are more easily missed. Though the church draws from a cross section of the occupational life of the community it nevertheless attracts like-minded people, whose religious beliefs are similar. Because of this the church as a group has a better opportunity to develop mutual interest and appreciation than almost any other group in the community.

6. The typical rural church group also exhibits multi-group aspects. Though the church group is made up of family membership, smaller age- and interest-groups invariably form within the church.

These, if effectively coordinated, can mean much to the success of the church program. In many rural, and especially open-country, churches the groups work together with considerable ease, for in them participation is a family affair. This is as it should be. But groups within the church can become self-centered and develop conflicts both within the church organization and with groups outside the church. When this happens some of the best leaders of the church may lose interest and turn to other forms of group life.

7. Each church group has its own system of organization. In some the pastor is the leader of most groups, or selects the leaders for the groups and acts as chairman of the official policy-making board of the church. In others, the various boards, committees, and other groups select their own leaders and determine their own policies. In still others, the congregation selects its pastor from among its own membership; the pastors of some groups thus selected are not paid.[3]

In general, the pastor is the interpreter of the Scriptures, adapting them to modern conditions affecting his people. He also administers the rites of the church such as baptism, communion, marriage, and burial ceremonies, and acts as the family counselor to whom the people go for advice on almost any problem of life. Of recent years the pastor has been expected to know something about social and economic issues and to be able to give ethical guidance to so-called secular groups and institutions in the community. To gain the confidence and be the all-round counselor of his people a pastor must have adequate training, an ability to work with people, and the opportunity to stay in one church over a period of years.

8. Almost every local church has organic relationships with an overhead body or denomination. In some groups this relationship exercises considerable influence over the local church, and may help or hinder it in working out cooperative relationships with other churches and groups in the community. In the past few years there has been an increasing amount of interdenominational cooperation, especially among Protestant denominations in rural areas. Inter-Protestant cooperation in setting up larger parishes, and even cooperation among certain denominations in establishing new, federated, or community churches is increasing.

------

[3] R. F. Eshleman and D. E. Lindstrom, *The Church of the Brethren in the Rural Community*, Rural Sociology Mimeograph 16, Univ. of Illinois Agr. Exp. Sta., 1945; and Hudson A. McNair and D. E. Lindstrom, *A Study of Presbyterian Churches in Illinois*, Rural Sociology Mimeograph 17, Univ. of Illinois Agr. Exp. Sta., 1946.

Changes in the Rural Church

Most Protestant denominations in the United States are still predominantly rural. Even the Catholic Church, which has most of its members in urban areas, has more than half of its churches in rural areas. But even in urban areas the influence of the rural church is significant, for studies have shown that a large percentage of the members of urban churches either were members of rural churches or came from families who lived in rural areas. Hence, urban churches must come to a realization of the need to help support rural churches.

Numbers of Churches.—Most of the churches of twelve major denominations, enrolling over 40,000,000 members according to the 1936 Religious Census, were located in rural areas. Of these twelve, the denominations having more than three fourths of their churches in rural areas were the Southern Baptist with 86.7 per cent, the Methodist with approximately 85.0 per cent, the American Lutheran Conference with 79.5 per cent, the Church of the Brethren with 76.1 per cent, and the United Brethren with 79.3 per cent. All of the other seven denominations had 55 per cent or more of their churches in rural areas. We recognize, of course, that the number of churches is not necessarily an indication of strength; for even though most of the churches are in rural areas, they include considerably less than half of the total church membership in the United States. Note in Figure 62 the large number of churches. The membership of village and especially country churches is small, as indicated in the explanation below the map. Nevertheless, the predominance of churches in rural areas is socially significant, for where there is an active church there is also a social group, and these groups in rural areas contribute an important human product to the rest of society.

The plight of the rural church is indicated, however, by the decline in the number of churches in rural areas, a decline which far exceeds that of the less vulnerable village church. This is true of almost all denominations. When an open-country church closes, some of its members inevitably seek transfer to the village church. Some members, however, do not and this means a net loss of membership in both country and village churches.[4] The preservation of strong country churches will be reflected in strong village and city churches.

---

[4] LeRoy J. Day, *What Makes a Church Vital?* New York: The American Baptist Home Mission Society, 1944, p. 3. See also Edmund deS. Brunner and Irving Lorge, *Rural Trends in Depression Years,* New York, Columbia University Press, 1937, p. 299.

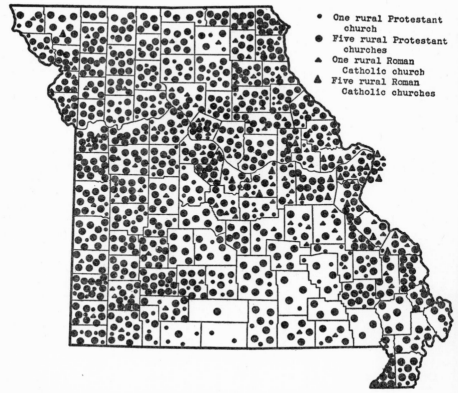

One rural Protestant
    church
Five rural Protestant
    churches
One rural Roman
    Catholic church
Five rural Roman
    Catholic churches

Figure 62. Location of 4,108 Churches in Missouri; 2,590 Rural Churches Averaged 107 Members per Church

(C. E. Lively and Ronald Almack, *Rural Social Agencies in Missouri*, Res. Bull. 307, Univ. of Missouri Agr. Exp. Sta., 1939)

Many of the rural churches which have closed were of the major Protestant denominational groups, such as Methodist and Presbyterian. The Lutheran, Church of the Brethren, Amish, and Mennonite, however, have gained somewhat in the number of village and open-country churches. The Catholic Church started in 1921 to build a rural church program, and the programs of the Amish and Dunkers are by their very nature rural-life centered. The open-country Lutheran rural church congregations of the Middle West are normally larger than those of other Protestant denominations, and their groups are in general more close-knit than others.

Members per Church.—The number of members per church in rural areas has increased, but this increase has not kept pace with the general increase in population (Table 11). As we have indicated, the increase came chiefly because of a shift in membership from the open-country church to the village church, but this shift has meant a smaller total of the families in rural areas in church, some areas dropping below one third of the total population.

TABLE 11. PERCENTAGE COMPARISONS, 1936 MEMBERSHIP OF
CHURCHES AND 1940 POPULATION, RURAL AND URBAN,
IN TEN SELECTED STATES *

State	Percentage the 1936 Urban Church Membership Was of the 1940 Urban Population	Percentage the 1936 Rural Church Membership Was of the 1940 Rural Population
Total 10 states	47	35
Minnesota	51	45
Iowa	46	40
North Dakota	56	47
South Dakota	43	43
Nebraska	48	39
Kansas	47	31
Indiana	46	32
Illinois	50	30
Michigan	41	20
Wisconsin	50	43

* From A. D. Mattson, *A Study of the Mid-West Churches of the Augustana Lutheran Synod,* Augustana Book Concern, 1944, p. 6.

Though most of our churches are in rural areas and most of the church members in the United States live in urban areas, yet five of the twelve major denominations, previously referred to, reported to the 1936 Religious Census that more than half of their members lived in rural areas. In order of percentage of rural members these were:

Church	Per Cent of Members Who Were Rural
Church of the Brethren	63.4
Southern Baptist Convention	62.1
American Lutheran Conference	56.3
Methodist	52.8
Negro Baptists	50.5

Six of the other seven groups had more than one fourth of their members in rural areas. Only the Catholic Church had fewer than one fourth of its members in rural areas.

The church is an important rural institution and the ideal is for everyone to belong to and take part in some church. A check of the relative memberships of churches in rural and urban areas will reveal how far short we are of achieving these goals. A study of 140 villages made by Brunner and his associates showed that only in the South were more than a third of the people counted as church members in 1936. Since Brunner made his study, Osmond has reported that of the approximately 26,000,000 rural people in fifteen Southern states less than 10,000,000 are church members.[5] In the Far West only 25.5 per cent were church members, according to the 1936 Religious Census.

Over-all gains have been made since 1936. In urban areas some 52 per cent of the people are now reported as church members; for rural areas the figure is probably a little over one third. An Iowa study, for instance, showed an over-all gain in rural church membership in ten denominations of 7 per cent from 1929-1931 to 1943-1945; the enrollment in Sunday school, however, was only 80 per cent in 1943-1945 of what it was 15 years earlier.[6] Forty-three of the larger Protestant denominations showed a combined rate of growth from 1926 to 1941-1942 of nearly 24 per cent; the Catholic Church had almost an identical growth. The Baptists gained 35 per cent, the Lutherans 27 per cent, the Methodists 19 per cent, and all Presbyterians about 9 per cent. A few of the largest denominations —notably the Presbyterian bodies and the Protestant Episcopal Church—failed to grow as rapidly as average church membership or as population during the 15-year period; and 48 of 132 smaller denominations actually lost members in the period.[7]

Attendance at Church.—Church membership does not necessarily mean church participation. In Brunner's village study one fifth of the members were reported as inactive in 1930. By 1936 the average membership in village churches was 171 members, and in the country, 93 members. According to this study, each member attended church on the average of 2.8 times in each month in 1936. A study of attendance in sample rural areas throughout the country reveals a falling off of more than one fifth in rural church attendance from 1930 to 1936, a decline three times more rapid than from 1926 to 1930.[8] A Virginia study showed that one out of four persons attended church and one out of seven attended Sunday School.[9] A study in Jasper County presents a high proportion of non-attenders to attenders of church in Jasper county. A study of the churches in 29 counties in North Mississippi concluded that "the average monthly attendance per person in rural areas for 1943, counting the whole

[5] "The School and the Changing Pattern of Country Life," *Report of the Southern Rural Life Council*, Nashville, Tenn.: George Peabody College, 1943, p. 48.
[6] H. Paul Douglass, *Some Iowa Rural Churches*, Des Moines: Iowa Interchurch Council and Iowa Christian Rural Fellowship, 1946.
[7] J. Frederick Dewhurst and Associates, *America's Needs and Resources*, New York: The Twentieth Century Fund, 1947, p. 333.
[8] Brunner and Lorge, *op. cit.*, p. 302-304.
[9] Douglas Ensminger and John S. Page, *A study of Rural Churches in Culpepper County, Virginia*, BAE, USDA, 1940 (mimeographed).

membership for those twelve years of age and above, was 46 per cent. That means that less than half the people attended church as much as once a month." [10]

Though membership in the Roman Catholic Church does not by any means depend upon regular attendance, nevertheless regularity of attendance is constantly insisted upon by the clergy and, as is natural, the standing of the communicant is to some degree dependent upon the regularity with which he attends Mass, goes to Confession, and partakes of Communion. As a consequence, most Roman Catholics attend church far more regularly than do most Protestants. If the same strictness regarding attendance were to apply in the Protestant denominations, the actual participating membership in Protestant rural churches would probably rise considerably. Something is wrong if, for the country as a whole, only a third of the population in rural areas were reported as church members, and only half of these were in regular attendance, which makes the participating rural church membership only about 15 per cent of the total rural population.

The Causes for Rural Church Decline

The quite universally recognized decline of the rural church is due to a number of reasons. Some of these were or are beyond the power of the churches to remedy; others are plainly attributable to neglect on the part of the church leadership.

Decline in Rural Population.—We have already seen that in normal or prosperous periods the rural-farm population tends to decline. In the 1920-1930 decade many rural areas lost from a third to half of their population. There was an increase in the rural populations in the years 1930-1935, and a slight increase in rural church membership in this period. From 1935-1945, however, there was a loss of from half to two thirds in the population of some school districts and townships. This decline in population inevitably carried with it a decline in rural church membership.

Increase in Tenancy.—It is well known that tenants move more often than do owners and that they do not participate in church nearly as much as do owners. A more highly mobile population in rural areas has added to the numbers who do not go to church. There may be a number of reasons for this, one of which certainly

---

[10] See W. A. Tyson, *White Harvest Fields*, Nashville: Methodist Publishing House, 1944, pp. 74-75.

is that when tenants move into a community which has no church of their chosen denomination, they may just stop going to church. The growth of tenancy has become of deep concern to an increasing number of church leaders.

Too Many Churches.—Much has been written, especially by social scientists, about the overchurched situation in the average rural community. This seemed to be the inevitable outcome of the early American mission policy that "where there is one of our faith, there also must we have a church." Distress came to many of the church groups when the population declined or changed. With old members moving out or dying off and new people of different faiths coming in, the situation became unbearable for the remaining members. The result has been that many of these churches have ceased to function, or have carried on with a pitifully inadequate program. Figure 63 (page 238) pictures the situation in one Illinois neighborhood.

Overconstruction.—The rural church has been hurt by the tendency to overbuild in a period of prosperity, leaving heavy bonded indebtedness for a declining membership to support. The afflicted church properties are allowed to deteriorate, and many stand idle or are sold at a loss.

Increase in Secular Groups.—Studies have shown the rapid growth of economic, social, and educational organizations in the last three decades. Many of them have developed as a result of outside stimulation, as was shown in the chapter on interest groups. These groups have offered real competition to the church programs in rural areas, even though the groups and their leaders have recognized the importance of the church in the community. Even more keen has been the competition of commercial amusements, such as Sunday night movies, so that church services have had to give way to them. The ease of travel for Sunday visiting and recreation also contributes to the difficulties of the church in rural areas.

Inadequate Leadership.—The policy of so many church bodies of assigning their best professional leaders to urban churches, and to train the professional church leadership for urban positions, has led to a decline in the quality of the church leadership in rural areas. The rural church is looked upon as a steppingstone to a better job in the city, and many theological seminaries still look upon the rural parish as a means to provide in-service training for urban churches. There has grown up a feeling among professional church leaders, therefore, that the man who must take a rural parish is to be pitied, and if he remains in the rural area from year to year he comes to be considered inferior. The result of this policy is that many rural people merely tolerate the minister they get, and remain at home rather than "endure" his sermon. This is especially true if their minister is a very young man who knows little about their special problems, or an old man who is just "waiting his time" serving in the country church.

Properly trained men would have something of an understanding of farmers' production, management, and marketing problems; would know of the findings of the experimental stations; would encourage the people in their communities to take part in extension programs; would know what the various Federal service agencies such as the Soil Conservation Service, Production and Marketing Administration, Farmers Home Administration, Rural Electrification Administration, and Farm Credit Administration, have to offer; and could talk intelligently about rural health, library, school, social welfare, recreation, and similar matters. They then can be strong spiritual leaders and rural people will have confidence in them because of their understanding of rural problems.

Numerous opportunities are open for training. The Conference on Cooperation between Colleges of Agriculture and Theological Seminaries has brought into being an excellent program of cooperation between these institutions. (1) A student going to a college of agriculture can take a pre-theological major giving him full credit for entry into several leading seminaries. (2) An increasing number of seminaries are giving courses in rural sociology and related fields, and some are holding summer schools for rural pastors, such as the Interdenominational School for Rural Leaders at Garrett Biblical Institute. (3) Summer and winter short courses are held at colleges of agriculture to give rural pastors the information and training they need to serve adequately their rural pastorates.[11] (4) County and regional rural pastors' conferences are increasing in number to give opportunities for acquaintance with agricultural leaders, both professional and lay, and agricultural programs in the county. (5) A wealth of materials is available, not only from church groups, but from agricultural agencies, on agricultural programs and their importance to the rural church.

Financing the pastor's salary, however, is only part of the task of adequately financing a church program in a rural community. Most active rural churches require an equal sum for other needs: building

---

[11] See list issued by the Committees on Town and Country, Home Missions Council, New York, 1948.

maintenance, heat, secretarial help, travel, books and pamphlets, home and foreign missions, etc. If there are enough families in each church group to provide the financial support, a rural church should not continue to be a "mission" church. Its chief financial support should come from its members, though some churches in poorer sections may need outside help for a time. Rural people will contribute freely to a church with good leadership but will give only grudgingly to a church with poor leadership.

Church financing must be planned on the basis of needs. Some church groups depend on the pledges made each year for the support of the church, working out a budget and going to the people to raise it. In others special enterprises are carried on, such as church picnics, bazaars, suppers, rummage sales, etc. Nationwide attention has been centered on the Lord's Acre Project developed by the Reverend Dumont Clark, who claims for it certain stewardship values which are impressive for adults as well as for children.[12] A few rural pastors can get part of their living from a small plot of land. Arguments for this practice, and an illustration of how one pastor carried on his work and farmed about 25 acres, are told by Russell Hoy.[13] By doing so he feels his family makes "our whole life a form of ministry . . . We are content to serve our little church indefinitely."

Inadequate Finances.—The total church income for the average village Protestant church in 140 villages in 1936 was $1,910. The Iowa study in 1946 reported that two fifths of the churches spent less than $2,500 per year for all purposes. In such cases more than half of the church budget goes to the pastor's salary. Even so, the salary is so low that it is difficult if not impossible for a minister and his family to have the kind of food, clothing, and various comforts that are in keeping with their position. Even in 1946 four fifths of the pastors, according to the Iowa study, were receiving a total for all church work of $2,500 or less.[14] On this income, which in many cases is less than that paid to school teachers, the rural pastor must rear and educate a family. The net income for living is further reduced because the rural pastor must have a car, for many of them have several churches. It is little wonder, then, that there is such a strong desire to move on the part of these men, and that the average number of years spent in one charge is pitiably small.

---

[12] See Clarence B. Gould, "The Lord's Acres," *Town and Country Church*, No. 16, March, 1945.

[13] "A Small Farm for the Pastor," *Town and Country Church*, No. 16, March, 1945.

[14] Douglass, *op. cit.*, pp. 26, 31.

Figure 63. Two Open-Country Churches, Side by Side

Such duplication results in ineffective leadership in both places and a loss of interest in religion.

Figure 64. The Interior of a Country Church Before and After Remodeling

Much of the work was donated. Now the congregation fills the church each Sunday.

Figure 65. A Modern Rural High School in the Corn Belt

Such a school can be the center of a 12-grade rural-life program of education. (Courtesy Illinois Education Association)

Efforts are also being made to increase salaries of rural pastors. The chief feature of present programs is to set a minimum salary, usually $1,500 to $2,000 for all pastors, and to assess the churches or pastors in a conference, district, or state to provide the fund to insure the minimum. Another approach is to pay all pastors the same basic salary irrespective of the field of service, and assign pastors to parishes on the basis of their qualifications to serve the needs of that particular parish.

The financial condition of rural churches becomes more acute as the church declines in membership; studies have shown that expenditures per church decrease as the number of churches per 1,000 population increases.[15] Inadequate finances greatly limit the program that can be provided, and many rural churches must depend on a visiting minister. The usual program in Protestant churches is to have weekly preaching services, preceded or followed by church Sunday School. Resident pastors can have much more elaborate programs, including men's, women's, and youth meetings, not only on Sunday but during the week. Programs of the more successful rural churches, however, cover more than the program of the church itself. As we will see later, the most successful rural churches are those which help build a total program, including, for example, not only the provision of religious services and training on Sunday, but also a weekday religious program. To be completely successful, this program must be in cooperation with other agencies such as the school.

There are, of course, many fine village and open-country church buildings. However, with the right kind of leadership the most drab and forbidding of buildings and interiors can be changed into attractive places of assembly and worship as is shown in the accompanying illustrations (Figure 64). If the church has carried on an effective program the people will support improvements willingly and, in depression times, sacrificially.

Churches Fail to Cooperate.—If the majority of rural people rather than the minority were to participate, probably all of the remaining rural churches would be needed. A deterrent influence, however, is the un-Christian and divisive influence of the lack of cooperation among the denominations with churches in the rural community.[16] The situation is most acute in overchurched small villages in which there may be from five to nine active or struggling churches. Recent efforts on the part of national and state denomina-

---

[15] Douglass, *op. cit.*, p. 32.

[16] See Eshleman and Lindstrom, *op. cit.*, for data on the Church of the Brethren, and McNair and Lindstrom, *op. cit.*, for data on the Presbyterian Church.

tional bodies to limit the granting of mission funds in areas in which there is evident competition and lack of adequate local support are to be commended. Another needed approach is for the church leaders in the communities themselves to work toward greater co-operation in the provision of trained leadership and effective pro-grams. Only thus can the majority of the rural people be induced to participate in church activities.[17]

Efforts to Strengthen the Rural Church

"The great spiritual needs of the country community just at present are higher personal and community ideals," stated the Theodore Roosevelt Country Life Commission in 1908. A nation's greatness cannot be measured entirely by its material resources, nor does the well-being of a people depend alone upon the abundance of things they possess. Any plans for building a better agriculture must include provisions for revitalizing the rural church.

National Rural Church Movements.—There are many encouraging signs. Several national rural church movements are under way. One of the first significant movements, which grew out of the first American Country Life Conference in 1919, was the organization of the National Catholic Rural Life Conference. Its "Manifesto on Rural Life" [18] was prophetic, for it placed chief emphasis upon the welfare of the family on the land and encouraged church participation in establishing an enduring farm and rural family life.

In 1943, the first National Convocation of the Church in Town and Country was called by the Committee on Town and Country of the Home Missions Council of the Federal Council of Churches of Christ in America. The 1947 Convocation, which attracted over 900 rural leaders, including some Catholics (it is significant that there has been an exchange of participants between the Catholic and the Protestant conferences) concerned itself with such matters as rural reconstruction, farm tenure, farm laborers and sharecroppers, the church and community agencies, the theological seminary and the rural church, the agricultural colleges and the rural church, rural church extension, financing the rural church, and rural religious education.[19]

Many national and state bodies are taking an interest in working

---

17 See Louis Bultena, "Rural Churches and Community Integration," *Rural Sociology*, Vol. IX, No. 3, September, 1944, p. 259.
18 Published by the Bruce Publishing Co., Milwaukee, 1939.
19 See *The Rural Church in These Moving Times*, New York: A Report of the National Convocation of the Church in Town and Country, Committee on Town and Country, Home Missions Council, 1947.

for a stable and secure farm and rural family. For example, the Grainger Homestead Project at Grainger, Iowa, gave encouragement to Catholic Land Associations to establish and develop Catholic communities by investing Catholic money in Catholic land projects.[20] Its interest goes beyond this, however, as is shown by its Manifesto. It is concerned with the farm family and its welfare, rural education, spiritual and secular youth interests, community life, rural leadership, rural health, rural social charity, the farm laborer, taxation, and rural credit.[21]

The Methodist Church is developing a nationwide rural church program which stresses the need for social security for the rural family. Leadership is now being taken by a Bishop's Committee of Six, and a national committee of the outstanding leaders in rural life, including the heads of the various church departments carrying on rural work. District, state, area, jurisdictional, and national conferences are being encouraged by this committee. The Methodists are also taking part in the establishment of farmers on the land, and in the development of a rural semi-professional leadership, called agricultural missionaries.

The Church of the Brethren is working for the family-type farm by encouraging rental-purchase payments, father-son partnerships, equitable forms of leasing, and, in cooperation with other groups, farm tenancy conferences.[22] The Jewish Agricultural Society was specifically organized to help Jewish people who wished to settle upon the land on farm units large enough to secure a decent living. Today Jews are represented in every branch of farming.[23]

Catholic, Protestant, and Jewish rural leaders have set forth a statement of principles underlying national, state, and individual actions.[24] The principles call attention: (1) to the stewardship aspect of land use "to enable the possessor to develop his personality, maintain a decent standard of living for his family, and fulfil his social obligation . . . to enrich the soil," (2) to the family as a primary institution and to the fact that "access to land and stewardship of land must be planned with the family unit in view," (3) to

[20] See L. G. Ligutti and J. C. Rawe, *Rural Roads to Security*, Milwaukee: Bruce Publishing Co., 1942, Ch. XI.

[21] See *Rural Life in a Peaceful World*, Des Moines, Iowa: National Catholic Rural Life Conference, 1944, p. 6.

[22] See I. W. Moomaw, *Rural Life Objectives of the Church of the Brethren*, Elgin, Ill.: The Brethren Publishing House, 1945.

[23] See Gabriel Davidson, *Our Jewish Farmers*, New York: L. B. Fischer Co., 1943. See also the *Annual Report of the Director*, New York: Jewish Agricultural Society, Inc., 1947.

[24] "Man's Relation to the Land," published by the Catholic Rural Life Conference, the National Town and Country Committee, and the Jewish Agricultural Society, cooperating. Available also from the Christian Rural Fellowship, New York.

efficiency in land use judged by spiritual, social, and material values that "redound therefrom to person, family, and society," and (4) to the rights and duties of the tillers "to the fruits of their toil and for a decent standard of living" and "to receive their just shares of the economic, social, and religious benefits in organized society."

Church cooperation in the community implies church cooperation on other bases as well. Here, again, significant results are being attained.

1. The simplest type of cooperation is that which will give church leaders a picture of the church membership of the community. A wide-awake pastor will have as his first task in a new community the location on a map of his members in the community. To get a composite map made by having all pastors work together should not be difficult. This should be done on an interfaith basis and to show not only active members by denomination, but by church preference as well. Then recruitment programs for getting people to become members of the church of their choice can be more effectively carried on.

2. Some denominations are developing larger parishes, in which eight or ten churches over a larger territory cooperate in developing programs. In some cases it is a group ministry plan in which there is interchurch cooperation in a natural area. Or it may be extended so as to provide a supervisor, a system of pastor and layman training, and an effort to provide some such specialized training as is being provided by the Illinois Synod of the Presbyterian Church in several areas of the state. Some denominations are working on training centers in rural areas, such as Merom Institute, Indiana, which also became the supervisory center for church activities in the rural areas of the surrounding region. The "Family-Community Project" at Addison, Michigan, is also a significant experiment.

3. The larger parish plan may also be interdenominational, organized through a larger parish council and a larger parish staff to serve the people of the area with a diversified ministry.

4. Numerous denominational and interdenominational efforts are resulting in some consolidation of rural churches. Among these are denominational community churches, denominational united churches, and undenominational rural churches in which each denomination keeps its organizational identity, though cooperating in services. Some are affiliated churches which combine the characteristics of the undenominational or the denominational united church.[25]

25 See A. D. Mattson, *Midwest Rural Churches*, Rock Island, Ill.: Augustana Book Concern, 1943; Ralph Williamson, et al., *Are Federated Churches Succeeding?*, Ithaca, N. Y.:

Cooperative efforts can be developed in any community which has the will to do something about the situation. Protestants and Catholics in many communities are now cooperating on weekday programs of religious education for children which are financed and staffed by the churches. In a number of communities a majority of the children of certain ages are enrolled in such classes. Summer programs of religious training and recreation are a regular part of the interchurch work of many communities. Union services and joint meetings are encouraged. Community and youth recreation centers and programs of year-round nature are sponsored.

The most effective way to secure such cooperation is to organize a church council in the community. The council should be made up of a group of people chosen by the different organizations of the church to represent them in a committee. The committees from all churches should meet monthly to plan and administer projects having to do with the cooperative church program.[26]

A third significant service to the rural church has been the National Christian Rural Fellowship, whose chief contribution has been the issuing of some of the best available bulletin literature dealing with rural church welfare.[27] In addition, this organization has stimulated the formation of state and denominational fellowships which have meant much to the improvement of the programs of rural churches.

A fourth recent development is the formation of a national Lutheran office for rural work. This has been an outgrowth of the National Lutheran Council, representing most of the Lutheran bodies of the country.

A Good Rural Church Program.—The most important task of a functioning rural church is the development of a complete program of religious education. The elements in such a program are (1) a church school that is in session every Sunday, (2) an annual vacation Bible School, (3) a program of adult education that operates both through Sunday school and weekday programs, (4) weekday religious instruction, and (5) a religious instruction course.[28]

It is obvious that such a program requires the attention of full-time, professionally trained leadership. If it is to embrace promotion

Rural Church Institute, 1945; Ralph Felton, *Local Church Cooperation in the United States,* New York: Town and Country Department Board of Home Missions, Congregational and Christian Churches, undated.

[26] K. A. Roadermel, *Town and Country Church,* Home Missions Council, New York, January, 1945.

[27] See *List of Publications,* The Christian Rural Fellowship, New York.

[28] See the *Proceedings of the American Country Life Association,* 1944, pp. 77-79; and the 1946 *Proceedings,* pp. 61-95.

of family religion, foreign and home missionary education, and develop a sufficient number of organizations to meet the needs of the young people of various age groups, as is also recommended, a specialized leadership is desirable. Advances are being made in the development of community programs for the religious life of the people in rural areas. But a great deal of educational work is still necessary if this goal is really to be achieved. Recognizing that many rural churches cannot undertake such a program, the American Country Life Association Committee suggested that wherever this proves to be the case, "the various churches in the community consider some sort of cooperative effort to do so. . . . Recognizing the principle of complete separation of church and state, it is nevertheless desirable that plans for cooperation between churches and public schools be developed for religious instruction of children and youth." [29]

A Church-Community Approach.—The church occupies a unique position in the community. It can be, as it historically has been, an initiator of many of the fine movements to improve the secular life of the people of the community. The program of the extension department of St. Francis University in Antigonish, N. S., Canada, significantly illustrates what has been and can be done through cooperatives to raise the living levels of the people.[30] The work of the Big Lick Presbyterian Church in remolding the lives of the people of its parish is another significant social experiment.[31] Many other illustrations could be cited of the work of the church in changing the economic and social conditions of the people of the community. This is a vital part of the program of the rural church.

Some of the more obvious of the church's secular responsibilities have been set forth by a noteworthy Wisconsin statement: (1) joining in a community-wide voluntary survey concerning church preferences, followed by denominational and interdenominational programs; (2) arranging for released time from regular school-studies for weekday religious instruction; (3) participation with other social institutions and agencies in community councils, harvest festivals, health clinics, discussion forums, and dedication exercises; (4) supporting worthy projects, such as parks, playgrounds, or other civic improvements; (5) assisting with citizen survey committees in studying local social and economic problems; (6) promoting local

29 1944 *Proceedings*, p. 79.
30 See M. M. Coady, *The Significance of the Cooperative Movement*, Chicago: The Co-operative League of the U. S. A., 1945.
31 See Ralph A. Felton, "The Church at the Center," *The Progressive Farmer*, December, 1943.

interest and understanding of county, state, or national programs which may be of benefit to the community and its people; and (7) helping to maintain moral standards and law enforcement, speaking out against intolerances, injustices, and hidden or flagrant wrongs.[32]

Such a church-community approach will require first of all the formation of a community-church fellowship of the pastors and lay-men of the community. The same principles of procedure in community organization that were discussed in Chapter 9 would then apply. The professional leadership of the church, especially the pastor, should have the training and the incentive to lead in carrying out desired community programs. Usually he will not find it difficult to interest other leaders, especially if he has had the right kind of specialized training for community life in theological seminaries, teachers' colleges, and colleges of agriculture.

The church in the rural community can be, should be, and must be an effective institution in the development of a better rural life. It should tie the people to the community, giving men and women a feeling of happiness and satisfaction in what they are doing and where they are going. The church has a great opportunity and responsibility for leadership in getting people to work together for community welfare, for by developing an effective interchurch fellowship many things seemingly impossible can come to fruition.

The Rural Church and World Peace

O. E. Baker includes among rural values a recognition of the divine in man and the necessity for peace if we are to promote public welfare, protect life and property, and see the growth of freedom and service.[33] World peace must establish in principle, and seek to achieve in practice, the right of individuals everywhere to religious and intellectual liberty. The task ahead for the church is a monumental one. Since more than three fourths of the world's people are rural, it must seek to improve rural church life everywhere in the world. If it is to be effective in building rural and open-country churches throughout the world, especially in areas of great economic, social, and spiritual stress, it must minister to all of the rural-life interests of the people.

---

[32] *Rural Communities of Wisconsin*, Madison: Cir. 353, Ext. Ser. of the Coll. of Agr., Univ. of Wisconsin, 1945, p. 15. See also Rockwell C. Smith, *The Church in Our Town*, New York: Abingdon-Cokesbury Press, 1945, pp. 143-156.
[33] O. E. Baker, Ralph Borsodi, and M. L. Wilson, *Agriculture in Modern Life*, New York: Harper & Bros., 1939, p. 181.

DISCUSSION

1. What evidences can you find regarding the place of religion in the culture of rural people?
2. Analyze the reasons for rural church decline. Which seem to be subject to solution by the people of the community? Which need the help of outside forces?
3. Check the program of a typical rural church. What elements need strengthening?
4. What are the opportunities and possibilities for church cooperation in the average rural community?
5. Study the various methods and opportunities for religious education. What should be the contents of such a program in the rural community? How can it be carried out in the community?
6. What are the elements in a desirable policy for the strengthening of the church in rural areas? Discuss what you consider to be the role of the church in the rural community of the future.

READINGS

The Christian Mission Among Rural People, A Group Study. New York: The Christian Rural Fellowship, 1946.

Davidson, Gabriel. *Our Jewish Farmers.* New York: L. B. Fischer Co., 1943, Ch. VI.

Dawber, Mark A. *Rebuilding Rural America.* New York: Friendship Press, 1937.

Douglass, H. Paul. *Some Iowa Rural Churches.* Des Moines: Iowa Interchurch Council, 1947.

Felton, Ralph A. *Local Church Co-operation in Rural Areas.* New York: Town and Country Department, Congregational and Christian Churches, undated.

Lindstrom, D. E. *Rural Life and the Church.* Champaign, Ill.: Garrard Press, 1946.

Manifesto on Rural Life. Milwaukee: Bruce Publishing Co., 1939, Part I.

Morgan, Arthur E. *The Small Community.* New York: Harper & Bros., 1942, Ch. XXIV.

Randolph, H. S. *A Manual for Town and Country Churches.* New York: Board of Missions of the Presbyterian Church of the United States of America, 1945, Chs. VII, XIV.

Sanderson, Dwight. *Rural Sociology and Rural Social Organization.* New York: John Wiley & Sons, Inc., 1942, Ch. XV.

Smith, Rockwell C. *The Church in Our Town.* New York: Abingdon-Cokesbury Press, 1945, Chs. 13, 14.

Tyson, W. A. *White Harvest Fields.* Nashville: Methodist Publishing House, 1944, Chs. VI, VII.

Urgent Tasks for the Church in Town and Country. Committee on Town and Country, Home Missions Council of North America, 1945.

Chapter 13

SOCIAL PROBLEMS OF THE RURAL SCHOOL

It is an obvious but nevertheless essential truth that a real democracy must provide a good education for *all* children in *all*
communities.[1] Providing a good education for rural people is quite
largely an organizational problem, a problem that has become complex
because of the way farm people settled on the scattered farmstead
plan, and because schools were developed in a haphazard, planless
manner.

The Changing Purpose of Education

The pioneer concept of education deemed it sufficient for farm
children to have a working knowledge of the fundamental skills:
reading, writing, and arithmetic. The most elementary methods used
in the city schools were transplanted to the country schools. Advanced education was for those who wished to do something other
than farm; the rudiments of farming could be learned at home on
the farm.

The passing of frontier society in rural life has changed our
ideas with respect to the function of the schools and education. The
modernization of agriculture and new and baffling rural social conditions also called for new educational approaches. Education in a
democracy is now looked upon as a primary method of bringing
about social change. Educational methods for rural areas, then,
must be as effective as in any other area, for schools in rural
areas must educate for urban as well as for rural life.

Modern Objectives of Education.—School authorities have seven
cardinal objectives of education for life in the modern world: health,
citizenship, worthy home membership, mastery of the fundamental
tool subjects, vocational fitness, avocational interests, and ethical
character.[2] These objectives are as valid for rural schools as they

---

[1] See Roscoe Pulliam, *Still Sits the Schoolhouse by the Road,* Chicago: University of
Chicago Press, 1943.
[2] Howard A. Dawson, *Trouble at the Crossroads,* The White House Conference on Rural
Education, NEA, Washington, 1945. See also *American Education in Transition,* pamphlet
published by *The New York Times,* 1945, p. 30.

are for urban schools. This concept of education is a great step in advance of that offered in many rural schools, too many of which concentrate on the "mere imparting of literacy" and give training only in subject matter that will enable children to climb the educational ladder to higher academic levels. Rural schools need to place more emphasis upon earning a living and learning to live in the rural community.

Types of School Districts in Rural Areas

A public school is, essentially, a group method of meeting the educational needs of a people. Therefore, the emphasis will be upon how rural people work together to meet their educational needs: the types of rural school district organizations, and the changes which are needed in these organizations.

The Country School.—The elementary school, offering grades one to eight, has been the traditional, basic type of rural school. In most rural areas it started as a one-room, one-teacher country school. In fact, the one-room school has come to be looked upon as the farmers' school. So much sentiment has grown up about the little one-room school that there is an immediate reaction against change when consolidation of small schools is proposed. In spite of a definite trend toward consolidation, there are still more one-room schools in the United States than any other kind. The latest educational survey showed more than 96,000 such schools, with an estimated attendance of nearly 2,500,000 children.[3]

The Village Elementary School.—Other types of elementary schools include the two-teacher school, of which there are some 23,000, enrolling 1,300,000 pupils. These two-room schools and the one-room schools enroll 40 per cent of all rural pupils. Schools with three to six teachers enroll 22 per cent of the rural pupils, and schools with seven or more teachers account for the remaining 38 per cent of rural pupils.

Most of the elementary schools with three or more teachers are in village and town centers. The national importance of these and the open-country schools can be seen in the fact that 13,000,000 pupils are enrolled in all rural elementary schools, or about half of the pupils enrolled in all schools in the United States.

---

[3] *Statistics of State School Systems,* 1941-42, Biennial Survey of Education in the United States, U. S. Office of Education, p. 38. See also "Statistics of State School Programs in Public Education," NEA Res. Bull., Vol. XXV, No. 4, 1947, p. 161.

The Town High School.—Whereas the rural elementary (and especially the one-room) school is traditionally a farmers' neighborhood school, the high school is characteristically a townsman's school. High schools were first organized for urban children and for farm children who were going to "make something of themselves." Consequently, high school districts were originally organized to take in only town people and property. But as more and more rural, especially village, people wanted their children to go to high school, an effort was made to provide a wider tax property base by including farming territory in the district. The addition of farms as tax property more than compensated for the added pupils from the farms. This was particularly true in the smaller communities, for when village property alone could not support the schools it became necessary to add farm property as well. The rural high school is typically a small institution; about one fifth enroll fewer than fifty pupils and have but two or three teachers. In all, there are more than 17,000 rural high schools, enrolling more than 2,000,000 pupils.

The high school districts which include farming territory have been of two chief types: the township high school which originally limited its area to the area of the township, and the community high school with boundaries sometimes cutting across not only townships but also county lines. Though originally organized as townsmen's schools, high schools have become an important part of rural life. In the fifteen Southeastern and Southwestern states, for example, over 72 per cent of the public school buildings are in rural areas. Figure 65 (page 239) shows a typical setting of a rural high school.

Non-High School Districts.—A third type of school district, namely, non-high school districts, came into being after high schools had been organized on a widespread scale. Such districts embraced territory in a county with no high school. Their governing boards were empowered to raise money to enable children in these areas to attend some high school in another district.

Processes in the Organization of Schools

The processes involved in organizing school districts were essentially social. They began with a recognition of needs, followed by group discussions about means of meeting needs, leading to group action, based usually on rules or procedures of law.

The Elementary School District.—In the earliest times country people provided schools in their homes. Then they built log schoolhouses, and each family with children contributed to the support of the "schoolmaster." It was not long, then, until they began to tax themselves to support their schools. The Ordinance of 1787 provided that one section of land out of each thirty-six was to be school land, the proceeds of which were to be used for school purposes. School districts were so set up that those families having children in school could have a legal means, through taxation, to support their schools. Then those who had no children could petition to have their property removed from the district. Thus elementary school districts were formed which took all shapes and designs.

Later it came to be generally agreed that all children should have an elementary education and that all people owning property should help to support these schools. Township officials, called trustees, were empowered to form school districts. Illinois, for example, had included in its constitution provisions for universal education, which made the state legislature the state's supreme school board. As early as 1841, the Illinois legislature created school districts and gave them their taxing power. But township trustees did not progress very fast in getting all areas in the state included in some school district. So, in 1855, the legislature set up a basic taxing unit, the local school district, with a board of directors, for the support of schools for all the children in the district by all property owners. All local officials were ordered to organize their territory into some local school district.[4]

The High School District.—When high schools were organized in several Eastern states, and in California, a new taxing district was provided, to be superimposed on the existing elementary districts. These had no relation either to the elementary districts or to the township trustee system. Some efforts were made to set up systems providing for the support of elementary and secondary education in one district organization, but it was soon discovered that, under state law, such "unit" districts could not levy taxes for amounts greater than could be levied either in the elementary or the high school district. Therefore, in order to have sufficient funds on which to operate, it seemed desirable to form two districts, making possible two tax levies for school purposes.

Progress in Rural School Reorganization.—Rural school district lines tend to become set and changes in them come slowly, especially if left to the action of the people in the neighborhood or locality. A

---

[4] *Report of the Illinois Agricultural Association School Committee,* 1945.

desirable form of reorganization would be to preserve the open-country attendance unit which has sufficient numbers to provide a good program, and to form a larger administrative unit to supply professional supervision and adequate financial support. It is significant that legislation in a number of states looks in the direction of just such reorganization. In some areas, however, sweeping changes have come. In West Virginia, a state law passed in 1933 abolished all existing school districts and set up the county as the school district, with a school board empowered to establish elementary and high school attendance units as and where needed. In this way many open-country schools were kept open, but only if they were doing a good educational job. In several states laws have been passed giving the state superintendent the power to close rural schools. Under such a law, in Arizona, all schools having fewer than twelve in average daily attendance were closed; in Wisconsin all school districts having assessed valuations of less than $100,000 were combined with other school districts to provide adequate finances.

Such laws help to enlarge the attendance unit but, of course, do not provide for community unit schools. The organization of unit or centralized systems is provided for by the laws of New York State. Under them the State Commissioner of Education is authorized to lay out boundaries for proposed central districts, which may be adopted by a majority of the qualified voters attending special meetings called upon the petition of fifteen residents and taxpayers. Half of the transportation costs and one fourth of the building costs approved by the commissioner of education are made available to central districts from state funds.

Legislation Providing for School Surveys.—County and state committees have been set up in the state of Washington, under a law enacted in 1941. These committees are required to make studies and submit reorganization plans to the voters to form new districts, so that there will be provided more nearly equalized educational opportunities for pupils of the elementary and high schools, a higher degree of uniformity of school tax rates among districts, and a wise use of public funds. A large percentage of the local cost of reorganization is provided from state funds.

Permissive legislation has been enacted in Illinois, under which the members of the school boards in a county vote whether or not to elect a school survey committee. If the vote is favorable the committee is empowered to make recommendations for reorganiza-

tion, and the county superintendent is required to call elections in all
newly proposed districts. Significantly, town and country people
vote separately on the proposals; a favorable vote on the part of
both groups is required to reorganize according to recommendations.

The above illustrations make clear the types of legal action being
taken to improve rural education in the United States. The trend in
school reorganization has been away from efforts confined to local
areas toward action taken on a state basis. Primary efforts are
directed toward school district reorganization, which, sociologically
interpreted, means a change in group alignments. Significant social
changes take place in the process of reorganization of schools, such
as the disintegration of old and traditional group lines and the
formation of new, and at first strange, group relationships. There
is a real struggle in many areas to retain the old primary groups,
for when a school leaves the neighborhood one of the chief bonds
of neighborhood affiliation is broken. Where efforts to reorganize
on the basis of the natural primary and secondary groups are successful, the results are much more satisfactory. If elementary neighborhood attendance units can be organized, they will strengthen this
basic unit in our democracy. Organizing the administrative unit on
the larger community or county basis, however, will widen group
contacts, and overcome the provincialism and self-satisfaction which
now seem to characterize the people in many of our self-contained
one-room school districts.

Persistence of Traditional Patterns.—Even so, rural school modernization moves slowly. The elementary school for grades one to
eight and the high school for grades nine to twelve still remains the
general pattern of organization. Illinois still has over eight thousand active one-room schools. In Michigan by far the largest number
of districts are one-room school districts; other states—Iowa, Indiana, Missouri, Wisconsin, to name a few—still have a large number
of small, and sometimes old, schools. But it is socially significant
that concern for rural school reorganization has risen from a local to
a state and now to a national level.

The National Rural School Situation

In most rural communities the definite break between the elementary school and the high school requires drastic social adjustments on the part of the children. In many rural areas, therefore,
most children do not go beyond the eighth grade. The last census
showed that, for the nation as a whole, only 56.8 per cent of those

sixteen and seventeen years old in rural areas, contrasted with 75.6 per cent of this age group in urban areas, were enrolled in school.[5] In one Illinois county in 1940, for example, two thirds of the youth from eighteen to thirty years old had not gone beyond the eighth grade.[6]

We are told that "many of the best and most of the poorest schools in the nation are found in rural areas." [7] Rural schools, *as a class*, are so much poorer than schools in urban areas that millions of rural children are seriously handicapped educationally. Table 12 shows the differences between rural and urban areas for grade completed, almost a fourth of the heads of rural-farm families going no farther than the fifth year. Note also the large percentages in this group for the South, especially among nonwhites.

TABLE 12. PERCENTAGES OF HEADS OF FAMILIES COMPLETING SPECIFIED GRADE, FOR URBAN, RURAL, AND RURAL-FARM POPULATIONS FOR THE UNITED STATES, AND BY REGIONS: 1940 *

| Area | Percentage of Family Heads Having Completed: | | | | | | | |
| | Grade School | | | High School | | College | | |
	Less than 5 years	5 or 6 years	7 or 8 years	1 to 3 years	4 years	1 to 3 years	4 or more	No report
Urban	12.5	10.3	33.6	15.4	14.6	5.9	6.6	1.1
Rural-nonfarm	15.0	12.6	35.9	14.9	11.0	4.9	4.6	1.1
Rural-farm	23.6	16.4	39.0	10.8	5.5	2.5	1.1	1.1

Farm Family Heads by Year of School Completed, by Regions:								
Northeast	9.6	12.0	51.6	12.5	7.6	3.1	2.2	1.4
North Central......	10.1	12.2	55.6	10.3	7.1	2.8	1.0	0.9
South—total	35.9	20.6	25.8	10.2	3.5	1.9	0.8	1.3
South—nonwhite ...	65.5	19.7	9.4	2.6	0.6	0.4	0.2	1.6
West	14.2	10.8	43.2	14.3	9.3	4.8	2.3	1.0

* U. S. Dept. of Commerce, Bureau of the Census, Sixteenth Census of the United States, *Families*, pp. 33, 37.

Financial Support.—Rural areas, with more than half the nation's children, receive only 38 per cent of the nation's annual expenditure for the support of schools. Inevitably, this disproportion has resulted in inadequate school facilities in rural areas. The average salary of rural school teachers in 1939-1940 was $957; for urban teachers it was $1,937. The World War II period caused a considerable increase in these salaries, but rural teachers even in this

---

[5] U. S. Dept. of Commerce, Bureau of the Census, Sixteenth Census of the United States, Vol. II, *Character of the Population*, pp. 33, 37.
[6] D. E. Lindstrom, et al., *Rural Youth in Wartime Illinois*, Rural Sociology Mimeograph 10, Univ. of Illinois Agr. Exp. Sta., 1942.
[7] Dawson, *Trouble at the Crossroads, op. cit.*, pp. 31-32.

period were not so well paid, by and large, as were those in the urban areas. More than 44,000 rural teachers in 1943 received $660 or less. Despite some improvement in postwar years, the salary levels of school teachers are still critically, even disastrously, low.

Training Received by Rural Teachers.—The majority of all teachers in this country are in rural areas. As a group, the rural teachers are woefully undertrained. Nearly 60 per cent of the teachers in rural elementary schools staffed by one or two teachers had less than two years of education beyond high school. The turn-over is naturally very large. In normal times two out of every five rural teachers are new, each year, to their positions. With very little except low salaries in prospect, few students taking teacher training plan to teach in rural schools, thus creating a great deficiency in the supply of good rural teachers.

Expenditures per Pupil.—Total expenditures per pupil in rural schools are only about two thirds the amount expended per pupil in urban areas. The value of school property in rural areas, per pupil, is less than half that of urban areas.[8] The low average expenditure per rural pupil results in painfully inadequate schools in many rural areas, especially in the South. Furthermore, farm areas are obliged to make a much greater effort to support their schools than do urban communities. In Iowa, for instance, the assessed value per child is more than three times as great in the rural as in the town areas.[9] Rural property tax rates also vary widely. Farmers on the best lands may have tax rates for the support of schools as low as three cents per $100 valuation, whereas those on poorer lands must assess themselves to the legal limit. Even so, if they were to depend upon the returns from such rates alone some districts could not support a school. A district would have to have a valuation of at least $100,-000 to raise $1,000 at a $1.00 rate, and many country school districts have valuations as low as $25,000.

Social Organization of the Rural School

Group processes are learned in school quite largely outside the schoolroom. One of the most significant duties of a teacher—whenever she has time and nervous energy to spare—is to encourage group activities in the school program that will prepare the child for group participation in adult life.

---

[8] Dawson, *Trouble at the Crossroads, op. cit.*, p. 30.
[9] W. H. Lancelot and Barton Morgan, *Iowa's Vanishing Farm Youth and Their Schools*, Bull. P81, Iowa State College Exp. Sta. and Ext. Service cooperating, 1946.

Figure 66. A Typical One-Room School in the Middle West

The program is limited, the equipment meager, and the pupils per grade too few for good work. (Courtesy Illinois Agricultural Association)

Figure 67. Country Children on Their Way to School

The hazards of walking are far greater than of transportation by bus. (Courtesy Extension Service, USDA)

Figure 68. Small Buses, Operating over Short Routes, Provide Efficient, Effective, and Safe School Transportation

(Courtesy Illinois Agricultural Association)

Group Activities in the One-Room School.—With its mixture of age levels the one-room school differs from the graded school, wherein play groups are of the same age. Moreover, when the enrollment in a one-room school becomes too small there is danger of psychic isolation, because a school with but one child in some of its grades fails to provide for that child the essential social contacts for the most desirable development of personality. Hence many small rural schools endeavor to group the grades to secure the cooperation and competition of group activities so desirable in the proper development of personal and group life.

Furthermore, the average eight grade school throws age groups with different interests together. Adolescent boys and girls do not have the same interests as younger pupils; they need the association of their own age group. It now seems desirable to begin a pupil's high school years at the sixth grade rather than at the eighth grade, a change that has been made by many city systems.

Although there is some question as to the extent to which such domestic group life is really encouraged in many country schools, certainly a better opportunity for such activity is offered there than in the average city system. In the establishment of larger rural schools, one of the chief values of an all-grade rural school, that of a family-type situation in which the older children are encouraged to help the younger ones, may be lost. If the country school as a whole could maintain the enrollment and the program that is now being carried on in some of the best country schools, and in addition provide modern facilities, probably few city schools would excel it in educational possibilities.

The Rural School in Community Life.—The rural school, as a part of its community, influences, and is influenced by, the community. As Brunner says:

The idea that the school is an institution apart from and impervious to the life of the community, never valid, should be entirely abandoned. . . A school cannot rise above the level of its community. If it is to progress, it must sometimes help lift the community to broader, more purposeful concepts, especially about education, if it is to improve the quality of its own work. Comparably, in the long run the community cannot rise above the level of its school. It is no accident that those states in which the educational status of the rural population is lowest, as measured by the 1940 Census, are also those which have the smallest proportions of their school age population actually in attendance, which have shorter terms and smaller proportions of those enrolled in daily attendance.[10]

[10] Edmund deS. Brunner, *Major Problems Affecting Education in Rural Areas*, Yearbook of the Department of Rural Education, NEA, 1945, p. 22.

Reasons for the Inferiority of Rural Schools

The chief reasons given for the inferiority of rural, and especially one-room, schools are (a) they do not attract competent teachers, (b) they have become too costly per pupil and costs have been unequally distributed, (c) they have not adjusted themselves to changing population and community conditions, (d) they have become inefficient from the standpoint of modern educational needs, both in curriculum and facilities, and (e) they have been too much a separate entity, not an organic part of an educational system in a community.[11] Of these, the teacher situation is the most important. The success of a school depends quite largely on the kind of teacher provided for that school, and her success in turn depends not only on how well she can teach but also on her ability to understand and work with the people of the community in which the school is located. Let us examine this problem further.

1. Teaching in a rural school is a more difficult task than teaching in town. The one-room school teacher has all eight grades, and her teaching equipment is usually quite meager. (See Figure 66, page 254.) (She or he) must be her own janitor. Often she finds it difficult to become a part of the community in which she is teaching. Hence, the only way some areas can assure themselves of a supply of teachers is to maintain lower training requirements.

2. Perhaps the chief reason that teachers in rural schools are not so competent as urban teachers is that the hiring—for the average country school—is in the hands of a locally elected board of directors, many of whom are more sensitive to demands to keep taxes low than to provide a good teacher. The net result of this shortsighted attitude is that many teachers are hired at little more than a subsistence salary.

3. The problem of securing a good teacher is aggravated in areas in which numerous people without children are property owners, and in areas in which the absentee landlord makes it clear to his tenant that he wants no increase in taxes. The problem is further increased in areas in which most of the children come from poor-land tenant or laborer families.[12]

Rural schools have high per-pupil costs. When the average daily

---

11 See *Education of Teachers,* Yearbook of the Department of Rural Education, Washington: NEA, 1946, Ch. 2; also D. E. Lindstrom, *A Guide for the Study of Rural School District Reorganization,* Urbana: Ext. Service in Agr. and Home Econ., Univ. of Illinois, 1946, p. 8.

12 See D. E. Lindstrom, "What Rural People Think Are Changes Needed in Rural Schools," *Illinois Farm Economics,* April. 1945.

attendance at a school falls below fifteen or twenty the social costs of maintaining the school become exorbitant, if the school is to provide a good education. Yet many country schools are being operated for as few as ten, and some with as few as five, pupils. Since the yearly cost of conducting a one-room school ranges from $1,000 up, it is common to find per pupil costs ranging from $200 to as high as $1,600 (as in one school in a central Illinois county in 1945).

4. In depression times there is competition for teaching positions and rural school directors can pay low teacher salaries. Indeed, the depression years of the 1930's saw many teachers who had trained for specialized teaching positions in the cities forced to take teaching jobs in country schools, something for which they were not prepared. In wartime, teachers become scarce and teacher requirements were lowered. But most of the wartime "emergency" teachers, usually with wholly inadequate training, go to rural schools to replace rural school teachers who have accepted better-paying jobs elsewhere.

5. Some means must be provided to secure more properly qualified teachers for rural schools. At least one teachers college has solved the problem by requiring all its student teachers to take basic training for teaching in rural schools. Recognizing the fact that rural teachers have a more difficult task and greater discomforts than those who teach in towns and cities, some states and foreign countries have solved the problem by paying somewhat higher salaries to rural teachers than to those in comparable positions in urban areas.[13]

6. Most rural schools still depend primarily upon local real estate taxation for their support. In view of the fact that the largest numbers of children are reared on lands least able to support an adequate educational system, reliance upon local property taxation is clearly not enough. People living in the wealthier sections of the country who insist that each locality should educate its own children are not assuming their full responsibility to society.

The failure to accept social responsibility is shown in the resistance to efforts to equalize the differences in valuations and tax rates for the support of schools. Valuations in a single county in Illinois varied as much as from $27,000 in one school district to over $4,000,000 in a nearby district, both in the open country.

The variations in assessed property valuations are not so great, however, as variations in wealth per pupil. In Pulaski County, Arkansas, for instance, the assessed valuation per pupil ranged from

---

[13] See Iman Elsie Schatzmann, *The Country School,* Chicago: University of Chicago Press, 1942, p. 145.

$246 in one district to $4,407 in another.[14] In Arizona the assessed wealth per pupil in the poorest district just before the war was $42; in the richest district, $187,859.[15] Such astonishing variations in taxable wealth per child mean that poor areas, if they were to depend entirely upon their own property tax resources, could provide for their many children only a woeful minimum of education. No longer can adequate schools for all of the children be provided by local property taxation. Yet when efforts are made to spread the burden of taxation, persons on the best lands and in districts with the most valuable property resist such efforts. Measures to limit taxation on property and to get revenues from other sources thus become necessary.

The School Population

Rural and especially farm populations are remaining stationary or are declining slightly. Yet the rural reproduction rates are so much higher than the urban that if all of the children born in rural areas were to remain there, serious overpopulation would soon result. People *must* move from rural to urban areas, for "only one man in ten is really needed at present in agriculture, and if improved scientific practices were followed everywhere, one man in twenty would suffice." [16] Then, too, the element in the rural population that is growing most rapidly is the rural-nonfarm element, which means that the increase is in the part-time farming sections near large urban centers and in the growing villages.

The result of these changes in population has been that some small rural school districts have lost from half to two thirds of their school population. Fifty years ago it was common to find one-room schools with as many as fifty pupils; today, the average has dropped to as low as ten in average daily attendance. Likewise, in villages with declining populations one can frequently find buildings with unused rooms. On the other hand, there are villages with crowded schools, part of the reason being that the nearby one-room schools have closed and the children come to the village schools. An acute situation results with the development of suburban housing areas, the children flocking into the small one-room schools.

The increase in farm tenancy and the presence of a mobile farm labor population have further aggravated the situation. When ten-

[14] Floyd W. Reeves, *Education for Rural America*, Chicago: University of Chicago Press, 1945, p. 138.
[15] George A. Works and Simon O. Lesser, *Rural America Today*, Chicago: University of Chicago Press, 1942, p. 47.
[16] See O. E. Baker, "The Family and Rural Nonfarm Residence," *Land and Home*, Vol. VIII, No. 1, March, 1945.

ants move they usually do so in the middle of the school term, and from one small district to another. As a result, a change of as much as half, or more, in the number of pupils in a particular school has often occurred in a very short period. The movement of farm labor families makes the situation even more acute, for many of the children are taken out of school before the end of the year in order to follow the harvests.

Results of Unplanned Expansion.—Too often, when rural people realize that their schools need improvements, their remedy is to put two or three small districts together. The result is a school with a few more pupils but with little change in school program. The arrangements are often temporary, that is, one district with but two or three pupils transports them to a nearby school, tuition being paid by the one school district for pupil attendance in the other. Usually, districts whose children have been transferred gain the advantage because the cost of transferring a few pupils is usually less than that for keeping a school open. Partially, at least, they are educated at the expense of the district to which they are transferred. This is especially true when children are transferred into village schools, for tax rates in villages are usually higher than those in the country.

The situation is just as acute in high schools as in elementary schools, but the problems are somewhat different. Most town high schools, especially in smaller villages, cannot be supported by the townspeople alone; a valuation of at least $10,000,000 is needed to support a high school adequately. Since few villages have such valuations it has been necessary to extend high school districts into country areas in order to have enough taxable wealth to support the school. Many states, therefore, have enacted township and community high school laws to make it possible to "vote in" country territory. A rapid expansion of such high schools has taken place because village populations could outvote those in the country part of the proposed district. The movement spread so rapidly in some states, and on such an unplanned basis, that many small and inefficient schools were formed, some floating huge bond issues to build fine structures on a local tax base too small even to support the school, much less pay off the bonds.

Proposals for Rural School Improvement

The plight of the rural school—its inefficiencies, shortcomings, and handicaps—has become a matter of national concern. In 1944, the White House Conference on Rural Education brought together some of the best minds in the country to consider the needs, ways, and means for the improvement of rural education in the United States. One of its significant conclusions was "that every child has the right to educational service and guidance during the entire year, and full-time attendance in a school that is open for not less than nine months for at least twelve years." [17] The report stressed the need for units of administration large enough to include several schools. This recommendation does not mean "that small schools will be done away with, rather that they will become a part of the larger administrative district so that all of the schools in that administrative district will have enough resources through which to develop a good schools system." [18] Let us review, therefore, some Conference proposals for rural school improvement.

1. Desirable Units of Administration.—A desirable unit for elementary schools is seven teachers for six grades with an enrollment of 240 to 280 pupils. The minimum attendance unit for an elementary school should be three teachers with twenty pupils per teacher if population density is low, or if necessary neighborhood conditions do not permit larger units. The high school should have twelve to fourteen teachers and 240 to 350 pupils. If there is low population density, and community conditions do not permit these standards, the minimum high school attendance unit should be seven or eight teachers and 150 pupils. These attendance units should be a part of a larger administrative and finance unit.

The advantage of larger community or county administrative or finance units would be a more equitable spreading of the tax load. In general, the cost of consolidated schools is greater than the cost of smaller schools because of improved and more adequate facilities. But the per capita costs of consolidated schools are less than the per capita cost of small schools for the same grades. However, in West Virginia the reduction from 398 to 55 districts did result in a saving of over $4,000,000 the first year the law was in effect.[19]

Attendance Units. We are recognizing that elementary and high school districts should be combined, so far as administration is concerned, though as attendance units they can remain separate. The neighborhood, because it is an important and persisting area of social contact, should continue to be recognized as an attendance unit for the open-country school.

[17] See the *Report of the White House Conference on Rural Education,* published by the National Education Association, Washington, 1945, pp. 14-15.
[18] *Ibid.,* p. 17.
[19] Works and Lesser, *Rural America Today, op. cit.,* pp. 46-47.

Administrative Units. The towns or larger villages are becoming more and more the community centers, especially those which, with their surrounding territory, can support a good high school. The high school, we have seen, is the most important single factor in determining the area of a rural community. When the percentage of farm youth in high school is as large as the percentage which now attends from villages—and soon most farmers will want their children to go to high school—there will be more farm than village youth in the smaller of our rural high schools. Moreover, when the boundaries of a village are extended to include the rural areas of which it is the service center, the assessed valuation for the rural property will be greater than that of the village, in many areas. Thus, the rural community may well become the local administrative area for both elementary and high school attendance units. This does not mean, let us repeat, the passing of the open-country school, for the organization of such administrative areas can and should mean that there will be several attendance units or schools, especially for elementary school purposes.

2. A Modern Curricular Program.—It is now recognized that any good school program should provide for work in seven distinct fields:

(a) A periodic physical examination of all children, and corrective treatment for those who need it; instruction and guidance in healthful living, including instruction in diet and provision for hot lunches; adequate means to prevent and control contagious diseases; recreation; physical exercise and play suited to the interests and needs of the child.

(b) Mastery of the basic skills—reading, writing, and arithmetic.

(c) Attention to the especially talented, or to those who are handicapped, socially, physically, or mentally.

(d) Attention to the development of appreciations, abilities, and expression through the creative arts.

(e) Guidance in social living, culminating in a social-studies program that fits youth to take part in adult society.

(f) Opportunity for growth through manual activity, with practical arts for the younger and industrial (including agricultural) and homemaking arts for the older children.

(g) Organization of materials around the idea of child growth and development.[20]

---

[20] D. E. Lindstrom, et al., "We Can Have Modern Schools in Illinois," Univ. of Illinois, Agr. Ext. Service, RSE 106. 1947.

Efforts should be made to develop a twelve-month program including a community health program, summer library services, crafts, art and dramatics, community forums, business and industrial education, a summer physical education program, and a summer music program. In an increasing number of communities many of the teachers needed for such a program are employed for a twelve-month term.[21]

Obviously, such training cannot be given in the average one-room school. In the first place, properly trained teachers are not available. Secondly, library, laboratory, and similar facilities are also not available, although the rural community itself is one of the finest laboratories that a school could have. Such facilities can be provided only through larger administrative units, in schools financed from a larger base, and with adequate state and Federal aid.

3. A Community Center.—The rural school should be a neighborhood and community center. Its facilities should be planned not only for adequate classroom, library, gymnasium, play yard, and laboratory use, but also as a center for community meetings, entertainments, special group meetings—and in these ways become a genuine community facility.

4. Transportation.—If a school is to provide facilities for the educational needs of all of the people it must not overlook transportation. One of the chief reasons farm people resist consolidation is the fear of hazard to their children. Yet studies have shown that a good system of transportation affords a much greater degree of safety than when children walk, often as much as three miles and along roads with heavy traffic, to school. (See Figure 67, page 254.) In larger administrative districts it is possible to provide adequate bus service at reasonable cost which in many areas is partially met by state funds. Where attendance units are separate, some remaining in the open country, the purchase of small buses, running over short routes, may be desirable.

Experience has shown that where transportation has been developed properly, most farm people would never go back to the old system. Routes can be arranged so that no pupil is on the bus longer than a half hour; bus schedules can be sufficiently regular so that few pupils will have to wait more than a few minutes at the side of the road. Bus supervision can be such that the same discipline as is

---

21 See *Education for Rural Wisconsin's Tomorrow*, Madison: State Department of Education, 1946, pp. 4-6.

found in school can be maintained in the bus. Costs can be kept low enough so that, with state aid, no larger administrative unit need hesitate to provide transportation. (See Figure 68, page 255.) Poor road conditions may be a factor in some cases, but the usual experience has been that road improvement quickly follows school reorganization. Indeed, the need for better schools is one of the best arguments for securing aid for improved country roads.

5. Training and Keeping Rural Teachers.—We have previously indicated that competent rural teachers can be secured if adequate salaries are provided. It is desirable to include, with this pay, facilities for keeping the teacher in the community so that he or she may become a part of the community life. Some areas are now providing teacherages—dwelling places in which the teachers live, doing their own cooking and housework, or having the housekeeping provided for them.

The payment of adequate salaries—turning rural teaching jobs into attractive positions—will make it possible to require the same training for rural as for other teachers, plus special training in a rural school. "A rural teacher should know the interests and ways of farm people, their problems, and how they make a living. She should understand what science, the radio, the motion picture, and the automobile mean to rural living and rural education and how towns and larger urban cities have influenced and changed rural life." [22] She should know about new inventions relating to agriculture and what they mean to the farm family, and should help introduce them in rural life.[23] She should know something about farm neighborhoods, farm groups, and farm communities, and how to work effectively in them, helping to relate the school to life in the community.[24] The prospective teacher whose training or experience clearly indicates inability to meet these requirements should not be allowed to teach in a rural school.

These basic requirements apply equally to professional administrators of rural schools as well as to the teachers themselves. The principal of a rural high school who has no training in the fundamentals of rural life or no concept of the significance of the rural way of life may actually hinder the development of rural-centered school programs. Sometimes administrators who lack training for

---

[22] Pulliam, *Still Sits the Schoolhouse by the Road, op. cit.,* p. 42.
[23] John D. Black, "Factors Conditioning Innovations in Agriculture," *Mechanical Engineering,* March, 1945, p. 180.
[24] See "On-the-Job Education in Rural Communities," 1947 Yearbook of the Department of Rural Education, NEA.

rural life even prevent the organization of departments of vocational agriculture and home economics in the high school. Hence land-grant colleges and universities should provide adequate opportunities for such training and cooperate with teachers' colleges in providing it.

6. Need for Increased State and Federal Aid.—The magnitude of the rural migration to urban areas emphasizes the need for Federal and state support for the education of these youth. In brief, since half or more of the rural-educated youth moves to urban areas, half of the financial support of rural schools should come from state and Federal sources. In some states more than half of the support of rural schools now comes from state funds.

The great fear that farmers have of accepting increased state and Federal aid is that control of their schools will pass from their hands to state and Federal authorities. There is, of course, real danger that this will happen if the body politic is not alert. It won't happen if state and Federal funds are given to counties and local communities strictly on a grants-in-aid basis, or if financial aid be given only when the resources of the local tax unit have been used to the legal limit. By preserving these principles and insisting that rural people merit outside financial support for their schools because of their human and material contributions to urban areas, such aid could be made available without loss of local control.

Rural Education in a Democracy

This review of the social processes operating to change the rural school system reveals a definite movement in many areas of the United States toward a modern rural community school. Where this objective has not been attained—which is too often the case—it has doubtless been due to a lack of understanding of group and community processes. Summarized, the elements in a modern rural community school system are:

(a) Provision of at least twelve grades—with opportunity to expand to include kindergarten and grades thirteen and fourteen—organized, staffed, and supervised to serve rural interests.

(b) Neighborhood elementary schools, preferably for the first six grades with at least twenty pupils per teacher; smaller community junior high schools, and at least one senior high school.

(c) State and Federal financial aid as needed above that which should be provided locally to insure interest, participation, and control.

(d) Supervision by county, state, and Federal administrators who are qualified and who are permitted to carry on their work with as little political interference as possible.

(e) Adequate transportation.

If education in a democracy is fundamental to the existence of the democratic way, the system of school administration and control must be such as to nurture and advance that objective. The people for whom a modern educational program is developed must participate in its development and must maintain an active interest in and an intelligent control over the system provided to carry on that program.[25]

DISCUSSION

1. Discuss the social aspects of a modern rural school program. How do rural schools measure up to these objectives?

2. What types of group activity are carried on in the formal rural school program? To what extent are rural youth and children given experience in group activity?

3. Analyze the chief causes for the inferiority of rural schools. What measures are needed to bring rural schools up to desirable standards?

4. What training should be received by a person who is to teach in a rural school? What must be included in a school program to make it rural-life centered? In what ways can a school be made a community center?

5. Outline what you feel are the functions of the school in rural life.

READINGS

Dawson, Howard, Reeves, Floyd, and others. *Your School District.* Washington, Dept. of Rural Ed., NEA, 1948.

Education for Rural Wisconsin's Tomorrow. Madison: State Department of Education, 1946.

Lancelot, W. H., and Morgan, Barton. *Iowa's Vanishing Farm Youth and Their Schools.* Bull. P81, Iowa State Agr. Exp. Sta. and Ext. Service cooperating, 1946.

Lindstrom, D. E., et al. "We Can Have Modern Schools in Illinois." Univ. of Illinois, Agr. Ext. Service, RSE 106, 1947.

Olsen, Edward G. *School and Community.* New York: Prentice-Hall, Inc., 1945, Part II.

Planning for American Youth. National Association of Secondary School Principals, 1944, pp. 15-35.

Proceedings of the Governor's Conference on Rural Education. State of Illinois, Springfield, 1946.

Reeves, Floyd W. *Education for Rural America.* Chicago: University of Chicago Press, 1945, Chs. VI, VIII.

---

[25] See the section on "Rural Education in the Structure and Function of Democracy," in the *Report of the White House Conference on Rural Education,* 1945, pp. 250 ff.

Rural Schools of Tomorrow. Yearbook of the Department of Rural Education. Washington: NEA, 1945.

Schatzmann, Iman Elsie. *The Country School.* Chicago: University of Chicago Press, 1942, Part II.

The White House Conference on Rural Education. Washington: NEA, 1945.

Works, George A., and Lesser, Simon O. *Rural America Today.* Chicago: University of Chicago Press, 1942, Chs. IX, X, XI.

Chapter 14

SYSTEMS OF ADULT EDUCATION IN RURAL AREAS

We do not stop learning when we leave school, for our education continues as long as we are learning new things, or learning new ways of doing things. Furthermore, the idea that we learn more slowly or with more difficulty as we grow into adulthood is a mistaken one. We may actually learn faster as adults than we do in school because we have a different kind of drive or motive for learning, directed toward solving a particular problem.[1] Adult education has come to be recognized as a very important field in which many groups, organizations, and agencies, both public and private, are participating. They include not only the traditional family, church, and school groups, but also extension service, libraries, newspapers, radio, magazines, farm organizations, community or neighborhood discussion groups, community councils, and other special-interest groups formed in the community, plus government agencies, and recreational programs. Because of their special importance to rural life, particular attention will be given here to the adult education work of extension services, adult education in schools, libraries, the rural and agricultural press, radio, and moving pictures.

Extension Service to Rural People

Farm people, since their earliest settlements, have had group meetings to discuss and to deal with various problems. Agricultural societies were formed even before the Revolutionary War, and farmers' clubs were an important means for enlightenment and social intercourse in the period before and after the Civil War.[2] After the establishment of the land-grant colleges and the experiment stations, new information relating to farming began to be available, but means of getting it to farm people were inadequate. Hence farmers' institutes were organized in the 1880's to bring college of agriculture experts and their materials to the rural community for annual one-

---

[1] Harry A. Overstreet and Bonaro W. Overstreet, *Leaders for Adult Education*, New York: American Association for Adult Education, 1941, p. 11.
[2] D. E. Lindstrom, *American Farmers and Rural Organizations*, Champaign, Ill., Garrard Press, 1948, p. 12.

or two-day meetings. Lectures on farm and home practices for men and women and exhibits of produce and handiwork were arranged. The institutes spread throughout many states and still are an important form of adult education in some states.[3]

Early Forerunners of Extension Work.—The main impetus for the organization of an extension system for demonstrating experimental work to rural people came in the first few years of this century. The U. S. Department of Agriculture had carried on experiments in which "county agents" were employed in the South to demonstrate the new methods for the control of the boll weevil, which threatened to destroy the cotton crop. Seaman A. Knapp, who had been connected with the department, was asked to establish the first demonstration.[4] He had to secure the cooperation of a farmer, but the farmer selected refused to cooperate unless guaranteed against the loss of his crop. Thereupon, the merchants of the nearby town raised a fund for the guarantee. Knapp's experiment was successful and was followed by demonstrations all over the South, requiring the work of county agents.

Spread of the County Agent Idea.—County agents were selected to demonstrate better farming methods in other parts of the country. In New York state a city chamber of commerce, realizing the close dependence of town business upon farm prosperity, secured the cooperation of the state college, the U. S. Department of Agriculture, and the Lackawanna Railroad in hiring a county agent. In Illinois two county soil and crop improvement associations were formed and, with the help of townspeople, hired county "soil doctors" in 1912. An Ohio lawyer, whose health required open-country work, stimulated the organization of similar work in Pennsylvania and became by popular choice one of the first county agents.

These efforts to get farmers to use new methods of farming were achieved by personal contact and demonstration. It was soon discovered that it was necessary for the farmers to help plan and set up demonstrations. In New York and Illinois, especially, success was attained only after group methods were used; farmers' clubs were formed to initiate and organize the work. Only after several years, however, was there national recognition of the need for adult educational work among farmers. As early as 1908 the Theodore Roose-

---

3 See J. P. Schmidt, *Ohio Farmers Institute,* Special Report, Dept. of Rural Economics, Ohio State University, 1944.

4 See J. C. Bailey, *Seaman A. Knapp,* New York: Columbia University Press, 1945, Part II; M. L. Wilson, *The Extension Service Marches On,* Extension Service Circular 348, USDA, 1940.

velt Country Life Commission pointed out the need for encouraging a system of extension work in rural communities through the land-grant colleges. The Commission specifically recommended a nation-wide organization to take stock of country life, a nationalized extension service to reach every person on the land, and a campaign to secure the cooperation of rural teachers, librarians, clergymen, editors, physicians, and others in rebuilding country life.

The Smith-Lever Act of 1914.—These movements led to the enactment of the Federal Smith-Lever Act of 1914 "to aid in diffusing among the people of the United States useful and practical information on agriculture and home economics and to encourage the application of the same . . . through field demonstrations, publications, and otherwise . . . to persons not resident" at some college of agriculture. The broad objectives of the act—to deal with all rural problems, social and economic, looking to the betterment of rural life in its entirety—have been only partially realized in practice. Even today too many state extension services concentrate on the economic aspects, particularly production, and seriously neglect the social, especially human and group improvement aspects.

The Extension System of Organization

State and National Aspects.—A cooperative system of organization for extension work has been developed, according to law, between the U. S. Department of Agriculture and the land-grant colleges of agriculture. Under a memorandum of understanding signed by the head of the college, Federal funds, to be matched by the state, were made available to set up a state extension service. Each state then hired extension administrators and state subject-matter specialists, who were to go from college to teach and demonstrate new methods of crop, soil, animal, or household care. County agents (called farm or home advisers in some states and county extension directors in others) were also hired.

Local Cooperative Aspects.—In some states the extension service sought the cooperation of county boards for raising local funds to match or supplement state funds. To support a county agent these counties had to secure a certain number of farmers to petition the county board to appropriate funds. Special efforts were made to secure the cooperation of farmers' organizations. In Illinois, for example, a county can get a farm adviser only if a certain number of farmers will join in forming a county farm bureau. Likewise, a home adviser can be employed only when a certain number of rural women sign up as members of a county home bureau. Of course, such local cooperation did not always succeed. In some states, reverse action was taken—petitions were circulated to cut off county funds and eliminate the work in the county!

Extension Organization.—Though most state extension services are quite similar, including administrators, district supervisors, and extension specialists in various fields of subject matter, the county systems vary. In general, there are three plans:

1. In some states the county agent is appointed by the state extension service; the type of county organization and program resulting is usually approved by the state leaders.
2. In other states, a county advisory committee or council represents the various farmers' organizations, rural neighborhoods, or communities of the county, to help formulate and carry out programs.
3. In still other states, the county agent is hired and is in part paid by a local farmers' or homemakers' organization. The governing board of such a county organization, with the help of the state extension representatives, formulates and helps carry out the program.

Chief Phases of Extension Work.—As we have noted, the Smith-Lever Law specifies "diffusing practical and useful information on agriculture and home economics," and through the years much effort has been made to do this. As a result somewhat different systems have been developed for the work of men and of women. In addition, boys and girls have been encouraged through 4-H clubs to take on projects in out-of-school time. Recently, special attention has been given to older youth or rural youth activities. In some states attention is also given to rural community organization.

The first emphasis in all phases of extension work was to get new farm or home practices adopted; in many areas this is still the primary objective. More and more attention is being given to the quality of the farm people, their social attitudes, and the kinds of groups to which they belong. People with some spark of the progressive spirit are much more willing to accept new methods: to help the county agent bring about the transformation of an invention to an innovation.

Functioning of the System.—Since most counties have only one or two county extension workers much attention has been paid to the problem of how to make their work most effective. The methods vary, as has been indicated, from work with individuals to work with community organizations. Figure 69 summarizes the ways in which farmers take part in the work.

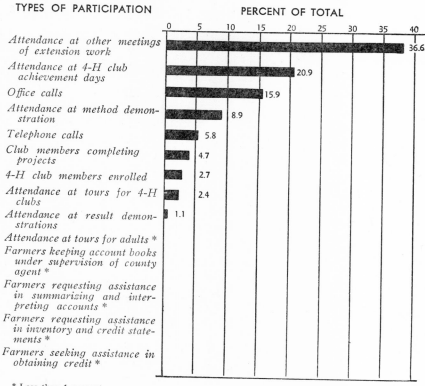

TYPES OF PARTICIPATION   PERCENT OF TOTAL

Attendance at other meetings of extension work — 36.6
Attendance at 4-H club achievement days — 20.9
Office calls — 15.9
Attendance at method demon-stration — 8.9
Telephone calls — 5.8
Club members completing projects — 4.7
4-H club members enrolled — 2.7
Attendance at tours for 4-H clubs — 2.4
Attendance at result demon-strations — 1.1
Attendance at tours for adults *
Farmers keeping account books under supervision of county agent *
Farmers requesting assistance in summarizing and inter-preting accounts *
Farmers requesting assistance in inventory and credit state-ments *
Farmers seeking assistance in obtaining credit *

* Less than 1 percent.

Figure 69. Participation by Farmers in Various Types of Extension Work in Michigan

Note the predominance of attendance at "other meetings" which include community meetings, both those attended by the agents and those held by local leaders. Even 4-H club achievement days are in the nature of community meetings, for usually all members of the family attend. From Charles R. Hoffer, *Participation of Farmers in Agricultural Extension Work*, Univ. of Michigan, AES Spec. Bull. 331, 1944.

1. The demonstration method. Probably the most widely used method is the demonstration method, whereby a farmer agrees to have a new practice tried out on his farm and to have his neighbor come to see the results. The cooperation of a local leader is essential in demonstrations. The methods used in the demonstration and the results obtained should be discussed at community meetings, tours, and shows.

Under the demonstration method project cooperators are used. The agent urges a farmer to enroll in specific projects—for example, using new methods to control weeds. He hopes and expects that neighbors will see the benefit of, and imitate, the new practice. Often the farms or homes of these project cooperators are used as stopping places on tours.

2. Indirect influences. Seed dealers or salesmen who have had considerable success in getting new types of seed used are important as indirect influences.[5] Bankers, merchants, and to some extent, teachers and pastors, are also helpful in spreading information on new practices.

3. Personal contacts. Personal contacts, both on the farm and in the county agent's office, can be very beneficial, especially if directed to possible group use.

4. The local or community group. One of the most effective means of carrying on extension work is group effort. In fact, it would be impossible for a county extension agent to work effectively without the cooperation of groups and their leaders. The work in home economics and especially with youth—through 4-H and Rural Youth—has been conducted through groups.[6] In most states local home bureaus or home demonstration units are organized with officers, program committees, and local leaders to do the work. In some areas community units, including all members of the family, are organized.

Program Planning and Execution.—Each extension specialist is requested to develop a plan of work for the project for which he is responsible. The plan is based on the evident needs of farm people in the state, as found in surveys, data from crop reports, outlook information, and—to some extent—as recognized by the farm people themselves and relayed to the specialists through the county agents and their local leaders. The projects thus outlined in the state plans of work are the basis for county program planning, which is different in almost every county. County agents usually attend two or three state program-planning conferences and some go to district conferences in order to "make dates" with the specialists.

Local Leader Training.—The county programs of work which make use of the state specialist usually include some form of training for local leaders, especially leaders who—it is hoped—will cooperate

---

5 Bryce Ryan and Neal C. Cross, "The Diffusion of Hybrid Seed Corn in Two Iowa Communities," *Rural Sociology*, Vol. VIII, No. 1, pp. 15-24.
6 Gertrude L. Warren, *Organization of 4-H Club Work*, Misc. Pub. 320, BAE, USDA, 1938.

with the county agent and extension specialist in demonstrations of new practices. Demonstrations in methods of carrying out a project, such as building a movable hog house or planning a kitchen, are usually followed by result demonstrations, which show the results of the complete project. (See Figure 70, page 286.)

The role of the local leader, therefore, is important in extension work. Some so-called leaders or cooperators, as has been indicated, merely help establish and carry on a project; others, especially in home demonstration work, go to county leader training schools, then present the material before their own local community or neighborhood group. Thus the local leader becomes more than a demonstrator; he (or she) becomes a teacher of subject matter.[7]

Integration with Governmental Agencies.—The extension service gave valuable educational and organizational assistance to a number of Federal agencies during the depression and war years 1934-1945. For example, specialists and county agents devoted much of their time from 1934 to 1936 to the organization and supervision of the work of the Agricultural Adjustment Administration (AAA). They held training schools, helped conduct community meetings and made selections for community and county committeemen, conducted local sign-up schools, supervised the check up to determine eligibility for benefits, and were responsible until personnel drawn from the field could be worked into the full-time county, district, state, and regional offices. After that, the AAA carried on alone. Soon it began to develop its own educational program, drawing upon colleges of agriculture and U. S. Department of Agriculture material. In some areas the AAA and county agents conflicted, a few AAA leaders going so far as to say that since the AAA was manned by farmers chosen by farmers there was no need for an Agricultural Extension Service. Some regional and national leaders actually stimulated agitation against the extension service and even threatened to set up a new national farmers' organization based upon the widespread AAA organizational framework.

Other Federal agencies were also given valuable help by the extension service in developing their own educational programs. To cite another example, the Rural Electrification Administration (REA) found a very intensive program necessary, first, to secure full coverage in an area, and then to show the desirability of using maximum rather than minimum loads. It employed teachers to in-

---

[7] See Lucinda Crile, *Lay Leadership in Extension Service,* Ext. Service Circ. 428, USDA, 1945.

struct farmers and farm women in the installation and use of farm and home electrical equipment.

In general these agencies usually checked closely with the county agents and worked with them on coordinated programs. But conflict situations did develop between various agencies, and in some instances grew serious. Farmers were not only confused but often exasperated by the numerous duplicating approaches by these agencies. Something had to be done to eliminate the conflicts between these agencies, especially since most of them were located in the U. S. Department of Agriculture. Recognition of these conflicts came in 1938 when a national conference, called by the director of extension, formulated an agreement—the Mt. Weather Agreement. It was agreed that the extension service should have the chief responsibility for educational work and that the other agencies were to look to it for educational service in order to get their programs into action.

In some states it has long been the policy of the extension service that if farmers in a county were to receive extension service they should organize. So farmers did form their own organizations, but did not limit their activities to educational functions. They soon set up cooperatives and commercial concerns in competition with existing enterprises. Therefore, it was necessary to define the county agent's function; the resulting definition of policy forbade the extension agent to engage in any form of promotional work for the setting up of any kind of business enterprise. His function was to provide educational material and to act as an educational adviser. Strict adherence to this principle and to the principle of serving the educational needs of all groups has kept many a county agent out of serious difficulties. The hand of the extension man has been strengthened by the Mt. Weather Agreement.

Out of the Mt. Weather conference came, also, a new national effort to coordinate the work of all Federal agencies in a county and set up a system of neighborhood and community organization that would make the work of the agencies more effective. Under this system, a planning division in the Washington office, called county and local planning, provided the impetus for regional, state, and county planning efforts to determine present uses of land, and the best uses of that land. Part of the plan was to set up county committees on which all Federal agencies would be represented, also to form community committees with one or more elected representatives in each neighborhood. There was objection, however, on the part of some farm organization leaders to this kind of Federal, state, and local coordination. Whereupon, the Federal appropriations were withdrawn.

The Extension Service in Wartime.—In both World War I and World War II, emphasis was given to food production and food conservation. The government turned to the Agricultural Extension Service as the agency in the best position to help obtain widespread cooperation. In World War II the extension service was given charge of special programs, such as the farm labor program. It also helped to organize bond drives, war chest drives, scrap drives, and similar activities, so that it became a wartime service agency, sacrificing, to an alarming extent, its original educational function.

The charge to carry the wartime food production and conservation program to the "last family down the last road" led to a reconsideration of the neighborhood leader plan. In some states the system was set up on the basis of areas which were found to be actual, "natural" neighborhoods. Leaders in these neighborhoods were selected differently. In some states an effort was made to appoint leaders in every school district or neighborhood; in others, leaders were selected by the local people. What was expected of neighborhood leaders also varied in different areas. Some were expected to be contact persons—to tell their neighbors about the various programs and drives and to get their cooperation. Others were called upon to discuss a variety of subjects. Still others were asked to call and hold neighborhood discussion meetings. As a result, success was spotty. In general, the system was short-lived, chiefly because it was superimposed. It asked the same leaders to do too many different things, and had insufficient time for finding the true leaders in the various neighborhoods.

The whole wartime production program, however, was very successful. Even with a short labor supply, farmers increased production over 35 per cent in four years. Without question the widespread educational program, even if it was inefficient, had its influence.

The postwar years have brought a pressing need for careful revaluation of extension service activities in terms of the future needs of "farmers in a changing world." Extension methods have contributed significantly toward the rehabilitation of war-torn countries. After the First World War, agricultural workers and technicians came to the United States to learn about research and methods of extending the findings of science to farm people. Soon after the close of the Second World War an international conference was called jointly by the Office of Foreign Agricultural Relations and the Extension Service, to bring together information on extension methods to be made available to all countries that might find it useful.[8]

Problems Facing the Extension Service

Many new agencies have been set up to serve the interests of farmers. Each of them has developed its own system of education. In some cases the teachings of the various agencies implemented and in others conflicted with those of the extension service.

Cooperation with Adult Education.—One system of education for farmers, which later developed adult educational services, was made possible through the Smith-Hughes Act for teaching vocational agriculture and home economics in high schools. This system will be described in greater detail later. Suffice it to say here that it became a twelve months' program with projects in the summer months supervised by the teachers. Thus there was an early duplication of 4-H club work which in some communities has been ironed out satisfactorily. Some youths are in one, some in the other, and a few are in both types of work. Some teachers are 4-H club leaders; others help to find local lay leaders, which seems to be a better arrangement.

An extension worker can exert social control only through his influence as a teacher in possession of authoritative information. The great strength of the extension worker's position has been that he has access to results of research from experiment stations, results which can be demonstrated as reliable by experiments in his own county. His care in exercising control over these local demonstrations often has much to do with the acceptance or rejection of his teachings. By developing a confidence in his ability to demonstrate his teachings, the extension worker can command respect and a real following—probably the finest kind of social control possible.

Because he has access to sources of information, other agencies and organizations look to the extension worker for guidance and service. The Farmers Home Administration, for example, can exert more control over its clients than can almost any other agency. But even its system of control breaks down if the information used to guide clients in their farming or homemaking operations proves faulty. The same may be said of the Soil Conservation Service. Its

---

8 *Conference Report on the Contribution of Extension Methods and Techniques Toward the Rehabilitation of War-Torn Countries*, USDA Extension Service and Office of Foreign Agricultural Relations, 1945.

ordinances for some form of conservation will fail if the information on which they are based is not sound.

Local Leader Selection and Training.—The extension service depends for its effectiveness largely upon local, unpaid leaders. Hence, since its beginning, many farm and rural people, numbering hundreds of thousands, have acted in one way or another as officers, as local leaders, or as demonstrators. The same person may serve all three functions, but the selection and training of leaders for each function differ. Because the extension service has had few professional leaders these functions have not always been well executed.

Since the extension service must depend upon local leadership to help get the job done, the selection of any type of local leader should be made through the participation of the local group. Sometimes leader selection can be left entirely to the local group if the qualifications of the leader are made clear. It is usually desirable, however, to have the local group make the selection with some guidance. A demonstrator, for example, may conduct a good demonstration, but may have no local following. A subject-matter leader may have the confidence of his group but may not be able to speak before a group. A local officer or group leader, if selected by a county agent, may be notorious as an office seeker, and thus have no following.

Local leadership should be extended wherever possible. In general, there is a tendency toward overspecialization in extension work, various project leaders seeking their own local leaders. This too often results in an overloading of certain local willing workers, some of whom may not have too much influence in the community. This tendency can be minimized somewhat through local organization. Many 4-H club leaders find that almost every 4-H club member has potential leadership in some field. The same is true in other local organizations, especially in those in which everyone is expected to take part at one time or another. Thus, the various forms of leadership can be spread throughout the entire membership. Without local organization such a process is impossible; the same few leaders must be used over and over again.

Expanding Extension Organization.—Though extension workers have been charged by law to take new information in agriculture and home economics to every farm family, this has not been done except in rare cases. In too many states each extension specialist has developed his own group of cooperators, or each type of extension service has developed its own system of organization. Recent efforts have aimed at developing a neighborhood-community form of organization. These efforts are taking advantage of the impetus gained by the wartime necessity to reach every farm family, which impelled the development of a widespread system of community and neighborhood leaders.[9] In most areas it was phenomenally successful, especially where the chosen neighborhood representatives were the natural leaders. But in many areas it failed so miserably that future efforts in these areas may have discouraging results.

Extension service needs neighborhood and community leaders if it is to carry on its present program. A wise approach for finding leaders is to inquire of the people of the neighborhood: (1) who in the neighborhood is visited frequently, (2) who is frequently consulted about problems, and (c) who is the person to whose judgment the people defer. This person may not look on himself as a leader, and may act only when his counsel is sought. But once the leader is found and his cooperation secured, the desired performance of the leadership function is usually assured.

Providing an adequate and effective system of community organization is another problem which the extension service has not yet solved. There are various forms of extension organization in the community. 4-H clubs, home bureau or home demonstration clubs, and project demonstrations are organized in most communities in counties in which such extension work is carried on. In some areas extension work is organized on the community club or community or township unit basis, calling for participation of the family as a group. A few counties have tried to organize the community for extension work, but these are exceptions. Real efforts to study and experiment with various forms of community organization for extension service are needed. Extension work needs an effective system of neighborhood and community organization to provide extension information for the majority of farm families. This system will require community and neighborhood analysis, leader selection and development, as well as program planning to find and meet local needs through local participation. Such a system will also call for the employment of county workers not only in agriculture and home economics but also in rural community organization and rural youth work. These workers should have training not only in technical agriculture and home economics, but also in agricultural economics and rural sociology.[10]

9 D. E. Lindstrom, "Extension Service Jumps Back to the Neighborhood," *Rural Sociology*, Vol. VIII, No. 4, pp. 412-415, December, 1943. See also Extension Service Circular 402, USDA, 1943.

10 See D. E. Lindstrom, "Postwar Needs and Proposals for Extension in Rural Sociology," *Rural Sociology*, Vol. X, No. 4, December, 1945.

Cooperation Among Rural Agencies and Organizations.—Much closer cooperation is necessary among Federal and state agencies, especially on the county and community level, in making and carrying out programs. A county professional workers' council, supported by farmer, homemaker, and youth representatives from the various communities, seems essential. The county agricultural agent could well take the first steps to organize such a council. The professional workers in the community—especially the vocational agricultural and home economics teachers, as well as rural pastors, librarians, and similar local leaders—should help develop the community programs of work, based on local needs. These local needs should be the basis for making up the county program.

State and county U. S. Department of Agriculture councils help to coordinate the work of the various Department agency activities on state and county levels. The state councils consist of the heads of the state offices of the constituent agencies of the Department, membership being extended to the director of the extension service and to the director of the state experiment station. Membership may also be extended to the head of any interested state agricultural agency. In the county the council membership is made up of the constituent agencies of the Department in the county, the heads of the Production Credit Association, the National Farm Loan Association, the Rural Electrification Administration Cooperative in the county, the county agent, the county home demonstration agent, and the county FHA farm and home supervisor. Each state and county council is headed by a chairman and a secretary, elected once each year in December. Each council, also, is required to meet at least once a month.

Greater Usefulness.—The attainment of the material objectives of the extension service will be immeasurably aided if extension work is broadened and deepened by more emphasis on human and group values. Family life, school, church, health, library, social welfare, recreation, and similar social factors must have a greater place in the future. Furthermore, the extension service might well be extended to other than farm people, especially to village and town people. A truly effective and useful extension service is one which deals with life as it is lived in a total rural community. The local professional and lay leaders of the community must recognize its value and take upon themselves the job of bringing it to the community. Therefore, they must know more about the extension service and its benefits. If its program is broadened to include social as well as economic materials, it will command the attention and support of these leaders. Otherwise it will remain a special service to a select group, and be superseded by programs of other agencies so far as rural adult education is concerned.

Adult Education Through the Public School

The Agricultural Extension Service has, to a considerable degree, operated independently of the school system. Up to the present time its chief emphasis has been on vocational education—to improve farming and homemaking practices—and on youth work, principally 4-H club work for both in-school youth and out-of-school youth.

Federal Action for Vocational Education.—The public school system has been gradually extending its service into the adult field. The Smith-Hughes Law of 1917 provided Federal and state funds, administered by the U. S. Office of Education and by state boards, to teach vocational agriculture and home economics in communities which supplied facilities and local funds to match those coming from state and Federal sources. In these communities, two teachers—one in agriculture and one in home economics—conduct regular high school classes in crops, soils, livestock feeding, sewing, cooking, home management, and similar subjects. Here, then, is a second major educational effort in rural areas administered by a different Federal department, and organized on the state and community basis, with no form of county organization.

The unique nature of the vocational program in high schools, especially among boys, is that classroom instruction is usually tied to project work on the farm. Hence, the instructor remains in the community all during the year, in direct contact with the parents. An informal type of adult education was therefore possible from the outset. Also, the program includes the organization of the youth into Future Farmers clubs, which hold regular meetings. The members enter their projects in competitive shows; take part in judging teams; have their own series of inter-school and inter-community contests; and take part in local, county, and state fairs. Their activities are to some extent a counterpart of 4-H club work. They also have indirect adult educational values, for many adults are influenced by them.[11]

Expansion into Evening and Part-Time Classes.—The programs of many schools are expanding to include evening schools. During the war the number of evening schools increased greatly because

---

[11] W. A. Ross, *The Future Farmers of America Organization*, U. S. Office of Education, 1945.

many classes, with paid local leaders, were held in the open-country neighborhoods. In some communities the vocational agricultural and home economics teachers cooperate by having general sessions followed by separate sessions for men and women. Classes usually meet once a week for nine or ten weeks in the winter. The final meeting quite often is a community meeting, open to all who may be interested in coming.

The adult educational work is planned and managed with the help of local committees of farmers and homemakers, who in turn help get enrollment. A large percentage of the farm families of the community are usually enrolled, though not all are interested in every course. Since teaching personnel is usually limited, the courses must be restricted to one or two per season.

The programs of some vocational instructors are as broad as those of extension agents. Their supervised farm or home practice program fosters a close relationship between the home and the school and many parents are thus led to seek advice from the teacher. The teacher usually enjoys the confidence of his community because he is associated (sometimes in positions of leadership) not only with its economic life but also with general programs of community improvement. Instruction increasingly stresses the community and broad social aspects of farm management, marketing, soil conservation, land use planning, and the developing of social understandings and cooperative attitudes. Home economics instructors emphasize not only management of personal finances, home management, child care, health, and family and social cooperation, but also community and social relationships.

The public school adult education program has unquestionably made progress. Nevertheless, there is an obvious need for improving the program in a threefold manner:

1. Rural teachers should receive a better training in, a better understanding of, social and community problems, for the simple reason that they are becoming increasingly important as rural community workers.

2. The program should develop closer relations with the extension service, and similar county agencies, for the vocational teachers in a community can help to make extension service effective on the community level. Since both the extension workers and the vocational teachers secure their basic knowledge from the same source—the agricultural college—they might well cooperate in developing one community adult education program.

3. The program should work for closer cooperation between administrators on the state and national levels, not only to avoid conflicts in the county and community but also to provide for cooperative planning at all levels. A national liaison committee or office is needed to secure cooperation between the U. S. Department of Agriculture and the U. S. Office of Education; most other administrative problems would then solve themselves.

The Rural Library

Most farm people in the United States are denied free library service. Whereas 96 per cent of the urban population of the nation have access to free library service, only 40 per cent of the rural people have such services.[12] There are several reasons for such a startling deficiency. One is that farm people feel they cannot afford the service; they have high taxes already and hesitate to add another tax for library service. Another is that farm people think urban and town libraries have little which would interest them. The deplorable lack of system in the organization of libraries has only increased this belief.

A third reason is that farmers are furnished with a considerable amount of reading matter through the agricultural press and through farm bulletins and circulars from their college of agriculture and the U. S. Department of Agriculture. When they want literature to help them in their problems they go to these sources rather than to the library. Even rural schools have few library books; and these are not the kind which interest adults.

Lastly, farm people simply do not read so much as other people. One excuse is that they think they do not have the time; another is that reading, as taught by the rural school, is a painful process.

It has been demonstrated over and over again, however, that once rural people experience good library service, they "take to it."

. . . rural people turn to books for many reasons. Some are looking for specific information on cooperative marketing, building chicken houses, caring for babies, or repairing tractors. Some seek in books, pamphlets, magazines and newspapers, an understanding of the current social, economic, and governmental problems which vitally affect the life of every individual. Wise folks look for the background of current problems in the pages of history and in the biographies of great leaders. A few find inspiration in great

---

[12] See C. Arnold Anderson and Neal C. Gross, *Can Iowa Have Better Public Library Service?*, Bull. P50, Iowa State College Agr. Exp. Sta., 1943.

poetry and prose. Others see distant lands through books of travel. Many turn to good stories for entertainment and relaxation.[13]

What is said here of books is true also of other types of reading, for a good library has all kinds of educational material.

Rural Library Development.—The public library, primarily an adult educational organization, grew up through private library associations. Many village libraries are still supported by private donations and voluntary groups in the community.

The essential nature of library service has long been recognized. One of the earliest efforts to provide complete library service was the county library law enacted in California in 1909, although the first county library actually started was in Ohio in 1898.[14] Yet, fifty years later, only California, Ohio, Maryland, and New Jersey have established many county libraries, serving all of the people. Illinois has long had a law permitting county library organization, but only a few have so far been organized, though recently demonstration library services for rural areas have been organized in five areas of the state. These are county or district systems providing for bookmobile service from the State Library. Most of the rural people in these areas now have access to free public library service. (See Figure 71, page 286.)

Most rural libraries are operated through a locally selected library board, which hires the librarian or librarians. The success of the library obviously depends to a great extent on the quality and vision of the board members. If they are content to limit the service to book lending, chiefly fiction, and to hire a local, relatively untrained person to keep the place open two or three afternoons or evenings a week, the library service of the community certainly will be limited and ineffective.

One of the chief concerns of a board should be to select a librarian with the kind of training that will enable him or her to know the people and groups of the community and to serve their reading interests. Part of the task of such a person is to get to know and work with the various organizations of the community—the churches, the schools, farmers' and homemakers' organizations, as well as the various groups in the village itself.[15]

---

[13] *Rural Library Service*, Farmers Bull. 1847, USDA, 1940. See also Marion Humble, *Rural America Reads*, New York: American Association for Adult Education, 1938, pp. 16-17.

[14] Mildred W. Sandoe, *County Library Primer*, New York: H. W. Wilson Co., 1942, p. 15.

[15] *Ibid.*, pp. 55-57.

The library should be a community reading center and a source of information and material for all groups in the community, especially for the community's children. It should expand its service beyond books to periodicals, bulletins, pictures (sound, silent, film slide, and others), exhibits, news articles, and similar services, and provide a rural-trained, adequately paid librarian.

Units of Administration and Service.—Library service can be extended to all rural people through an integrated system of state, regional, county, and community library service. The state library performs numerous valuable services for rural areas. It provides library service by mail whereby books and other materials are sent to groups and individuals, on request, for two- or four-week periods. Too few farm people know of such services.

The state library also provides materials and services to any library in the state, and also serves schools and similar institutions. Most of them are depositories of materials that can be sent to other libraries. Close working relations should always be maintained between the state office of education and the state library so that rural schools, especially, can have new and up-to-date books. By the same token, close relations should be maintained with state extension services, especially those of colleges of agriculture, and the U. S. Department of Agriculture.

If rural areas are to be adequately served, a state library system should provide for regional libraries from which books and other materials can be taken to the remotest part of the region. These regional libraries may be county libraries or libraries covering the needs of several counties. They may serve rural communities either through branch libraries set up in every rural community (and many independent libraries in small villages would do well to become branch libraries) or through a bookmobile service, which could bring new stocks of books and materials to all parts of the county or region at regular intervals.[16]

The school library system should be thoroughly integrated into the state library system. The school library in many rural communities could well become the local community branch library, or the small elementary or one-room school could be the station at which the bookmobile makes one of its regular stops. Thus both the school and the community library needs could be met.[17]

16 *Ibid.*, Ch. VI.
17 George A. Works and Simon O. Lesser, *Rural America Today*, Chicago: University of Chicago Press, 1942, pp. 174-179.

The principle of local unit requirements and adequate support must be observed in library organization. Adequate support for a library requires an annual income of $3.00 per capita. The minimum is an annual income of $1.00 per person for libraries serving 25,000 or more people.[18] The most desirable form of organization is an integrated system of state, regional, county, branch, and bookmobile service.

If all rural communities are to have library service, moreover, adequate state and Federal financial aid is necessary. Numerous states are working for, and some have secured, such aid. State aid should be provided on a grants-in-aid basis so that the first consideration is the local need and the ability of the local area to provide funds.

Expanding Rural Library Service.—Library service will expand as rural people experience its value. Citizens' groups, called Friends of the Library in some areas, could study local needs, conduct education programs, and make the libraries serviceable. Members of all types of rural organizations should be included so that through their representation the kinds of materials needed could be provided.

Farm people would patronize and support the library movement if the librarian knew their problems and provided proper materials. For example, each rural library should have a complete list of college of agriculture bulletins and should be on mailing lists to receive notices of new publications. It should have a good selection of rural periodicals. It should keep an up-to-date check on new bulletins and books on agriculture and rural life. By thus being aware of rural problems a rural library can become a much used service agency. These services will result if libraries are organically connected and can exchange materials, the larger units helping the smaller ones.

The Rural Press, Radio, and Pictures

Almost every farm family takes some kind of newspaper, either a city daily or a country weekly. Almost every village has its newspaper which, in earlier days, gave space to national and international news. Too often, village newspapers deteriorated into partisan organs which often gave rise to two "party" papers in some of the larger places. Inevitably, village newspapers had to meet keen competition from large city newspapers. Those which have survived have done so

---

[18] Farmers Bull. 1847, *op. cit.*, p. 19.

by paying increasing attention to their function as a community service and educational medium.

Extent of Weekly News Service.—Many weekly newspapers are published in villages of under 2,500 population. Though a majority of the people in the vicinity of these villages take the local paper, those near the cities take the dailies rather than the weeklies. The competition of the city dailies is growing more acute as more and more of them report "local doings" and publish farm pages. Nevertheless, the well-managed weekly is still of considerable service.

The weekly is pre-eminently the newspaper of the rural community. Most of its advertising space is given to local business, thus furnishing a means for local merchants to "show their wares." To be effective, this advertising must be on a par with that of the city. Second in importance is the space given to local personal items. A "personal" usually tells who visited whom and where—a simple item, but keenly interesting to those in the locality. Articles, fiction, comics, and other "boiler plate" take up a good portion of the space. Some weekly newspapers also have excellent editorials dealing primarily with local issues, many of which are also current political issues. Increasing numbers of the good weeklies are giving space to agricultural information, most of it coming from the county agent or the college of agriculture. In some areas the local (county) farm organization takes space, sometimes a whole page, for its news and information. An increasing amount of space is being given, also, to school, church, and local organization news.

There are a few agricultural dailies in the country, such as the Bloomington *Pantagraph,* which serve both town and country interests in an agricultural area, with considerable space given to regional, state, and national events as well as to local news. These papers often report farmer opinion and action more accurately and sympathetically than do country weeklies, because they employ specially trained men who know farmers and who are on the job all of the time.

Large city newspapers have recently developed a farm page, hiring men and women trained in agriculture and home economics to handle the work. In addition, these dailies usually have access to their own or to a closely affiliated radio station which gives considerable time to a discussion of rural affairs, especially to markets and news items of special interest to farmers.

Though the country weekly still has a place in rural life, it must, in order to survive, be published in the larger villages. Its career is tied closely to the trade, school, church, and social interests of its

Figure 70. Result Demonstration

Research men of the Agricultural Experiment Station explain to farm leaders the results of small grain variety tests. (Courtesy Department of Agronomy, University of Illinois)

Figure 71. New Horizons!

The bookmobile extends library service to remote rural areas. (Courtesy Illinois State Library)

Figure 72. A Rural Youth Discussion Group
Camps provide excellent opportunities for small group discussion.

Figure 73. Participation by Farm People in a Discussion
Here is democracy at work. (Courtesy Extension Service, USDA)

larger community—its town-country community. It should be a "folk" newspaper with "folk" news that will make people both in town and country better neighbors. It will be of greater service if it is non- or bipartisan, expressing both or several sides of an issue.[19]

The Agricultural Magazine.—Editors of agricultural magazines have been influential in keeping rural people informed, encouraging innovations, and in leading new movements. They keep in close touch with current movements and the work of organizations and agencies affecting agriculture. Feature articles often describe the need for a new agency, the importance of integrating the work of agencies, etc. Such agricultural magazines report on activities in Washington which are of interest to farmers. They include material on applied farm practices, some of which are developed successfully by the farm people themselves, and others of which are successful applications of the findings of agricultural experiment stations. They have women's and youth sections, whose editors are well acquainted with farm homes, where they get their pictures and stories. Some also carry good serial stories.[20]

Almost every farm family takes one or more farm magazines. They must be recognized as a most important means for adult education in rural areas.

House Organs.—Of great significance, also, are the publications issued by agricultural organizations and agencies. Each of the three major farm organizations—American Farm Bureau Federation, the National Grange, and the Farmers' Union—issues a regular journal, magazine, or newspaper; these go to a total of more than 2,500,000 farm families. The cooperatives—the American Institute of Cooperation, the National Council of Farmers' Cooperatives, and the Co-operative League—also issue periodicals. In addition, each major Federal agricultural agency endeavors to have a "house organ," such as the *REA News,* which is sent free on request.

Many state and local groups also publish papers. Every county farm bureau in Illinois, for example, has a regular periodical, which is generally sent to all the farmers in the county.

The Radio.—It is probably true that more farm people prefer listening to the radio rather than reading farm papers. It is much easier to sit down in the easy chair after a heavy day's work, turn the

---

[19] See C. F. Reuss, *Content of Washington Weekly Newspapers,* Bull. 387, Washington State Coll. Agr. Exp. Sta., 1940, p. 46.

[20] See the makeup and content, for example, of the *Farm Journal,* the *Country Gentleman, Successful Farming,* or *Capper's Farmer.*

dial to a favorite program, and relax,[21] than it is to "go look up my 'specs,'" find the paper, and read. The radio near the dinner table or in the barn at milking time enables the farmer to listen to market and news reports.[22]

Special radio programs have been developed for farm people. The national chains have their farm hours, such as the National Farm and Home hour; state agricultural colleges have their farmers' and homemakers' hours; farm journals and newspapers have their stations and special farm programs; and local stations give special attention to the interests of farmers. Programs are highly varied, but they are timed so that farmers' programs come when farmers can listen. And listen they do! The average daily listening time for rural people is almost five hours.

The radio is a modern adult educational agency of great importance to rural life. It is being improved, for more and more programs of educational interest and value are being gauged to listeners' needs and demands. Farm people are voicing their protest against "hillbilly" music and stories and plays that put farm people in a bad light, and are now demanding intelligent discussions, better music, drama, reports, talks, and other features which give dignity and importance to agriculture and rural life.

The Movies.—The primary social function of the movie industry is entertainment. But, for rural areas especially, movies also provide stimulation, letting the people see how "folks" elsewhere live. They are, therefore, a great influence in modernizing modes of dress and in other ways educating the rural citizens as to the conditions of urban living, as well as to general social conditions.

Free movies, sponsored by trade-seeking merchants, are used as a means of attracting farm people to the village center. Since such movies may be of a very low order, they are a matter of important social concern. Here is a place where a local reviewing committee might be valuable. Movies in the village have also helped to "shut out" Sunday evening church services; to integrate movies with church programs should therefore be a valuable undertaking.[23] Movies, as well as film slides and similar visual aid materials, are being used by schools, farm organizations, and other groups to an increasing extent. Very fine showings are available from a variety of sources, which can help to enrich many rural community meet-

---

21 James Truslow Adams, *Frontiers of American Culture*, New York: Chas. Scribner's Sons, 1944, pp. 309-311.
22 See *Attitudes of Rural People Toward Radio Service*, BAE, USDA, 1946.
23 Adams, *Frontiers of American Culture, op. cit.*, p. 306.

ings.[24] As rural people make greater use of visual aids, these devices can be employed to bring actual situations before the group for discussion.

Rural Group Discussion

Farmers have always talked things over in their family and neighborhood groups. Though modern methods have speeded up farm practices, farmers still stop the tractor at the fence line or along the road to chat with a neighbor, meet him on the street corner in town on Saturday night, have several neighbors over for visiting on Sunday, and for exchanging ideas on work or mutual aid. This natural desire to talk it over with the neighbors has led to a national movement for the encouragement of discussion groups, and the recognition that good discussion groups need planning and that good leaders need training.

The discussion method has been widely used in all forms of adult education work, and is being employed to an increasing extent by extension workers. It is followed in groups such as farmers' and homemakers' clubs, youth groups, cooperatives, community organizations, schools, libraries, church societies, and all similar groups. Other groups are organized especially for discussions, with meetings in homes, school buildings, churches, or other private meeting places.

Small Group Discussion.—The most effective type of discussion group is the small group of fifteen to twenty people, who come together to solve a problem of mutual concern to the group. (See Figure 72, page 287.) In such a group the usual process is to state the problem so that each person present knows what it is and how it affects him; to have each member suggest a solution of the problem; and to come to an agreement on the best solution. Although this social process can sometimes be completed in one meeting, it usually requires two or more meetings, in order to obtain additional facts, test out suggested solutions, and to reach full agreement.

Not all discussion results in group action. Some causes a change of opinion or attitude, or may merely clarify the problem and place possible solutions before the group. But the discussion method is highly desirable, especially in rural groups, for it enables each person to have a part in finding the solution to problems, a process in which he takes a natural pride.

---

[24] Excellent lists of sound and silent movies and film slides are available from the U. S. Department of Agriculture.

Discussion and the Democratic Process.—Discussion is the democratic method of solving individual and group problems. As it is better understood and more widely accepted by people everywhere, it will increasingly become the method by which the democratic process of government will function (Figure 73, page 287). Only the fullest use of the discussion method has made cooperative endeavor possible. Certainly it is essential if we are to have an intelligent citizenship in our increasingly complex society.

The Future of Adult Education

Education is of the greatest importance to everybody, especially in helping him to develop his various abilities to the full. As Adams says, education should enable a person "to lead a more satisfying life, should assist the growth of his personality, prepare him for intelligent citizenship and make him feel that he is a person and not a slave, not a mere cog in the vast machine of modern life." [25] "Adult education," he adds, "is for that person who has passed beyond the age at which he would ordinarily have had education in school or college." This tremendously broad field is linked closely with our democratic form of society, which makes every individual work out his own salvation and at the same time offers him opportunity to develop his capabilities and improve his position among his fellows.

Perhaps as never before in our national history, this postwar world requires an intelligent, independent citizenry. We shall need more and more education. It cannot be of one kind or belong to one agency alone; it must be conducted in all kinds of groups and under all types of situations—in rural as well as urban areas.

DISCUSSION

1. Why was early rural adult education called extension service? Analyze the various plans of extension organization to discover the extent to which each depends on or uses group methods.
2. What are the chief problems facing extension work? How can these problems be met? What are some effective ways of exerting social control through extension organization?
3. What significant changes in adult education have come through the public school? What has been the role of local committees? What improvement is needed in the public school programs for adult education?

---

[25] Adams, *Frontiers of American Culture, op. cit.*, Ch. I.

4. What are the chief reasons why so many rural people are denied free library service? What are the values of library service to rural people? How have rural libraries developed? Discuss the chief factors in the success of a rural library.

5. What specific community functions are performed by the country weekly? What part does the city newspaper play in the life of the average rural community?

6. Discuss the influence that radio and pictures have had upon rural life. What is needed to improve these services to rural people?

7. What is the place of discussion in rural group life?

READINGS

Adams, James Truslow. *Frontiers of American Culture.* New York: Chas. Scribner's Sons, 1944, Ch. I.

Better Rural Living, Report of Cooperative Extension Work in Agriculture and Home Economics, USDA, 1947.

Brunner, Edmund deS. *Radio and the Farmer.* New York: Radio Institute of Audible Arts, 1941.

Hamlin, H. M. *The Community Program of Adult Education.* Champaign, Ill.: Stipes Publishing Co., 1943, Chs. III, IX, X.

Hoffer, C. R., and Gibson, D. L. *The Community Situation as it Affects Agricultural Extension Work.* Special Bull. 312, Michigan State College Agr. Exp. Sta., 1941.

Humble, Marion. *Rural America Reads.* New York: American Association for Adult Education, 1938, Ch. I.

Kolb, J. H., and Brunner, Edmund deS. *A Study of Rural Society.* New York: Houghton Mifflin Co., 1940, Ch. XIX.

Lindstrom, D. E. *American Farmers' and Rural Organizations.* Champaign, Ill.: Garrard Press, 1948, Chs. VIII, XVII.

Overstreet, Harry A., and Overstreet, Bonaro W. *Leaders for Adult Education.* New York: American Association for Adult Education, 1941, pp. 78-118.

Reuss, C. F. *Content of Washington Weekly Newspapers.* Bull. 387, Washington State College Agr. Exp. Sta., 1940.

Smith, C. B., and Wilson, M. C. *The Agricultural Extension System of the United States.* New York: John Wiley & Sons, Inc., 1930.

Works, George A., and Lesser, Simon O. *Rural America Today.* Chicago: University of Chicago Press, 1942, Ch. XIII.

Chapter 15

GOVERNMENT AND RURAL LIFE

The American farmer is today more conscious than ever before of the influence of government, for he is being provided with an increasing number of governmental services. It is significant that most of these services call for some form of group activity: informal or formal, local, county, state, or national.

The farmer once looked upon government as a system of protection whose strength was usually expressed in the form of police power. Now he recognizes government as a means of attaining equity with other groups, gaining services he cannot perform for himself, and increasing his security against hazard or disaster. Many farmers who at one time regarded government as a thing to be shunned and feared have more recently come to share the view that it gives "added freedom and development through adequate protection and ample services, with authority vested in certain men and agencies by the citizens." [1]

In rural areas even today, it should be noted here, written laws as a means of social control are still less important than the customs, habits, mores, organizations, and institutions affecting rural people. Though government is one of our basic institutions, children in rural areas grow up with little knowledge of its organization and its functions, so that only the exceptional youth have much interest in its methods of operation. Similarly, after election day many farmers take little or no further interest in their representatives, so that many inefficiencies and abuses have developed in government, even at the local level.

The primary support for governmental services comes from local taxes, especially the property tax. Property taxes are used primarily for the support of local institutions: schools, roads (see Figure 76, page 302), county and township government, etc. Property taxes usually fall most heavily on farm property. As long as farmers are called on to "foot the bill" they will scrutinize carefully the causes of the increases in local property taxes.

---

[1] Howard W. Odum, *Man's Quest for Social Guidance*, New York: Henry Holt & Co., 1940, p. 394.

A definite trend has manifested itself in levying of other kinds of taxes besides property taxes. Some states are now supported entirely by taxes from other sources. State and Federal tax revenues are being used, moreover, to an increasing extent to supplement tax revenues from local sources so that governmental services, such as schools, will be equally available to all people, irrespective of their economic status. Rural areas are justified in seeking state and Federal aid for local services, for, as we have seen, they transmit yearly a huge amount of wealth to urban areas.

Politics and Government

Rural people, and especially farmers, have not been without political influence. Throughout our history farmers have aligned themselves with one or another of the political parties. Their national political influence in recent times has been that exerted chiefly through the farmers' organizations, which have come to be recognized as major political pressure groups in the nation.[2] State farmers' organizations exert similar influence on state legislation.

Local Political Organization.—Political organizations in rural areas are grass-roots organizations, for each party has its system, beginning with the voting precinct. These systems take the main responsibility for selecting candidates for office; the rank and file of voters merely vote for the party representatives and the candidates. Party alignments are usually very strong in rural areas. The son remains loyal to his father in being a Republican or Democrat, and there is a tendency for many to vote "straight," thus taking the bad candidates with the good. The party spoils system, whereby workers are compensated by jobs irrespective of qualifications, is one thing which makes government expensive and inefficient.

Political groups are important in rural group life. In them one finds such group processes as leader and member selection and the formation of cliques, conflict, competition, cooperation, and selectivity. They are the local groups which exert the most influence in selecting local candidates for office. They are also related to county, state, and national political groups, and interest in national politics sometimes overshadows the importance of local issues. Loyalties to national candidates often determine the manner of voting in local elections.

---

[2] See Stuart Chase, *Democracy Under Pressure,* New York: The Twentieth Century Fund, 1945, Ch. IX; and Arthur Moore, *Farmers and the Rest of Us,* Boston: Little, Brown & Co., 1945.

Some of the conflicts which arise in local politics seem too trivial to be significant. But local political cliques are headed by politicians who, for money or for the gratification of ego which comes from controlling people and manipulating events, attempt to elect "their" candidates. This fact makes the process a significant matter in rural social life. It is a process, says West, which

involves skillfully "lining up"—and keepin' 'em lined up even between elections—the most influential neighborhood leaders, the most respected members of large kinship groups, preachers, church deacons, and so forth, all of whom can sway votes. This means direct and indirect bribes, contributions to churches, compliments to women, admiration of babies, head patting and ice cream cones for children, the lending of tools and disbursing of "trade information" to men, pressure on debtors, subtle threats of disclosing moral or financial "secrets," and the circulation of gossip, rumors, and outright lies "along the grapevine." [3]

In general, rural people become more interested in their government in times of economic and social crisis. During the last depression there was widespread rural interest in what the state and Federal governments were doing to alleviate distress. Many organizations were active in political campaigns. Their attention was quickened by the radio and other modern means of communication. Such active interest and participation of a people in the political and governmental life of the community and nation is highly desirable.

As long as farmers take part in politics as a means of reform a healthy democracy exists. The real tests of popular government are the participation of the electorate in the selection of local, state, and national elected officials, and the electorate's concern for the issues before these officials. Perhaps the weakest link in the chain is the participation of people in their local elections. Very often one finds that the only people at a country school election are the candidates themselves, and enough patrons to make it legal. On the other hand, when school "fights" arise, many people, who otherwise would not feel concerned, become emotionally stirred and too often vote down constructive measures. The trend toward making local studies or surveys and holding hearings or discussions prior to having elections is in the right direction.

Local Government

Systems of Rural Local Government.—Three types of local government have developed in the United States:

---

3 James West, *Plainville, U. S. A.*, New York: Columbia University Press, 1945, p. 87.

1. The New England town which has always been characterized by the town meeting. It includes the village center and the open country lying within the limits of the town.
2. The township system found mostly in New York, New Jersey, and in the Middle West. It includes all towns and villages except those which have separated themselves by being incorporated.
3. The precinct or commissioner form of local government, in which the county is the predominant unit. This came out of Virginia and the Southern group of colonies, where all administrative functions were vested in the county seat government.

Local Taxing Units.—In addition to these three forms, thousands of overlapping local government units with separate taxing powers have grown up for road building, schools, cities and villages, park districts, forest preserves, mosquito abatement districts, health units, fire control districts, etc. These multifarious units of government spend in excess of $7,000,000,000 of tax monies annually. Despite the magnitude of this sum, probably more than half of them do not have adequate methods of budgeting, accounting, auditing, and reporting.[4]

We should not overlook the importance of the various kinds of taxing bodies and the functions of these local governmental units. Hence in this book much attention has been devoted to rural school district organization (Chapter 13), to rural health services (see Chapter 16), and rural social welfare (see Chapter 17), which includes public support of public libraries (see Chapter 14), for we are coming to realize that everyone should have public library service paid for out of tax funds. Some attention needs to be given, also, to the extension of fire department services to rural areas, to mosquito abatement districts, to road districts, and to park districts. As more and more services are provided at public expense, increased attention should be given to efficiency of administration, effectiveness of service, and equitable financial support. These matters are considered briefly in connection with a discussion of each type of service provided by government or through taxation.

These units of local government are the means by which rural people provide protection and social services which they feel cannot be provided as well in any other way. Let us examine some of them, especially the township, village, and county forms of government.

---

[4] See H. K. Allen, *Control of Expenditures in the Local Governmental Units of Illinois*, Bull. 37, Bureau of Business, Univ. of Illinois, 1940.

Town and Township Government

New England Town Government.—The town antedated the county in the New England area. Before the Revolutionary War the governor of a province as well as the legislature could incorporate a town and give a charter. After the Revolution, New England towns could be incorporated only by act of the legislature.

The town is the major unit of local government, and the public services it provides are numerous and varied. Every town is required by public law to hold an annual meeting. The elected town officers include the moderator, selectmen, town clerk, collector of taxes, treasurer, highway agent, auditors, supervisors of check list, school committees, trustees of trust funds, trustees of the public library, police officer, and health officer. (See Figure 74.)

The town budget includes the school and precinct taxes which the selectmen are required to levy and pay over to the respective treasurers. Towns hold elections for county officers. Village districts may be established, including a part of one or more towns.

Township Government.—The township as a local government unit grew out of the New England town form. Unlike the New England town, however, townships more or less followed government survey lines, and were formed at the time of the establishment of government in a new territory or soon after. Thus, township boundary lines were arbitrary.

The township, as it developed, became more of an independent unit, conducting its own business of road improvement, care of paupers, health protection, etc., raising its own funds, and buying its own equipment. But, as an institution, the town or township is legally an arm of the state, just as are school districts and other forms of local government. Nevertheless, the people regard these units as their own and resent the encroachment of the state or any other larger unit on their "rights." The precinct was organized, also, to provide a local unit for voting purposes and to carry on certain other functions, such as road improvement.

The chief present-day functions of the township are to provide representation on the county board of supervisors, and to raise tax monies for road improvement, relief, fire protection, and libraries; and to care for or distribute to school districts the revenues from school lands or the proceeds of the sale of such public lands. The township officials, whose duties vary in different states, are elected. In Illinois the elected officials are the collector, supervisor, assistant

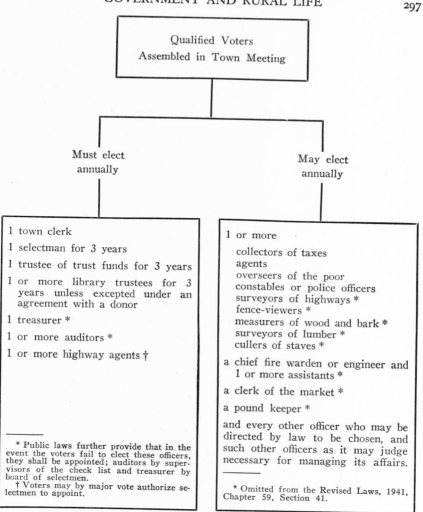

Figure 74. The Elected Officials in a New England Town

Note that the qualified voters assemble in town meeting to elect these officials. From Harold C. Grinnell, *Studies in Local Government and Taxation in Rural New Hampshire*, Univ. of New Hampshire AES, Bull. 436, 1943.

supervisor, assessor, clerk, and three trustees. Town meetings are usually called the second Tuesday in April, at which time levies are made for various purposes including bridges, roads, poor relief, etc. The law provides for the appointment of health officers, thistle commissioners, and other officials needed to keep order and provide for the welfare of the people.

Deficiencies in Township Government.—The township form of government is deficient in many respects. The principal criticism leveled at it is that it is too small for efficient operation under modern conditions. Many townships try to buy road building equipment, for example, although most of them have valuations too low to enable them to purchase anything but the most meager equipment. Many townships cannot furnish adequate public health service, library service, fire protection, or satisfactory halls for community meetings. The township official is usually untrained and quite often incapable. He sometimes falls under the influence of unscrupulous individuals who exact "terms" as a result of votes they can "throw" in elections.

A second criticism is that township officials usually are not elected or appointed on the basis of qualifications for office, but rather because of popularity, willingness to run, and in some cases because "they need the extra money." Most of these officials serve on a part-time basis.

A third criticism is that the township is an unnatural unit, for it was usually laid out on the basis of governmental surveys. All too frequently the people in the township are divided by community interests, some going to one community center and some to another. A township lacks political cohesiveness.

One of the chief weaknesses of local government is the failure to distinguish between the functions of policy-making and of administration. Both functions have been performed by the same elected officials on the township as well as on the county level. If these functions can be separated on the principle that policy-making should remain largely in the hands of locally elected officials, with administrative functions performed by qualified persons hired to carry out the policies, there may be a sound reason for the retention of the township or some similar unit as the basic unit for electing representatives on the county policy-making body. This principle is being observed by most farmers' organizations, for each has its locally elected representatives on a county board or executive committee. These county boards are policy-making bodies and place the administrative responsibilities in the hands of trained and paid administrators.

Changes in Township Government.—Any effort to take away the township form of government is hotly resisted by many rural people. It is close to them and they can see what is going on. The people they elect are "their" people. Hence throughout the years there has been little change in this form of governmental organization. Yet the township usually serves only incidentally as a rural social group.

Changes have come, however, in that more and more of the functions once carried on through townships are being carried on through county or larger units. Road improvement is being carried on more efficiently by counties and units larger than the township. Assessments, public health improvement, relief administration, library service, and even education, are functions which can be performed far more efficiently on the county level. Thus the township appears to be neither a necessary nor an economic governmental unit.[5] Viewed objectively, it has outlived its real usefulness.

The county, however, is not a good sociological unit. It has been advocated, therefore, that in order to maintain effective local contacts a new, more socially cohesive, local unit be formed, namely, the rural municipality. A rural municipality, as a *natural* community, would include the village and the area tributary to it. Although only a few such local governmental units have been formed, the entire plan is worthy of careful study and trial.[6] It may be that with the development of the high school community such "municipalities" will develop.

The Incorporated Rural Village

Incorporation by a village is a voluntary act performed to make possible the provision of services not otherwise possible: water systems, sewage systems, lighting, paved streets, etc. Incorporation permits taxation for these services. It makes possible a certain degree of social control, which is usually vested in a village board, headed by a mayor. These officials, elected by the people in the village, are given the job of administering the "ordinances" made for village government or services. Most of them do the kind of job they think the people want them to do.

An incorporated village is usually a sort of "in-group"; by incorporation it sets itself apart from the rest of the community. (See Figure 77, page 303.) In general, smaller villages which draw such arbitrary lines about themselves are primary groups, for everyone is intimately acquainted with everyone else. The larger incorporated villages, however, are secondary groups.

The village at one time tried to perform most of the necessary functions. Like the township, it is losing some of these functions to the larger unit. Nevertheless, the village is an important social

---

[5] H. K. Allen, *Costs and Services of Local Government in Illinois*, Bull. 33, Bureau of Business, Univ. of Illinois, 1936.
[6] T. B. Manny, *Rural Municipalities*, New York: D. Appleton-Century Co., Inc., 1930.

unit in its own right, and the real problem is to integrate its work progressively with that of its natural community.

We have seen that the village can become, and increasingly has become, the center for educational purposes. Some villages are supplying their fire department services to rural areas. They often extend tax boundaries to provide park facilities. Library facilities are also provided in townships which cooperate in levying library taxes. In rural areas the possibilities of extending such social services to the people of the "natural" community is limited only by the vision of the people, their willingness to cooperate, and their degree of tolerance. These qualities may be expressed in a readiness on the part of farm people to increase their taxes to meet those of the village for school or other purposes.

The County Form of Government

The traditional basic unit of local government is the county, for its origin goes back to the shire—the unit of local government established at the time of formation of the kingdom of England out of the Anglo-Saxon kingdoms in the ninth century.[7] Like the township, it is a creation of state law, being originally organized for maintaining order and for collecting taxes. As a governing body it has become relatively independent of the state, since most state constitutions restrain the state from interfering with county elections.

Functions.—The county government carries on legislative and executive functions, and in some counties provides judicial service. The governing in most counties is done by the county board or county commissioners. In some states county boards carry on legislative and executive functions, and in others legislative and judicial functions.[8] In addition to the county board, however, there are a number of elected county officers who have no responsibility to the county board, such as sheriff, clerk, prosecuting attorney, and judge. There are also other boards or commissions such as public health, welfare, education, etc. Few of these are held responsible to any one executive.

Deficiencies.—Like most townships, many county units are too small for the most effective service. The divided and overlapping

[7] See J. A. Fairlie and C. M. Kneier, *County Government and Administration*, New York: D. Appleton-Century Co., Inc., 1930.
[8] *Ibid.*, p. 116.

nature of services and functions of county government has led to serious deficiencies and abuses. The fee system, whereby fees are charged for such things as marriage licenses, land recordings, contracts, leases, and for making arrests, encourages inefficiency, for more attention is too often given to services for fees than to other services for which the person has been elected or hired by the county. With no official headship a county boss can and does distribute offices among his henchmen.

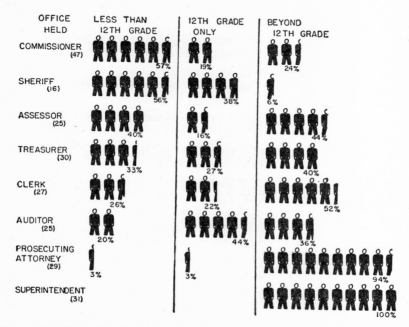

Figure 75. High School Grade Completed by County Officials, Classified by Office Held

(From Carl F. Reuss, *County Government in Washington*, Bull. 400, State Coll. of Washington Agr. Exp. Sta., 1941)

There are too many independent, elective, administrative offices, many of which are not of sufficient importance to demand the attention of the electorate. Elected officials are too frequently not qualified by training or experience. (See Figure 75). Furthermore, these officials often hire their own relatives whether the latter are qualified or not. There is no uniformity with regard to accounting, auditing, and reporting, and the county treasury is too often and too easily opened for plunder.

Governmental Centralization

Units of local government are human organizations. Many local units were laid out in horse and buggy days, and it is human nature to want to preserve them, and to retain a large degree of control over them. We must recognize that any minimum standards will really be set by the people themselves, based on what they believe to be adequate. Give farmers freedom of choice and they will vote to keep separate from village people to avoid paying taxes for village schools or poor relief.

But with the increase in number and variety of public services the old reliance on the "educational value of self-government," whereby a person elected to office is expected to learn his duties after assuming the office, is becoming too costly, not from the standpoint of money cost alone, but in social cost. Farmers in a one-room school district, for example, can keep their tax levies to the minimum by hiring a poor teacher. They fail to count the cost of the poor education their children receive. The best argument for larger units of government is their greater efficiency in maintaining and improving public services. For many purposes, as has been shown for schools, larger units providing better services can actually operate at lower cost. What, then, are minimum standards? On the basis of his studies, Anderson concludes that we can get along with one ninth of the number of units now in existence. "The average state, instead of having 3,500 local units, would have about 370." He feels the county should be the main unit for performing services of state-wide importance, including education, and also for providing rural local services.[9]

Anderson also feels that it is as desirable in rural areas as it is in urban areas to have only a single important administrative unit—the county—with coordinated boards for general county business, for schools, etc. Under such a plan most of the changes would have to come in the "northern" states (except New England), and particularly in the Middle West. New England, the Far Western states, and the South would require few changes.[10]

Proposed Reforms in County Government.—What can be done to improve county government? There are a number of local governmental official organizations, such as the County Sheriffs' Association, the Township Supervisors' Association, the County Clerks' Associa-

9 William Anderson, *Units of Government in the United States,* Chicago: Public Administration Service, 1942, p. 46.
10 *Ibid.,* pp. 45-46.

Figure 76. Unimproved Roads, with Only Local Government Support, Are Frequently Impassable. Consequently, They Are a Heavy Social Cost

(Courtesy Illinois State Library)

Figure 77. An Incorporated Village

The incorporated area might well be extended to include the adjacent farming territory, to provide better services and social control.
(Courtesy "Bloomington Pentagraph," Bloomington, Illinois)

tion, etc., all of which exert considerable influence on the state legislators to maintain the status quo. These associations could become an effective influence for needed reforms in rural government. To accomplish this, the leaders of these groups must be brought into discussion groups made up of local governmental officials, leaders from voluntary groups, and adult educational agencies. The result will often be that they will work for the reforms which are in the interest of public welfare.[11]

The core of most recommendations for the improvement of county government is the plan for a county manager plan, a county executive plan, or a commission form of government.[12] Since many county boards are now made up of from a dozen to several dozen members, this would mean cutting down the number of elected officials to three or five persons, who will be responsible to the voters for employing administrators for various county functions: the assessment, calculation, and collection of taxes and disbursing of county monies through a department of finance; the care of roads, bridges, drains, etc., through a department of public works; and the provision of relief, charitable, and correctional institutions, parks, playgrounds, etc., through a department of public welfare. Thus all present functions except those of county attorney, sheriff, and superintendent of schools would be under one executive.

A second significant recommendation for improvement is through functional consolidation, whereby two or more counties pool their resources to provide certain services, such as a hospital, a jail, a county health unit, or relief administration, which is then available equally to the residents of the participating counties.

The county is coming to be looked upon more and more as a local administrative unit for nonlocal government services such as the Production Marketing Administration, the Soil Conservation Service, the Farm Security Administration, the Farm Credit Administration, and state health, welfare, educational, and protective services. Thus, there has developed a real need for cooperative planning on the part of these agencies.

Evidences of interagency and interorganization cooperation are increasing. Health units are established more readily when cooperative planning takes place. School reorganization progresses more rapidly when organization and agency representatives, both on the state and the county level, meet frequently to discuss the situation.

[11] As is shown by *Adventure in Governmental Gearing*, Newcastle, Ind.: Council on Intergovernmental Relations, 1946.

[12] T. Hamp McGibony, *Governmental Cooperation in Greene County, Georgia*, Washington: Council on Intergovernmental Relations, 1945.

Soil conservation districts are formed in shorter time when interested county and community organizations and agencies work together on the project. Then, after the new service is established, its benefits are made more widespread and effective if there is close cooperation among the various interested groups. It may be that a single county coordinating or integrating council will be required to keep each of the agencies aware of what others are doing, to avoid overlapping, and to insure effective as well as efficient service.[13]

A properly organized county government may be more than an administrative unit, however. It could conceivably take over responsibility for the carrying out of functions now performed by special districts, such as fire protection. The county unit could provide full coverage by working through functional community units which include all of the territory in the county.

Physical planning in the county through a planning commission, the setting up of zoning regulations such as those in Wisconsin and Michigan,[14] for example, makes possible a program for the use of land and other natural resources in accordance with the character and adaptability of these resources. Such zoning regulations whose basic purpose is to promote the general welfare of the community limit improper use of land and promote public health and safety. This would be one way to prevent unwise settlement on new or public lands, and would enable the county to acquire misused land and put it to proper use. It would also make possible or more feasible plans for slum clearance in towns and villages and on land unsuited to agriculture.

Stimulating Citizen Interest.—Many local governmental officials have complained of the lack of public interest in their work. They complain that once they are elected the voters turn the job over to them and exhibit interest or come to them only when they pay their taxes, question their assessments, or work for the enactment of a desired regulation.

If local government is to be a government "by the people," it should be understood by them. A good starting point is the public schools, some of which in their courses in civics provide opportunities for students to visit the various officials and offices that have responsibility for the services, so they can see what is being offered. A knowledge of local government should be an important requirement of civics courses.

---

[13] *Ibid.*
[14] Louis A. Wolfanger, *Your Community and Township Zoning,* Circular Bull. 184, Michigan State College Agr. Exp. Sta., 1945.

An apathetic electorate will prevent the enactment of many constructive reforms and too often will let the "court house gang" do
as it pleases. Citizens' groups should be developed which will keep
abreast of new developments in their local government. The various
types of adult educational agencies described in the previous chapter
could well include a study of local government and needed reforms
in their programs.

Surveys or studies in which local people participate have been
among the most effective means of stimulating local interest. Such
studies have been carried on either by the people themselves on issues
on which they felt facts were needed, or with the help of service
agencies and organizations. The need for recreation facilities and
programs, more adequate health protection, libraries, and other services can be disclosed by such surveys. In some states legal provision
has been made for such surveys. In some areas voluntary groups
such as taxpayers' leagues have been formed to "keep tabs" on local
government. Too often, however, these groups have only one objective, such as to keep down real estate taxes.

State and National Aid to Local Governments

We have seen that, because of the great interdependence of interest and objectives, absolute local administration and control seems
almost impossible. We have recognized the fact that tax assessments
and rates vary and are inequitable, especially where rural people try
to support all of their local institutions out of their own resources.
(See Figure 78.) Some state and national aid is therefore essential. All rural people, it must again be remembered, contribute to
the wealth of urban areas. It is only right and just that urban
areas support the institutions in rural areas.

The great fear on the part of rural people is that the trend toward
governmental centralization will lead to state and national administrative and bureaucratic control. These fears are not unfounded. It
is a mistake to assume that the governmental unit furnishing the
funds should have control over the funds. A far sounder principle
would be that local units receiving state and Federal funds should
exercise control over them under the advisory direction of the larger
units of government. Moreover, loss of control of funds can carry
with it loss of interest in their administration.

The functioning local unit—the community—is essential, if intimate personal contacts are to be maintained, and if the rank and
file are to retain their interest in the making and administration of

policies. All people should bear costs on a basis commensurate with their ability to pay; when they bear part of the cost they have more interest in the quality of the service.

Government can remain local by insisting upon community or local representation on all county policy-making boards, and by the development and nurturing of local citizens' groups. They can be citizens' groups interested in governmental functions that promote the organization of county health units. Or they can be groups in the

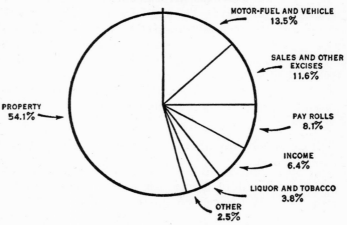

STATE AND LOCAL TAX REVENUES
UNITED STATES, 1938

MOTOR-FUEL AND VEHICLE
13.5%

SALES AND OTHER EXCISES
11.6%

PROPERTY
54.1%

PAY ROLLS
8.1%

INCOME
6.4%

LIQUOR AND TOBACCO
3.8%

OTHER
2.5%

Figure 78. Where the Tax Revenue Comes From

Note the high percentage coming from real estate taxes. (From Tyler F. Haygood, *Postwar Federal Finance and Agriculture*, BAE, USDA, 1945)

community made up of representatives of various voluntary organizations called together to do community planning or to form planning bodies. Or they can be groups, sponsored by voluntary organizations, formed to discuss governmental issues. These are ways in which a people can secure and retain control over government.

State and Federal participation in local government, however, is essential if standards of service are to be improved, if the burden of support is to be made more equitable, and if many areas are to be provided with any semblance of adequate services. Such state and Federal participation in local government should be on the basis of service where needed; helpful supervision, in some cases the setting of minimum standards; and assurance of equitable financial support to assure equality of opportunity.

Though there are minimum standards for efficiency and effectiveness of governmental services, there are also maximum limits—some units of government can become too large and too remote to be effective. In general, the farther removed a government service is from the people, the less human are likely to be the contacts. Also, the larger or more distant services can be more costly to society than local ones properly performed. Not the least important is the value of contributed services, most of which are given by people living in the community.

We are faced with greater, rather than less, centralization of supervision for most public services—with the prospect of more, rather than less, government service in various forms, especially to rural areas. As more state and Federal funds are used to support such services, the problems of interagency cooperation, cooperation with local units, and of maintaining interest and participation on the part of the layman, citizen, and taxpayer will assume greater importance. Changes in local government must come gradually, and with the fullest possible understanding and cooperation of rural people. It is not a problem of eliminating local self-government, but rather one of modernizing our forms of local government and of parceling out responsibility to bring about an efficient and effective system of public services.

DISCUSSION

1. Analyze local government, as you have experienced it through the years. What changes have you noted? Analyze the political groups in your rural community. Describe your experiences with political groups.

2. What evidences can you find concerning the influence of farmers on government throughout the years? What is your judgment as to the nature and value of these activities?

3. Make an analysis of the types of local government affecting the rural people in your home county. What are the chief deficiencies in these functions? What changes are needed?

4. What are the chief functions of county government? Discuss the proposed reforms in county government. Which can be worked out in your own home county? What are the chief obstacles to improvement?

5. What are the various ways in which people generally can be made to have more concern for local government? What are the principles of policy making and administration?

6. Discuss governmental centralization: its value and why it is needed, the possible outcomes, and how we can be insured against central government domination. Indicate what you consider should be the nature of future developments.

READINGS

Allen, H. K. *Control of Expenditures in the Local Government Units of Illinois.* Bull. Series Vol. XXXVII, Bureau of Business Research, No. 48, Univ. of Illinois, 1940.

Anderson, William. *The Units of Government in the United States.* Chicago: Public Administration Service, 1942.

Chase, Stuart. *Democracy Under Pressure.* New York: The Twentieth Century Fund, 1945, Ch. IX.

Cole, William E., and Crowe, Hugh Price. *Recent Trends in Rural Planning.* New York: Prentice Hall, Inc., 1937, Ch. XV.

Gee, Wilson. *The Social Economics of Agriculture.* New York: The Macmillan Co., 1942, Chs. XXI, XXIII.

Grinnell, Harold C. *Studies in Local Government and Taxation in Rural New Hampshire.* Bull. 346, New Hampshire Agr. Exp. Sta., 1943, Part I.

Landis, Paul T. *Rural Life in Process.* New York: McGraw-Hill Book Co., Inc., 1940, Ch. XXI.

Manny, Theodore B. *Rural Municipalities.* New York: D. Appleton-Century Co., Inc., 1930.

McGibony, T. Hamp. *Governmental Cooperation in Greene County, Georgia.* Washington: Council on Intergovernmental Relations, 1945.

Moore, Arthur. *The Farmers and the Rest of Us.* Boston: Little, Brown & Co., 1945.

West, James. *Plainville, U. S. A.* New York: Columbia University Press, 1945, pp. 85-91.

Chapter 16

HEALTH IN RURAL AREAS

The protection of the health of persons in rural areas, and the improvement of rural health conditions, have become matters of national concern. Health protection is best provided through group action. Control of contagious disease, for example, requires firm group cooperation. The provision of health insurance calls for special developments, among which is cooperative organization. Cooperative hospital plans and medical societies are being organized in increasing numbers in rural areas. Rural health protection is a social problem of the first importance.

Rural Health Conditions

Judging by comparative death rates, rural people have been gradually losing their health advantage over urban dwellers. In 1900 rural death rates were 50 per cent lower than urban; in 1940 they were only 10 per cent lower. The health of city people has been improving rapidly, but progress in the rural areas has been slow. A contributing cause, of course, has been the greater rural health hazard, due to the lack of adequate services: doctors, hospitals, and modern preventive means.[1]

Evidence that the present health conditions of rural people are below those of urban people, in spite of the lower death rate in rural areas, is revealed by the Selective Service rejection rates in World War II. Farm youth, eighteen and nineteen years old, showed the highest Selective Service rejection rate for physical, mental, or educational defects of any occupational group—41 per cent, compared to an average of 25 per cent for other groups.[2] Rates of Selective Service rejections by occupation show the unfavorable rejection rates for farmers and farm managers, followed closely by the rate for farm laborers and foremen (Table 13.) Only domestic service workers

---

[1] See *Medical Care and Health Services for Rural People,* Chicago: Farm Foundation, 1945, p. 54.

[2] See *Medical Care Services in North Carolina,* Progress Report RS-4, North Carolina State College Agr. Exp. Sta., 1944.

and emergency workers and unemployed showed rates in excess of these.

TABLE 13. REJECTION RATES PER 100 REGISTRANTS EXAMINED BY OCCUPATION, APRIL 1, 1942 TO DECEMBER 31, 1943 *

Occupational Group	Rate per 100 Registrants
All occupations	42.6
1. Domestic service workers	59.6
2. Emergency workers and unemployed	56.5
3. Farmers and farm managers	56.4
4. Farm laborers and foremen	52.8
5. Service workers, except domestic and protective	49.1
6. Laborers, except farm and mine	46.6
7. Proprietors, managers, and officials, except farm	46.4
8. Protective service workers	42.7
9. Professional and semiprofessional	42.2
10. Craftsmen, foremen, and kindred workers	40.7
11. Clerical, sales, and kindred workers	37.5
12. Operatives and kindred workers	37.2
13. Students	25.7
14. Others	44.5

* Source: Physical Examinations of Selective Service Registrants During Wartime, *Medical Statistics Bulletin* 3, Washington: Selective Service System, 1944, Table 3, p. 12.

The causes for rejection are important. A study made in one Ohio county through June, 1946, showed higher rejection for farm workers for mental disorders, heart and vascular weaknesses, hernia, weak eyes, neurological disorders, and mental deficiencies than for nonfarm workers: [3]

Cause for Rejection	Percentage of Farmers	Non-Farmers
Mental disorders	26.6	22.3
Heart and vascular	14.4	12.1
Hernia	11.4	8.0
Eyes	9.8	5.5
Neurological	6.8	3.5
Mental deficiency	6.8	3.2
All Others	24.2	45.4

We have noted that conditions conducive to good health have increased more rapidly in urban than in rural areas. In harsher language, this means that very many rural people are dying from *preventable* causes, as is shown by U. S. Bureau of the Census Mortality Summaries of death rates per 100,000 people:

[3] A. R. Mangus, *The Health of Farm People,* Ohio Agr. Exp. Sta., Farm and Home Research Bimonthly Bull., Vol. XXXII, No. 244, January-February, 1947, p. 18.

Disease	Urban	Rural
Infant mortality *	42.3	50.7
Maternal mortality *	3.4	4.0
Typhoid, paratyphoid fever	.6	1.6
Diphtheria	.6	1.5
Malaria	.3	1.8
Pellagra	.8	2.3
Pneumonia, influenza	63.4	76.6

* Rates per 1,000 live births.

Rural infant death rates are now over one fourth higher than infant death rates in urban areas. They are considerably higher for non-whites than for whites, though the urban nonwhite deaths of those under one year of age per 1,000 live births in 1944 was considerably higher than the rural nonwhite rate (63.0 in urban compared with 57.9 in rural areas). Maternal deaths in connection with childbirth are also higher in rural than in urban areas. These are, indeed, black marks against our supposedly dynamic, efficient, and forward-looking civilization! The principal reason, of course, is that whereas about nine out of ten urban babies are born in hospitals, a much smaller proportion of babies in rural areas are hospital-born. Figure 79 shows, for four sections of the United States, the proportion of births in hospitals in urban and rural areas.

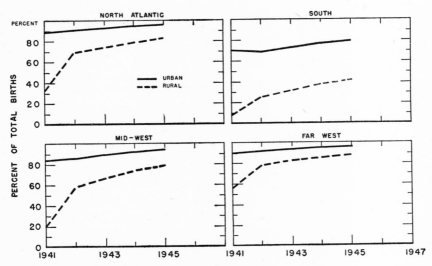

Figure 79. Proportion of Births in Hospitals, Urban and Rural, by Region, 1941-1945

(Bureau of Human Nutrition and Home Ec., USDA. Data from the Bureau of Census and National Office of Vital Statistics)

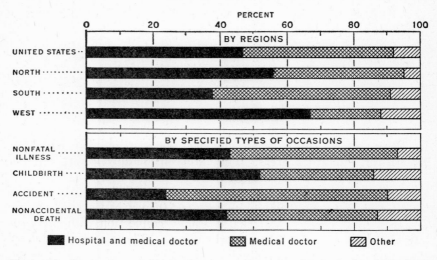

Figure 80. Percentage of Farm Operators Reporting Medical Care Received During Previous 12 Months, by Regions and by Specified Types of Occasion, United States, 1945

Most hospitalizations were for childbirth. (BAE, USDA)

Farm accidents, also, are a major cause of death. About one fourth of all persons killed at work are persons engaged in agriculture, although they represent but 16 per cent of all working people. That the farm is far less safe than the factory is indicated by the fact that the farm rate of deaths per 100,000 workers is almost three times as much as the rate of deaths per 100,000 workers in manufacturing industries.

Medical Deficiencies.—Lingering illnesses, though not a major cause of rural death, are a heavy burden and, at least, a heavy indirect cost upon rural people.[4] Recurring illnesses which are not properly attended by a doctor result in a high occurrence of chronic, physical defects, as high as three and four significant defects per person. Farm Security Administration studies in 17 states have shown that only 4 in every 100 rural persons were in top-notch condition:

7 out of 10 over five years of age had decayed teeth.
1 in 12 children under twelve were undernourished.
1 in 17 children had or showed after-effects of rickets.

---

[4] See Harold F. Kaufman, *Extent of Illness and Use of Medical Services in Rural Missouri*, Progress Report No. 5, Univ. of Missouri Agr. Exp. Sta., 1945.

2 in 5 white mothers had second or third degree injuries from child-bearing.

1 in 2 of all persons had defective tonsils.

1 in 12 heads of white families had hernia.[5]

Most of these conditions have resulted from inadequate care and could have been prevented. Even so, not all such illnesses were reported, for farm people are reluctant to admit that anything is wrong. Many a farm failure can be traced to a bad back or to an untreated heart condition! In addition to physical defects, there are tens of thousands of rural people suffering from diseases like malaria, hookworm infestation, and pellagra.

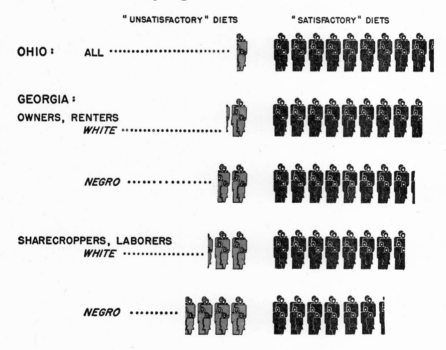

Figure 81. Comparative Percentages of Diets "Satisfactory" and "Unsatisfactory" in Calcium

(Farm families in an Ohio and a Georgia county, summer, 1945. Bureau of Human Nutrition and Home Ec., USDA)

[5] Gustav Larson, *Fact Sheet on Rural Health and Sanitation,* Office of Information, USDA, 1945.

Undernourishment.—Many of the illnesses, moreover, can be traced to undernourishment and the hidden hunger which is due to poor soils yielding poor food, low in nutritive value. (See Figure 81.) Farm people pride themselves on the amount of food which is served, but studies carried on by the National Research Council in five geographic regions have shown that only 35 per cent of white farm operators' families in the North and West and that only 27 per cent in the South had diets of the right kind of food.[6] In a spot survey carried on in Bond County, Illinois, in 1945, not one of 97 children had an adequate diet for the day. Of 667 children in Jasper County of which checks were made only 10 per cent had adequate diets for the day.

The Mental Health Situation.—More than one fourth of the rejections for military service, both for Negroes and for whites, were due to mental disease.[7] In Ohio, for example, 52 out of every 1,000 men from rural areas examined were reported by Mangus to have mental illness, which overshadowed all other defects. Only a small proportion of these, however, were cases of psychosis which needed special institutional attention; most were cases of neuroses or nervousness.

Both types of disorder are socially significant. According to Mangus, the high prevalence of neuroses "is indicative of a very great amount of human suffering," growing out of prolonged emotional strains and conflicts, which in turn

are generated by disturbances in interpersonal relations and maladjustments in family, school, and community contacts . . . Emotional turmoil gives rise to precisely the same aches, pains, and discomforts as are caused by organic diseases . . . Once neuroses have become established in the individual, they are difficult to cure . . . Prevention offers the more hopeful mode of attack on mental disease . . . In a mental hygiene program for the prevention of mental disease, more personal guidance is needed, but also needed is better organization of family and community life, and a decrease in the many cultural contradictions, conflicts, and inconsistencies with which the neurotic struggles without success to reconcile in his own personality.[8]

Social Diseases.—Some countries have almost wiped out venereal disease. This country, however, has not. At least 9 per cent of all new admissions to mental hospitals are due to syphilis, which curses

---

[6] *Inadequate Diets and Nutritional Deficiencies in the United States*, Bull. 109, Washington: National Research Council of the National Academy of Science, 1943, p. 3.

[7] *Statistics on Rural Health Conditions*, BAE, USDA, 1945.

[8] A. R. Mangus, *Health Defects of Selective Service Registrants in Rural Ohio*, Mimeographed Bull. 178, Ohio State Univ. Agr. Exp. Sta., 1944, pp. 9-11.

the lives of about 1 in 42 Americans. Gonorrhea is estimated to be from 3 to 5 times more frequent than syphilis. Three fourths of the new infections of gonorrhea occur in the age group fifteen to thirty years. In recent years, medical science has developed several effective methods for rapid treatment of syphilis, and the sulfa drugs have proved useful in treating many cases of gonorrhea. Penicillin and other treatments make possible the gradual eradication of both syphilis and gonorrhea.

The control of venereal disease lies in effective community and intercommunity cooperation. This cooperation must be carried out on the part of law enforcement and health agencies, courts, schools, churches, and social agencies if the program of control is to be effective. It cannot be done by one community acting alone. State laws requiring health examinations and blood tests before marriages are allowed are needed. Any program of prevention, however, must be accompanied by a vigorous and effective program of education.

Chief Contributing Causes of Poor Health

Perhaps the chief contributing causes of poor health in rural areas are (a) the lack of doctors and hospitals, (b) the great distances farm people must travel for medical services, (c) the high cost of medical service, (d) the inadequate development of public health services, and (e) the inadequacy of the health education program in rural areas.

Lack of Doctors and Medical Services.—There should be at least one doctor for every 1,000 people. Rural areas, however, average one doctor for every 1,700 people whereas urban areas have one for every 650 people. During the war period only one doctor for 3,000 or 5,000 or even 10,000 was quite common. The situation is even more appalling with regard to dentists. Moreover, doctors and dentists in rural areas are considerably older than those in urban areas. Many are past the age of retirement. Most are general practitioners; few are specialists. Not only is the rural patient usually quite unable to afford the consultation of a specialist, but also his country doctor is seldom in close professional contact with specialists to whom the patient might be referred.[9]

Farmers have always hesitated to seek the advice and help of a doctor because of the cost. Medical visits in the country cost more

----

[9] See, for example, Leland B. Tate, *The Health and Medical Care Situation in Rural Virginia,* Bull. 363, Virginia Polytechnic Institute Agr. Exp. Sta., 1944.

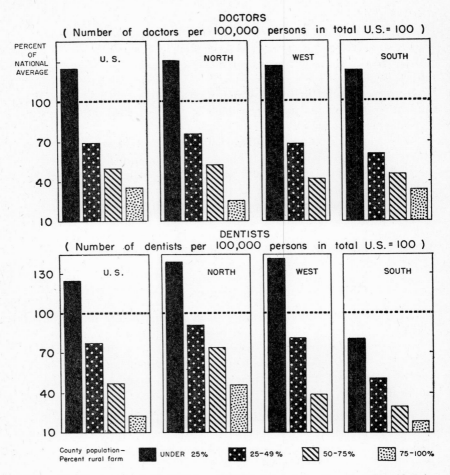

Figure 82. Doctors and Dentists per 100,000 Persons in Counties Classified by Percentage of Population Living on Farms, by Region, 1942

The most rural areas have the fewest doctors and dentists; the South has the fewest of all. (Computed by the BAE, USDA, from *American Medical Directory,* 1942, American Medical Association, and *Distribution of Dentists in the United States,* American Dental Association)

than they do in town, for besides the regular fee there is generally an additional charge per mile of travel, usually about $1.00 per mile. The result is that farmers living from three to ten miles away call the doctor only in extreme circumstances, often when it is too late.

As farm income goes up the amount spent for medical care is generally increased. Families with incomes under $500 usually spend less than $35 for medical care; those receiving over $2,000 about

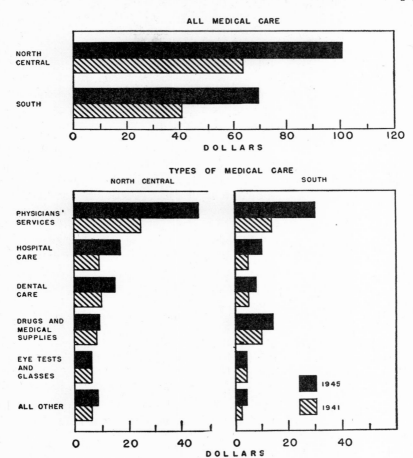

Figure 83. Average Expenditures of Farm Operator Families in the North Central
and Southern States for Medical Care, 1941 and 1945

(Bureau of Human Nutrition and Home Ec., USDA)

$120.[10] The average expenditure for medical care per farm family
is only about $60 a year, whereas a good program of health protec-
tion requires the expenditure of at least $100 a year. (See Figure
83.)

Rural areas have inadequate hospital services. There should be
4.5 hospital beds per 1,000 persons,[11] yet hundreds of counties have

---

[10] Jean L. Pennock and Grace M. Angle, *What Farm Families Spend for Medical Care*,
Misc. Pub. 561, USDA, 1945, p. 14.
[11] J. W. Mountin, E. H. Pennell, and V. M. Hoge, *Health Service Areas*, Public Health
Bull. 292, Federal Security Agency, U. S. Public Health Service, 1945, p. 5.

less than one bed per 1,000 people and over 1,200 counties are without any type of hospital, public or private. Most hospitals are privately owned and the costs are prohibitive for most rural people. As is to be expected, the states with lowest per capita income have the fewest hospital beds per 1,000 persons. Likewise, special sanatoria are lacking. In the South there are only thirty beds per 100,000 to take care of tuberculosis cases; in other areas there are as high as eighty-one. The facilities for caring for the mentally ill are likewise scandalously insufficient.

Inadequate Public Health Protection.—Public clinics for diagnosis or treatment and scientific laboratory facilities and well-trained specialists are almost unknown in rural areas. Most cities and larger towns have their public health protection units; it is the rural areas which are not so protected.

Furthermore, almost 1,400 of over 3,000 counties have no full-time departments of public health, and many existing departments are understaffed. Most rural schools are without adequate health education, examination, or protection programs. Very few one-room schools have even such elementary equipment as a clinical thermometer.

Inadequate Public Health Education.—The distressing conditions discussed above are certainly due in part to an inadequate health education program in rural areas. As we know, there is a tendency on the part of rural people to cling to the old ways—to resist movements for control of contagious disease and health examinations for children. As stated in a report of the Southern Rural Life Conference, the situation is too often that "most schools exhibit no well-designed programs of vital health education studies and learning experiences." [12] This report points out that teachers rarely have suitable preparation. Most subject material is conventional and academic in nature, as on such subjects as alcohol, tobacco, and narcotics, and usually presented only because required. The child often indulges in daily practices contradictory to textbook teaching. Little is being done in health education by doctors or health departments and even these efforts are not related to the school program. The "potentially valuable contributions from teachers of home economics and agriculture, county farm and home agents, physical education teachers, medical societies, and various voluntary health organiza-

---

[12] *The School and the Changing Pattern of Country Life,* Nashville: Southern Rural Life Council, George Peabody College, 1943, p. 2.

tions have been unrelated and far from integrated into a total community health program."

The Kellogg Foundation, in making a study preparatory to its program for the promotion of health in the Battle Creek area, reported that "health programs were practically nonexistent, many schools were neglected and inadequate, and community facilities, such as hospitals and libraries were either absent or of poor quality." [13]

Present-Day Rural Health Education

The traditional attitude toward health protection in rural areas has been that a person should keep well, and should call the doctor only when he became ill—and then not until the "home treatment" failed or seemed ineffective. Many times a cut or burn would be in such an advanced stage of infection by the time the doctor was called that it was too late to save the limb or even the life of the patient.

Dependence on Family and Neighbors.—The old tradition of dependence on the family or the neighbors for the care of all so-called minor ailments is still widely prevalent in rural areas. The country doctor, who often is more interested in saving lives than in getting his fees, still works in response to "last resort" calls in many rural communities.

The Local Health Official.—Usually the only form of rural health protection available is a county health nurse, most of whose time, obviously, has to be given to working with the most serious situations. It is impossible for one person to check all of the school children in a county. Some of the better health programs are designed to work through schools and voluntary organizations in immunizing against one or two of the most easily controlled diseases. Not all counties have even a county nurse, for in too many counties the boards of supervisors are still to be "sold" on the need, and there are no voluntary organizations interested enough or strong enough to accomplish anything.

Work of Voluntary Organizations.—Significant work has been done by voluntary organizations such as the American Red Cross, tuberculosis associations, parent-teachers' associations, and farmers' organizations, but until recently efforts have been scattered, uncoordinated, and not too well accepted in many rural communities. Each community may have its health program and its health com-

[13] *The First Eleven Years*, W. K. Kellogg Foundation, Battle Creek, Mich., 1942, p. 3.

mittee and it may take pride in doing its bit (the work of parent-teachers' associations in summer roundups for health examinations, for instance, has been excellent) but as long as these groups work independently, the task of overcoming the native inertia in respect to a positive health program is likely to prove too great. However, it can be recorded that groups are being formed here and there and that real progress is evident. The Kellogg Foundation's health program called into being both professional and lay community and county committees to study the local problems and to help make plans to meet them.

Measures to Meet the Need

If rural health protection is not to be left to chance a positive program must be developed. But to get rural people to believe that "an ounce of prevention is worth a pound of cure," and to get them to feel that good health is a social concern requires an extended, integrated, persistent program of education. Many organizations and agencies are interested in the matter, from the United States government—which stated the basic problems in the White House Conference on Child Health and Protection—down to local groups of citizens, such as the group in the small community in the sandhills of Nebraska, which organized its own medical cooperative.

County Health Departments.—An increasing number of counties are now organizing full-time health departments. These have been stimulated by the experience of the wartime health districts imposed by army regulation. In the wartime period all areas surrounding military camps or war production industries were placed under public health units. These units were disbanded within six months after the war. Many counties are therefore taking action to set up units in order to continue the protection afforded in wartime. In some states enabling legislation has only recently been enacted for setting up county health units.

The School-Community Health Program.—Real progress has been made in some areas toward developing a constructive school-health program. Such a program has the following important steps: [14]

1. Regular or periodic physical and mental health examinations.
2. Follow-ups to correct defects found.

---

[14] See *A Basic Plan for Health Education and the School Health Program,* Illinois Department of Public Health, 1944.

3. An effective program for controlling contagious diseases.
4. Instruction in good health practices.
5. A physical education program adapted to each child's needs.
6. An effective program in proper sanitation.
7. Instruction and practice in safety and first aid.
8. Instruction, demonstration, and practice with proper diet.
9. Integration of the program with those of the community agencies—health department, doctors, dentists, hospital, clinics, etc.
10. Proper instruction in character, personality, and social adjustment.
11. Effective extension of the program into the home.

The first concern in developing a good school health program is, of course, the preparation of teachers to help carry on the program. Since the average one-room school must depend on one teacher, it is essential that all teachers should have some basic training in health education. The least that one should expect is that the teacher (a) be required to take a complete health examination periodically, (b) know something about detection of contagious disease, (c) be able to cooperate on a health examination program for the children, (d) help in seeing that all discovered defects are corrected, (e) be able to help in handling a good program of hot lunches, (f) provide a minimum program of instruction with concrete applications in sanitation, safety, first aid, care of the sick, personal care, etc., and (g) supervise all play periods so that the most effective program of physical fitness compatible with the provision of free play and wholesome enjoyment will be forthcoming.

In larger schools the least that one should expect is that (a) the various teachers responsible for the health program—the physical education teachers, the teachers of hygiene, of home economics, etc.,—should formulate cooperatively the right kind of positive program; (b) the school administration should work out a cooperative program with the health agencies and the organizations in the community interested in health protection, for example, to make sure that children are really given thorough health examinations, that parents are present when those examinations are given, and that specific plans are made to correct any defects found; and (c) that the health program of the school will be accepted by the parents to the extent that practices taught in school will be carried out in the home.

The most effective means of attaining such a program is to have a school health committee which will be part of a school agency committee (doctor, dentist, hospital, clinic, health department, government official). In turn, this will be part of a school-agency-community health committee on which health committees of the various community organizations as well as parents will be represented. Many people will be involved, so a good working arrangement is to have a small executive committee, representing the school, agency, and community responsible for making detailed plans and formulating proposed policies.

Basic Organization for Health Protection.—We now know that a number of contagious diseases can be controlled through immunization. Many families are now being urged by their family doctors to take shots or vaccinations for typhoid fever, whooping cough, diphtheria, smallpox, and be X-rayed for possible traces of tuberculosis. It is not enough, however, to depend entirely on one's own doctor (or dentist), for too many people still wait until they get sick before they go to the doctor, and too many rural mothers have home deliveries without the prenatal and special care which they require. Hence the least that should be asked for rural areas is a public health department with at least one full-time doctor, sanitary engineer, and several nurses, for every 50,000 people. In addition a good hospital, as well as health centers providing care in the fields of internal medicine, obstetrics, eye, ear, nose, and throat treatment, dentistry, minor surgery, and laboratory facilities for X ray and bacteriology, should be available to every farm home. These health centers should be within an hour's driving distance of every rural home within the respective area.

A coordinated hospital service plan provides complete service, in the form of rural hospitals and health centers, that bring both general and specialized services to all rural people. A number of states have already authorized surveys of the extent and nature of hospital facilities. The plan provides for constant exchange of information, training, and consultation service and personnel between hospitals and centers, and for referral of patients when indicated.

The provision of hospital service is, however, but one part of the health program now being proposed for people in the United States. A complete plan would include health insurance, medical cooperatives, hospital associations (such as the Blue Cross which has been spreading rapidly in the country), and possibly tax supported medical service. An increasing number of farm people are now becoming members of hospital associations such as the Blue Cross plan, which provides complete hospital care and many special services. Many farmers' organizations are promoting these plans.

The entire cost of medical care is now being provided by several medical associations. Most of these plans provide for a membership payment of from $30 to $75 per year. They can include costs of doctors' care in the home and office and surgeons' services in a hospital. They include, also, costs of hospitalization, dental care, drugs, special nursing service, and administration. Usually the member can select his own doctor, and every family gets full protection for all members. They are urged to come early and often, in order to cut down the heavy costs of care when illnesses or injuries are ignored.

Federal Aid for Hospital Construction.—Public Law 725 provides for the making of complete hospital surveys in a state and Federal aid for hospital construction. The primary purpose of the law is to provide adequate hospital services, especially for rural areas. Though a 50-bed hospital is considered the minimum for adequate service, farmers' organization leaders are working to provide smaller units as health centers to attract doctors and dentists to many rural areas not now served. Under this law local hospitals are being built, with one third of the funds coming from the local community, one third from the state, and one third from Federal sources.

The Future of Rural Health Protection

Our health is now of concern to the whole of society. We cannot allow the illnesses of those with low incomes to jeopardize the health of the rest of us. Neither can we allow children to grow up with physical, organic, or mental handicaps which can be corrected. We must see, moreover, that the child's health is protected by good diets, proper sanitation, adequate safety measures, and effective control of disease. Rural areas must have protection and care comparable with that in urban areas: thorough health departments, adequate school health education programs, health clinics and centers, rural hospitals, sufficient doctors and dentists. These should be provided through cooperatives or, if necessary, by taxation.

In summary, the rural health situation is still unsatisfactory, but there are many encouraging trends. The problem *is* being attacked, and some definite improvement can be noted. Once again, it is to be hoped, the country will become a really healthful place in which to live. To achieve this goal will require abundant education and full-hearted cooperation on local, county, state, and national levels. Schools, churches, rural organizations and agencies should join in this nationwide educational effort to bring good health to rural people.

DISCUSSION

1. What are the chief contributing causes of poor health in your own community, especially in the rural districts?
2. What would be an effective school health program for your community? How should it be adapted to a small rural community? What should be the program in larger schools?
3. What would be an effective program for the control of contagious diseases? How should a program for treating patients with mental diseases be worked out for rural areas? What facilities are needed for adequate health protection and hospital care in rural areas? What should be the nature and extent of health insurance?
4. Discuss the nature and functioning of cooperative medical societies.
5. What government plans for medical service are needed? What safeguards are necessary in these plans? What are the arguments for and against tax-supported medical service?
6. How would you proceed in organizing a county health unit in your county?

READINGS

Almack, Ronald B. *The Rural Health Facilities of Lewis County, Missouri.* Research Bull. 365, Missouri Agr. Exp. Sta., 1943.

A Handbook on Health for Farm Families. Farm Security Administration Pub. 129, USDA, 1944.

Health Service Areas. Public Health Bull. 292, U. S. Public Health Service, Federal Security Agency, 1945.

Inadequate Diets and Nutritional Deficiencies in the United States. Bull. 109 of the National Research Council, National Academy of Sciences, Washington, 1943.

Kemp, Louise, and Smith, T. Lynn. *Health and Mortality in Louisiana.* Bull. 390, Louisiana Agr. Exp. Sta., 1945.

Mangus, A. R. *Health Defects of Selective Service Registrants in Rural Ohio.* Bull. 178, Ohio State Univ. Agr. Exp. Sta., 1944.

Medical Care and Hospital Services for Rural People. Chicago: Farm Foundation, 1944.

Medical Care Services in North Carolina. Progress Report No. RS-4, North Carolina Agr. Exp. Sta., 1944.

Pennock, Jean L., and Angle, Grace M. *What Farm Families Spend for Medical Care.* Misc. Pub. 561, USDA, 1945.

Pink, Louis H. *The Story of Blue Cross.* Public Affairs Pamphlets 101, New York: Public Affairs Committee, Inc., 1945.

Proceedings of the American Country Life Association, 1944, pp. 59-71.

Tate, Leland B. *The Health and Medical Care Situation in Rural Virginia.* Bull. 363, Virginia Polytechnic Institute Agr. Exp. Sta., 1944.

The Experimental Health Program of the United States Department of Agriculture. A study made for the Subcommittee on Wartime Health and Education for the Committee on Education and Labor, U. S. Senate, 1946, p. 2.

The First Eleven Years. Battle Creek, Mich.: W. K. Kellogg Foundation, 1942.

Chapter 17

SOCIAL WELFARE IN RURAL LIFE

Rural social welfare is more than charity or sentimental uplift. It is, in its broadest sense, a concern for the welfare of all people. Common usage, however, has tended to restrict the term "welfare" to those who are in need. When people are deprived of the means, economic or social, of attaining a decent standard of living on their own initiative and through their own efforts, someone else must have concern for their welfare. If other means fail or if there is no other source to which they may turn, these people can look only to society, public or government, to provide the necessities of life. To care adequately for the dependent, the delinquent, the lame, halt, or blind who need help is of importance not only to the people themselves, but also reflects a healthy moral tone in the whole of society.

Prior to 1933, in most rural communities, the only financial assistance available for persons in need was county or township poor relief funds. Expenditures from these funds were frequently limited to provision of almshouse care for the aged and chronically ill, medical relief in emergencies, and meager relief for the completely destitute. Administration of public relief was usually one of the many duties of the township supervisors, county commissioners, or town selectmen, depending on the type of government.[1]

It was only during the early depression years that we suddenly realized—one might almost say discovered—that millions of our rural people had a standard of living below the minimum necessary to preserve health and decency. We were, in effect, in full possession of some very fine rural slums. Many rural people, of course, became poor because of the disastrous lowering of price levels and because of drought and other hazards. These people, we knew, would probably fight back to their former scale of living. But the poverty of others had deeper roots in personal difficulties—illness, physical or mental—or because of the progressive, rather than sudden, deterioration of the environment in which they lived.

---

[1] Grace Browning, *Rural Public Welfare*, Chicago: University of Chicago Press, 1941, p. 3.

Rural poverty is not limited to families on the land. It is found in villages dependent on agriculture, and in regions of "rural" industries, especially mining, lumbering, and quarrying. Two of its basic causes are over-exploitation of natural resources and technological improvements, such as mechanical farming. Economic groups which are particularly subject to the hazards of rural poverty are farm laborers and their families, and sharecroppers and tenants, many of whom go on relief because they are displaced and cannot find other employment.[2]

Changes in Systems of Public Aid

The old idea that "the poor we have with us always" and that we must treat them as a different class of people—as paupers—is unfortunately still widespread in rural America. Farm families, especially, are expected to make their own living. If they cannot, it is felt, something must be wrong with them. Developments in the last two decades, however, have made us realize that no nation can be healthy if it permits the development, much less the existence, of rural decay. We are slowly beginning to realize that poverty can be a form of malady, either on the part of the individual or of the society in which we live, and that we must treat it as scientifically and intelligently as we know how.

Pauper Aid.—Aid to the poor or unfortunate was at one time dispensed primarily by the church, for charity and almsgiving were acts of mercy. The present legal conception of poor relief goes back to the reign of Queen Elizabeth, during whose reign two rather unjust "principles" characterizing poor relief were established:

1. Residence requirements—the idea that a person or family must have lived in a particular community for a specified period of time in order to become eligible for pauper aid.
2. "Less eligibility"—the belief that the recipient of pauper aid should receive less than the lowest-paid wage earner in the community in order to discourage a demand for aid.[3]

The first of these principles has caused untold misery for thousands, for those who must go on relief are usually the most unstable and migratory of our populations. The second tends to condemn the unfortunates to a life on relief, for they frequently cannot get enough to eat or to wear, much less the medical aid which so many

2 T. J. Woofter, Jr. and Ellen Winston, *Seven Lean Years*, Chapel Hill: University of North Carolina Press, 1939, Ch. II.
3 D. E. Lindstrom and Ida D. Johns, *Rural Relief in Illinois*, Bull. 480, Univ. of Illinois Agr. Exp. Sta., 1941, p. 398.

of them need, in order to have the initiative to become self-supporting again.

Indoor and Outdoor Relief.—Previous to the depression of the 1930's relief cases in rural areas were handled largely by lay or elected officials, such as the township supervisors. For some time the county poorhouse was the only means of aiding the poor. It sheltered the old, the sick, the insane, and dependent children. Gradually, another form of relief, called "outdoor" relief (that is, relief outside of the institution), was provided for widows of veterans, for the insane, for the blind, and for mothers with dependent children. This outdoor relief is still being administered in most rural areas by township and county overseers of the poor, who dole out food, clothing, or fuel in amounts sufficient merely to prevent starvation or freezing. The only efforts at rehabilitation of these unfortunates in times past were to castigate them, in the hope that shame would drive them to support themselves or to leave the community.

Social Case Work.—Professional social welfare work developed in the cities through organized charity groups, which found numerous families requiring help because of sickness, accident, desertion, and needing help in coping with delinquency. By degrees, it came to be recognized that effective aid in the reconstruction of dependent families required just as much ability and specialized knowledge as does the practice of medicine or law. Social welfare workers have been accepted slowly by rural people, not only because the latter felt capable of taking care of their own poor, but also because few professional workers are trained to understand rural problems and to work with rural people.

Relief for Unemployment.—The shattering depression of the 1930's saw millions of people thrown out of work. Thousands of them returned to rural areas, most of them going to poor-land areas in which they could get a foothold, and many to families on poor land from which they had gone in the "good" years of the 1920's. In 1930, when the depression began, about 42 per cent of America's families were classified as rural. About that time, even as late as 1932 and before Federal funds had become available, only about one per cent were on relief. By 1935, more than one in three rural families had been forced to seek public or private assistance at one time or another. Local relief officials simply could not handle the situation. Federal action had to be taken.

In 1932 and the following years a number of Federal relief agencies were set up to provide direct relief and to provide work relief. The Federal Emergency Relief Administration (FERA) was organized in 1933, and for a time provided both direct and work relief. Similar relief agencies were organized by the states which, by organizing county relief offices, took over the functions previously carried on by the township supervisors. An effort was made to get professionally trained workers, but most workers had to come out of the cities or be recruited from among local school teachers or others. In 1935 the Social Security Act was passed. In the same year FERA was liquidated and the Works Progress Administration created (see below). The employing of improperly trained personnel resulted in an ineffective handling of the work in many areas and a demand that the administration be turned back to the townships.

Work Relief.—By 1936 the Federal government turned back to the states the support of the direct relief program, on the principle that the states should support their own chronic dependents or unemployables. The Federal government did retain responsibility for those who could work, and these were taken care of through the Works Progress Administration.

The principle of "less eligibility" demanded that WPA employees be paid lower wages than others. However, since wage rates were usually set on the urban employment basis, farmers complained that they could not get WPA employees to do farm work because it paid less in cash than the workers could get in town. Since it was extremely difficult to get back on the WPA rolls again after leaving them, most workers preferred the security of WPA employment to farm work, especially work of a seasonal nature.

The cost of direct and work relief varied from region to region and from town to town. The actual amount received per family was highest for the New England areas, and lowest for Negroes in the South. In terms of the average amount of relief per family, the families receiving direct relief were least expensive, and those receiving work relief were next, with the average amount almost 50 per cent greater for the latter. Families receiving a combination of both work and direct relief were most expensive of all. In almost every case, however, the cost of each type of relief was greater in the villages than in the open country.

Categorical Relief.—But direct and work relief were not the only forms of relief in the period. Blind pensions, veterans' aid, and similar "categorical" forms still continued, and new ones were created under the Social Security Act. To the list, also, were added grants to farmers in distress because of drought or flood. These unfortunates, whose numbers were swelled by the widespread dis-possession of farmers due to disastrously low prices, led to the formation of the Farm Security Administration (FSA).

Farm Security.—By far the most important relief agency for destitute and low income farmers has been the Farm Security Administration, which was merged into the Farmers' Home Administration in 1946. Figure 84 shows that in 1939, 60.9 per cent of the 2,682,000 low income farms in the United States were classed as those on which the operators were potential borrowers. Some 596,000 families received standard loans between July 1, 1935 and September 30, 1943. By the end of 1945 the number had risen to 770,000—equivalent to 1 out of every 8 farm operators reported by the U. S. Census.[4]

The chief characteristics of the standard loan program of the FSA included (1) credit for normal farm and home operating expenses to farm families who are unable to obtain satisfactory financing from other private or Federal source; (2) supervision, or advisory assistance, which includes help in making farm and home plans and "on-the-farm" teaching of improved farm and home practices; and (3) rehabilitation *in place,* that is, without resettlement. Other techniques adapted or developed to aid borrowers include improvement of tenure; group services, established with or without loans, to provide needed services or facilities such as sires or machinery where family circumstances do not justify individual ownership; group health plans to provide medical and dental care, hospitalization and drugs; adjustment of debts, a service transferred from the Farm Credit Administration in 1935; environmental sanitation; special loans such as those for water facilities and 4-H club activity; and specialized programs in limited areas.

Examples of the specialized programs are farm-unit reorganization in the Southern Great Plains, a special Negro community program, and a noncommercial experimental program. Grants were used extensively during the depression years but during the war years were greatly restricted. Before they were prohibited by Congress in the 1944 Agriculture Appropriation Act and subsequent Acts, cooperative associations were established and were assisted to aid borrower families in marketing, purchasing, land leasing, veterinary care, and a wide variety of other purposes. Neighborhood study or "action" groups were at one time encouraged to help borrowers discuss their problems and ways of solving them.

---

[4] Olaf F. Larson, *Ten Years of Rural Rehabilitation in the United States,* BAE, USDA, 1947, pp. 2 ff.

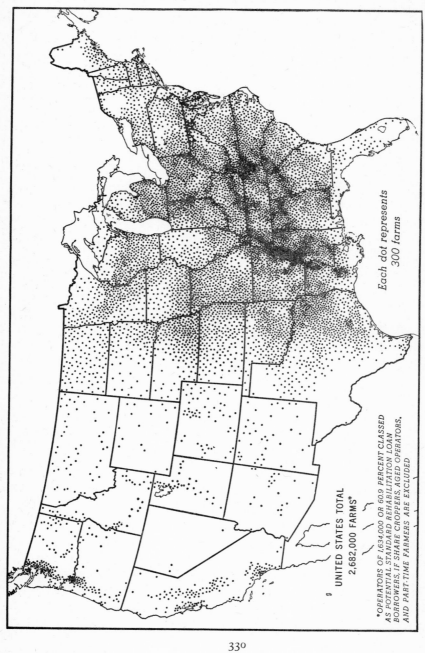

UNITED STATES TOTAL
2,682,000 FARMS*

*OPERATORS OF 1,634,000 OR 60.9 PERCENT CLASSED
AS POTENTIAL STANDARD REHABILITATION LOAN
BORROWERS. IF SHARE CROPPERS, AGED OPERATORS,
AND PART-TIME FARMERS ARE EXCLUDED

*Each dot represents
300 farms*

Figure 84. Distribution of the Low-Income Farms in the United States, on the Basis of Total Value of Products in 1939
(BAE, USDA)

The camps for migratory workers which were set up in areas with at least six months' work in the harvests were of a stationary type. Others were of a mobile type, following the workers from area to area. During World War II aid was given in the relocation of farm families displaced by new army posts and war industries. Since that time returning veterans have been aided in securing loans to buy farms.

When the program was an emergency function during the crisis in rural relief, its goals for individual families were to relieve their suffering and to restore them to permanent self-support. As time went on the objectives were broadened, to help the family obtain a physically healthful level of living, to acquire the skills and abilities needed to manage one's own affairs, to achieve security, to obtain land enough for a unit of economic size, to become a full participant in a democratic way of life, to obtain maximum employment of family labor in the production related to the war, and to obtain a socially desirable level of living for the family on the farm.

From the standpoint of society, the program objectives were to save the taxpayers money (the FSA was early recognized as the most economical of the relief agencies), by encouraging the family-type farm; bringing about better adjustment between land resources and population; securing full employment of the labor force on the land; rehabilitating farmers on the land without adverse effects on the commercial economy. This last objective was dropped in the course of the development of the program, as was the attempt to keep a maximum number of people on the land and to discourage undirected migration of the farm population.

The entire cost of the FSA program, including loans not likely to be paid and all administrative and supervisory functions, has been estimated at $75 per family helped per year. As a relief agency the FSA was both economical and effective, especially with respect to its loans in place program.

Use of "Surplus" Foods.—A food stamp plan was set up by the Surplus Marketing Administration to "eat up the surplus" and thus to help correct conditions of undernourishment among people with low incomes, especially in cities. The plan, as operated, gave a 50 per cent increased buying power to needy families in the form of surplus food order stamps. The plan was important to rural areas because it was a good way to dispose of unsold products. Long since abandoned, the plan may well be revived as a relief measure in the postwar period, should another depression disrupt our lives.

"Surplus" foods were used also by the school lunch program in rural as well as in urban areas. Not only were they used to provide a good lunch for the children, but every child also got a pint of milk for one cent. The program was, of course, not limited to the most needy.

Unemployment Insurance and Social Security.—The Social Security Act, passed in 1935, was designed to provide a framework for nationwide protection against economic and social insecurity. It recognized (a) that even in good times, about 8 per cent of the industrial workers in the country are without jobs, (b) that about one third of all men and women over sixty-five years old were dependent, and (c) that many children, in the absence of a breadwinner, were without financial support. The law, therefore, provides for:

1. Old-age and survivor's insurance, which is a Federal program. Monthly benefits under this program go to retired insured workers and their wives who are over the age of 65 and to survivors of insured workers who die. Benefits are paid out of a trust fund to which all industrial and commercial employees now contribute 1 per cent of income up to $3,000. Their employers contribute a like amount.

2. Unemployment compensation, which is a Federal-State system. In general the unemployed insured worker receives weekly unemployment benefits amounting to about half his average weekly wages, provided he is willing and able to work and is not unemployed through his own fault. In most states the top limit on benefits is $15 to $18 per week, and benefits are paid for not more than 16 to 20 weeks out of a year.

3. Aid for needy children, and needy blind, for maternal and child welfare, for vocational rehabilitation, and for public health, are also provided for in the Act, which called for the setting up of county departments of public welfare. These later took over the function of aid to dependent children. Whereas before the depression decade there were few such county departments in rural areas, welfare departments with their staffs of administrators and professional case workers have now been established in almost every county. Aid to dependent children provides security for the children in a family in case of the loss of parental support through death, in case of continued absence from the home, or in case of the physical or mental incapacity of the parents. Federal aid is given to the states, which in turn must set up a single agency to supervise the work in counties and in other local units. The work is placed, in most cases, with the

county welfare departments. Child welfare services include, also, maternal and child health services, foster-home care and adoption, and a nationwide program for a medical, surgical, and after-care service for the physical restoration and social adjustment of crippled children.

We have ample reason to be pleased, but by no means satisfied, with our national progress from pauper aid to social security. The intent of the former was merely to help keep "body and soul together." Social security implies that while we work the state and our employer will help us save to provide for emergencies and to care for ourselves in our declining years. New, also, is the idea that if economically distressed people can be rehabilitated, most of them will again acquire the will and desire to support themselves. It is also recognized that some people simply cannot take care of themselves, and that through the help of the state they should be assured a decent living and at least some elements of a good kind of life.

Wider Security Coverage.—Plans to extend social security include an extension of benefits to more of our citizens, as well as an extension of present social security services. The plans are of particular interest to rural, and especially farm, people.

1. Extension to farm people. It is proposed to bring into the social insurance program self-employed persons including unpaid family workers, except as they might qualify for benefits as dependents or survivors of insured workers. Among the current proposals the most important are:

(a) That old-age and survivor's insurance include farmers, household employees, nonfarm self-employed persons, and other groups not now covered.

(b) That old-age and survivor's benefits be increased, with the minimum retirement benefit raised to $20, and the age at which women could receive benefits as aged wives or widows of insured workers be lowered from 65 to 60.

(c) That personal disability be added to the risks covered by the old-age and survivor's insurance program.

(d) That insurance against temporary disability be provided for wage workers.

(e) That unemployment compensation be extended to cover hired workers at least on large industrial farms. They would also get temporary disability benefits if the program were extended to cover this risk.

The proposed new benefits for permanent disability would mean that if a farmer or his hired man became permanently disabled because of accident or sickness, no matter where it occurred, benefits would be paid him out of the old-age and survivors' insurance fund.[5]

2. Added protection. Insurance to prepay the cost of medical and hospital care is proposed. Under the plan the insured family would select its own physician and obtain services as needed.[6]

These proposals are based on the belief that "The growing complexity of our society has made it necessary for most people, including farmers, to rely on insurance and other group methods of protection, rather than on family or friends, for security against the emergencies and uncertainties of life. Even those who have acquired some security through farm ownership are frequently unable to enjoy assured comfort in their old age, because the return on their investments is uncertain or inadequate for a satisfactory living. A regular monthly cash income, such as would be provided by participation in the old-age and survivor's insurance program, would be a welcome source of additional income to most retired farmers and their wives. It would, moreover, be a certain and continuous source of income that they need not fear outliving."[7]

Rural Crime and Delinquency

Another aspect of the field of social welfare is concern for and attention needed by those who "cross the law" or become involved with the courts. Though costs for direct and work relief are high, the costs for the apprehension and care of the antisocial are even higher, both from a monetary and a social point of view, especially when one considers the cost of court procedures, law suits, prisons, and other institutional upkeep. Agencies and institutions to apprehend, try, and care for offenders and delinquents range from the lone village constable to fully staffed police departments. In general, the rural areas are inadequately protected. It is true that there are judges and justices of the peace in every county and town, probation officers and numerous other officers to enforce the law, apprehend, try, and incarcerate the offender. Nevertheless, officials in rural areas are almost invariably poorly trained.[8]

---

[5] *Social Security for Farm People*, USDA, prepared in cooperation with the Social Security Board, Federal Security Agency, 1946.
[6] I. S. Falk and Wilbur J. Cohen, "Social Security for Farm People," *Journal of Farm Economics*, Vol. XXVIII, No. 1, February, 1946, p. 92.
[7] *Social Security for Farmers and Farm Workers*, Office of Information, USDA, 1945.
[8] Austin H. MacCormick, "Adult Offenders," *Social Work Yearbook*, Russell Sage Foundation, 1943, pp. 33-45.

Agricultural people, especially farm owners and independent workers, are among the most law-abiding groups in the nation. Rural community pressures produced by the family, school, church, and neighborhood do more to coerce the individual and to shape his personality. Customs and mores in the rural community force many of the "undesirables" to leave. More rigid moral standards of the rural community result in conservative attitudes toward family re-

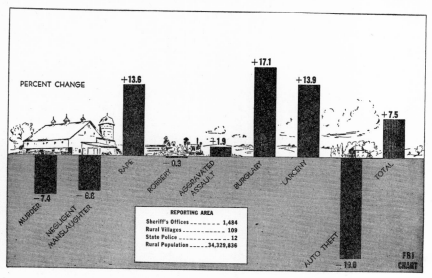

Figure 85. Offenses Known for Rural Areas—Changes from 1946 to 1947
(From Federal Bureau of Investigation, U. S. Dept. of Justice)

sponsibility—illegitimacy, birth control, nonsupport, and in some regions, drinking and smoking.[9]

Nature and Control of Crime in Rural Areas.—Rural areas are reputed to be freer of crime than urban areas. It is startling to learn, therefore, that recent trends have been for a greater increase in crime in rural than in urban areas. Federal Bureau of Investigation reports indicate, for example, that in 1947 the crime total for rural areas rose, whereas it fell in urban areas. Rapes, burglaries, and larcenies in rural areas showed unusually heavy increases. (See Figure 85.) Rural rates for crimes against property are generally lower than the corresponding urban rates. The decrease in murder

---

[9] Wilson Gee, *The Social Economics of Agriculture,* New York: The Macmillan Co., 1942, p. 493.

figures was greater for rural areas than for urban areas. However, rural negligency manslaughters did not decline as did urban, and there was only half the decline in auto thefts in rural areas as compared with urban. In general, rural areas have fewer cases of larceny with respect to other crimes, but more burglaries and more crimes against the person, such as assault, rape, and murder.[10]

Protection Against Crime.—The chief protection against crime in rural areas is the county sheriff's office. Too often, these offices are undermanned, and the sheriffs are not trained for the job. Advances are being made in permitting a competent man to succeed himself in office, in giving him the help of trained deputies, and by installation of modern equipment, such as two-way radios in patrol cars. Extension of the service of state police forces to protect rural property, and the close integration of local, county, state, interstate, and Federal forces is being developed. Citizens' committees are being formed to work with the law enforcement personnel.

Nevertheless, many rural areas are without adequate protection against armed desperadoes, the local police are untrained and incompetent, and the sheriff's office is staffed by inexperienced officials who possess no police, detective, or expert qualifications. Most local and county jails are disgracefully undermanned and ineffective. A system of regional jails, with professional staffs, which depend on the local jails merely for temporary detention purposes, would be cheaper and far more effective.

The principle of election of policy-makers and the appointment of administrators, which we discussed in Chapter 15, has specific application to law enforcement. Better services result when enforcement personnel are appointed on the basis of their qualifications.

Juvenile Delinquency.—Reliable over-all facts about juvenile delinquency in rural areas are not available, according to the 1946 National Conference on Prevention and Control of Juvenile Delinquency.[11] Such studies as have been made indicate (1) that there is generally less delinquency in rural areas than in urban, (2) that there is much more delinquency in *some* rural areas than in others and (3) that facilities for dealing with delinquency are very poor in many rural areas.

The unwholesome environment in many rural communities and the absence of recreational facilities are conducive to delinquency.

10 *Uniform Crime Rates,* Washington: FBI, U. S. Dept. of Justice, Vol. XVIII, No. 1, 1947, pp. 17-18.
11 *Rural Crime Reports, op. cit.,* pp. 3-4.

Poorly managed, distressed, or broken homes, and maladjusted relationships are responsible in many cases. The influence of irresponsible owners of public places in which youth find "bad" companions can be seen in almost every community. Schools in rural areas are not equipped to deal effectively with the miscreant. The rural school too often takes little interest in the general situation and offers no challenge through the curriculum to adolescents from economically deprived homes. Few of the children from such homes attend church. Too often little is done until the child is "caught by the law." If he is then placed in the local jail for detention, along with older offenders, he is well on the way to a career in crime. The pressure of the rural community for action is all too often directed toward getting something done about, or to, the individual who has offended rather than an attack on, and perhaps removal of, the general conditions that have brought about delinquency.[12]

Juvenile Courts.—Juvenile courts, completely separate from courts of general jurisdiction, are rarely found in rural areas. Generally, the hearing of juvenile cases is but one of the duties of the county judge, or the probate, circuit, or district court. Juvenile courts have come to have important judicial and administrative responsibilities including cases of neglected and dependent children, adults contributing to delinquency, and other functions. The judge of the juvenile court, because of his prestige in the community, should be of great help in the proper handling of juvenile cases in rural areas.

In some states the judges of the courts having juvenile jurisdiction are not required to be attorneys, and in almost no state is there real statutory guarantee either of legal skill or of a social point of view. In some jurisdictions provision has been made for the appointment of probation officers to serve the court. Unfortunately, in many places, standards for the selection of such persons have been low, and appointments have been made on a political basis. The prosecuting attorney cannot give sufficient time to juvenile delinquents since he also has responsibility for cases involving desertion and nonsupport, rape, incest, bastardy, and fraud.

Measures to meet the delinquency problem in a community must include a consideration of the many means of preventing delinquency,

---

[12] See *Report on Rural Aspects,* National Conference on Prevention and Control of Juvenile Delinquency, Washington: Office of Attorney General, 1946, pp. 3-4. This report shows that the highest concentration of Federal juvenile cases occcurred in the agricultural areas of the South and Southwest, where child welfare activities have been generally slow in developing. "The lack in most rural areas of any established means of caring for delinquents other than commitment to a reformatory is probably the main reason for a higher commitment rate for rural youths."

as well as proper care of those who do become the "patients" of the law enforcement and correctional institutions, and adequate treatment on the basis of the child's needs. In areas providing professional social case work service to neglected and dependent children, a number of resources can be used: the natural group solidarity of the family in rural areas, the church, the school, adult educational agencies such as the Agricultural Extension Service, libraries, the numerous interest groups already discussed, local public health services, the various governmental agencies, the American Red Cross, tuberculosis associations, child welfare committees of such groups as the American Legion or the woman's club, and local officials who have some responsibility in this field. The limitations of these groups are their lack of understanding of the proper treatment of the problem, their hesitancy to "meddle" in cases in which there may be a "kick back" on the organization, and a feeling that the best thing is for the police and the courts to handle the case.[13]

Causes for Dependency

Before we can adequately meet the requirements of those in need we must know why they became needy. Loss of a source of income is probably the major contributing factor of relief loads. Unwillingness to work is considered by the unthinking to be the reason why many go on relief. But where good jobs offering adequate security are available, practically all heads of families who are physically able will take work rather than stay on relief. The drastic reduction in relief rolls in the war period, moreover, was ample evidence that people prefer work to relief.

Six other causes of economic dependency, all of which must be understood, are:

1. Overpopulation. The presence of more people on the land than the land can support is a world-wide cause of poverty. This situation is aggravated by the fact that the people on the poorest land have the most children.

2. Lack of education and training. Lack of schooling is a major cause of poverty. Figure 86 shows the relationship of relief and educational status.

3. Sickness and a lack of health facilities. Poor health is a major contributing cause of indigence. If the breadwinner is sick or if

---

[13] See *Summaries of Recommendations for Action*, Washington: The National Conference on Prevention and Control of Juvenile Delinquency, 1947, pp. 122-136.

there are doctors', dentists', or hospital bills to pay, the situation often becomes hopeless and the family turns to relief agencies.

4. Too many dependents to support. This situation causes families in low-income brackets to go on relief. Four out of five rural families on relief had persons under sixteen and over sixty-five years old in the household.

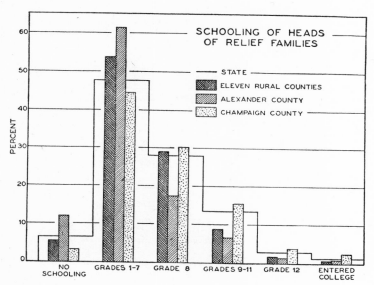

Figure 86. Schooling Received by Heads of Relief Families, as Indicated by an Illinois Survey

Three fourths had not completed the eighth grade; less than one tenth had completed high school. (From D. E. Lindstrom and Ida Johns, *Rural Relief in Illinois,* Bull. 480, Univ. of Illinois Agr. Exp. Sta., 1941.)

5. High mobility and instability. Migrant workers, farm laborers and renters particularly, and those who have no business of their own, contribute the greatest numbers to the relief population.

6. Adverse conditions affecting farmers. In the depression years drought and low prices caused many to go to the relief agencies for help.

Programs to Meet the Situation

A good program of social welfare depends on steady jobs, good working conditions, decent wages for the able, and adequate provision for those not able to help themselves. The needs for relief in rural areas will depend in large measure on the extent to which people in urban areas are employed, as well as on the prices farmers

get for their products. But it will depend, as well, on the adequacy
of a social welfare system that will do more than provide mere
subsistence for the needy.

Our peacetime labor force has exceeded 60,000,000, a figure at
least 3,000,000 more than thought possible before World War II.
Of these about 10,000,000 are in agriculture and 16,000,000 in
manufacturing and trade. The wartime unemployed low of 600,000
(See Figure 87) has since risen to about 1,500,000. It doubtless

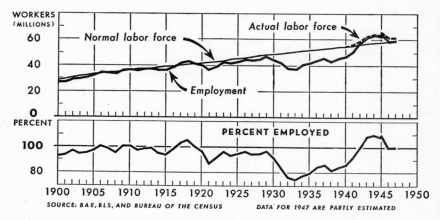

Figure 87. Normal Labor Force, Employment, and Employment as a Percentage
of the Normal Labor Force in the United States, 1910-1947

The actual labor force exceeded sixty million from 1943 to 1946. (BAE, USDA)

will rise to a more normal figure of around 4,000,000.[14] Our greatest employment increases must come, not in agriculture (for many in
agriculture are now underemployed), but in the service industries and
occupations. Nevertheless, it is the opinion of many authorities that
government-subsidized employment must continue, for though the
main employment reliance must be on private industry, public work,
and service—but not on a "made-work" basis—must continue to be
considered a second line of defense.

We have seen that a large number of people on the poorer farms
in America are underemployed. The principal corrective, of course,
has been the movement of people from farms to nonfarm occupations.[15] Evidence of such a movement has been the very heavy
migration from the Plains states, with the consequent enlargement

---

[14] J. Frederick Dewhirst and Associates, *America's Needs and Resources*, New York:
The Twentieth Century Fund, 1947, pp. 567-568.
[15] See Theodore W. Schultz, *Agriculture in an Unstable Economy*, New York: McGraw-
Hill Book Co., Inc., 1945, p. 88.

of farm units by the use of machines to a size more nearly calculated to insure a family adequate returns. To say, however, that the primary adjustment that is necessary to reach an equilibrium is to move large numbers out of agriculture into other fields is over-simplifying the problem. Farm people, especially in the older low-income sections, are not easily moved, because they have social and cultural roots in the communities in which they live.

A national policy for building up our smaller, and especially our rural, communities is needed. To these come the heaviest burden of relief in depression times. To these should be brought small in-dustries and other enterprises. Thus the underemployed in agricul-ture will have other-than-farm employment opportunities, which they had and took advantage of in the war period. Thus these under-employed could remain in the communities of their choice. Thus the nation would be engaged in a major effort to distribute industry to the areas in which there is a natural increase of population. And thus a real measure for national defense would be inaugurated, for the widespread dispersion of industry in smaller communities and in smaller units would greatly diminish the danger of its annihilation.

Local Responsibility.—In a society with a highly mobile popula-tion, with economic and industrial interdependence of rural and urban groups, the care of the needy breaks down unless local communities retain a real sense of responsibility for the support and care of their indigent. The soundest principle seems to be that local people should bear directly a part of the load and have a voice in policy-making, but that welfare administration should pass into professional hands.

Experience indicates that the county is the best unit for welfare administration, especially if a county board or committee representing the various communities or townships is made really responsible. The administration of relief is the job of professional workers with adequate training in social work, and knowledge of agriculture and rural life. There is imperative need for county and community coun-cils which will keep in focus the welfare of the whole community rather than push ahead the interests of special programs, each in competition with the others for funds and lay leadership. "It would seem that the problem in many rural communities is not so much a lack of resources as it is the fact that resources are still unevenly developed and are made less effective by the dissipation of available funds in the hands of a variety of local officials. Sound organization for public welfare must precede adequate case-work service." [16]

---

[16] Grace Browning, *Rural Public Welfare,* Chicago: University of Chicago Press, 1941, pp. 91 ff.

Need for State and Federal Aid.—Certain services will have to be financed by state and Federal aid and organized on a district or state basis. Skillful use of these services by local workers, whose community must often transcend township and county lines, will mean more effective work, especially if the case loads are small enough to permit the use of resources on the basis of individual needs. It is a matter, however, not only of good individual case work, but also of the stimulation and organization of the community resources so as to make possible better work with individuals.[17]

There is need for integration and correlation of these efforts on community and county levels. This is a major task in social engineering which has not yet been done in most rural communities. The usual procedure is for each agency to go its own way, endeavoring to get as much glory out of its own program as it can. The result is confusion or uncertainty in the mind of the man for whom the programs are meant. If he is confused or uncertain he will probably prefer to seek his own means of salvation. Noncooperation opens the door to another depression; cooperative efforts on the community, county, state, and national levels can prevent much of the suffering similar to that caused by the last depression, and bring real social welfare.

The Outlook for Rural Welfare

If, in our complex economic and social structure, farm people are expected to continue to produce such a vital share of the human and material wealth of our nation, they must be protected against economic and social disasters. This protection must include more than safeguards against low prices for bumper crops. The health of the rural family must also be given adequate attention; the educational facilities available to it must be on a par with those in the cities and attuned to rural needs; and farmers—owners, farm tenants, and farm laborers—must share in the nation's social security program, at least to the extent of some insurance against old age. Such a program can be a social and economic asset to the nation; the lack of such a program can cost more in human suffering and misery than we have ever before experienced.

---

[17] *Ibid.*, pp. 346-347.

DISCUSSION

1. What were the chief causes for changes in the forms of relief? What forms of relief operate in a typical rural area of your state?
2. Compare the nature of criminal acts in villages and in the open country in your home county. How are these cases apprehended and handled? How should rural areas be given adequate protection against crime? What are the situations which give rise to juvenile delinquency? What are the methods used to control it?
3. Is the trend of present employment such that a public works program is justified? What should be the nature of this program? How does the Farmers' Home Administration function to meet the situation?
4. How should services in a county be coordinated? What services should be included in such a plan? What type of training is needed for professional workers in the field of rural social welfare?
5. Discuss the proposals for rural social security. How do these affect rural people?

READINGS

Annual Report of the Federal Security Agency for the Fiscal Year 1947.

Brown, Josephine C. *The Rural Community and Social Case Work.* New York: Family Welfare Assn. of America, 1933, Ch. II.

Browning, Grace. *Rural Public Welfare.* Chicago: University of Chicago Press, 1941, pp. 3-17, 91-99, 315-348.

Gillette, John M. *Rural Sociology.* New York: The Macmillan Co., 1936, pp. 359 ff.

Landis, Paul H. *Rural Life in Process.* New York: McGraw Hill Book Co., Inc., 1940, Ch. XXVI.

Larson, Olaf F. *Ten Years of Rural Rehabilitation in the United States.* BAE, USDA, 1947.

Lindstrom, D. E., and Johns, Ida. *Rural Relief in Illinois.* Bull. 480, Univ. of Illinois Agr. Exp. Sta., 1941.

Mangus, A. R. *Changing Aspects of Rural Relief.* Research Monograph XIV, BAE, USDA, 1938.

Schultz, Theodore W. *Agriculture in an Unstable Economy.* New York: McGraw-Hill Book Co., Inc., 1945, pp. 89-100.

Uniform Crime Reports. FBI, U. S. Dept of Justice. Vol. XVIII, No. 1, 1947.

Woofter, T. J., Jr., and Winston, Ellen. *Seven Lean Years.* Chapel Hill: University of North Carolina Press, 1939, Chs. VIII, IX.

Chapter 18

RURAL SOCIAL RECREATION

Recreation is essential to a good kind of life, whether in rural or in urban areas. Morgan, in *The Small Community,* points out the essential nature of play as a primary need and declares that if a people were to choose between freedom and recreation, it would give up freedom and choose recreation.[1] Farm communities must recognize that what they do, or fail to do, in making the locality socially satisfying to both youth and adults, will sharply influence the kind of agriculture they will have in the years ahead. Adequate recreational facilities are of real importance and cannot safely be neglected or indefinitely postponed.

Nature of Rural Social Recreation

The term "rural social recreation" has come to include all forms of relaxing and recreative activities which are carried on in groups. Recreative activity implies that which is re-creative to relieve the monotony of work, quicken thinking, and make one more alert and more resourceful. Recreation also releases surplus nervous energy, removes discouragements, and brings refreshment to tired minds.

Recreation as Socialization.—Social recreation is a promoter of the easiest and often most enjoyable forms of association. Finding pleasurable activities in groups can submerge race, class, or religious difference, allay or destroy conflicts or animosities, and promote positive social sympathies. The right kind of play in groups fosters cooperation and social discipline. It is the natural manner of association in children's groups—out of their play activities children learn many lessons of social discipline essential to them in later life.

Rural recreational activities have been more social than individualistic. Even when one goes hunting or fishing one likes to have someone along—it's not much fun doing it alone. The old-time husking bees, barn warmings, birthday celebrations, picnics, and parties were characteristic rural forms of social recreation.

---

[1] Arthur E. Morgan, *The Small Community,* New York: Harper & Bros., 1942, pp. 216-217.

344

Recreation as Social Reform.—Recreational programs and activities are coming to be increasingly used to prevent delinquency and to keep children happily occupied in their spare time. Modern means of transportation enable a farm boy to "go quickly and far" to seek companionship in a community where he is little known, too often in an impersonalized and commercialized amusement hall. If no forms of recreation other than commercial amusements are available to these youth they may break away from normal, socially accepted behavior. Interesting recreation, of a sensible, wholesome, "home-grown" kind, is an obvious antidote to unsavory, tawdry, crime-breeding amusement.

Recreation as an Organizational "Tool."—Recreation programs are usually an integral part of the work of clubs and organizations. This is especially true of rural youth groups, simply because attendance at many such meetings depends to a great extent on the kind and quality of good times that can be had. Not only do rural clubs and organizations have recreation as a part of their regular meetings, but they also sponsor special recreation activities to which their members usually look forward with considerable anticipation. Sometimes conflicts arise between youth and older folks as to whether dancing, for example, should be permitted as part of the meeting. If denied, the youth are likely to find their own places for dancing, often at disreputable taverns.

The Nature of Rural Recreation Activities

Play and Rural Social Recreation.—The traditional rural attitude toward the use of leisure time has had much to do with the quality of its use.[2] Though the line between work and play is an indefinite one, there always has been a feeling in rural areas that play of any kind is a waste of time. Even going hunting or fishing was for some just a means of providing needed food. The old-fashioned folk games, square dances, husking bees, and similar get-togethers were relegated to an older generation with the advent of the automobile, radio, hard surface road, movie, and professionalized sports programs.

Hence, many rural people have lost the art of play. When they are urged to take part in a folk dance, for example, they are hesitant or may refuse because it is strange or new or because it is related to forms of activity which in their youth may have been taboo. To rural people, recreation is too often limited to such things as visiting

[2] Foster Rhea Dulles, *America Learns to Play*, New York: D. Appleton-Century Co., Inc., 1940, Ch. XXII.

relatives or friends. Their tendency is to restrict their children and young people to the same forms.

Recreation in Church and School Programs.—Rural churches, schools, and other organizations have provided various forms of recreational activity, especially for youth. Church-sponsored recreational activities range from simple church parties to ball tournaments, drama festivals, and folk dances. (See Figure 88, page 350.) The recreational programs in rural elementary schools are too often limited to informal play at recess time. In high schools, the programs are more varied, and include football, baseball, track, and other sports. But these, too, are confined to a small group who "come out for the team," and to a few classes in physical education which are "squeezed" into an already overcrowded curriculum. Some high schools also try to have programs in band, chorus, choir, dramatics, art, and debate; too often these are denied farm children because of lack of time or inability to get instruments. During a depression period these curriculum activities are the first to be sacrificed. Though schools might well become fine community centers, many are closed during the hours when they might be of use, and the gymnasiums are often restricted to the use of the basketball team only.

Family and Home Recreation.—Home recreation is a natural part of the life of many rural people. It takes on a wide variety of forms ranging all the way from listening to the radio, reading, or family visiting, family orchestras, production of art or "fancy work," to the development of fine or exceptional breeds of livestock or plant life. Often these activities are regarded as hobbies, but they are more likely to be the activities which make all the difference between a humdrum existence on the farm and a creative, ever-engrossing type of country life.

Rural Handicrafts.—"Art is just the best way of doing something that needs to be done." Certain arts are said to belong to the country —"objects made of materials native to the country, designs and motifs growing out of the country, and things that, through design and material, express something of the locality from which they come, or record the reaction of the countryman to his environment." [3] Rural art and handicrafts are valuable not alone because they may furnish the creators an income, but also because they are a real part of a rural culture. They definitely help to make rural life a richer and finer kind of life.

---

[3] Allen Eaton and Lucinda Crile, *Rural Handicrafts in the United States*, Misc. Pub. No. 610, USDA, in cooperation with Russell Sage Foundation, 1946, p. 7.

Recreation Through Expressive Arts.—The desire of rural people to have fun together, though too often repressed, was latent. When a number of enterprising leaders began to "spotlight" the musical, dramatic, artistic, and folk games and dance activities through contests, tournaments, and festivals, there was a heartening response. It was found that there was a real desire to sing, act, draw, or dance; and the quality and grace with which they performed these arts bespoke the fine creative ability possessed by many rural people.

Music and drama in the form of community singing, solos, duets, quartets, choruses, pageants, one-act or three-act plays, are now often a part of the program of rural organization meetings. Winners in an Illinois Rural Drama Tournament are shown in Figure 89, page 350. It is only because rural people like to do these things that it has been possible to organize and conduct music and drama tournaments,[4] rural county and state chorus festivals, and other forms of intergroup social recreational activities.

The rural arts are as varied as the flowers in an old-fashioned garden. They appear in all the different patterns of rural life; now in acting streaked and shot through with genius, on every kind of stage, from the makeshift platform on wheels to the beautifully equipped laboratory on a campus; now in circles of dancing figures weaving in and out among the shadows in the brilliant costumes of many lands; now in music with great choruses gathered together from crossroads communities, some of them as far as a day's journey in fast cars; in games and coverlets, in rugs and in paintings; in revivals of old folk art and music; in pageants bringing to life the whole vivid development of this country of ours.[5]

Good illustrations of such stimulated types of rural social recreation are the Carolina Folk Play Movement, the Little Country Theatre Movement in North Dakota, the Wisconsin Music and Drama Tournaments, the New York State rural drama development, and the Illinois Rural Chorus. So important have these forms of stimulated recreational programs become that recreation specialists are being added to the extension staffs of many colleges of agriculture and numerous special bulletins have been printed.[6]

---

[4] See D. E. Lindstrom, *Organizing for Rural Home-Talent Tournaments*, Circular 376, Univ. of Illinois Service in Agr. and Home Econ., 1931.

[5] Marjorie Patton, *The Arts Workshop of Rural America*, New York: Columbia University Press, 1937, p. 198.

[6] See, for example, J. W. Scott, R. A. Sandberg, and D. E. Lindstrom, *A Dramatics Guide for Rural Groups*, Circular 519, Univ. of Illinois Ext. Service in Agr. and Home Econ., 1941.

Much credit must go to the National Recreation Association for its continuing interest in rural recreation. Early in the depression period the Association loaned several of its specialists to the Agricultural Extension Service of the U. S. Department of Agriculture. They were used by the various state extension services in district and county four-day recreation leader training schools, and in other ways. The result was a widespread use of many of the finest of the Old World and the New World folk games (Figure 90, page 351), dances, and music, and a revival in many areas of folk drama and art. The materials, bulletins, and periodicals issued by the National Recreation Association have been widely used.

Worthy of attention, also, is the work of the Cooperative Recreation Service of Delaware, Ohio. Their materials, especially the "Handy" books, have wide usage by rural groups. Likewise, such services as the Co-op Parish Activities Services at Effingham, Illinois, have been used by rural groups both in this and in foreign countries.

Camps and Camping.—Camping, also, has become a significant form of recreation for rural people. Church groups, school groups, 4-H clubs, rural youth, and an increasing number of adults are going to camps for a day, a week end, and in some cases for longer periods of time. Camps are increasingly popular as places for programs especially built around outdoor activities and as places which offer opportunity for group companionship and the pursuit of mutual interests. Thus, many of them afford a real recreative opportunity.[7]

Commercial Amusements.—Most rural communities have no form of organized recreational program besides that offered in the schools, churches, or other organizations. The reason usually given for lack of such a program is that the community cannot afford it. Yet were a study to be made of the actual money spent in commercial amusements in and about the rural community, much of it for questionable forms, the result would be astonishing. Stupendous sums are spent for liquor, movies, pool halls, degrading literature, and public dance halls. The only feature which commercial amusements have in common is that one has to "pay to play."

Almost every village has its movie theater, pool hall, tavern, or dance hall. Except for the movie theater, many of these places of amusement are of such demoralizing nature that they need policing which they seldom get, and hence continue to spew up a costly anti-

---

[7] See, for example, Ella Gardner, *Short-Time Camps*, Misc. Pub. 346, USDA, 1939.

social product. Were the average rural community to count the actual, to say nothing of the social, cost of such amusement places, it would doubtless find that it could well afford an adequately paid, full-time, community recreation director and staff in a well-equipped recreation center around which might be built a constructive community recreation program.

This is not all of the unsatisfactory side of the picture. Almost every large village thinks it must have a carnival each year, or that a carnival troupe must be included with every county or community fair that is held. The chief attractions at most carnivals are the weird amusement devices, most of which are designed to give momentary physical thrills, and petty gambling devices which are always costly, not only because those who can least afford it lose their money at them, but also because they are bad examples for youth. Were efforts made to replace these commercial amusements with local productions in music, drama, and the arts, as is being done in some communities, the gain would be not only in attracting much larger crowds, but also in providing a constructive program in place of one which is destructive of the best morals and good character. These, then, are questions of social value which come out of the kind of community life one finds in rural areas.

In some communities commercial amusements and recreation places are used to good purpose. Teams among trade or occupational groups are formed and tournaments are held, out of which comes a wholesome kind of recreational activity. Such activities are usually stimulated by the managements of such places as bowling alleys. It would be excellent if more could be done to build community or cooperative voluntary organization interest in such activities, even among church groups. Then there would be a real incentive to keep these places clean and wholesome.

Individualized Recreation.—A universal desire in America is to go away on a trip to some park, playground, resort, or favorite fishing ground at some time during the year. At first this seemed the prerogative only of the rich. Then, when automobiles became universal, many city people took to the roads. Now an increasing number of farm people look forward to the time when they too can take a trip to the Rockies, into Canada, or to California. The preservation of our places of natural beauty and of our wild life has become a major national project worthy of the strongest support. This form of recreation is destined to play an even greater part in the lives of rural people of the future. Some states, moreover, such as Indiana, have developed an excellent system of state parks.

Many types of facilities are coming into being to provide for such forms of individualized (which are really family or group) forms of recreation. The cabin camp type has sprung up almost everywhere. Many of these have to be shunned by decent people, especially those cabins outside town limits, which are often used for immoral purposes. In wartime, some openly refused legitimate trade in favor of the more lucrative business of itinerant amateur and professional prostitution. But there has been a movement in many areas to provide state regulated or owned camping places. Perhaps these postwar years will see a renaissance of the wholesome prewar movement toward the establishment of youth hostels.

The average village has its public square and some have a park area. But aside from a bandstand, few have any equipment for recreational purposes. Most large villages could afford to find a good wooded acreage, possibly near a stream or body of water, and build a community center [8] with a variety of outdoor facilities—for picnicking, softball, tennis, and numerous other games. They would find these facilities used and enjoyed by the people far beyond the cost of construction and upkeep.

Community Celebrations.—An increasing number of village-centered rural communities are organizing annual celebrations of various sorts. In some, as in Eureka, Illinois, the festival is built around its specialized industry, growing pumpkins, and everyone is given a pumpkin pie. Thousands of people come. Business houses remain open. The local band is kept busy. Stands are erected by this or that local organization to raise funds through the sale of "hot dogs" or some other similar article. Speeches are made, and there is much visiting, milling around the streets, taking part in the various contests. The net results are an increased pride in the community and increased goodwill toward the local commercial institutions. The organizational efforts which are put into such celebrations are indicative of the more lasting things of community betterment that are possible. Too often the intergroup efforts end with the celebration, or one group, the original initiator, is depended on to carry on from year to year.

The Youth Center Movement.—World War II, like World War I, saw a widespread development of youth centers, in rural as well as in urban areas. The youth center movement, however, is mainly a

---

[8] See D. E. Lindstrom, W. A. Foster, and Max G. Fuller, *Rural Community Buildings*, Circular 470, Univ. of Illinois Ext. Service in Agr. and Home Econ., 1937.

Figure 88.   Folk Dances in Costume Form a Picturesque Part of a Farm Sports Festival
(Courtesy Univ. of Illinois Ext. Service in Agr. and Home Ec.)

Figure 89.   Dramatics Are an Excellent Form of Rural Recreation
The farm boys in this "heavy" dramatic production were winners in a rural drama tournament.

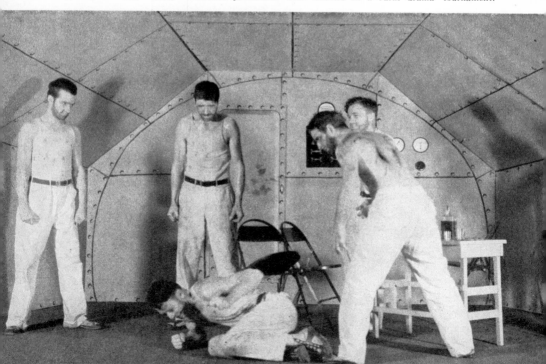

Figure 90. Folk Dancing

The revival of folk dancing is nation-wide in scope among rural groups and is finding its way into urban groups. This is an excellent form of social recreation.

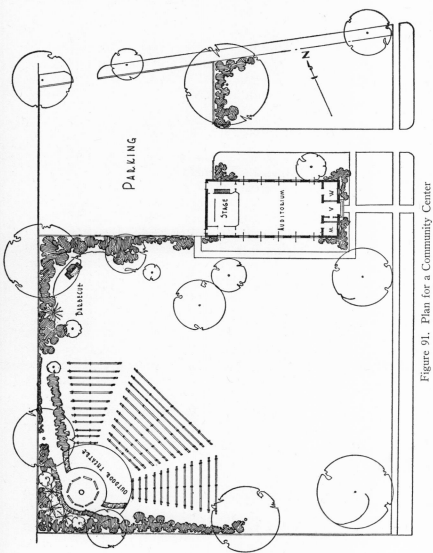

Figure 91. Plan for a Community Center

(D. E. Lindstrom, W. A. Foster, and Max G. Fuller, *Rural Community Buildings*, Univ. of Ill. Coll. of Agr. Ext. Service in Agr. & Home Econ. Cir. 470, 1937, p. 45)

town-centered movement. Many of these centers are designed to meet the leisure-time or loafing-time needs of town youth, especially in the junior and senior high school ages. Most of them are set up to provide facilities for games, a little social dancing to the tunes of juke boxes, and for social discussion over soft drinks. Efforts are made in most of them to give youth free rein in organizing and running the places. These youth centers are worthy of study to determine whether such programs can be developed to serve the informal activity needs of youth in the village-centered community.[9]

Organization, Program, and Leadership

The foregoing analysis indicates that in many rural communities social recreation is varied, sporadic, and lacking in effectiveness. In the future rural people, especially rural youth, will seek recreation more than they have in the past, not only because the mechanization of agriculture makes it possible and even necessary, but also because recreation is coming to form an integral and needed part of life in all areas. An increasing number of rural leaders are becoming so concerned that they will no longer allow it to develop haphazardly. If recreation is essential to individual and group life, and if the rural community is to form a unit of future organizational activity—is to be an area of direct action—what should be its approach to recreation?

A School-Community Program.—Schools in America, especially in rural areas, are being reorganized. In the process of reorganization it is hoped that they can become neighborhood and community centers. If the neighborhood attendance units are reorganized into larger administrative units, it is believed that adequate play space, equipment, program, and leadership will be provided. The modern emphasis is on health and recreation—the two are closely related.

1. Facilities. Adequate play space at a neighborhood school means making available (a) several acres of ground for tennis courts, baseball diamonds, etc.; and (b) housing facilities, the least of which would be a combination gymnasium-auditorium with a stage. In larger centers these should be separate, for gymnasiums are not usually good auditoriums. When provided, they should be adapted not only to the use of the school children but to the people of the community as well.

---

9 D. E. Lindstrom, *Youth Centers in Illinois*, Univ. of Illinois Agr. Exp. Sta., and Department of Public Welfare, Div. of Delinquency Prevention, cooperating, 1947.

2. Programs in the school. An adequate program is no less essential than are adequate facilities. The average school-health-recreation or athletic program is not really recreation-centered because too many are centered on winning tournaments in sports, drama, music, and public speaking. To secure winning teams, a rigid selective process is carried on, which of course denies the activities to most of the student body. Athletics in high school should be so organized that every boy and girl will be given the opportunity to play in every type of sport, and the participation must be made less rigid and more enjoyable. Centering on one outstanding individual denies others the opportunity to participate, and it may do untold injury to the individual. The athletic program in rural schools should include all who are physically able to take part; it should include, also, the people in the community as participants, not merely as spectators.

An enlarged athletic program, however, should be only a part of the school recreation program. There should also be folk games and dances as well as round dancing; music in which school and community people join (the school orchestra or chorus might well be the nucleus for the community orchestra or chorus); drama conducted on the same basis; public speaking; arts and crafts. If there is virtue in parent-child cooperation in these activities, then certainly the school might well encourage such cooperative participation. Out of such activities could grow a good community recreational program.

3. Leadership needs. The rural community which undertakes such a program will have need for properly trained leaders who are employed the year around.[10] Instead of hiring an athletic coach,[11] a school or community might engage a recreation director. The school music, drama, speech, and arts teachers and the school librarian should be employed on the basis of service to the community as well as to the school. If this were done these teachers, with the agricultural and home economics teachers, could work with a community committee in formulating a school and community winter and summer leisure-time program. The school facilities, including the library, gymnasium, playing fields, playing equipment, staging and properties, public address and visual aids equipment, and the available parks and playgrounds with the equipment of courts, diamonds, tables, outdoor ovens, etc., should all be considered in the

---

[10] See Ella Gardner, *Handbook for Recreation Leaders,* Bull. No. 231, Children's Bureau, U. S. Dept. of Labor, for the nature of material available.

[11] Note in C. O. Jackson, "Activities Engaged in by Teachers of Physical Education in the High Schools of Illinois," *Research Quarterly,* Vol. XIII, No. 2, 1943, how few physical education teachers go beyond teaching physical education and some academic subject.

program of planning. Then and then only would the school become a community center. In the rural community this is the most feasible and logical development.

4. Training essentials. The school-community recreation program outlined above will require professional leaders with more adequate training than is now possessed by most high school personnel such as coaches and drama, music, art, library, vocational, agricultural, and home economics teachers.

The average person training for a school health and education program, which is to become a well-rounded school-community leisure-time program, must be trained in more than skills (like coaching basketball teams). He must be trained in working with people —adults as well as youth—in building good school and community programs. This special training should enable the program director to understand rural people and their problems, economic and social, so that he can adapt his work to the needs of rural people and obtain their help in developing the program.

The Role of the Rural Church.—After a school-community leisure-time program is developed it should be integrated with the church program and with other voluntary group recreation programs. Conversely, rural churches can strengthen the community leisure-time program by relating church activities to others in the community. A highly desirable approach by rural church leaders would be to cooperate with the school leaders (a) in avoiding overlapping events, (b) in planning especially for summertime events, and (c) in offering additional facilities and opportunities for leadership training.

The traditional limitation of church recreational programs to children's parlor games may have become a contributing cause to the loss of youth's interest in the church. Youth are idealistic but they are also fun-loving, and if the church fails to provide for this outlet, youth will seek it elsewhere. If young people want to dance it is better that they dance with church approval than to be forced to find this outlet for natural expression in taverns or roadhouses. A church can also furnish a wide variety of other recreational opportunities, from basket dinners and potluck suppers to music, drama, and sports festivals.

An excellent illustration of church-sponsored recreational programs is the highly popular annual softball tournament, culminating on an afternoon in August, which has been sponsored for years by the Island Grove Church in Jasper County, Illinois. The leaders in this church are themselves outstanding leaders of folk or social recreation and have been in demand in social recreation leader training schools all over the country.

Opportunities for Interest Organizations.—Most adult-interest organizations have some form of social and recreational activity in their meetings. These activities vary all the way from a little half-hearted community singing, a few recitations by school children, and "just visiting," to the production of full-length plays, the organization of orchestras or bands, the sponsorship of tournaments and group excursions. The general tendency is for each group to develop its own recreational programs, and this is to be encouraged, especially on the part of open-country groups. Such efforts can be made part of a community program, however, (a) by encouraging their participation in festivals, homecomings, fairs, etc., and (b) by offering help in training leaders and making programs. Delightful results have come from exchanging programs between groups in different neighborhoods or communities.

Institutes for training leaders in recreation are increasingly being held on a county, district, and state basis. In these leader-training schools the aim is usually to train in skills. This is important, for one can learn best how to direct a game by actually directing it. Some emphasis is also placed on working with groups, for recreation in rural areas is largely a matter of handling groups. Special attention should be given in colleges, especially land-grant colleges and universities, to the development of a curriculum for rural recreation leaders. Most of the training for such leaders has come through experience and through a smattering of courses, mostly in physical education.

Future Needs in Rural Recreation

The primary future need in the field of rural recreation is a re-education of people generally in the value and art of participation. Except for individualized recreation, most people now participate only on a spectator basis. To secure such general participation will require better trained leaders, both professional and lay, in social recreation and in community organization for recreation. Most of our professional leaders, especially in schools, have too narrow a training.

A community approach in cooperative planning on the part of coaches, teachers, pastors, and lay leaders is very greatly needed and could result in tremendous benefits. These leaders, as a community recreation council, need to re-evaluate the place of athletics, music, drama, art, public speaking, and the various forms of social recreation (a) in terms of the value of recreation for itself alone, (b) as a means of bolstering good health, (c) as a means of socialization, for a desire to play is universal, (d) as a means of artistic expression, and (e) to develop a freedom of expression so essential to a democratic way of life.

A community recreation council would work with and tie together the school, church, town government, and interest organization programs, and maintain contacts with county, state, and national service agencies. The following ten-point scale can be used as a guide to community planning.[12]

1. Know your community—the people, their traditions, needs and problems, and the resources of the community.

2. Pool your resources—for full use of assets from public and private agencies, neighborhood groups, organizations and individual leaders.

3. Check your legislation—what you need and what you have and work to get new laws passed if necessary.

4. Establish a legal managing authority—a responsible lay board with legal authority to administer the program in accordance with needs.

5. Get good leadership—a trained, full-time executive responsible to the board, with paid and volunteer helpers carefully chosen and trained.

6. Make the most of present facilities—schools, town-owned buildings, parks, playfields, water areas, supplemented by privately owned property.

7. Secure a separate budget—a definite, adequate amount of public funds through special tax levy or other public appropriations.

8. See that the program is community-wide—with interests for young and old, indoor and outdoor, with sports, games, music, arts, crafts, drama, lectures, forums, social recreation, and community events.

9. Maintain public partnership—interpret program to the public and win public support for it.

10. Plan for the future—make long-range plans to include physical facilities, program, leadership, and finance.

---

[12] *Community Recreation Comes of Age,* Federal Security Agency, 1944.

DISCUSSION

1. State reasons why recreation is an essential part of rural life. In what ways can recreation be considered an end in itself? For what purposes are recreational activities used?
2. What is the nature of recreational programs in your home, church, and school? What influences keep the youth from taking part? How can these programs be strengthened?
3. What guidance or supervision is given commercial amusements in the rural community? How can their programs be improved?
4. Discuss the elements that should go into a good school-community recreational program to make it a complete, all-year school-community program.

READINGS

Dulles, Foster Rhea. *America Learns to Play.* New York: D. Appleton-Century Co., 1940, Ch. XXII.

Eaton, Allen, and Crile, Lucinda. *Rural Handicrafts in the United States.* Misc. Pub. No. 610, USDA, in cooperation with Russell Sage Foundation, 1946.

Gardner, Ella. *Handbook for Recreation Leaders.* Bull. 231, Children's Bureau, U. S. Dept. of Labor, 1936.

Harbin, E. O. *The Fun Encyclopedia.* Nashville: The Cokesbury Press, 1940.

Lindstrom, D. E., Foster, W. A., and Fuller, Max G. *Rural Community Buildings.* Circ. 470, Univ. of Illinois Ext. Service in Agr. and Home Econ., 1937.

Morgan, Arthur E. *The Small Community.* New York: Harper & Bros., 1942, Ch. XXI.

Patton, Marjorie. *The Arts Workshop of Rural America.* New York: Columbia University Press, 1937.

Rohrbaugh, Lynn. *Handy Series.* Cooperative Recreation Service, Delaware, Ohio, dated as issued.

Scott, Joseph W., Sandberg, R. A., and Lindstrom, D. E. *A Dramatics Guide for Rural Groups.* Circ. 519, Univ. of Illinois Ext. Service in Agr. and Home Econ., 1941.

Sims, N. L. *Elements of Rural Sociology.* New York: Thomas Y. Crowell Co., 1940, Ch. XXVI.

Smith, Charles F. *Games and Game Leadership.* New York: Dodd, Mead & Co., 1942, Ch. I.

Works, George A., and Lesser, Simon O. *Rural America Today.* Chicago: University of Chicago Press, 1942, Ch. X.

Chapter 19

THE COUNTRY LIFE MOVEMENT

The country life movement in America has one basic objective: "to make rural living as effective and satisfying as that in any other civilization." [1] This objective was tacitly expressed in the movements which led to the formation of the earlier agricultural societies and farmers' organizations, but it was most clearly stated by the Theodore Roosevelt Country Life Commission.

The Country Life Commission.—The Commission was organized upon the insistence of Liberty Hyde Bailey, Kenyon S. Butterfield (to mention only two), and others who saw both economic and social deficiencies in rural life and their relation to the welfare of society as a whole. The report of this Commission grew out of a series of "hearings" held in all parts of the country in which rural people had the chance to offer their views.

The chief recommendations of the report may be summarized:

1. The need for making agricultural or country life surveys which take into account, among other things, rural institutions and organizations, the adaptability of the neighborhood to the establishment of handicrafts and local industries, the general economic and social status of the people, and the character of the people themselves.

2. The need for redirected education, so that it may have a fuller relation to living. Schools should express the daily life, and those in rural districts should educate by means of agriculture and country life subjects. They must express the best cooperation of all social and economic forces that make for the welfare of the community.

3. The need for greater efforts by country people to work together, not only to further their economic interests, but also to develop themselves and to establish an effective community spirit.

4. The need for higher personal and community ideals for the country community. The spiritual nature of the individual must be kept thoroughly alive. In this, the church has an indispensable function.

---

[1] See *Report of the Theodore Roosevelt Country Life Commission*, Chapel Hill: Univ. of North Carolina Press, 1944.

5. The need for realizing that better institutions and more attractive homes do not necessarily follow profitableness of farming.
The complacent contentment in many rural neighborhoods, the Commission found, is itself the very evidence of social incapacity or decay.

The results were a fourfold stimulus, to: (a) the organization
of the national and state system of extension work; (b) the development of a more effective system of rural education, which led to
the Smith-Hughes Vocational Agricultural and Home Economics
work; (c) the organization of state and national country life associations; and (d) the efforts being made in several institutions to
study the social problems in rural life, a project which later grew
into the triple aspects of rural sociology: teaching, research, and
extension. The Country Life Movement, however, is broader and
more inclusive than the field of rural sociology, though rural sociologists did make significant contributions to the movement.

The American Country Life Association.—Soon after the close
of World War I a few outstanding leaders in rural life gathered in
Baltimore to organize what they called the American Country Life
Conference. It was formed by some of the same leaders who had
had a part in the work of the Roosevelt Country Life Commission.
The first and present objectives of the Association are: "(1) to fa-
cilitate discussion of the problems and objectives in country life
and the means of their solution and attainment; (2) to further the
efforts and increase the efficiency of persons, agencies, and institutions engaged in this field; (3) to disseminate information calculated
to promote a better understanding of rural life; and (4) to aid in
rural improvement." [2]
The American Country Life Association was not and did not
pretend to be an action agency or a policy-making group or even one
directly attempting to influence policies affecting rural people. Its
functions were performed through:

1. Annual conferences held in different parts of the country attended by many national leaders and by local people in the area
   in which the conference was held. The conferences were held
   to present, through addresses and discussions, the most recent
   findings and suggestions on the basic issues confronting rural
   people. In attendance at these conferences were many rural
   leaders whose whole outlook on the approach to the solutions
   of rural problems was profoundly affected.

---

[2] See *Proceedings of the First National Country Life Conference, Baltimore, 1919,*
American Country Life Association, Lafayette, Ind., pp. 15-24.

2. Publications of proceedings at the conference which contained the addresses and discussions at the conferences. These are among the best literature available on rural life today.[3]

3. A house organ, which contained current articles, presented in popular fashion, giving the best experiments and projects being carried on to solve the social problems of rural life.

4. Supporting the formation of the Catholic Rural Life Conference, the Youth Section of the American Country Life Association, and the National Rural Education Committee.

5. Stimulating state country life associations, such as the Pennsylvania Country Life Association, the Michigan Country Life Association, the Illinois Rural Life Conference, and the Mississippi Rural Life Council.

6. Sponsoring state conferences on rural life, with the cooperation of interested organizations.

The Association was financed by membership dues from individuals and organizations and by grants from foundations. It functioned with a full program during the twenty years from 1920 to 1940. In 1941 the foundation grants were not renewed, due to wartime pressures, and most of the functions of the Association were dropped. The offices were moved from New York to Lafayette, Indiana, a continuation committee was appointed, and restricted conferences were continued in 1942, 1943, 1944, 1946, and 1947, with proceedings of the 1946 Conference on *Rural Life in a Changing World* being the last published. Plans are being made to refinance the Association and to develop full-scale programs again.

Accompanying Movements.—Some of the notable movements accompanying the work of the Association have been the following:

1. The Rural Sociological Society. This Society grew out of the fellowship that developed among teachers, and research and extension workers in rural sociology, as they met in the annual meetings of the ACLA and the American Sociological Society. At first this group was a division of the Society's work; it afterwards formed its own society and published its own magazine: *Rural Sociology.*

2. The Southern Rural Life Council. This is a cooperative project sponsored by four Nashville, Tennessee, institutions—Pea-

[3] Titles of recent Conference Proceedings are: *Religion in Rural Life; Farm Youth; Standards of Living; Rural Government; Rural Health; Farm and Rural Life After the War; Disadvantaged Classes in Rural Society;* and *National Planning and Rural Life.* Most large libraries have a complete set of the Proceedings.

body College, Scarritt College, Vanderbilt University, and Fisk University. Its purpose is to utilize available resources, human, institutional, and natural, in developing a comprehensive continuing program of community development. The Council, through its director and staff, cooperates with institutions, agencies, and individuals working to improve the quality of rural life in the South.

3. The Rural Life Association. This new country life group, organized when it appeared that the American Country Life Association might become inactive, is made up of individuals and groups throughout the country (but chiefly in the Middle West) who are interested in enabling all kinds of groups in rural life to work together for its improvement. It was sponsored by the Friends, Brethren, Mennonites, and others concerned about the decline of rural life and the marked trend toward urbanism. It plans and conducts local conferences, helps in surveys, encourages rural people to write articles on rural life, aids in forming local study groups, maintains a lending library and a "placement service and clearing house for people, jobs, and ideas pertaining to rural life." [4]

The Rural Church Movement.—The stimulus given by the Roosevelt Country Life Commission and the American Country Life Association helped give rise to nation-wide concern for the plight of the rural church.

1. The Catholic Rural Life Conference. This Conference was established by rural leaders of the Catholic Church soon after the first meetings of the American Country Life Association. It has supported movements to strengthen the Catholic Church in rural areas, not the least notable of which is the effort to stimulate the settlement of Catholic families on the land. Other significant contributions of the Conference are (a) publication of the Catholic Manifesto on Rural Life, (b) publication of the periodical, *Land and Home,* and (c) holding local, state, and national conferences for the improvement of rural life.

2. Other denominational movements. The Church of the Brethren has an outstanding program for contributing to the improvement of rural life, giving primary emphasis to the improvement of farm tenure.[5] The Presbyterian Church has developed a program to encourage its state or other units to set up basic salary plans, to employ properly trained men for rural churches, to buy land and

---

[4] *Agencies Concerned with the Quality of Rural Life in the South,* Nashville, Tenn.: Southern Rural Life Council, 1944.

[5] See I. W. Moomaw, *Rural Life Objectives,* Elgin, Ill.: The Church of the Brethren Publishing House, 1945.

help "settle" families on it, and to organize rural cooperative parishes. The Congregational Christian Church has a rural training center at Merom, Indiana, which serves as a laboratory and rural leader meeting center for a firsthand study of rural problems. The Methodist Church, through a committee formed by its Council of Bishops and with the support of the Methodist Rural Christian Fellowship, has a rural life movement under way. It held an outstanding rural life conference in Lincoln, Nebraska, in 1947 (Figure 92, page 366) which was attended by more than 2,500 persons. The various denominations of the Lutheran Church have formed a National Lutheran Council, which is giving major attention to the work of Lutheran churches in rural areas. Similar efforts on behalf of the church in rural areas are being put forth by the Baptist, Evangelical and United Brethren, and other denominational groups with churches in rural areas.

3. The Town and Country Committee. Most of the national offices of church denominations are in or near New York City. Many of these denominations have professional rural workers. Under the stimulus of the National Home Missions Council of the Federal Council of Churches of Christ in America, a Town and Country Committee was formed. On this committee are the national rural workers for the various Protestant denominations of the Home Missions Council. Stimulated by the example of the Catholic Rural Life Conference, this committee has called annual meetings since its first national conference of rural church workers in Columbus in 1943. The 1947 conference, at Rochester, New York, attracted more than 1,000 people from most states of the Union. It was notable that not only did many Protestant rural church leaders attend, but an invitation was extended to and accepted by Catholic leaders as well.

The Town and Country Committee holds regular meetings, publishes the proceedings of the conferences, and issues a "house organ." It has also helped to encourage and sponsor rural pastors' short courses at colleges of agriculture and theological seminaries.

4. The Rural Christian Fellowship. The Rural Christian Fellowship grew out of the Agricultural Missions Foundation. It publishes a regular series of pamphlets or leaflets containing some of the best literature on the rural church and rural affairs, and has stimulated the organization of state and denominational fellowships which have not only benefited from the national fellowship literature but which also have carried on their own activities.

5. Conference between Theological Seminaries and Colleges of Agriculture. A recognition of the need for more men trained in

rural life led to the calling of a joint conference of representatives of theological seminaries and colleges of agriculture in 1939, in order to develop better understanding and cooperative projects. Subsequently, several conferences were held, resulting in the setting up of pre-theological majors in more than two dozen colleges of agriculture, and the acceptance of such training by the theological seminaries as meeting entrance requirements. Now young men who prefer to serve in rural churches can attend a college of agriculture for their first four years, and by taking the pre-theological major, be eligible to enter one of the seminaries working on this cooperative plan.[6]

Interest in rural church revitalization has been shown by colleges of agriculture in such activities as their rural pastors' schools, short courses, and state and county conferences; by the Farm Foundation in cooperation with the Town and Country Committee in holding a series of regional church-land tenure conferences; and by the agricultural magazines, such as *Capper's Farmer, Country Gentleman,* and *Successful Farming,* in publishing articles on the needs of the rural church.

The Rural Education Movement.—Both the Roosevelt Country Life Commission and the American Country Life Association can be given considerable credit for the national movement to improve rural schools. With the organization of the Department of Rural Education in the National Education Association in 1919, more emphasis was given to the need of reorganization, though shortly after the report of the Country Life Commission (1911), Mabel Carney in her *Country Life and the Country School* had pointed out the possibility of the country school being a social force in its neighborhood.

The organization of the Committee on Rural Education, sponsored by the American Country Life Association and supported by the Farm Foundation, resulted in the publication of two excellent pamphlets [7] on rural education, and led to the development of a rural education department at the University of Chicago. State committees on rural education and rural life have been formed in Michigan, Illinois, Missouri, Oklahoma, and other states. These committees have stimulated widespread interest in the need for rural school reorganization. The Illinois Rural Education Committee, for

---

[6] See *Minutes of the Conference Between Theological Seminaries and Colleges of Agriculture,* Garrett Biblical Institute, Evanston, Ill., 1942.
[7] *Still Sits the Schoolhouse by the Road* and *The Rural Child and the War Emergency,* The Committee on Rural Education, Chicago, 1942.

example, stimulated the calling of the first Governor's Conference on Rural Education ever held in the United States.[8]

Several regional and tri-state rural education conferences have been held, such as the Great Lakes Rural Education Conferences, to which the rural department of the National Education Association has given help. The Southern Rural Life Conference devotes especial attention to the rural education situation in the South.

The most notable rural education conference, however, was the 1944 White House Conference on Rural Education, attended by two hundred and fifty laymen, educators, and organization leaders from every state in the nation. Its report and charter for the Education of Rural Children will be important guideposts for many years to come.[9]

The Farm Foundation.—The movement to form foundations for the purpose of carrying on meritorious social work was extended to the rural field by Alexander Legge in 1933, in organizing the Farm Foundation.[10] Its aim is to supplement and help coordinate the work of other agencies seeking to improve living conditions of rural people. Its work includes studies and sponsorship of conferences in land tenure and similar problems, making grants for holding conferences, and carrying on work to improve rural life.

Other foundations, such as the Kellogg Foundation (in Michigan), the General Education Board, and the Russell Sage Foundation, have developed significant projects in rural health and rural education. Recent years have seen the establishment of the Foundation for American Agriculture, the Sears, Roebuck Foundation, the American Rural Youth Foundation, and others.

Related Farmers' Movements

A complete picture cannot be had of the country life movement without describing the related farmers' movements, some of which have contributed to or have in themselves become country life movements. Only a brief review, however, can be given here of these movements, for we have already studied some of the organizations which grew out of these movements.

---

8 See *Proceedings of the Governor's Conference on Rural Education,* Springfield, Ill., 1946.
9 *The White House Conference on Rural Education,* Washington: NEA, 1945.
10 *The Farm Foundation—Its First Ten Years, 1933-1943,* Chicago: Farm Foundation, 1944.

The Granger Movement.—The Granger movement grew out of a movement which has been characterized as "The Groundswell" [11] and included the activities of agricultural societies, farmers' clubs and farmers' fairs. Many groups besides the Grange had a part in the movement, though the Grange was the driving spirit behind it. Out of the movement came many changes, notably the Granger Laws, which placed public utilities under the watchful eye of government.

The Alliance and Populist Movements.—On the heels of the Granger movement came the Alliance movement, which soon merged into the Populist movement. At one time the Alliance movement drew into its fold most of the farmers of the nation, the Northern groups as well as the Southern. It never had complete unanimity, however, for there were rifts in the organization over the admission of Negroes, the use of secrecy in meetings, the support of political activities, and the nature of the organization itself. When the Alliance of the North joined the Free Silver movement at the end of the 19th century for the formation of an Agrarian political third party, the Southern faction fell away, as did the Grange elements, and the first major efforts of farmers to form a political party ended in failure.

The Cooperative Movement.—This movement had its start in the Granger and Alliance movements but, after many sad experiences with consumer cooperation, changed its emphasis in the early 1900's to concentrate on producer cooperation. Whereas it started as a part of the general farmer movement, it later carried on independently, though it has always enjoyed the full support of farmers' organizations. Three important national groups have crystallized from the cooperative movement: (1) the Cooperative League, (2) the National Council of Farmers' Cooperatives, and (3) the American Institute of Cooperation, which bring together the leaders of these three groups in a common understanding of the basic purpose of economic cooperation, and results in working out positive rather than negative attitudes toward interagency cooperation.

The Movement for Adult Education.—Farmers' institutes, which started late in the 19th century, paced the widespread adult education movement among rural people which crystallized into the Extension Service in Agriculture and Home Economics. It has grown to be much broader than this, however, for there are now vocational groups

[11] D. E. Lindstrom, *American Farmers' and Rural Organizations,* Champaign, Ill.: Garrard Press, 1948, pp. 80-81.

in the high schools, carrying on programs which have expanded to the farmers, to the veterans, and to the community as a whole. A part of the movement, also, is the farm women's organizations, most of which are sponsored by the Extension Service. They, also, have contributed much to the improvement of the quality of rural life.

The Movement for Agricultural Adjustment and Direct Action. —The rural unrest which expressed itself in demands for legislation leading to the establishment of such government agencies as the AAA, the SCS, the REA, and others, had profound effects on the farmer's attitude toward his government. He became convinced, for example, that there ought to be some control over the effect on prices of bumper crops. He was willing, though reluctantly, to submit to a degree of governmental regulation. The sporadic resort to direct action, such as milk strikes, has been replaced by the organization of direct-action agencies of government, most of which look to farmers for local administration. How far it will be necessary to use direct action and governmental regulation and control to insure the effectiveness of certain farm programs is yet to be determined. It is hoped that the trend from exploitation to conservation of soil in this country, for example, can be attained through democratic and educational means. But if it cannot, we may be forced to use government edict to accomplish the change.

The Planning Movement. —The prewar efforts of the U. S. Department of Agriculture for land use planning on the neighborhood, community, and county levels, were terminated by withdrawal of appropriations. Planning took on another aspect during and immediately following World War II through efforts by the Land-Grant Colleges, which recommended national, state, and county agricultural policy committees to "make an end to unadapted programs, to uncoordinated efforts, to wasteful duplication of facilities, and to working at cross-purposes." [12] The movement has now become of concern to agricultural committees of the United States Congress. They are working for the development of a new national agricultural policy to replace the present so-called farm program. It will provide for effective soil conservation, the encouragement of the family farm, the stabilization of prices, and the production of abundant food supplies. The program for soil conservation, for example, envisages the coordination of all governmental agencies working on the problem,

---

[12] *Postwar Agricultural Policy*, Report of the Committee on Postwar Agricultural Policy of the Association of Land-Grant Colleges and Universities, Univ. of Wisconsin Agr. Exp. Sta., 1944, p. 59.

Figure 92. The Assembly of the 1947 National Methodist Rural Life Conference at Lincoln, Nebraska
(Courtesy Methodist Christian Rural Fellowship)

and the formation of local, county, state, and national farmer committees. Planning will then again become a nationwide movement.

The country life movement needs more unity in thought, study, and action on the part of the various organizations and agencies working to improve rural life. The number of such voluntary and governmental agencies has grown rapidly in the past two decades, each without much regard or concern for the work of the others. It is evident that misunderstanding and confusion have resulted. To secure greater intergroup cooperation, more means must be found whereby, on a local, county, state, national, and even international basis, all rural groups can effectively cooperate in solving rural problems. Basic problems on which the country life movement must continue to center its attention are:

1. Man-land adjustments. Making realistic policies and programs that will provide rural people with a good kind of life and preserve our land resources.

2. Collective action. Stimulating and securing the kind of group action which would provide farm people with means of solving their own problems.

3. Equalization and control. Assuring rural people adequate resource for supporting and retaining a large measure of control of their institutions.

4. Policy making. Developing means whereby more farm people take part in making local, state, and national policies.

Unity Through the Country Life Movement.—Improving understanding and cooperation in activities through intergroup contacts should begin on the neighborhood and community level (neighborhood and community meetings, discussion groups, projects, and similar activities) and should then be carried on at the county level. State rural life conferences, in turn, can bring together many leaders and agencies which would have a common goal.[13] Each state should have its own conference group or groups.

On the national level, the need for carrying forward the objectives and programs of the American Country Life Association must be recognized. It is the only group which seems able to provide a common meeting ground for leaders from farmers' organizations, cooperative groups, rural church groups, rural education groups, rural health groups, and all other organizations and agencies working for

---

[13] See, for example, *"A Survey of Agencies at Work in Rural Mississippi,"* in *Rural Life,* Vol. I, Nos. 2 & 3, October, 1944, and January, 1945.

the advancement of rural life.[14] Therein the great common basic issues can be threshed out. Therein each group can see more clearly how it can work on its own, and how it can cooperate with other groups in solving these problems. Therein mutual confidence and good will can displace suspicion, ill will, lack of confidence, misunderstanding, and conflict. A cooperative attitude and cooperative group action on neighborhood, community, county, state, national, and international levels are essential if the fullest potentialities in rural life are to be realized.

DISCUSSION

1. Discuss the nature of the Country Life Movement—its constituent groups, and the nature of their programs or activities.
2. What are the problems in rural life that might be solved more easily through the approach made by the country life groups? What is the procedure for securing concerted action on country life issues?
3. Analyze the major problems whose solution can be aided by using the intergroup cooperation provided by the Country Life Movement. How may the effectiveness of the movement itself be improved?

READINGS

Agencies Concerned with the Quality of Rural Life in the South. Nashville, Tenn.: Southern Rural Life Council, 1944.

Buck, S. J. *The Granger Movement.* Cambridge: Harvard University Press, 1913.

Davidson, Gabriel. *Our Jewish Farmers.* New York: L. B. Fischer Co., 1943.

Kile, O. M. *The Farm Bureau Movement.* New York: The Macmillan Co., 1921.

Land Use Planning Under Way. BAE, USDA, 1940.

Ligutti, L. G., and Rawe, John C. *Rural Roads to Security.* Milwaukee: Bruce Publishing Co., 1940, Ch. XI.

Proceedings of the American Country Life Association, 1947.

Sanderson, Dwight. *Rural Sociology and Rural Social Organization.* New York: John Wiley & Sons, Inc., 1942, Ch. XXX.

Standing on Both Feet. Des Moines: National Catholic Rural Life Conference, 1945.

The Farm Foundation—Its First Ten Years, 1933-1943. Chicago: Farm Foundation, 1944.

The Methodist Church in Town and Country. New York: Department of Town and Country Work of the Methodist Church, 1944.

The Theodore Roosevelt Country Life Commission. Chapel Hill: University of North Carolina Press, 1944.

The 1919 Proceedings of the American Country Life Conference. Lafayette, Ind.: American Country Life Assn., 1919.

The Rural Church in These Moving Times. New York: Town and Country Committee of the Home Missions Council, 1947.

---

[14] See *Agencies Concerned with the Quality of Rural Life,* Nashville, Tenn.: Southern Rural Life Council, 1944.

Chapter 20

FUTURE TRENDS FOR RURAL LIFE

Rural life has always been in a state of flux. It is now, more than ever, in a transitional stage because it is being modernized by home conveniences such as modern plumbing, modern heating, and electricity; by better communication: roads, telephones, radio, automobile; by more farms of a size suitable for economic handling with mechanical equipment; and by new governmental services (FCA, REA, SCS, etc.). It is also being modernized by new concepts such as the functions of the larger rural community relative to education, health protection, governmental, and other services.

With modernization comes the penalty of greater dependence upon other forms of group life. The farm family is no longer self-sufficient, in spite of all efforts to make it so.[1] In this modern world, the economic, social, religious, and educational welfare of farm, town, and city people are so closely related as to be inseparable. Likewise, the rural neighborhood and community are part and parcel of the larger social order—county, state, national, and international. Ideas, as much as products, which come from other lands now make an impression on people living in rural areas. In Sunday Schools, clubs, and farm organization meetings, such topics as the system of social control over agriculture in Great Britain, the plans for social security in Australia or New Zealand, or the effectiveness of the cooperative movement in the Scandinavian countries, are of increasing interest. Our rural people are coming to participate more and more in their world community.

The Essential Nature of Rural Life

We have noted the difference in reproduction rates between rural and urban areas. The full significance of the fact that 7 adults have 10 children in rural areas, whereas 7 adults in urban areas have only 5 children—that rural areas are the human seedbed of this nation—is slowly coming to be recognized by national and state leaders, especially in urban areas. Since all urban areas depend upon rural areas

---

[1] See Ralph Borsodi's argument in O. E. Baker, Ralph Borsodi, and M. L. Wilson, *Agriculture in Modern Life*, New York: Harper & Bros., 1939, Ch. XI.

for food, fiber, and people, the quality of the human stock in rural areas is of great concern to the whole of society.

The essential function performed by rural people as custodians of our national resources—what farm people do to the land, for example—is now coming to be a national and an international concern. This is as much a social as an economic problem, for it can be economically feasible to exploit the land and yet socially desirable to conserve it. What measures will be needed to make it both economically and socially desirable to conserve the soil have not yet been fully worked out.

The essential nature of rural people, moreover, is reflected in the present international concern for food and good nutrition. This is also a social problem of the first magnitude. We are beginning to realize, although slowly, that nutritional poverty itself is a basic cause of world-wide strife. To raise the level of living of one group, and especially of those who live on the land, can result in higher living levels for every group.

But economic systems alone cannot accomplish these ends. Better social systems—education, government, health protection—especially for rural areas, are essential.

A great part of our concern, therefore, must be for a sound and progressive social organization which insures democratic processes. We want and must have a predominance of family-sized owner-operated farms. But we also want a farm and rural citizenry able, willing, and downright anxious to discuss their own problems and to take action to solve them, depending on nonrural sources only for essential social services and equitable financial support in exchange for the essential rural economic and social contributions to the rest of society.

Future Trends in Rural Society

An increasing recognition of the essential contributions of rural society and of rural society's need for democratic systems of social organization can and should mean (a) greater emphasis on group and intergroup cooperation, (b) greater emphasis on rural community and country life planning and action largely on the initiative of and by the rural people themselves, (c) greater unity in country life movements, (d) greater national and international concern for the welfare and security of people on the land, and (e) more inclusive social security.

These rural life trends should result in (a) using, protecting, and conserving our land resources as a social trust, (b) the protection and nurture of the family as the basic and most essential social group and economic unit, (c) the fullest possible *continuing* educational development of both those who remain on the land and those who go into other fields of activity, (d) the use of all possible public and cooperative means for the protection and care of health, (e) the development of professional, as well as humanitarian, treatment of rural social welfare conditions, and (f) the organization of the rural community for carrying on essential democratic policy-making processes, and to provide for direct action in solving rural problems.

Group and Intergroup Cooperation.—We know that rural people take part more and more in groups, with the family as the most important of all groups. We know, too, that there has been a tendency to individualize farm family life by the groups that have been formed to serve their interests. Now the time has come to re-emphasize the family nature of occupations in rural life both on the farm and in the village. Large-scale operation tends to urbanize and in some respects destroy this natural form of family cooperation. The family type of economic and social life in rural areas can mean more people working for themselves, more consumer goods desired and used, more desire for education, more participation in local government, more memberships in social and educational organizations, more religious activity, more and better modern houses, and more interest by youth as well as adults in constructive use of leisure time.[2]

If our emphasis is to be upon family unity and cooperation, greater attention will have to be paid to the neighborhood as a basic unit of social organization. The issues discussed or acted on in neighborhood groups are those most vital to the day-in and day-out life of the people. The neighborhood, like the family, is always there, and rural people can in the future make greater use of these vital primary groups in working for improved human welfare in rural areas.

Interest groups are too often divisive because they are selective and self-centered. Nevertheless, we know they exist and we must give opportunity for intergroup cooperation (a) to avoid conflict, (b) to do together many things which cannot be accomplished by each group working alone, and (c) to establish local control, preventing state domination, yet making the greatest possible effective use of state services. Whether or not we will move in the direction

---

[2] See results of studies of two communities in the San Joaquin Valley in California by the BAE, as reported in Carey McWilliams, *Small Farm and Big Farm*, Public Affairs Pamphlet 100, 1945.

of more inclusive group activity and more effective intergroup cooperation will depend upon the ability of the leaders of our interest
groups—local, county, state, and national—to envision the great
possibilities in such social cooperation and to place it on a par, if not
above, the special individual and group interests.

The most effective way in which rural leaders can enlarge their
vision of intergroup cooperation is to face up to some specific task.
The recent efforts to organize for land-use planning emphasized planning with, for, and by groups, both locality and interest groups,
to discover, develop plans for, and get action on basic social and
economic issues. Each community must learn to work out its own
procedures. The leaders of the community who should feel especially responsible for initiating and helping carry forward these
procedures are the church and school leaders.[3]

These processes in the rural community must have outside stimulation and help. But this help cannot be given by agency and
organization leaders who are operating without regard for or interest
in what the others are doing. We have already seen the disastrous
results on attitudes and morale by conflicting agricultural policies—
AAA, SCS, FSA, extension, and others. Too little attention has
been given to the various country life movements and their implications by leaders of these agencies, and even by farm organization
leaders. It is to be hoped that such integrating movements as the
American Country Life Association, the National Catholic Rural
Life Conference, the National Convocation of the Church in Town
and Country, the Rural Life Department of the National Education
Association, the Rural Life Association, the Southern Rural Life
Conference, and the various state rural life groups will broaden and
deepen the vision of the so-called "practical" leaders in extension,
farmers' organizations, cooperatives, etc. We are now in a position
to make the most of such movements. We can make the most of them
if leaders of farmers' organizations, cooperatives, interest groups,
churches, schools, health and welfare agencies will get together and
discuss their problems and programs of mutual interest.

More Inclusive Rural Social Security.—Throughout history the
people on the land have always had a feeling of insecurity—even
those on their own land—because they have been increasingly subject
to economic conditions over which they have little or no control and
which can deprive them of the very means of their livelihood. If

---

[3] See Henry S. Randolph, "The Church in the Rural Life Movement," in *Urgent Tasks
of the Church in Town and Country*, Committee on Town and Country, New York: Home
Missions Council, 1945.

rural people are to build up the soil, produce efficiently, rear moderately large families, provide an adequate education for them, and continue to contribute to the total culture of the society in which they live, they must be given adequate social security, against the background of a modern rural cultural environment. In order to encourage the right kind of youth to stay on the farms it will be necessary that they should have not only an opportunity to make a good income, but also that they be given the outlook for a good kind of life on the farm. This should mean both modern equipment and conveniences, and a cultural environment which will nurture a wholesome family life with good schools, churches, and recreation.

Adequate Economic and Social Farm Units.—Basic to more inclusive social security is security on the land. Some change is needed, for example, in our inheritance laws so that farms which are transferred from generation to generation will remain or become adequate economic and social units. This means that some farms should be combined, especially in the poor-land areas where there is now the tendency to further divide them among the large number of heirs. It should mean, on the other hand, dividing some large farms in the better-land areas to make them adequate economic and social units. Attention must be given, also, to other types of land transfer: from non-operator-owner to operator-owner, as well as stability of tenancy which will look to eventual operator-ownership.

We know that the best kind of farm life is that which is found on the family size farm, and that the family size farm differs in size from area to area. The adequate social unit, it would seem, is the unit which provides for a good kind of family life in a neighborhood and community in which a modern rural culture can be nurtured.

We do not yet know as much as we should about what constitutes a good social and economic farm unit, nor what social and economic policies are desirable to stimulate the establishment of such units. It is certain, however, that consideration of production or economic conditions alone will fall short of solving the problems. Major attention to the entire cultural environment is necessary.

The Role of the State.—The chief concern of a democracy is nurturing the initiative and self-reliance of its people. Hostility to the kind of social security that would afford a living wage or income to idle workers is particularly marked, especially among those who have "made their own way" and who have never faced dire need or starvation. To them the best form of security is a good price system, resulting in a good demand for farm products. An economic system which will assure good farm prices and good incomes, however, would not provide security for everyone, for even under such a system there are those who are forced to a low living level because of circumstances beyond their control.

Though farmers are now receiving excellent prices for their products, they are not yet assured of stable farm incomes. The extension of social security to all farmers, especially low-income farmers who supply the human raw materials, seems to be justified. The extension of such security can mean not only a better living for most farmers, but also a far less costly system than direct or work relief. Our present system places an undue burden of costs in terms of food, shelter, clothing, medical service, and education on large families with low incomes. These costs often exceed the ability of the family to provide the minimum essentials. As a result, many children on farms and in nonfarm communities are not privileged to eat enough nutritious foods, obtain needed medical attention, nor even attend school (often taught by poor teachers) more than a few months in a year.

We cannot expect to limit the population on the land to those who produce efficiently. To do so might be a good economic policy but it would require effective—and therefore obnoxious—state control over agriculture. We must, therefore, have concern for *all* those who live on the land or who make part or all of their living there. Hence plans to establish people on land, even though it be on small parcels on a subsistence basis or on a part-time basis, must have our serious attention. It may be that with adequate forms of social security such people can become the chief and proper stock on which our entire population is based. George Russell's admonition that a healthy society requires that 30 per cent of its population remain on the land then becomes of real importance.[4]

The first test of any policy of social security is its effect on the people. A desirable program of social security will result in improving the quality of the rural population. The provision of adequate educational and health facilities has this in view.

The right kind of social security program would put some kind of a premium on the proper rearing of a large family. The provision of adequate social services—for religion, education, social welfare, health, and recreation—is one effective means of improving the quality of the human stock produced. However, no satisfactory measures have been devised or even discussed to deal effectively with

[4] George Russell, *The National Being*, New York: The Macmillan Co., 1930, p. 33.

the genetic aspects of the problem.   There is as much real need for a
national population policy relating to rural areas as there is for a
national policy on production and marketing of agricultural commodities.

Greater International Concern.—We must trade if we are to increase our living levels and those of peoples in other parts of the
world.   We can and must trade with each other, in economic and in
social goods.   "The country as a whole, and the world as a whole,
can gain only from using its inheritance of productive resources to
produce more and better goods and services for mankind." [5]   This
country has recognized the postwar world's basic need for food by
its participation in the Food and Agriculture Organization of the
United Nations, and by its sponsorship of the European Recovery
(Marshall) Plan.   In the long run our living levels will be protected
and advanced as those of other peoples advance—for advancing living
levels mean greater consumption.   Hence there are definite movements in this country in the direction of freer international trade.   It
is a good omen!

But trade on the international scale can be in ideas as well as
goods.   The last international conference of farmers' organizations
(1947) confined itself too much to narrow economic issues.   Larger
issues, such as the serious lack of education in many rural areas of
the world, health protection, and even family and community
planning, should have come into the picture.   People in rural communities all over the world probably have more social interests in
common than they have economic.   By recognizing these broader
rural community interests, international conferences might lay the
kind of foundation that would make much easier the discussion of
purely economic problems.   It is on this basis—the human basis—
that greater international understanding and accord can be soundly
built. [6]

The Rural Community and the General Welfare

"The genius of democracy," says Morgan, "is to eliminate compulsion to uniformity, whether that compulsion be physical force or
social pressure, and to develop common outlooks and aims by mutual
inquiry, mutual interest, and mutual regard.   The process seldom if
ever takes place on a large scale.   Rapid large-scale changes generally

---

[5] Norman S. Buchanan and Friedrich A. Lutz, *Rebuilding the World Economy,* New
York: The Twentieth Century Fund, 1947, p. 285.
[6] See *Preamble to the UNESCO Constitution,* Educational Policies Commission, NEA,
Washington, 1946.

come by ignoring individual variations and by enforcing large-scale uniformities. True democracy results from intimate relations and understandings, with emergences of common purposes. The community is the natural home of tolerance and freedom." [7]

People living in rural communities should realize that most of them will live there all of their lives and that they should do something to make the community a better place in which to live. To do so they need to be led to look at themselves critically. Then, recognizing their shortcomings, they should be helped to build up their business, religious, educational, health, social, and recreational life to the level enjoyed by urban people. This is the task—and the obligation —of the rural sociologist.

READINGS

Butterworth, Julian E. *Goals for Rural Living in America.* Yearbook of the Department of Rural Education, NEA, New York, 1945, pp. 12-21.

Lindstrom, D. E. *Rural Life and the Church.* Champaign, Ill.: Garrard Press, 1946, Ch. VIII.

Moore, Arthur. *Farmers and the Rest of Us.* Boston: Little, Brown & Co., 1944.

Morgan, Arthur E. *The Small Community.* New York: Harper & Bros., 1942, Ch. XXVI.

Russell, George. *The National Being.* New York: The Macmillan Co., 1930, Ch. VI.

Schultz, T. W. *Agriculture in an Unstable Economy.* New York: McGraw-Hill Book Co., Inc., 1945, Ch. X.

Standing on Both Feet. Des Moines: The National Catholic Rural Life Conference, 1945.

---

[7] Arthur E. Morgan, *The Small Community,* New York: Harper & Bros., 1942, p. 282.

INDEX